SPACE FOR COMMUNICANT'S PHOTOGRAPH.

Use triangle corner tabs.
Sold at all stationery stores.

I was present at your first Holy Communion:

Nihil Obstat: JOHN M. A. FEARNS. S. T. D. Censor Librorum
IMPRIMATUR: FRANCIS CARDINAL SPELLMAN Archbishop of New York

Litho in Italy

FEAST

CHRISTY JOHNSON
AND 33 CONFESSORS

PREFACE

'The bride's modesty is a delicate thing; and I feel that at the Bridegroom's reproof a warm flush suffused her face, so heightening her beauty that she immediately was greeted with: *'Your cheeks are beautiful as the turtle dove's.'* You must not give an earthbound meaning to this coloring of the corruptible flesh, to this gathering of blood-red liquid that spreads evenly beneath the surface of her pearly skin, quietly mingling with it to enhance her physical beauty by the pink and white loveliness of her cheeks. For the substance of the soul is incorporeal and invisible, possessing neither bodily limbs nor any visible coloring. Try then as best you can to grasp the nature of this spiritual entity by means of a spiritual insight; and to conserve the fittingness of the proposed comparison, take note that the mind's intention is the soul's face.'

BERNARD OF CLAIRVAUX
Sermon 40, *The Face of the Bride*, 1136 AD

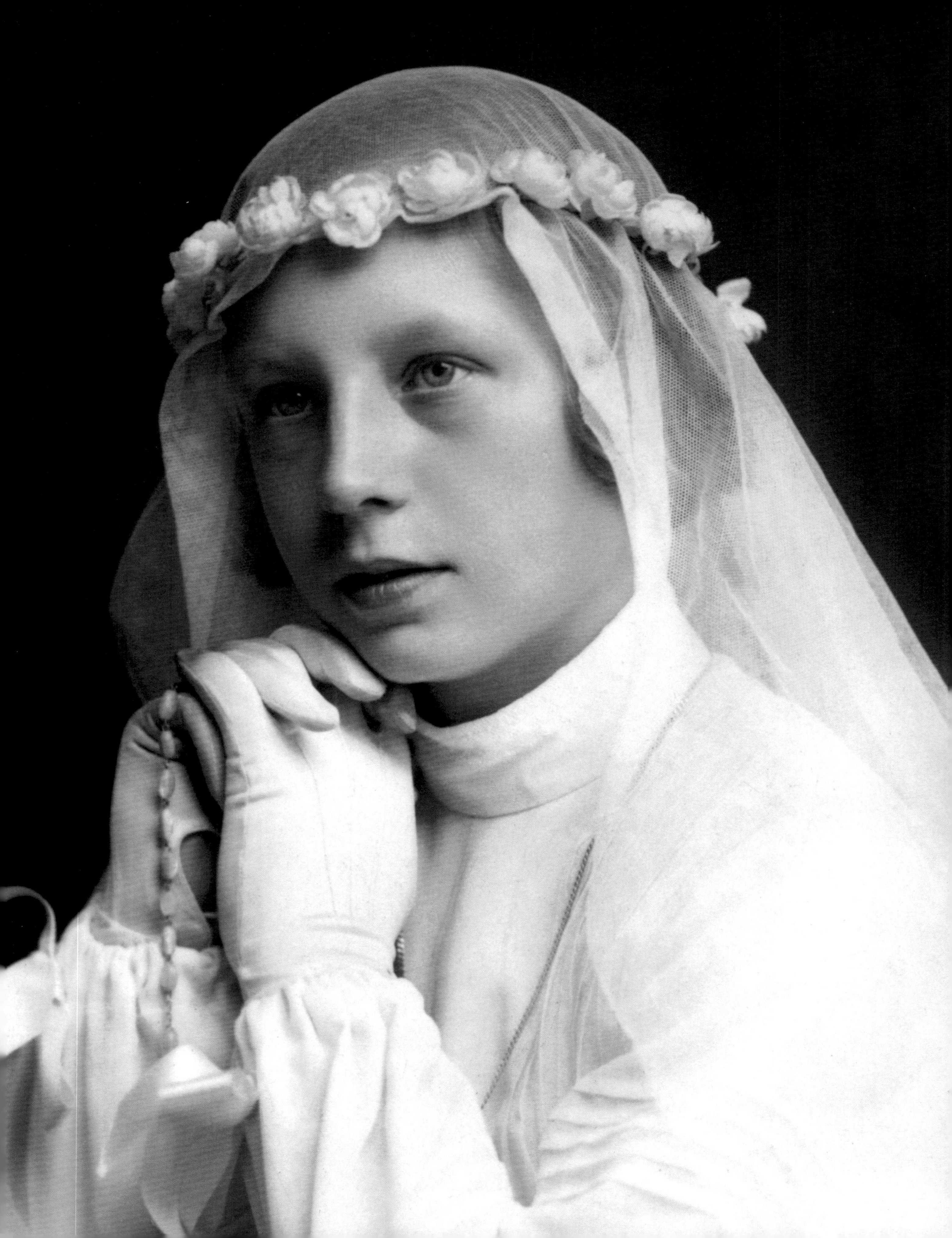

For Phyllis Marillyn Rivers Johnson

CONTENTS

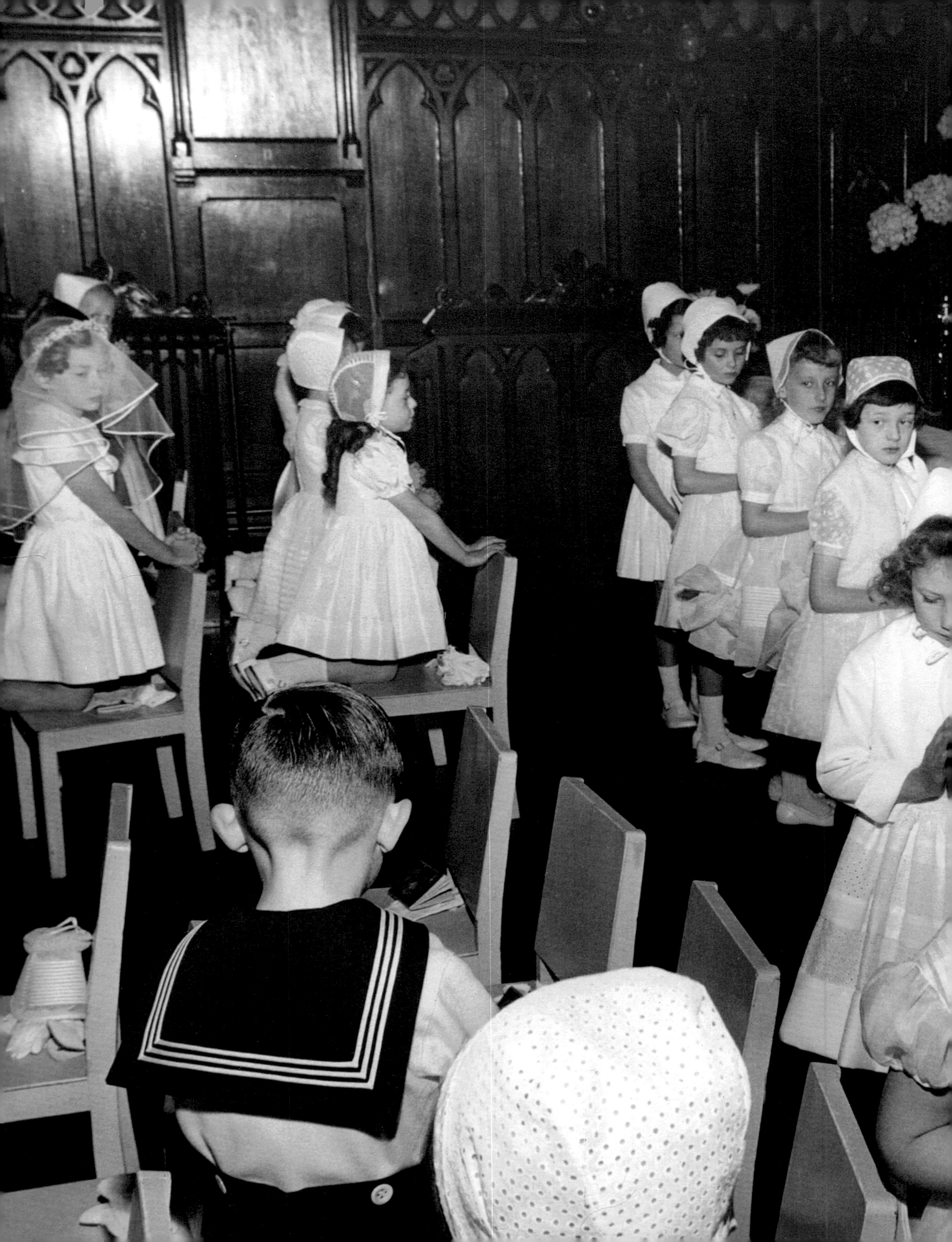

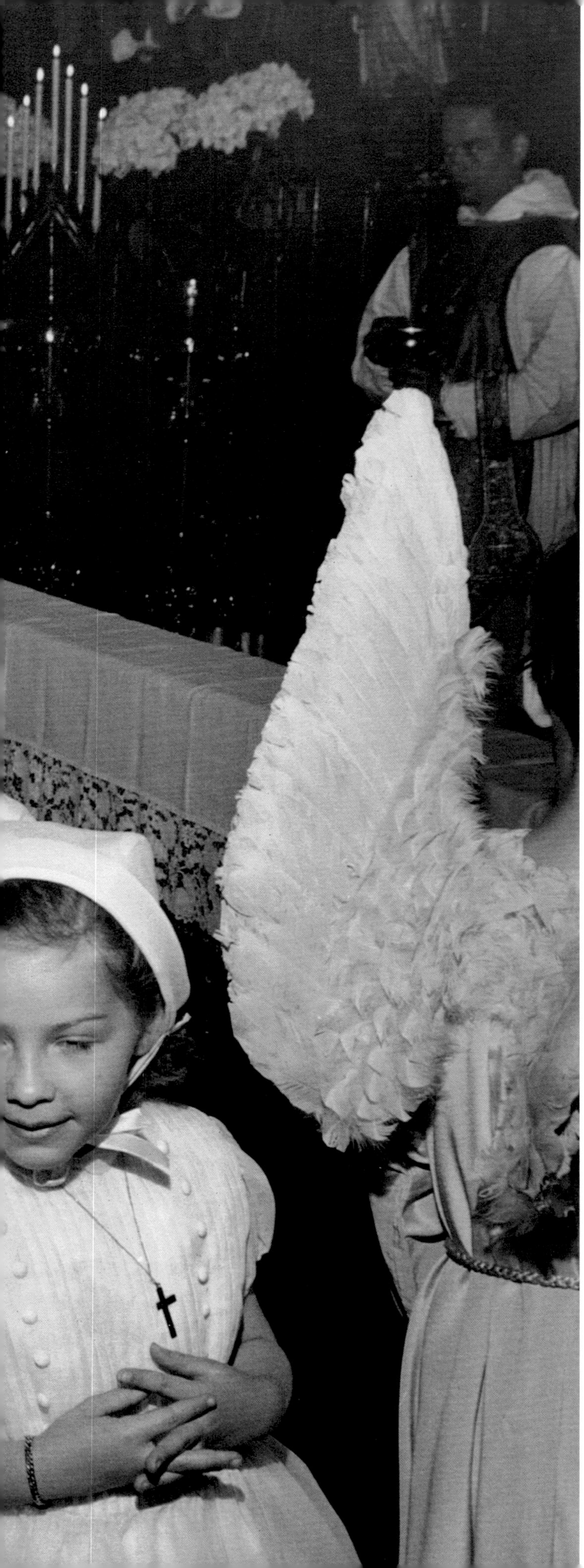

I

WASH ME
CLEAN FROM
EVERY STAIN
OF SIN

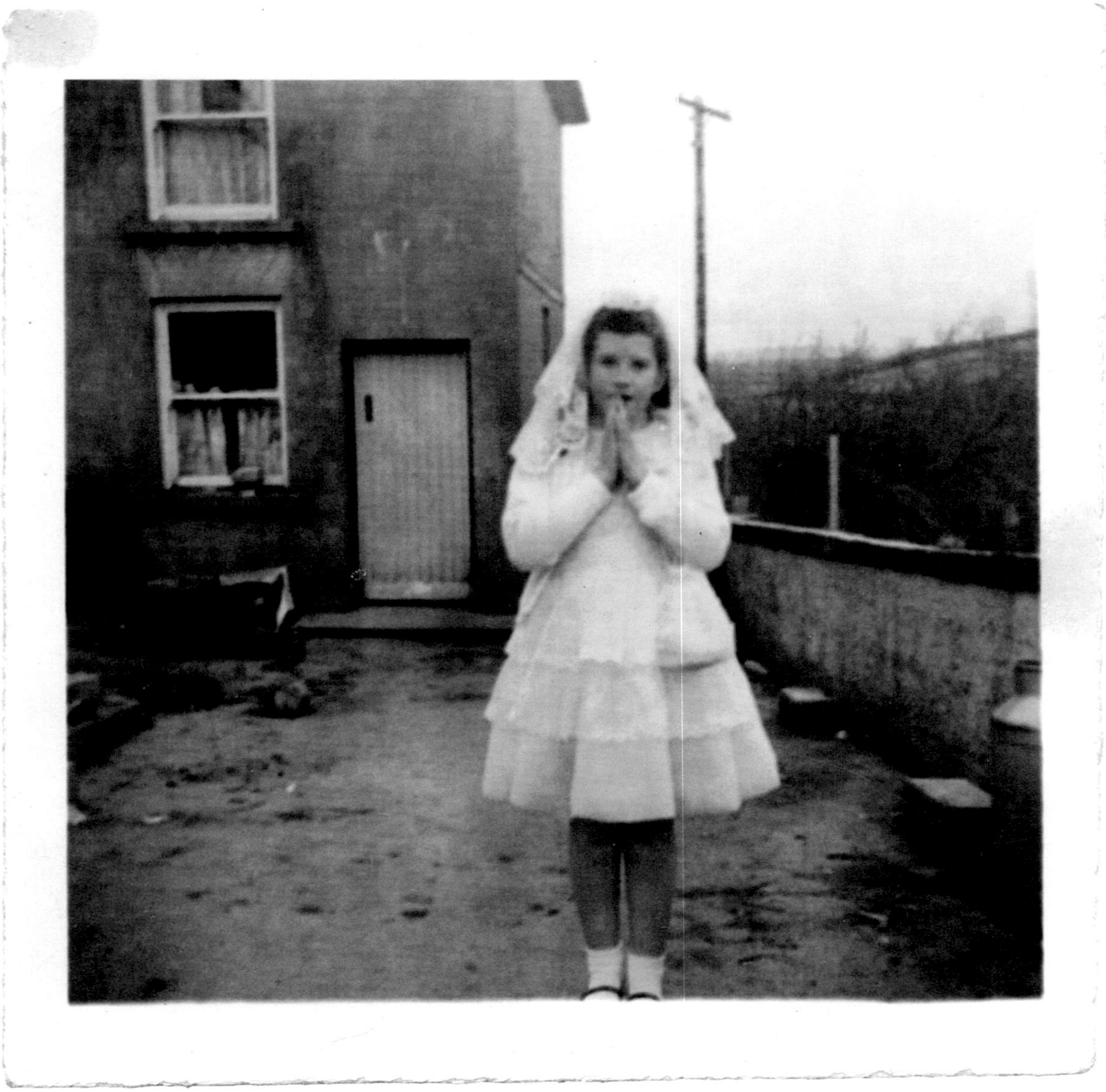

I remember very much liking white.

Why do you think you liked white so much?

I don't know. I used to be quite a tomboy and I used to like getting dirty. I played with worms and made mud pies and things like that. And I think the idea of being dressed completely, spotlessly clean – and my mum would have curled my hair and everything – I just thought, oh, you know, this is quite angelic. I think there's a great association with being angelic, because of all the preparation.

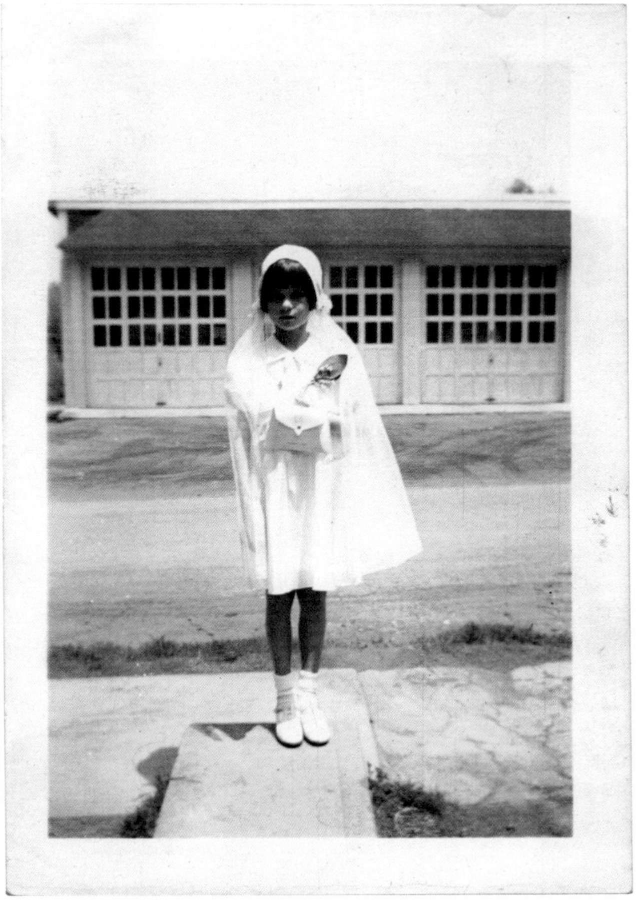

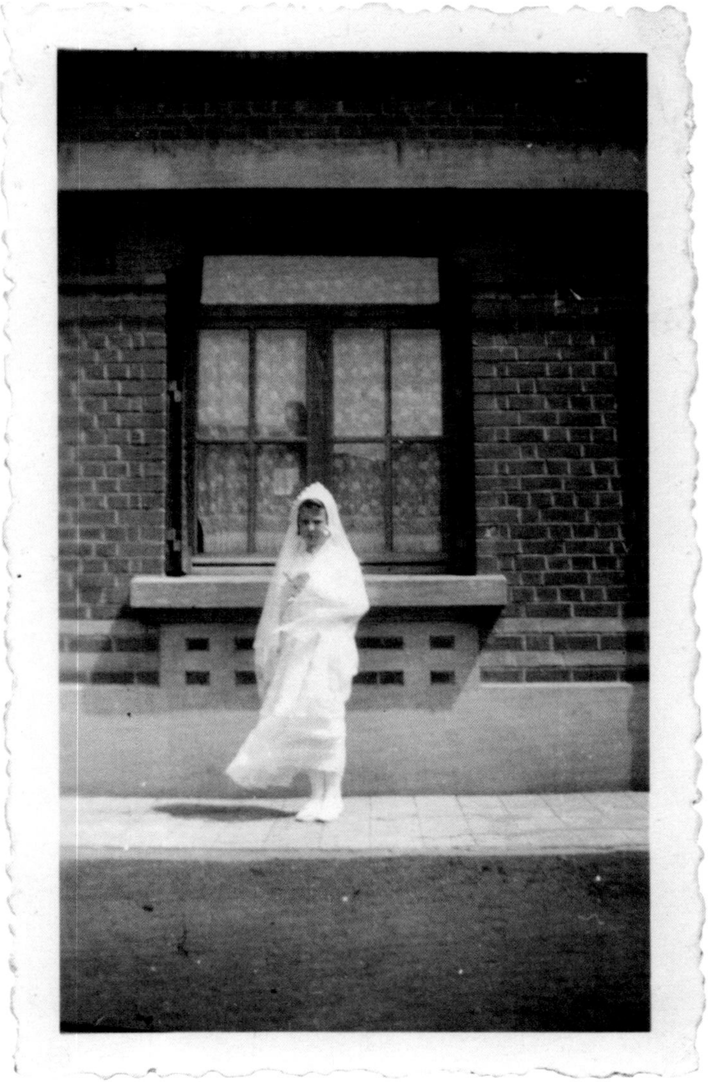

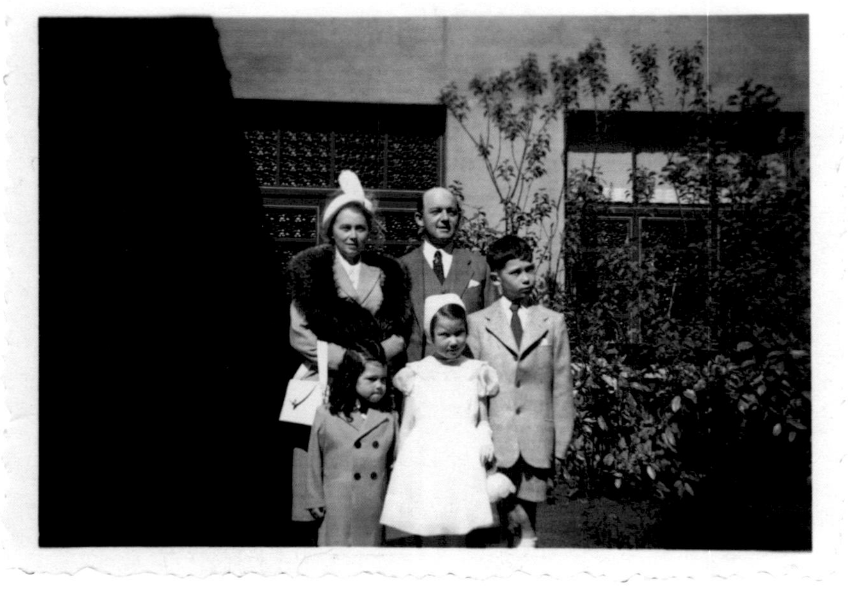

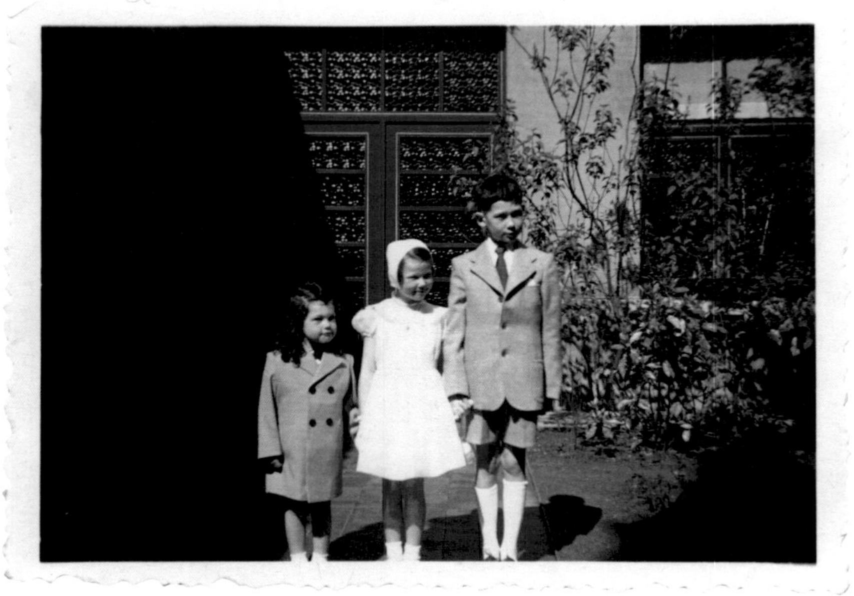

Mum would be getting everybody ready and making sure their collars were straight and their ties were straight and their jackets were straight and their socks were pulled up and, you know, everything was clean and so on, and she was like the manager of the children. She was a working mother, so she was busy and bustling, you know. Get it done and get on with it and don't you dare, don't you dare go outside until I say so. She would stand there and say that. But then you could make her laugh. I mean, she wasn't horrible. But, yeah – don't you dare.

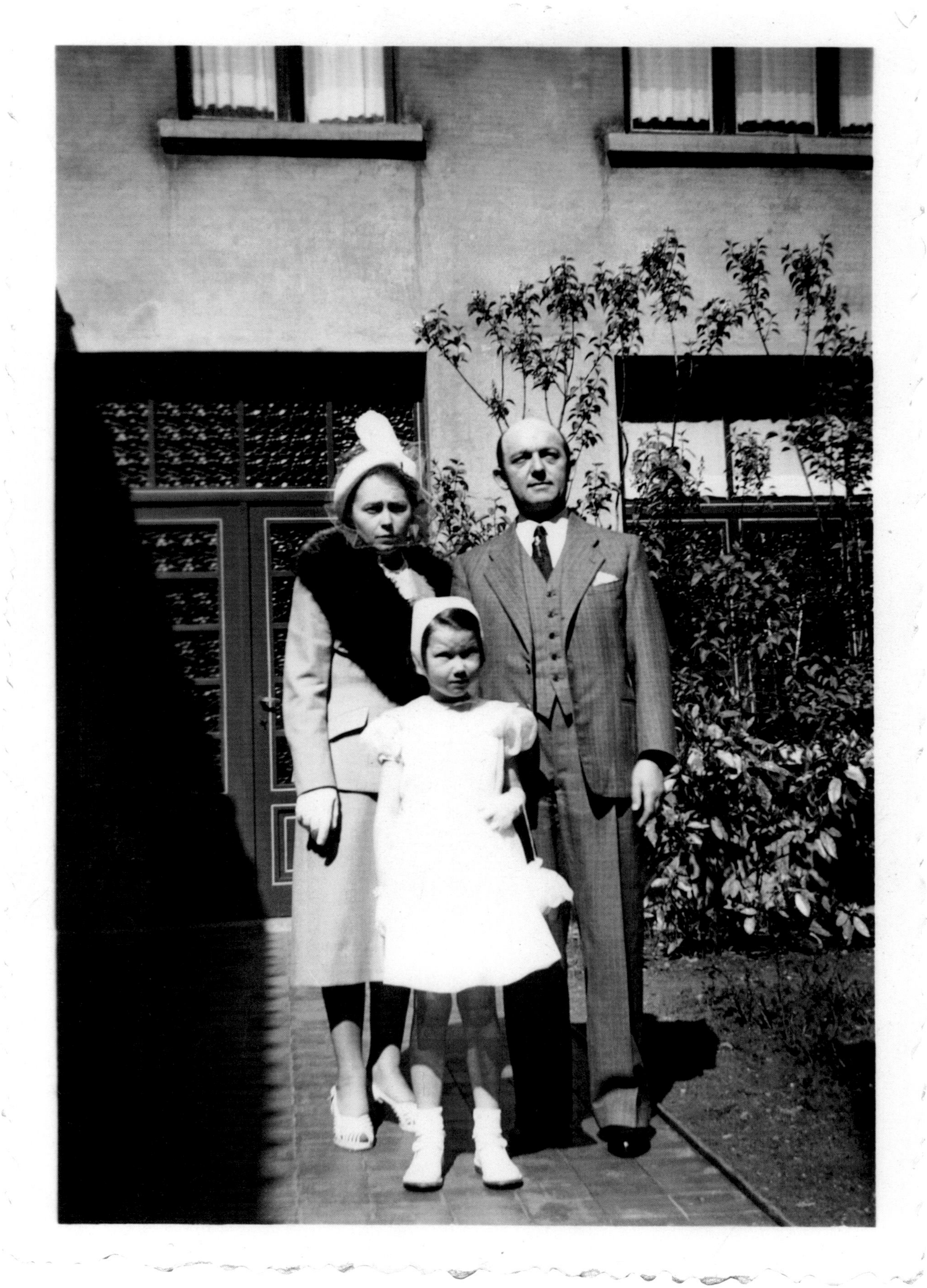

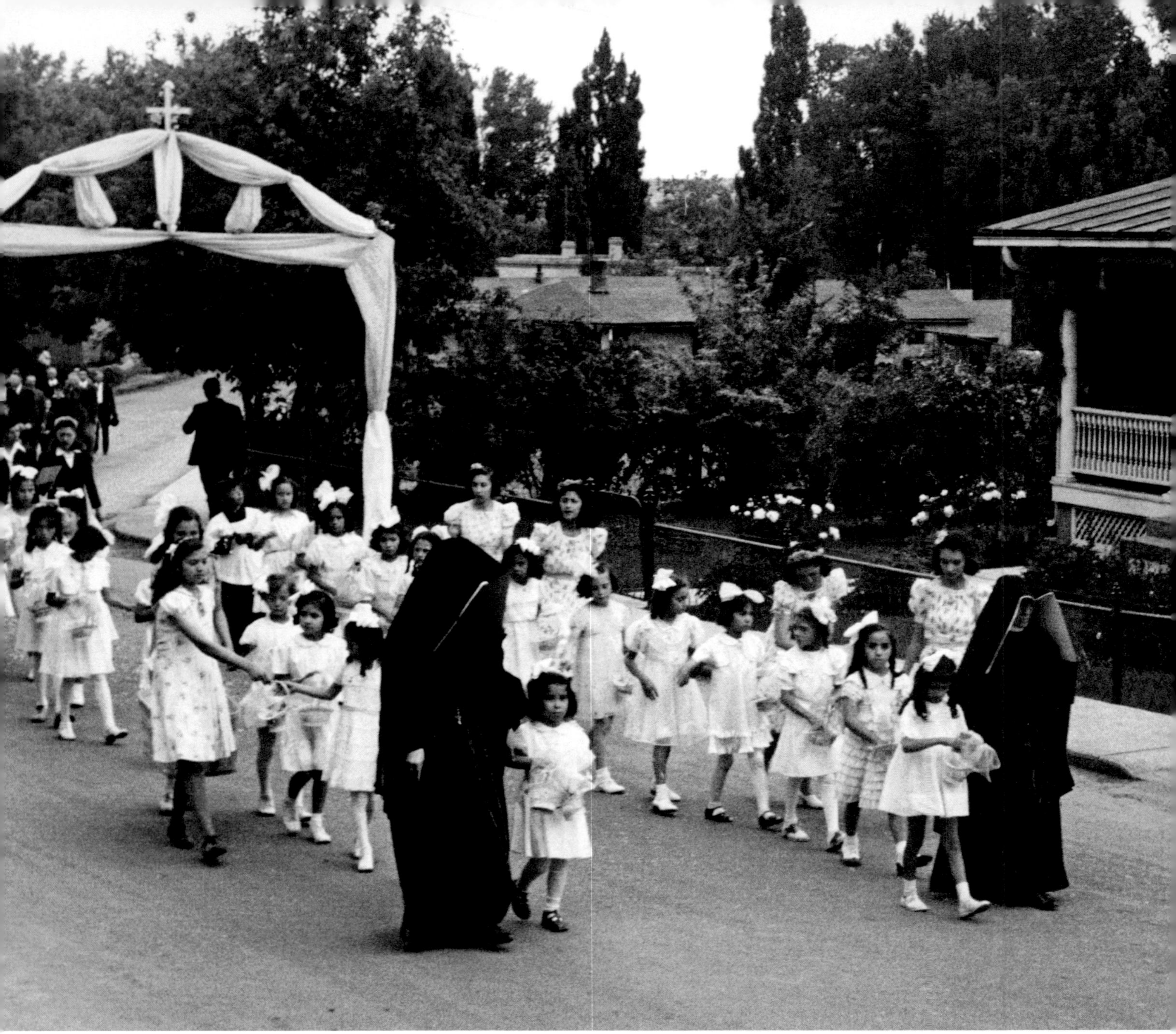

When you're walking you're a robot; you've been trained to walk a certain way and act a certain way. And it's something about the significance of white that happens again when you get married. When you're older you're still wearing white, but there's something about – my gosh, you can't even get dirt or a smudge … and, boy, they go in there and they clean all the pews off, so that you stay white. And, gosh, if you even had a scar on your knee from playing in the yard, say a week ago and you skid your knees … I noticed that sometimes some of the girls would take make-up and cover it because, you know, there's this whole thing about …

… being immaculate.

I think, you know, somewhere along the line, that white – no matter where you look it up, whether it's the lily or the dress or whatever, it always signifies purity. That I've always known.

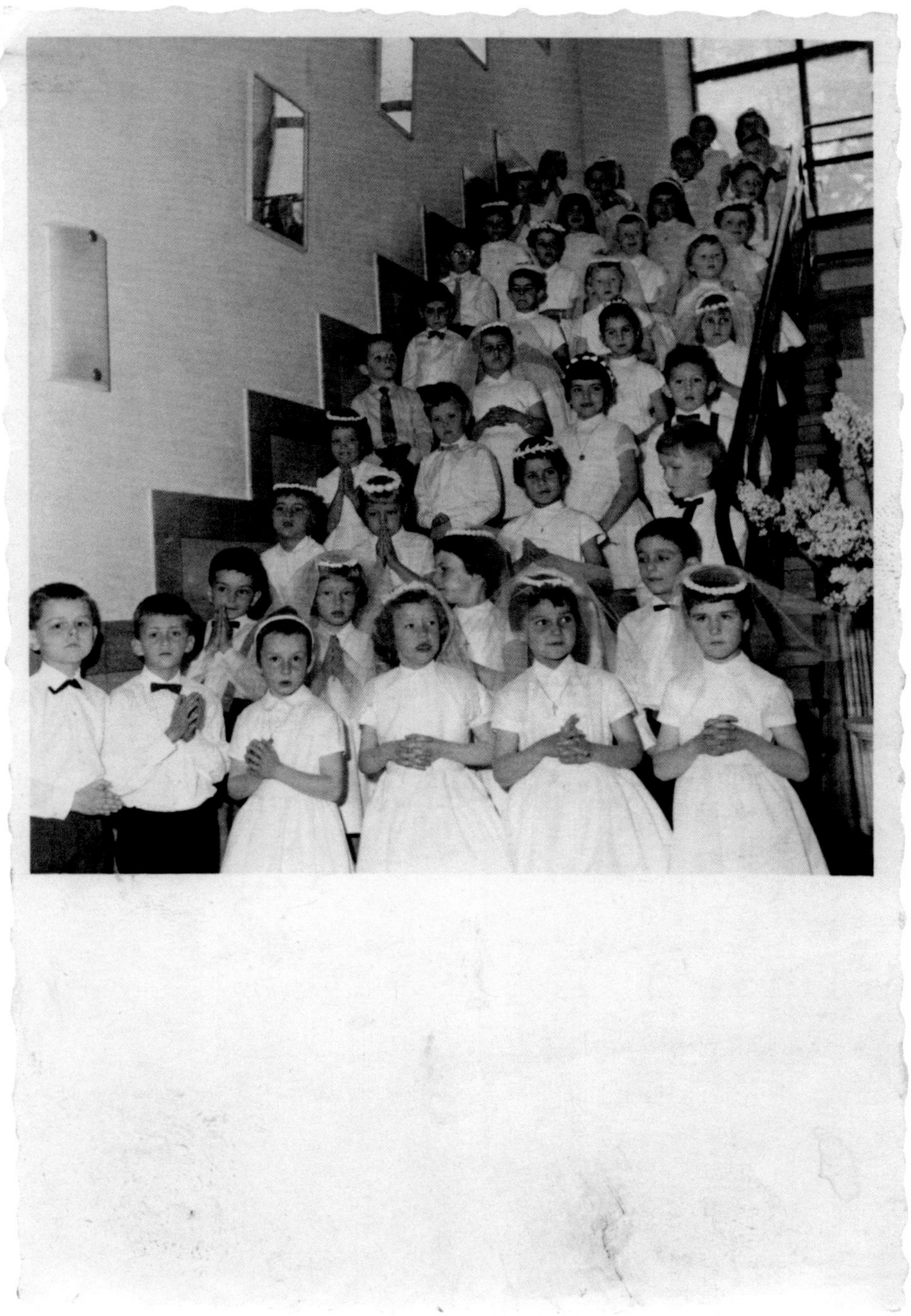

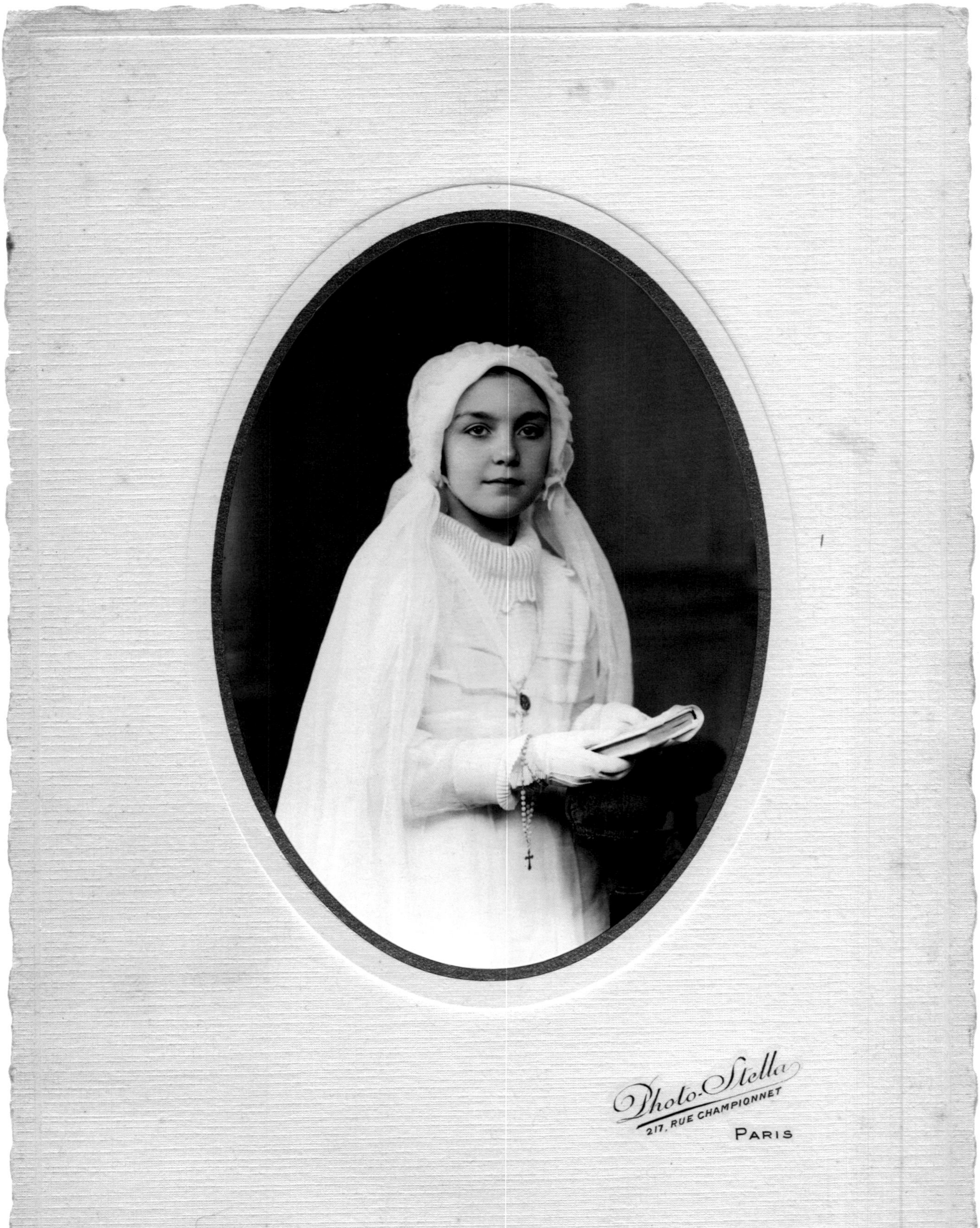
Photo-Stella
217, RUE CHAMPIONNET
PARIS

You were in your dress at the zoo?

You wore your dress all day, but you took your veil off.

What animals come to mind?

I remember the smell of the reptile house, but I don't know if it was from that visit or another day. The smell of the reptile house was gross. And I remember the polar bears.

Oh, that's interesting – white.

The polar bears always looked so cool – it was always so hot in the zoo and smelly and the animals looked a bit depressed, didn't they? But the polar bears always looked nice and clean.

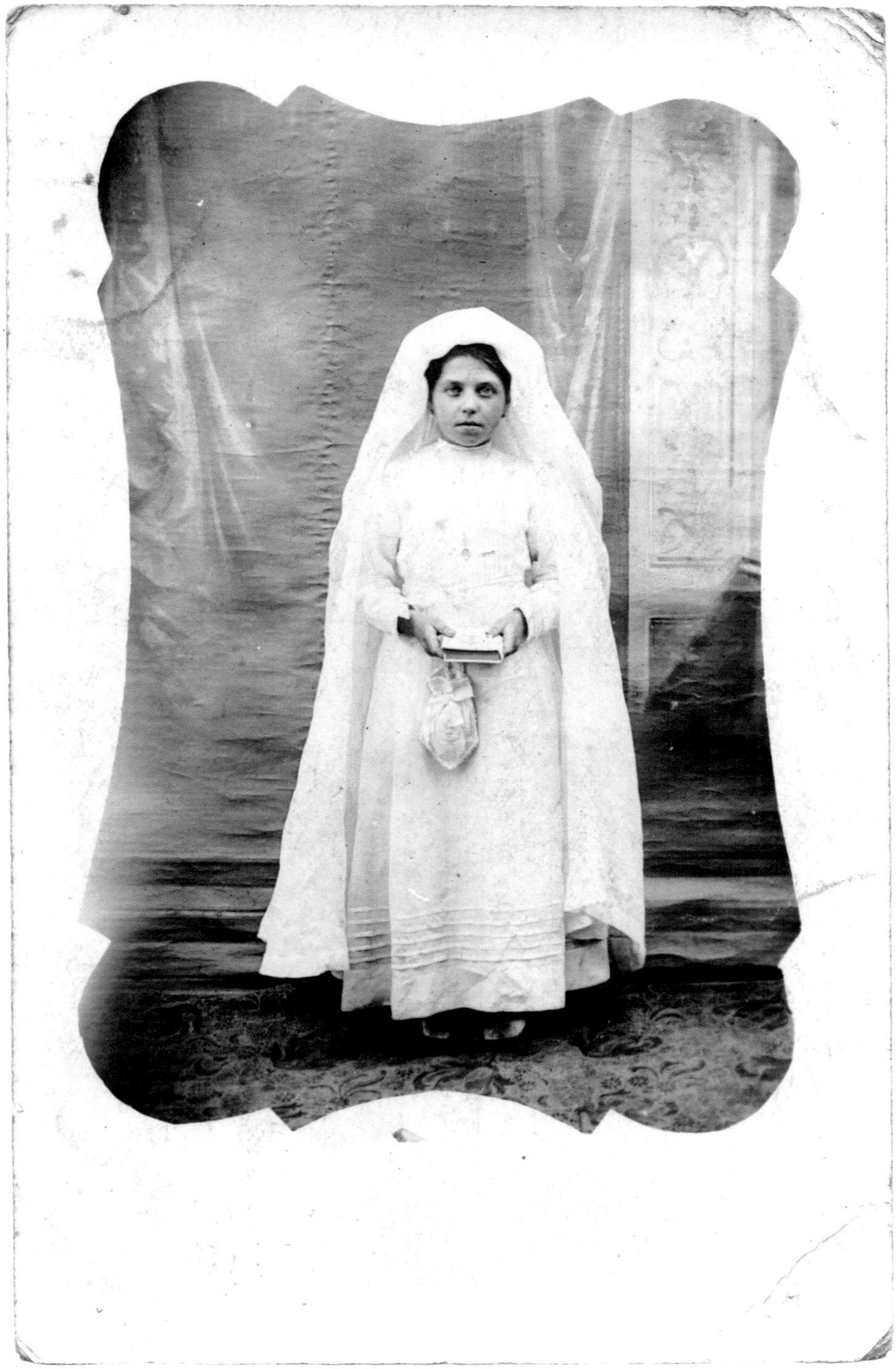

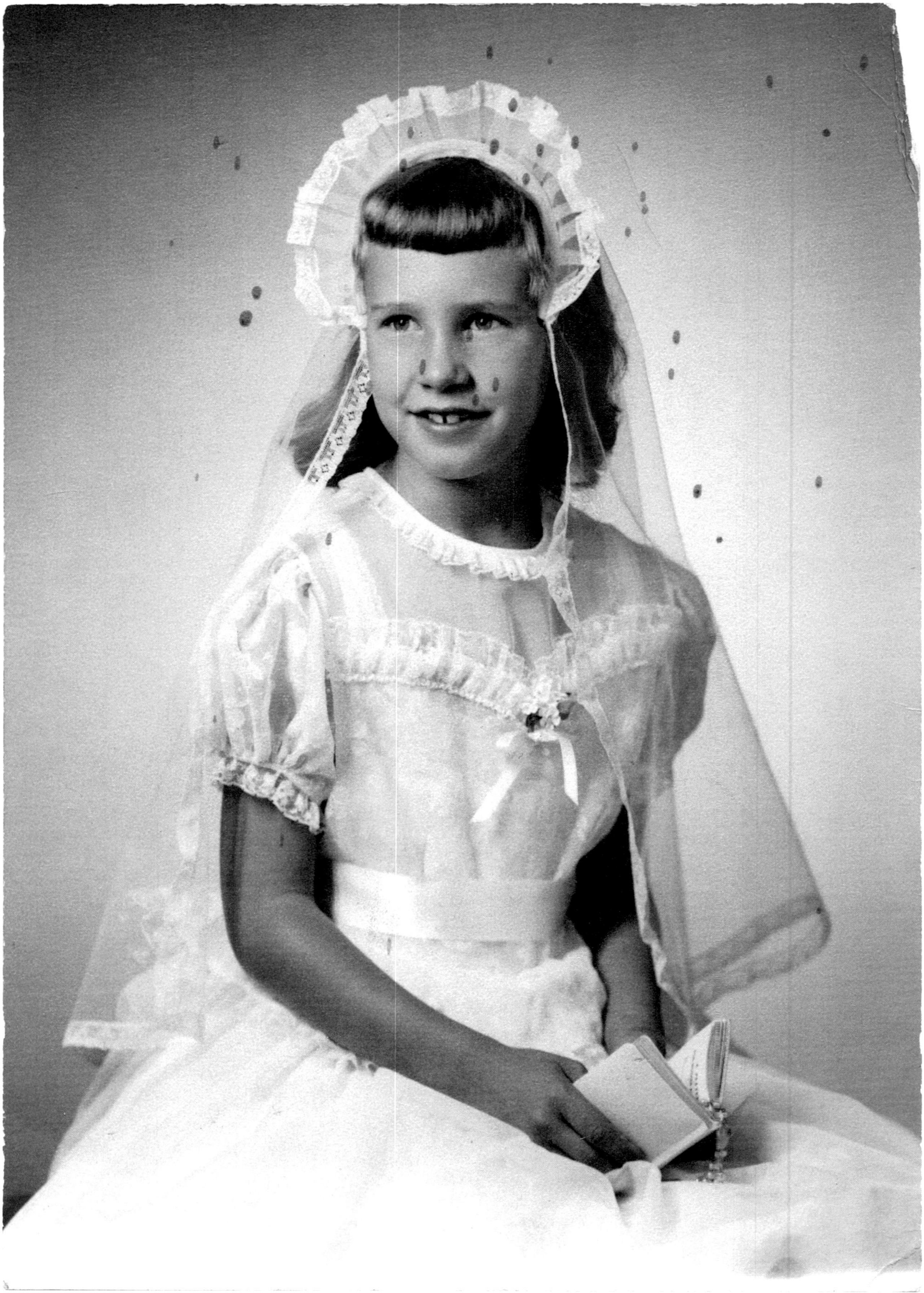

And um, yeah, I got blood on it but no one knew. I always had these nosebleeds. I was playing with my cousin and afterwards – because I've a big family everyone was there – we went off, snuck off, and she was very jealous because she's from Church of England and she didn't get to have the white dress. We were playing and I always had nosebleeds at that stage and she kind of jolted me and I had a nosebleed on the dress – little spots of blood. We went back to her house 'cause we lived very near each other, and we washed it off.

It didn't stain the white?

It came off. We did it very quickly. Unbelievable. Obviously someone was on our side. Yeah, that's something that I remember: panic.

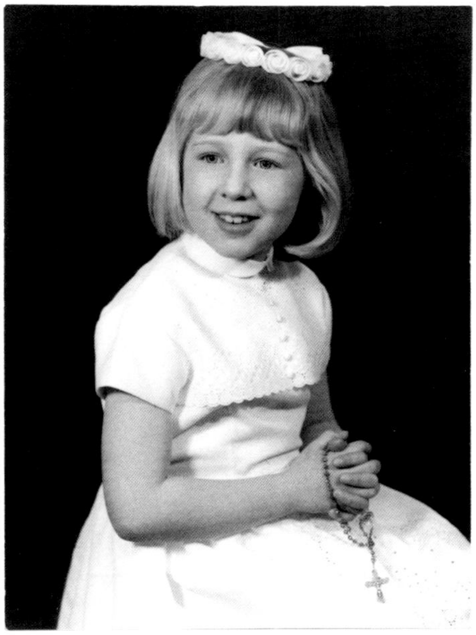

We had a nun who taught us you couldn't pray without your feet flat on the ground, you shouldn't have your feet crossed or anything. If you dropped a pencil it remained there during the whole class. You did not speak to anyone in the class out of turn. And everything was so regimented that all I can remember about that class is the discipline and the exactness of this nun, the control and being fearful of dropping a pencil.

In first grade, or maybe second grade, I remember the nun telling us when we went out to lunch that if we spilled our milk we would have to lick it up. And we met under an open arbour, you know, with picnic tables and on the ground it was dirt, and I remember being afraid. I mean, you know, kids are clumsy sometimes. You bring a lunchbox with the thermos and you can slip. I used to be so afraid that I would spill my milk and have to lick up the milk in the dirt all together – so afraid.

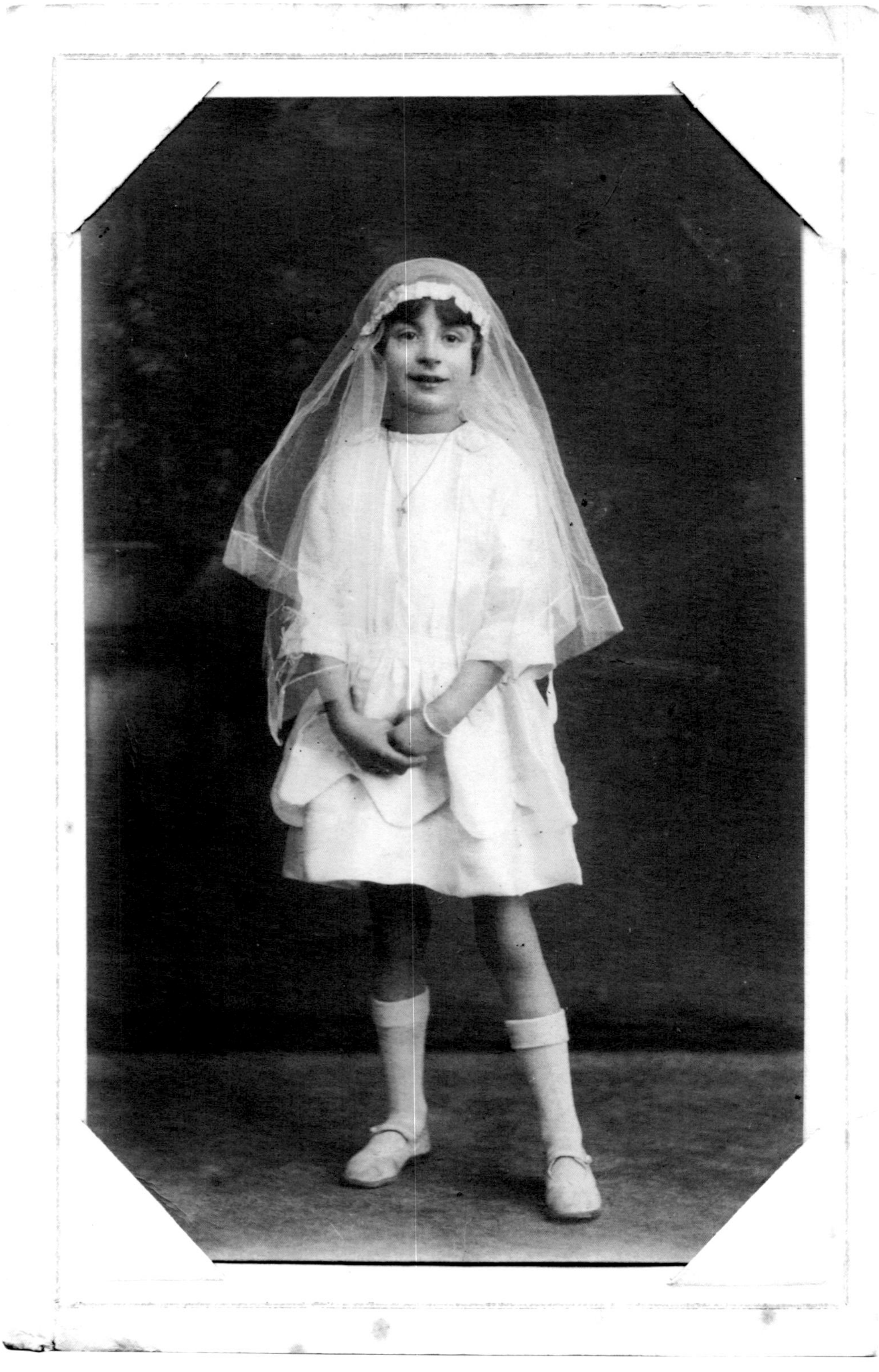

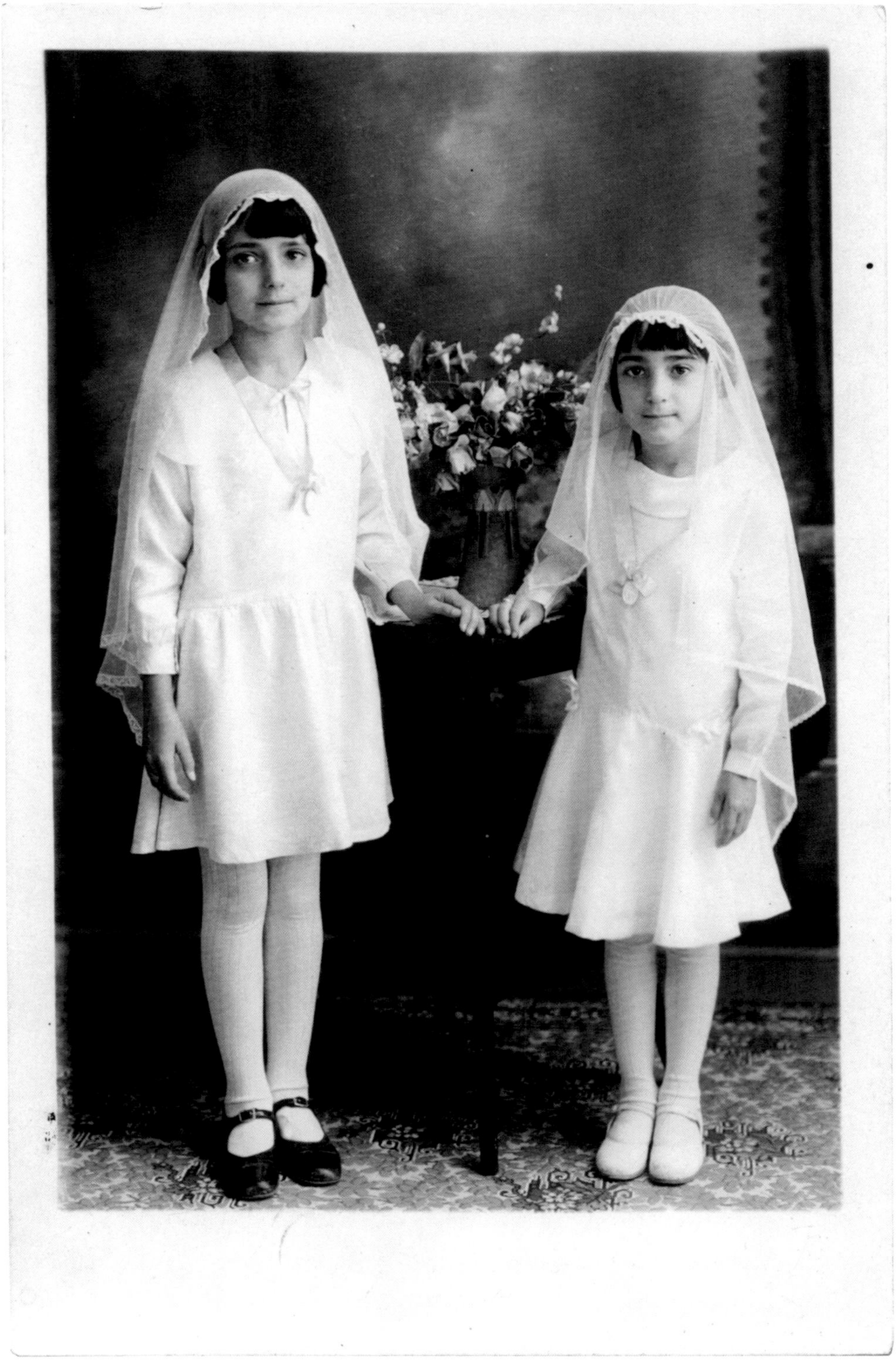

My way of getting back at the system was that I dyed my underwear a lot because you had to wear everything white under a uniform. And nobody could tell whether – 'cause who's going to look at your underwear? So I would dye my underwear because that was my way of, you know, having more control.

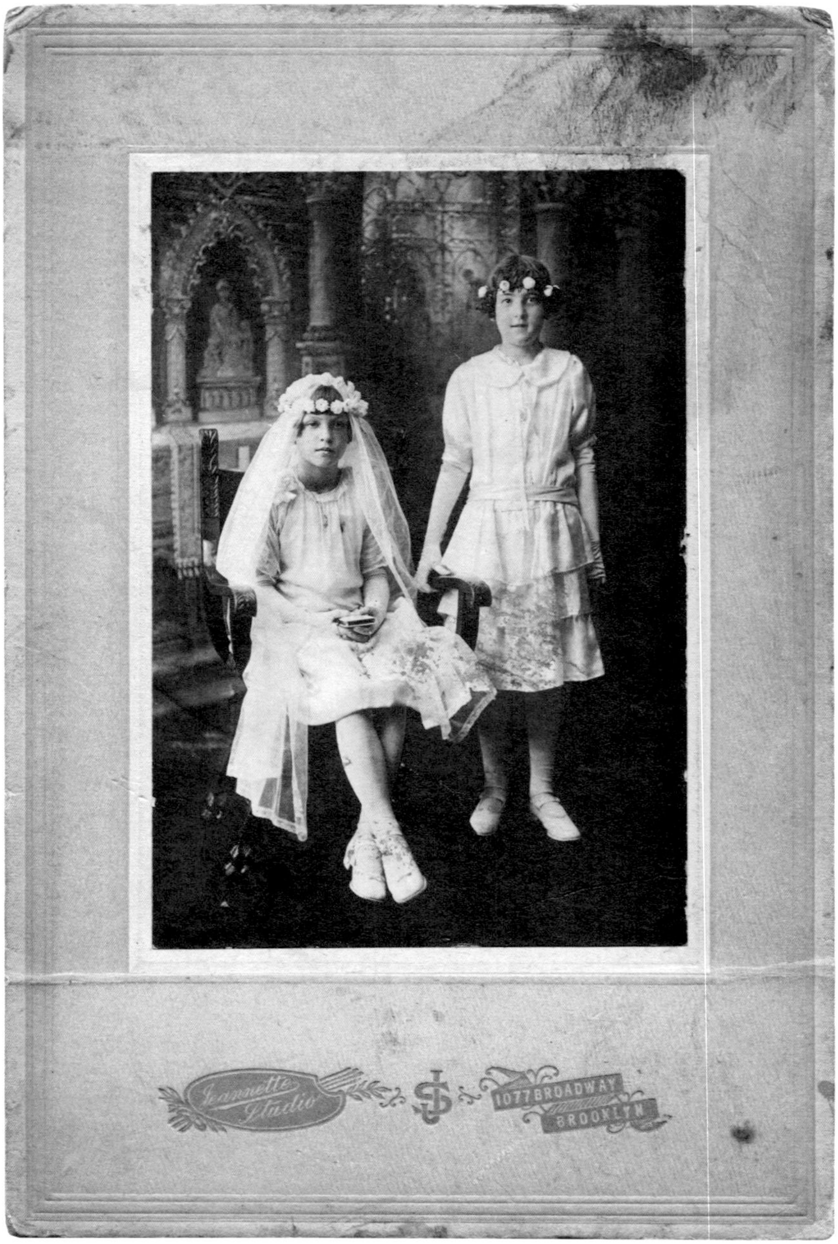
Jeannette Studio
1077 BROADWAY
BROOKLYN

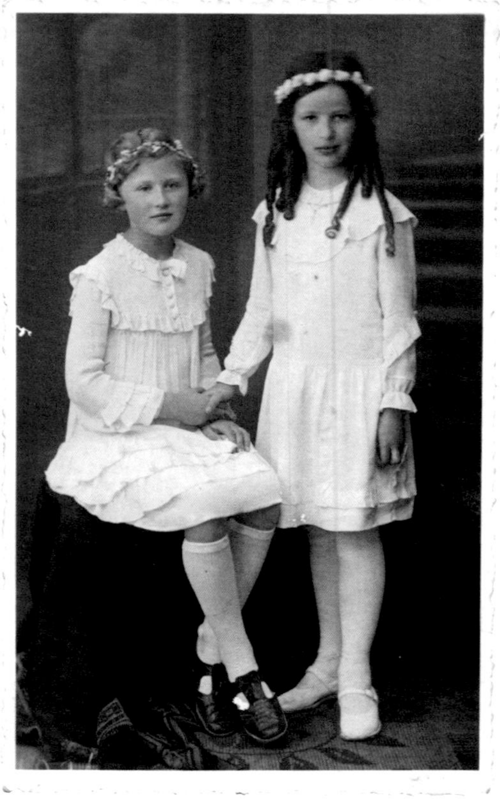

On the day my aunt had a visitor, quite an important visitor. And I sat – I was sitting there while they were talking and I think I sat with my hands between my thighs – and afterwards she was so ashamed of me.

She thought it was suggestive?

Yeah, but when you are little ... She absolutely went ballistic. She really did give me a good hiding. She hit me. But I think it wasn't so much the impact of the smacks. It was the shock. I was in shock, and I was so shocked, so shocked that I messed myself, honestly. It was so embarrassing. I was just absolutely, you know when you're so shocked ...

... that your body loses control?

Yeah, because I just didn't know what I'd done wrong. And the worst thing was that, where she lived, there were people living on either side. All the people, they could hear her shouting – out there when something goes wrong they all gather. They were all gathering by the front, you know, by her door, while I was getting this hiding, and she was chasing me around too. I just don't remember anything much after that. I just remember ... messing myself ... just being ... I just couldn't understand what I'd done.

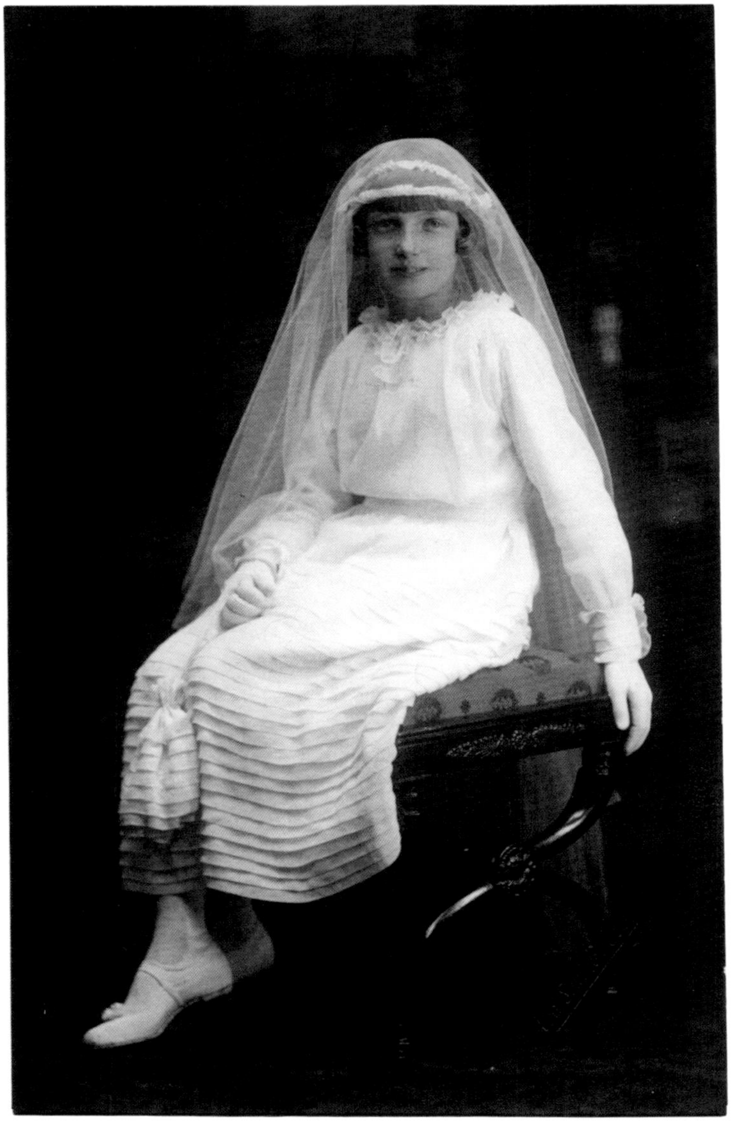

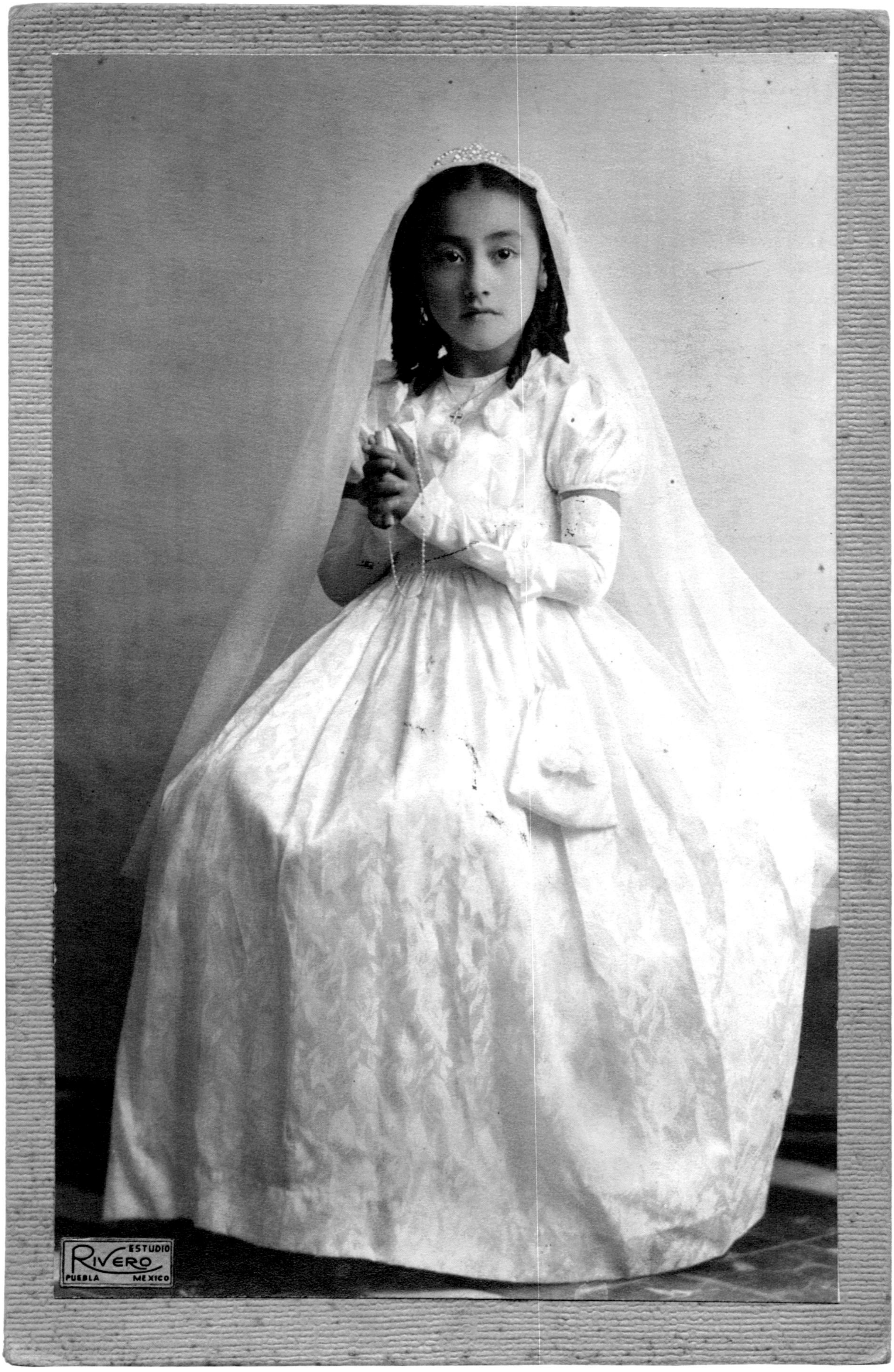
ESTUDIO
RIVERO
PUEBLA MEXICO

They said, 'Do you repent all your sins?' and we said, 'Yes.' And they said, 'Do you take the body of Christ?' and we said, 'Yes,' and then they gave us the Host. I felt like I was cleansed, or I felt so different.

Did you really? How?

Yes I did. I felt like a whole different person, you know. I felt clean. I didn't feel like a dirty person with evil thoughts. I don't know, I felt so like, wow, because it was the first time I ever had felt that. I wish I could go back to that day – it was special. Yeah, it changed me inside. And I still have the dress, still.

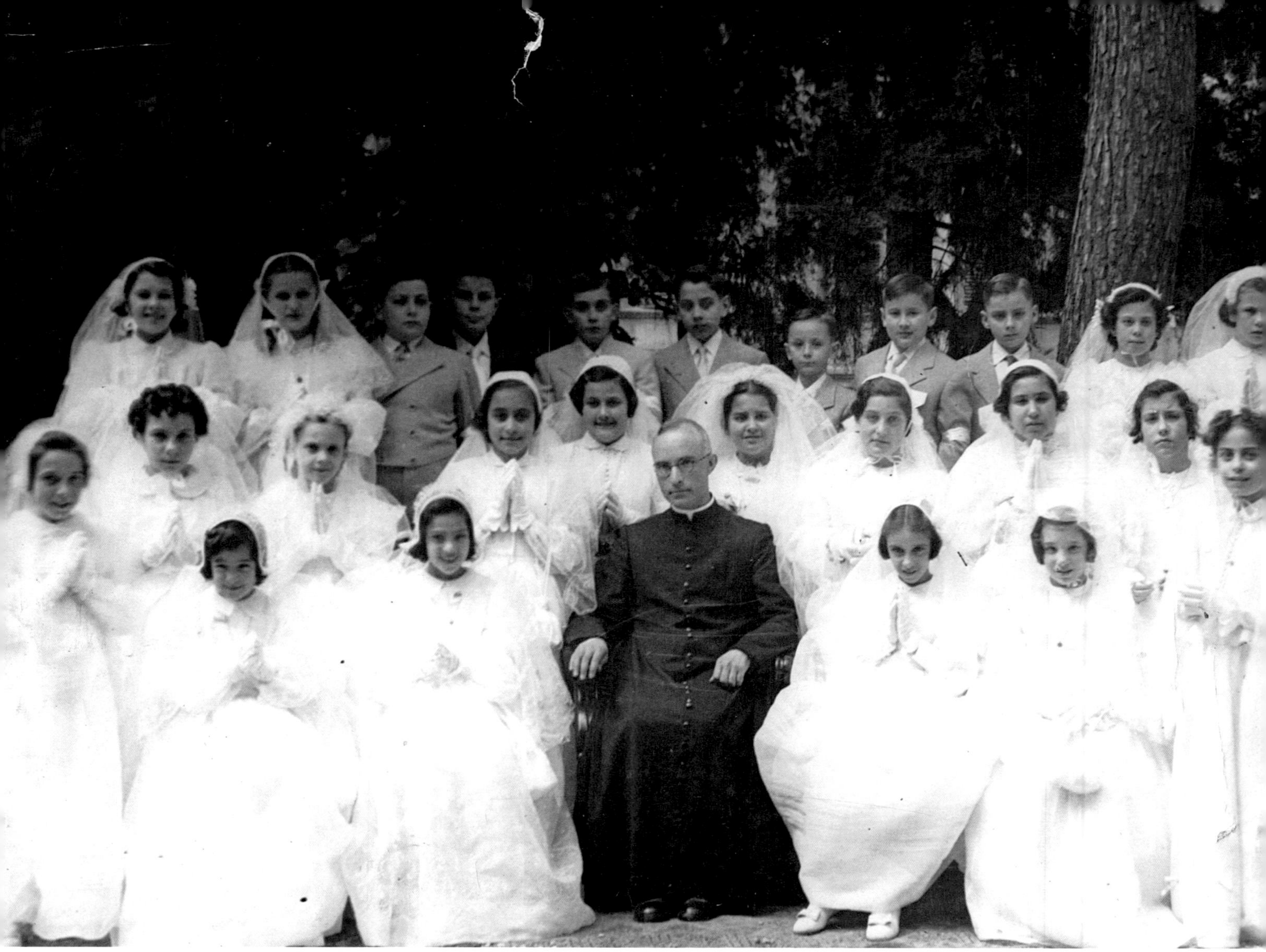

In the shop I looked fine, but when I actually put it on at home it didn't look good and I was sort of – I started the day off very tearful because I didn't want to wear it. Because I was the only little brown face stuck in a sea of white faces and I felt odd. And it made me scared as well 'cause we were told that we had to starve; we weren't allowed to eat from the previous midnight, basically to cleanse your body and soul and all that. And I thought, well, I haven't changed colour so I can't be pure yet.

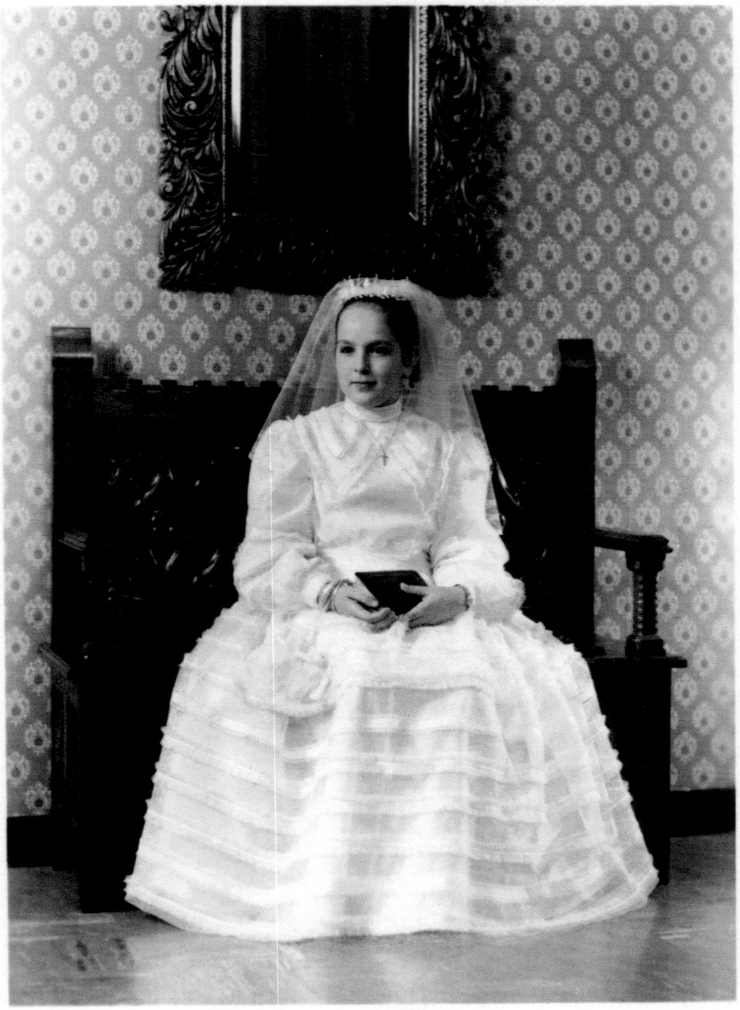

And the photographs – I think, oh my God, back drawer, underneath, don't look at them. Yeah, I do, yeah. But they were awful. We've got a couple of group ones that my father took as well, and it is just this little brown face stuck in this sea of white … And that is the first time I realised I was a different colour. A different colour, yeah, 'cause I'd never seen myself as a colour before then, you know? My mum was brown, my dad was white. It didn't matter to me what colour one was or the other. My friends were white, you know. I'd met brown people, but I'd never had much to do with them. But it wasn't until I was surrounded by them, and I was actually being photographed group-wise, that I realised it, yeah. It was a real eye-opener for me. Not only in the fact that, you know, I took Holy Communion but the fact that I realised who I was.

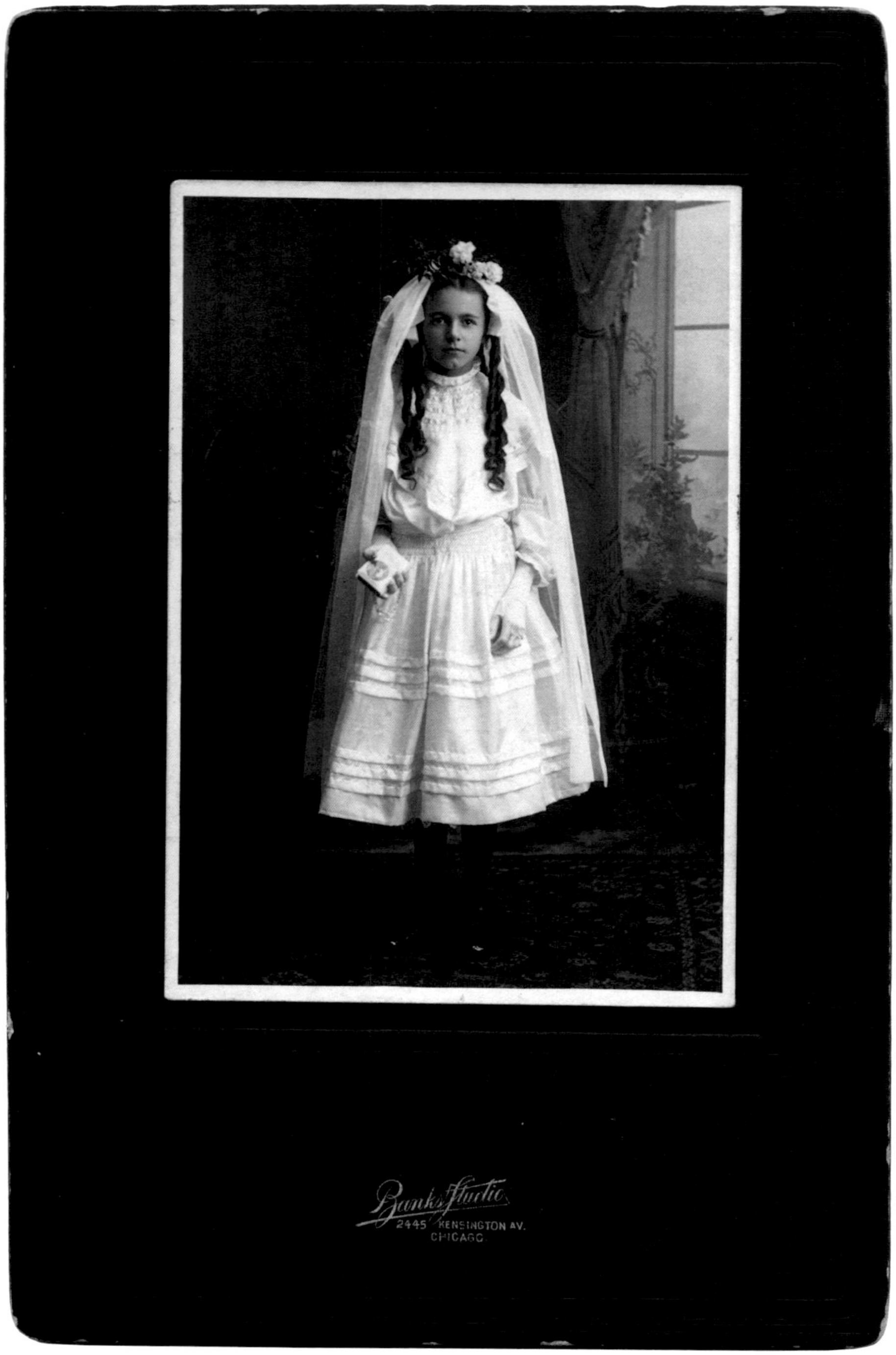

I was known as 'La Negrita Consentita' by my grandmother. I was her favourite. Consentita is, I think – and I was going to look it up for you – I think it means spoiled, endeared, you know, one that – I could get away with anything. I mean, I had power like you would not believe. Oh, incredible power. I was the eldest of two girls. And not only that, I was the favourite grandchild out of all the grandchildren. And I think it had to do with being the darkest one. That was very intriguing to my grandmother for some reason.

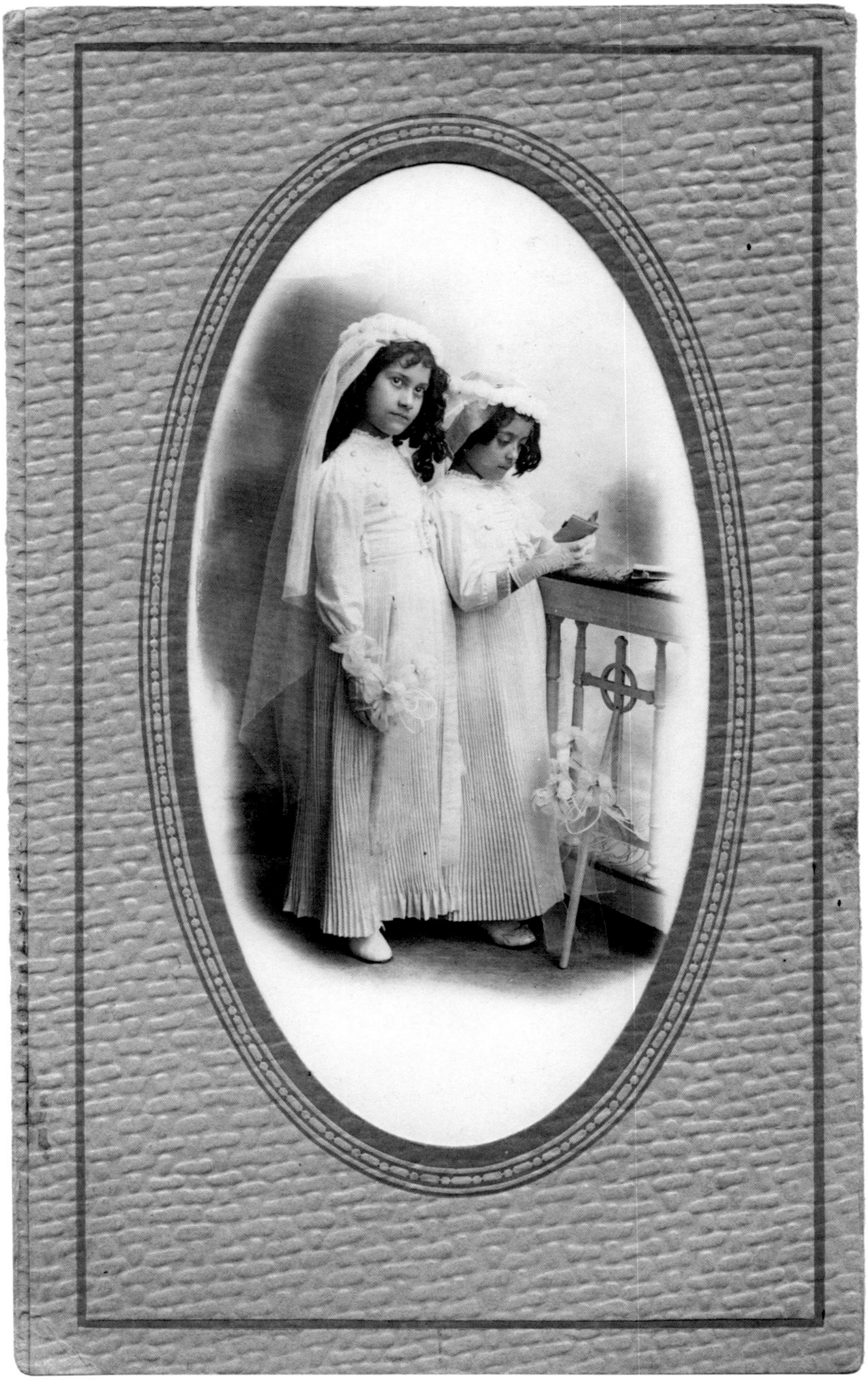

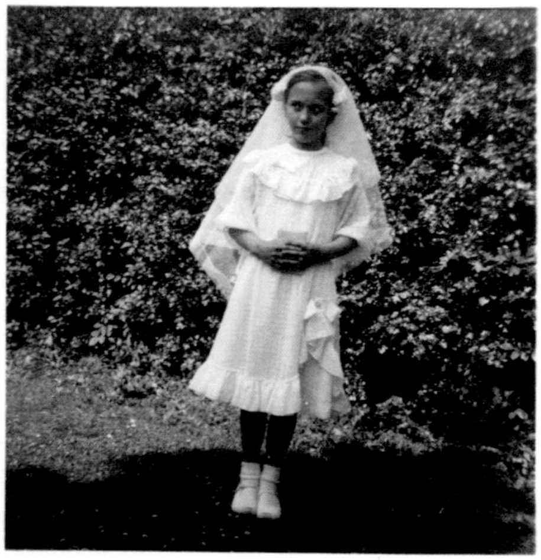

I remember something about them telling us that our soul – was it our soul? Yeah, it was – was like this white mass that was covered in … The way they described it, to try and describe what our soul was, was this white mass with lots of little black dots on, which were the sins. And there was always loads of black and you had to try and get rid of all the black.

Did they give you a size and shape?

I just remember them saying it was this white mass that's covered in black dots. Oh, I've suddenly remembered this other thing. We were in the church hall for some reason, doing all these different activities. And you had to write down, really secretly on a piece of paper, all the bad things that you'd done – sins. And there was this big bowl, a giant bowl in the middle of the table. You had to throw them all in and burn them. So all these sins were burning in the middle of the table.

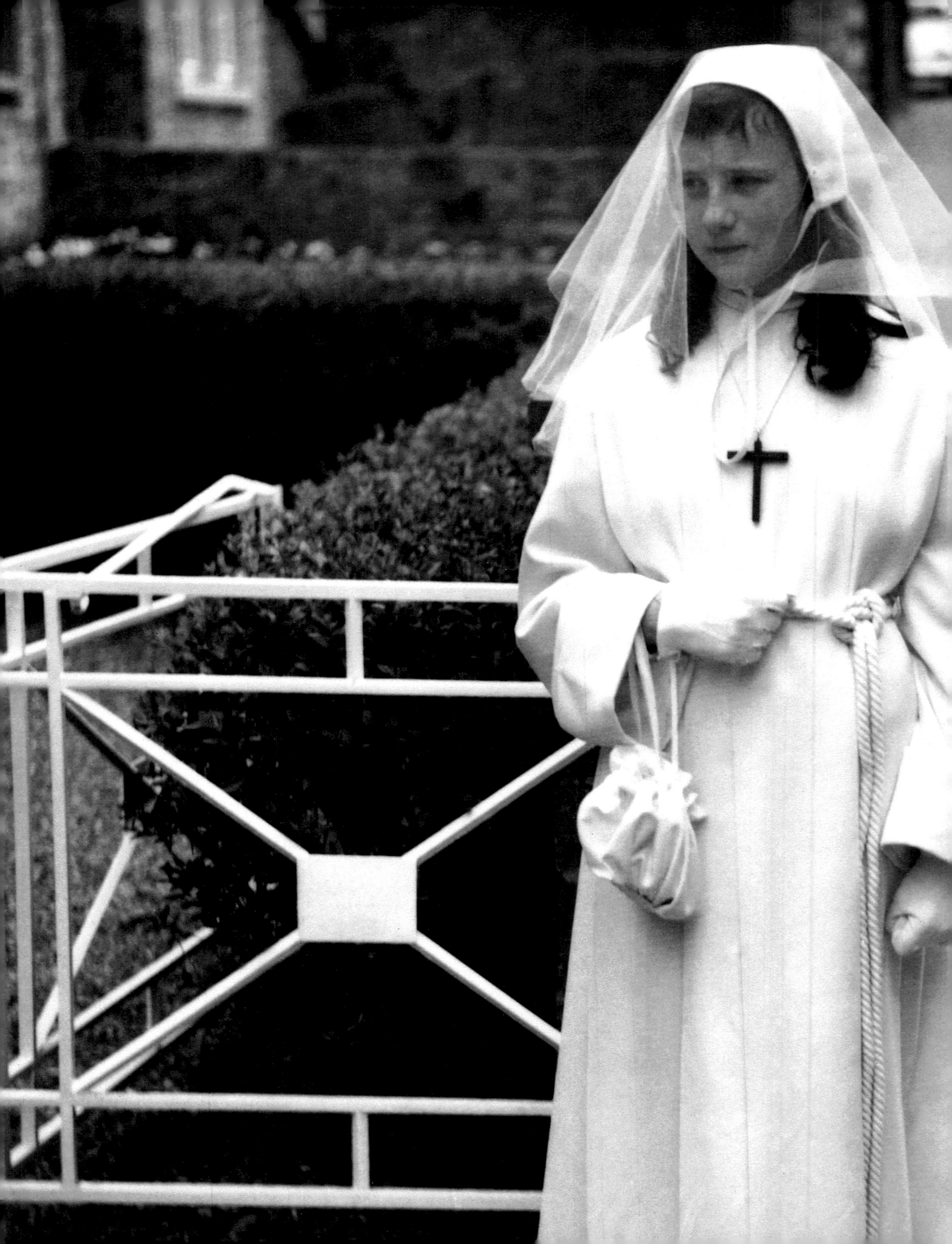

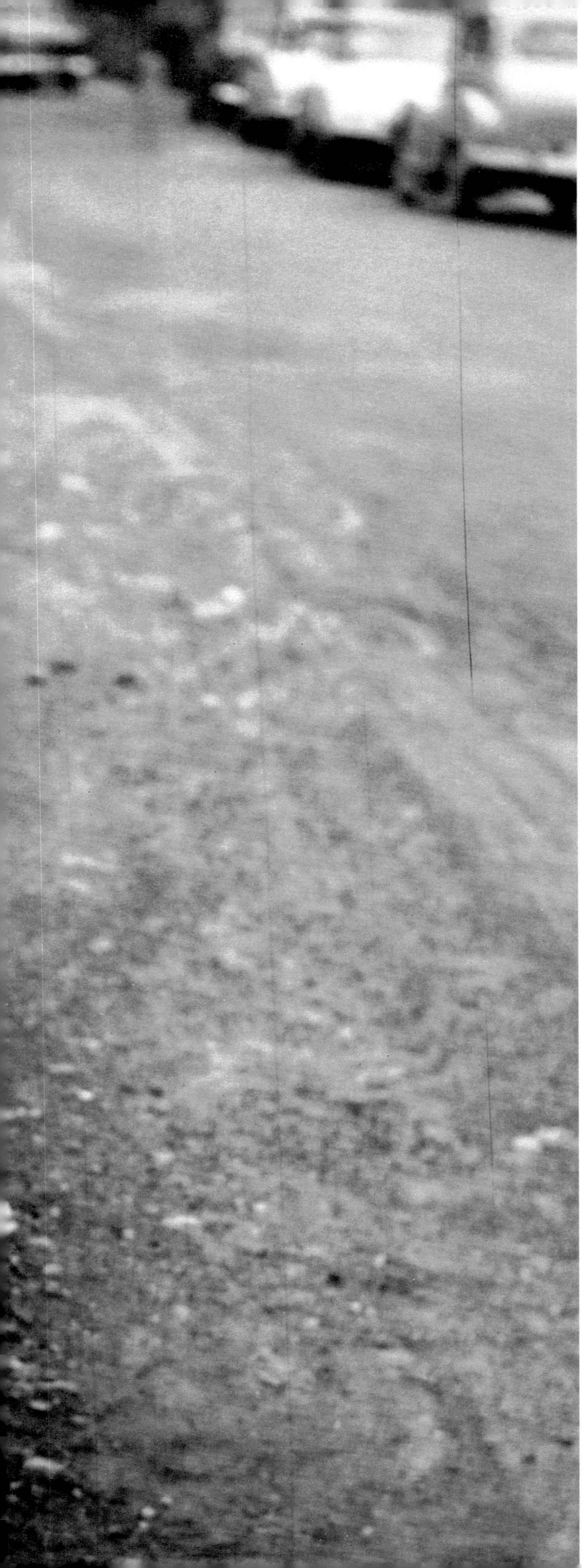

2

THIS IS MY BODY

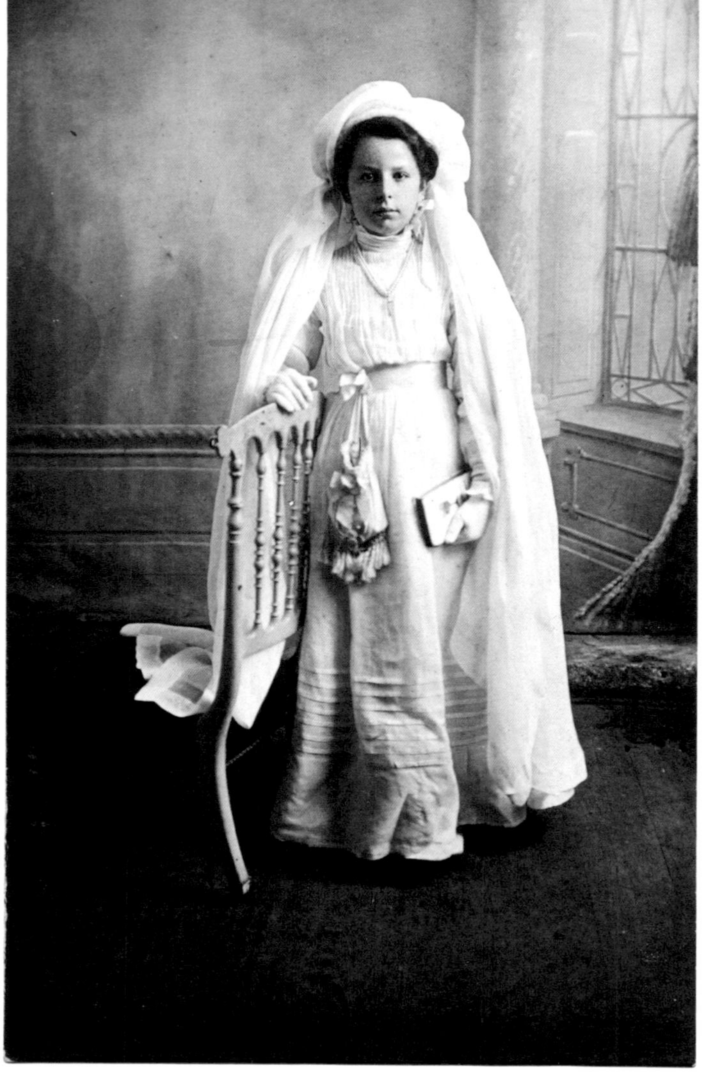

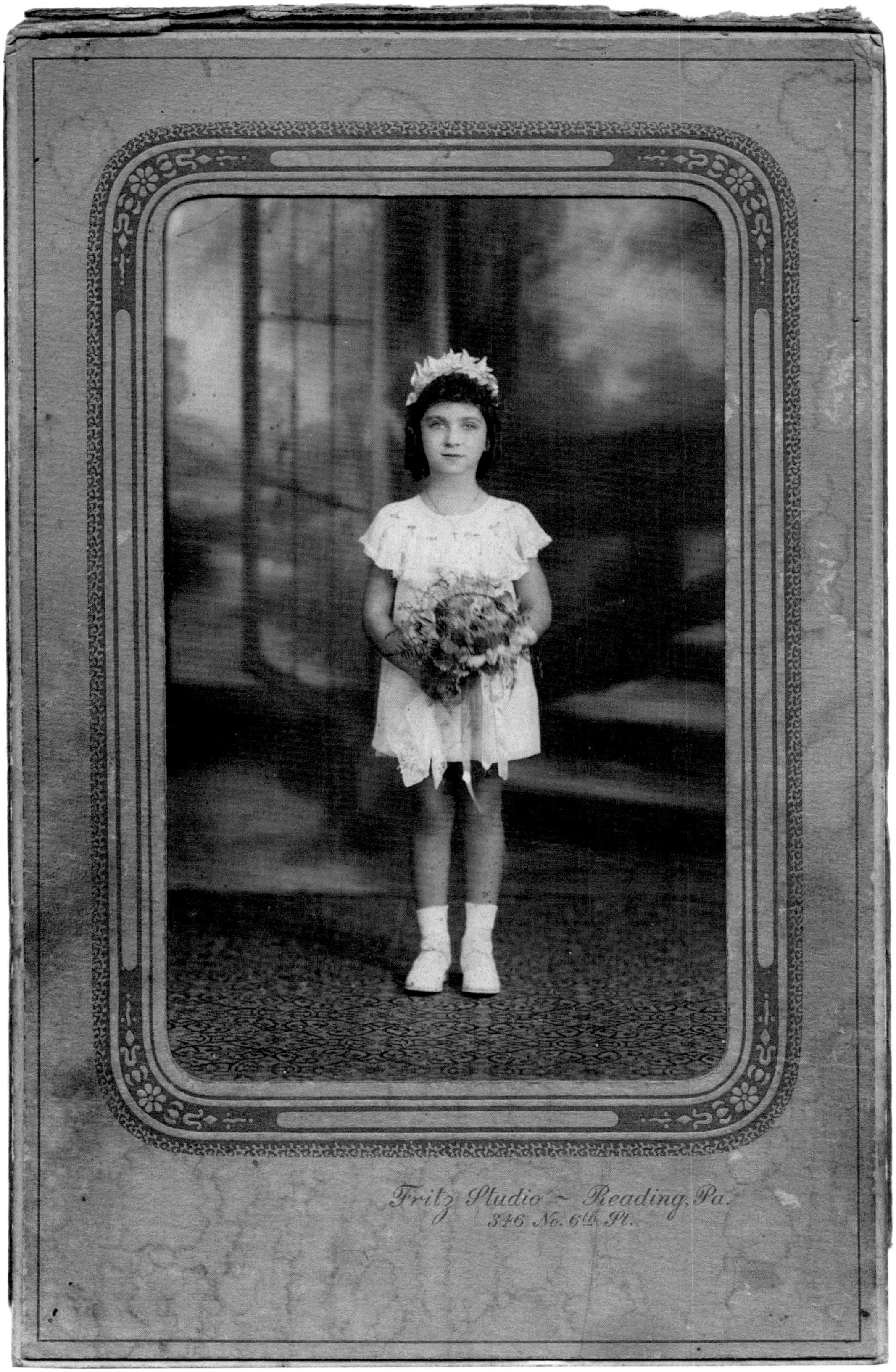
Fritz Studio ~ Reading, Pa.
346 No. 6th St.

The dress came over to Canada with us from England. It was that and my mother's pressure cooker. I can remember the two items that were most necessary, yes. I think the chipper as well you know, for cooking chips, that came over too. There were a few relics of our life in England that came with us. Anyway, the dress was one of them. But the dress was a long, sort of floor-length dress that had already been used by my grandmother and my mother and my mother's older sister and a couple of other aunties and my sister, of course. And so this was the dress I would wear on the day. But the other girls were having short dresses and this was a floor-length one so I made a fuss. It was cut down so that it just came to my knees. And so a wonderful little late-Victorian dress was ruined.

My grandmother bought my dress. I wasn't conscious of the dress at the time, that it was a pretty dress or that other dresses were prettier. But after the Communion my mother lent that dress to one of her sisters, for her child – a girl obviously. They destroyed the dress and it never came back to me. I was angry with my mom always for doing that. Even into my twenties, I was very angry with my mom and I told her. It wasn't her dress to lend to anybody, it was my dress. My mom didn't recognise the dress as that special.

How soon after your Communion was it given away?

Within five years. My aunt was struggling financially so, I mean, it was a nice thing that my mom did. And I don't know that I would have worn that Communion dress, because who wears a little white, puffy, lacy dress? But I was very sore about the fact that I never got that dress back. So, for me, it was very important. And maybe the day was more important to me than it was to my parents actually, in the long run. Because I liked it and it was the first sacrament that you receive, or that I received, that I was conscious of. So it was the first 'something' that I could begin to contemplate and I did like it. I was fairly intrigued by the whole thing, but she gave my dress away and it pissed me off.

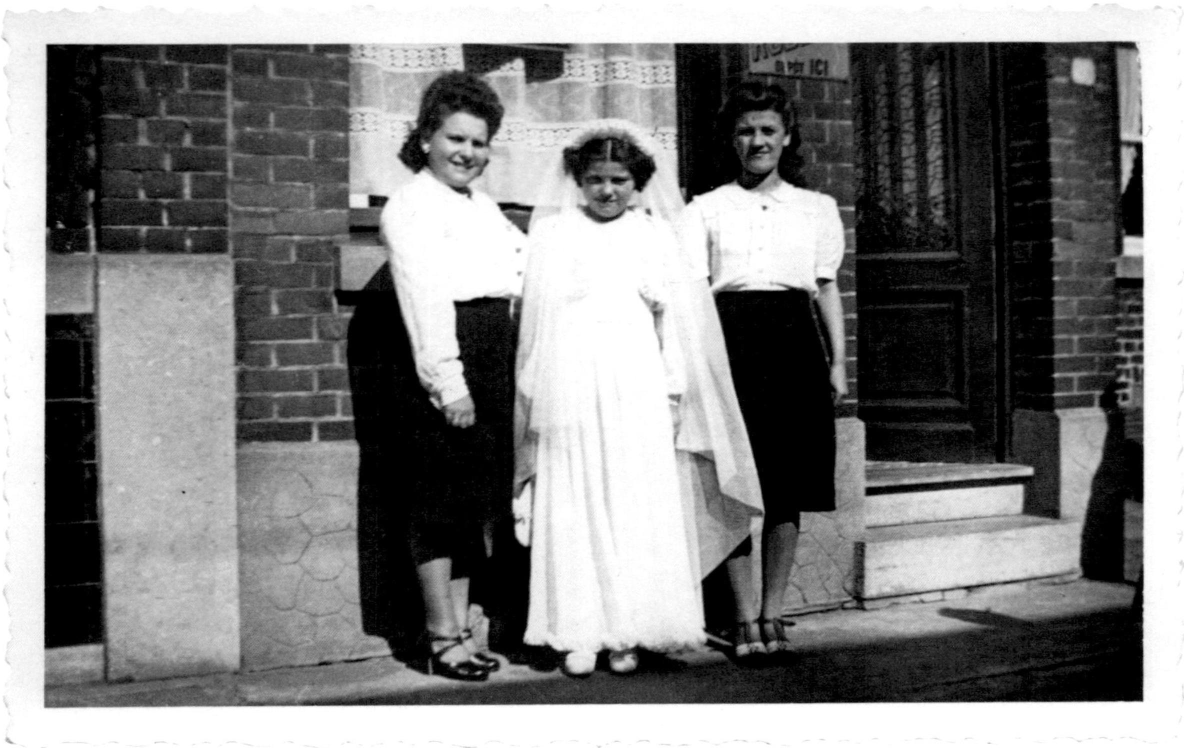

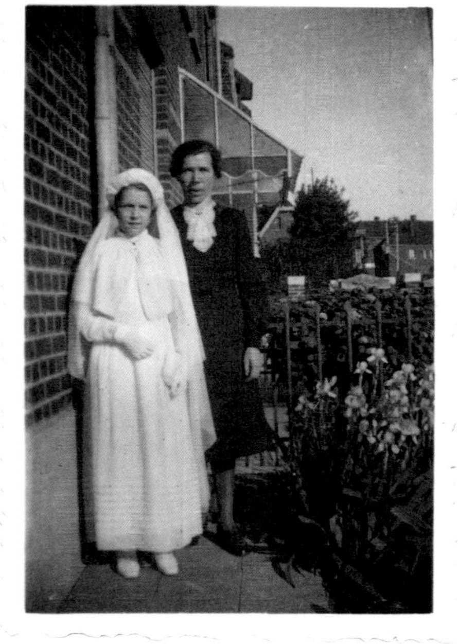

It's funny, I was just thinking – my mother's wedding dress was very similar to my Communion dress, which says it all really. Very similar – I just spotted it.

Do you find that odd?

No. It's a bit obvious really, isn't it? She picked the dress.

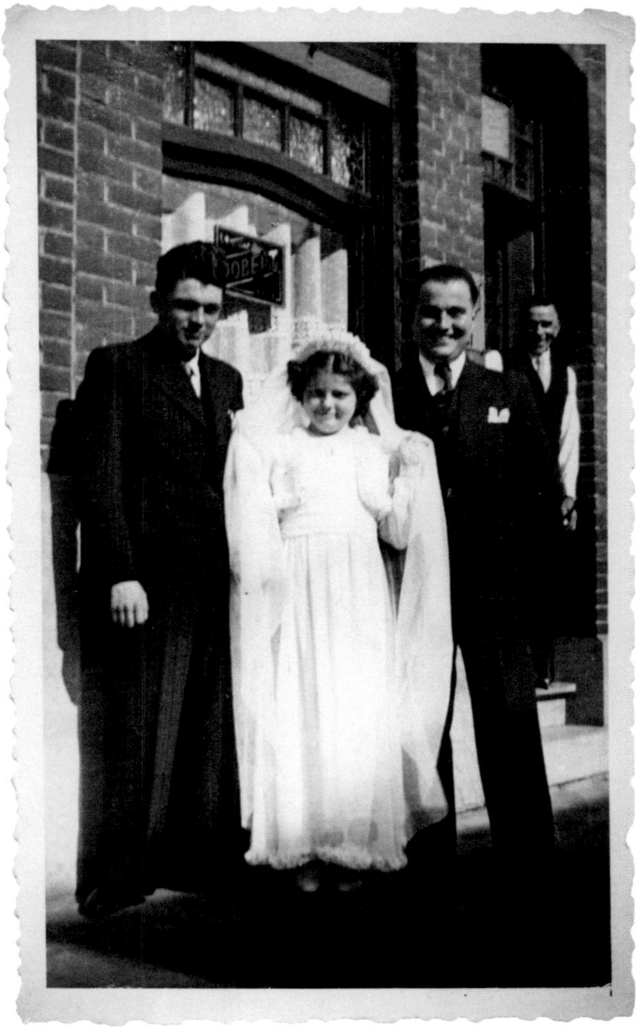

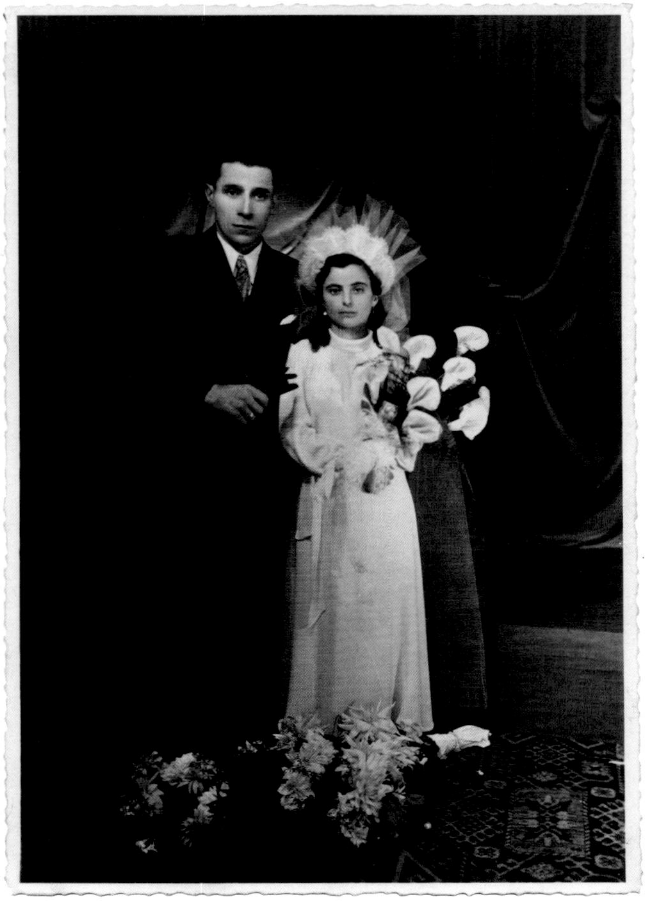

Fathers … do they really play a role?

I get the impression – from memory and various other things – that the whole buying of the dress is something that the father would have saved up for – you know, if they were poor. It would have been a big thing and it would be a gift from the father to the daughter, you know, in a tradition where the mother doesn't work. But I didn't have that because my father's not a Catholic and my mother made the dress. So, yeah, I did get the impression that father–daughter thing was quite important, you know, but not in my particular instance.

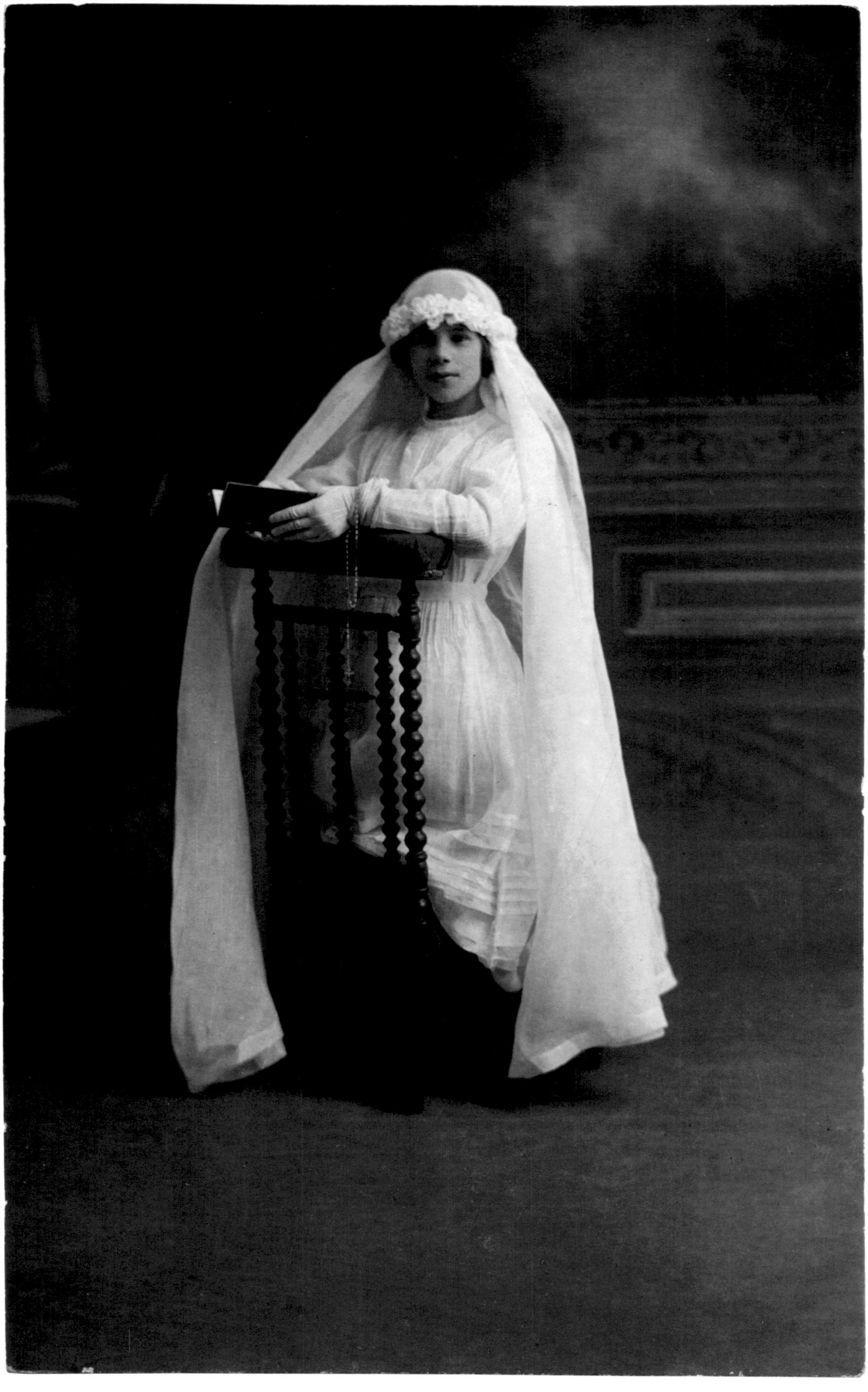

There's a kind of grown-up look
on the face.

But it's sort of fake, because it's a great age, I think. That age is fantastic 'cause you don't know whether you're pretty or not. You put on your new clothes and you think, aren't I fantastic? Whereas even three years later you'd be worrying because your nose is too big, your this is too big. But at that age you think the trappings make the creature, don't you? I mean you really believe in dressing up, that it can transform you. I just wanted to be more transformed.

Into what?

I don't know.

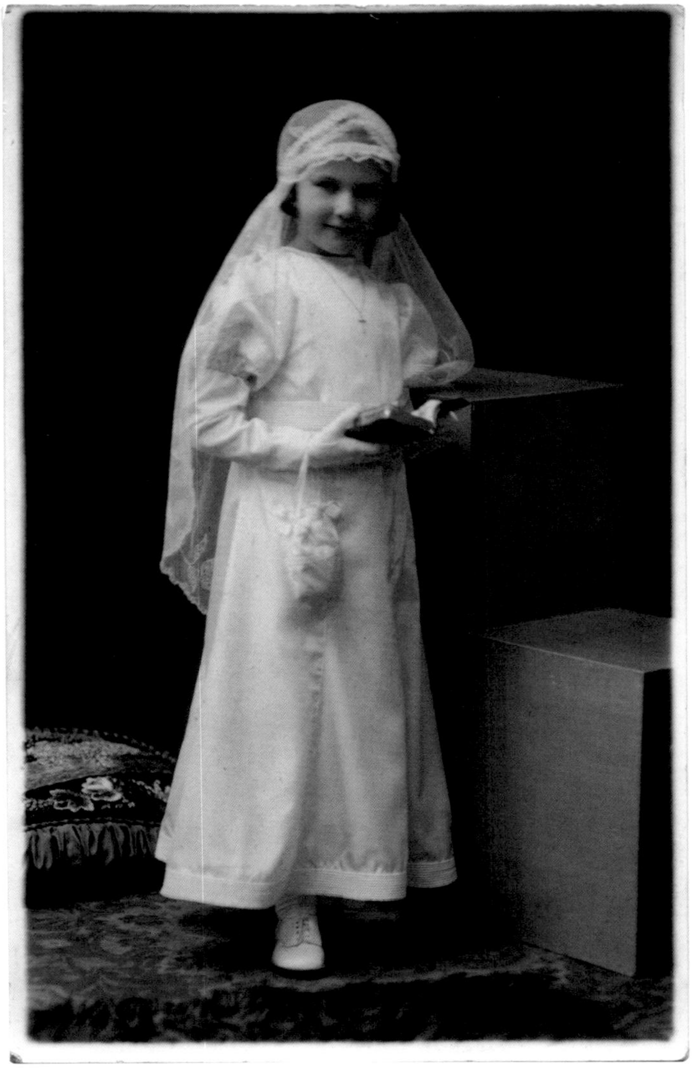

When you go to have your photograph taken, there's this really strange set-up in the back of the studio that makes you feel like you're in church … you look like this absolutely perfect virgin. You're innocent, you're perfect, you're having your First Communion, there are no blemishes. You have been to the confessional and have had everything wiped clean and here you are: the perfect virgin at Communion. And that persona is just instilled in you for weeks before, that you have to be this perfect lady. It is so interesting because it's all about the soul versus the body. And I see that.

You know, I don't think most people realise that this is what little girls go through, because you're already starting to compete. You go and pick out your dress and your hair is done … It's like we got started in Catholicism with this competition thing because I didn't care about those sort of things until then. It's like you're the show dog, you're the horse at the races, you're the beauty queen at the pageant.

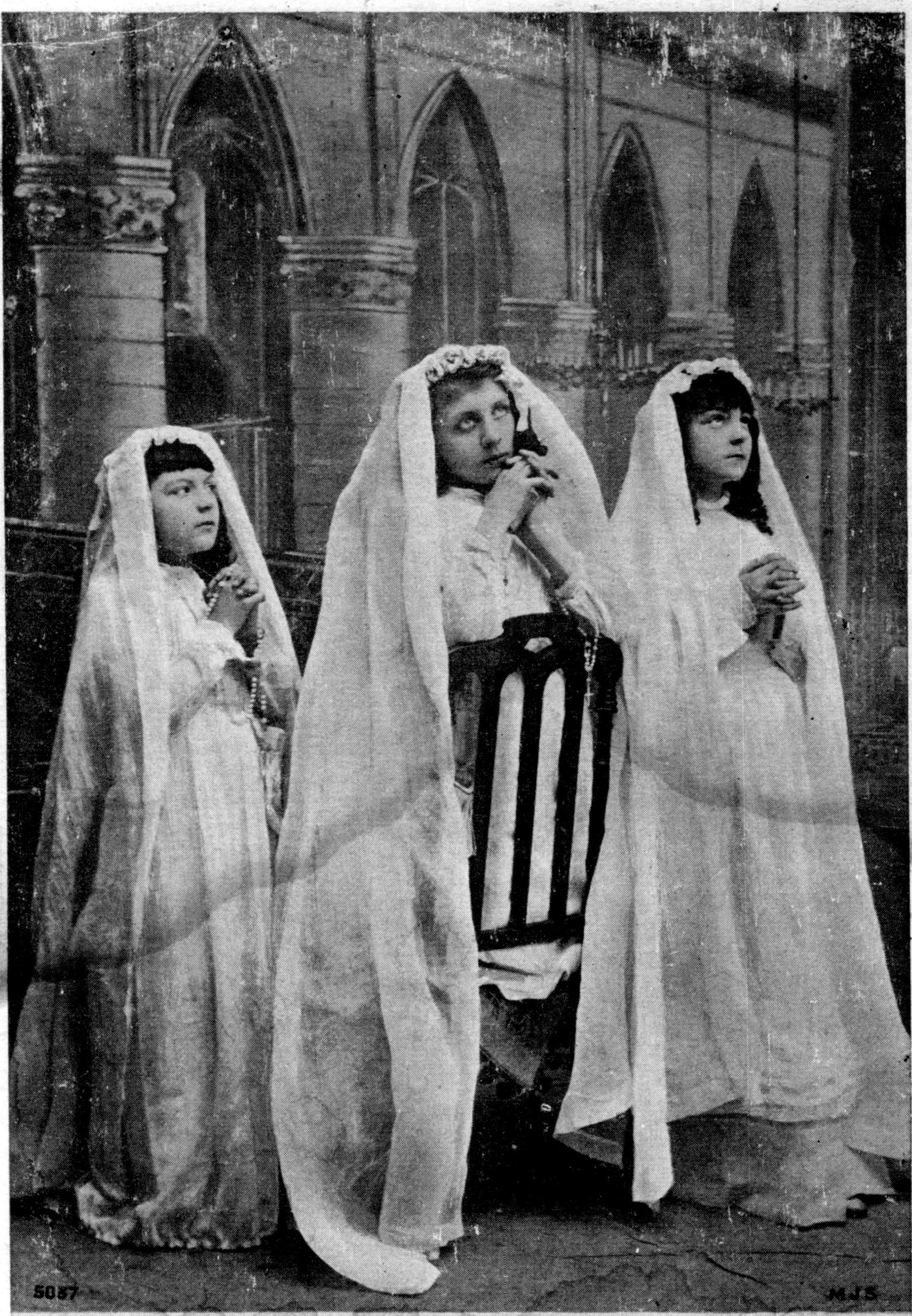

Souvenir de ma Première Communion

faite en l'Eglise d le 190

I have an identical twin sister and my mother took us both – we were making our Communion at the same time – she took us both to a store to get shoes. Somehow we got hand-me-down Communion dresses from our cousins in New York. My mother was very frugal, you know: whenever and whatever could be passed on – down, up, down, whatever – that's what happened. And she took us to buy shoes because they didn't have any. So maybe that's why they were so special – because they were bought just for me, with me in mind. Anyway, there were only two pairs of white shoes that fit us, but they were two different styles. And my mother bought these shoes, and one was far prettier than the other. I was kind of a manipulator, I guess, because we had somewhat of a large family, you had to do what you could to get what you wanted. I was a little more sneaky, more manipulative than my sister and I always got my way. So I somehow got her believing that the ugly pair was actually the nicer one so that I got the nicer pair. But I always got the nicer of everything.

Describe the two pairs of shoes.

Do you know, I can only remember my pair and I don't remember hers. Mine were just a kind of ballet slipper with a bow on it and a gold clasp and I think hers looked more like, I don't know, boys' shoes. But they were white, almost like loafers or something. But mine were just far more feminine and dainty and pretty. Actually my dress I think was prettier also. I always managed to get my way in these things.

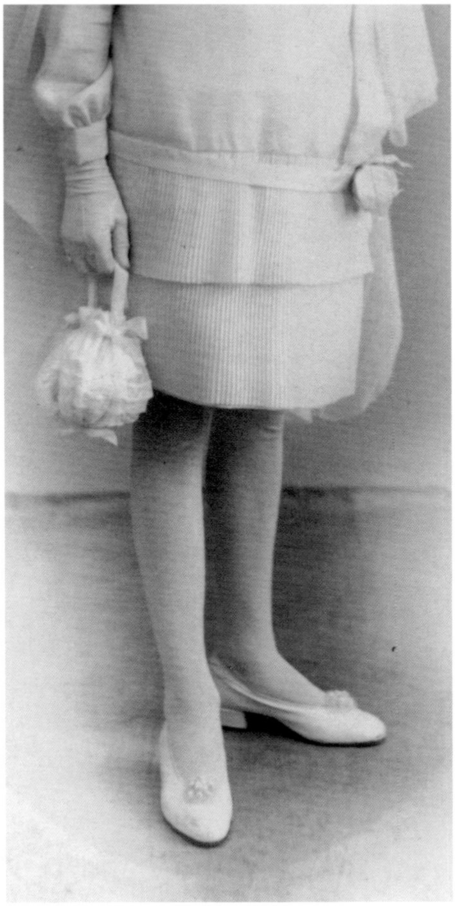
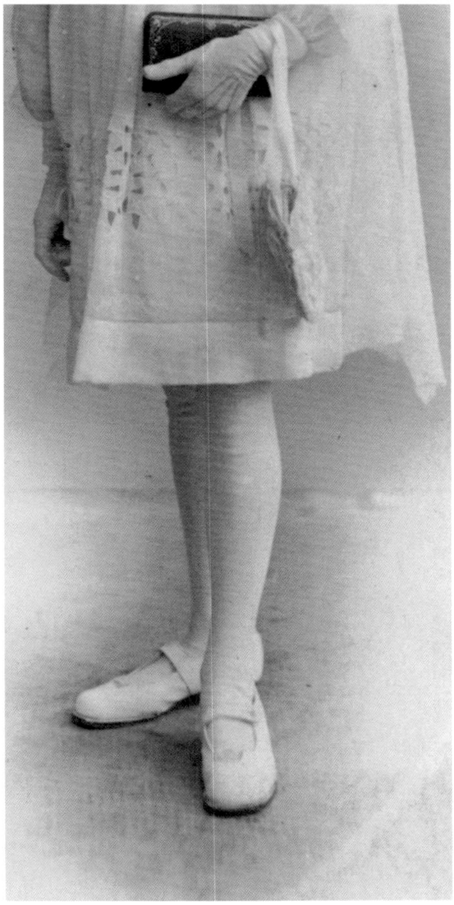

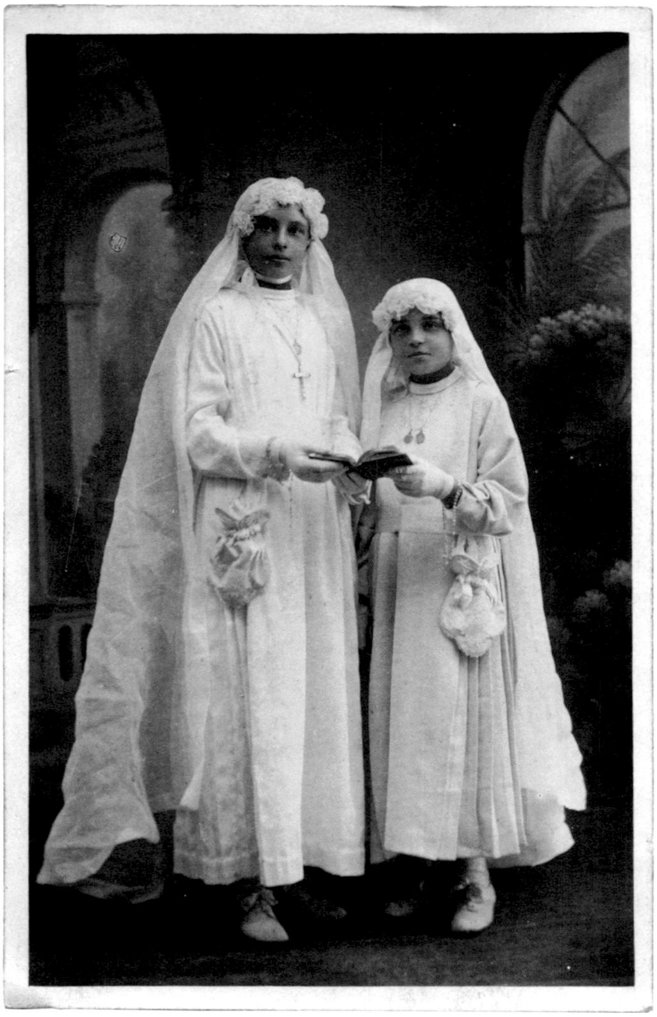

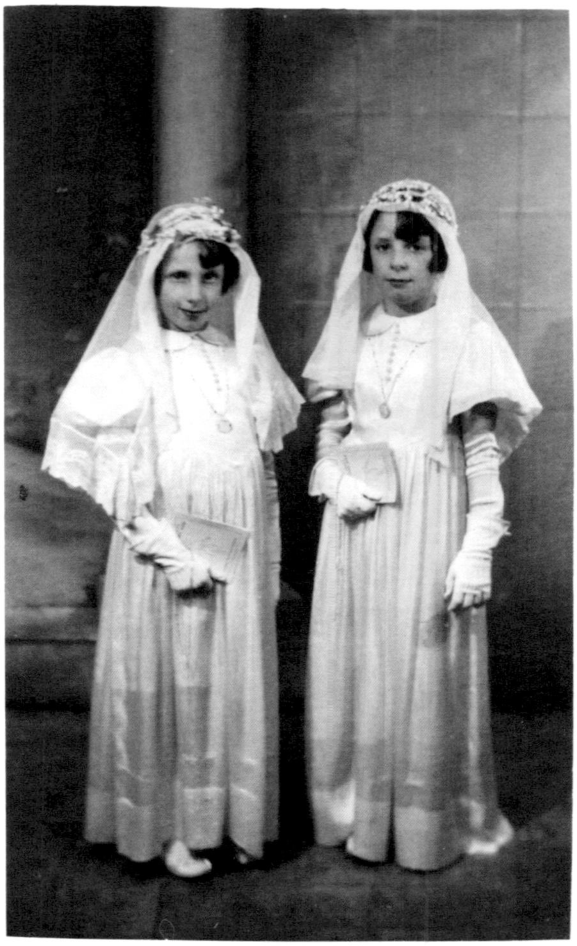

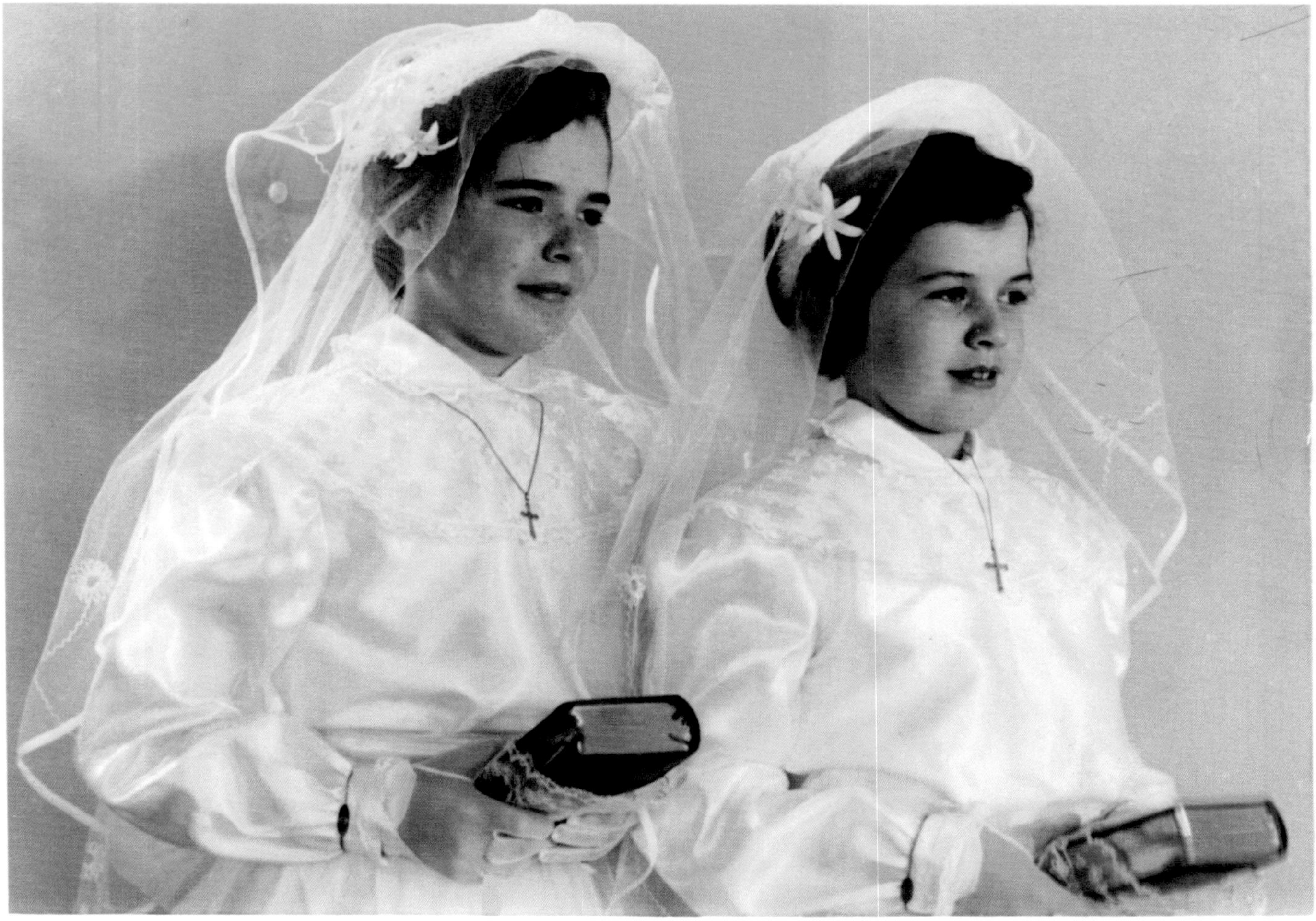

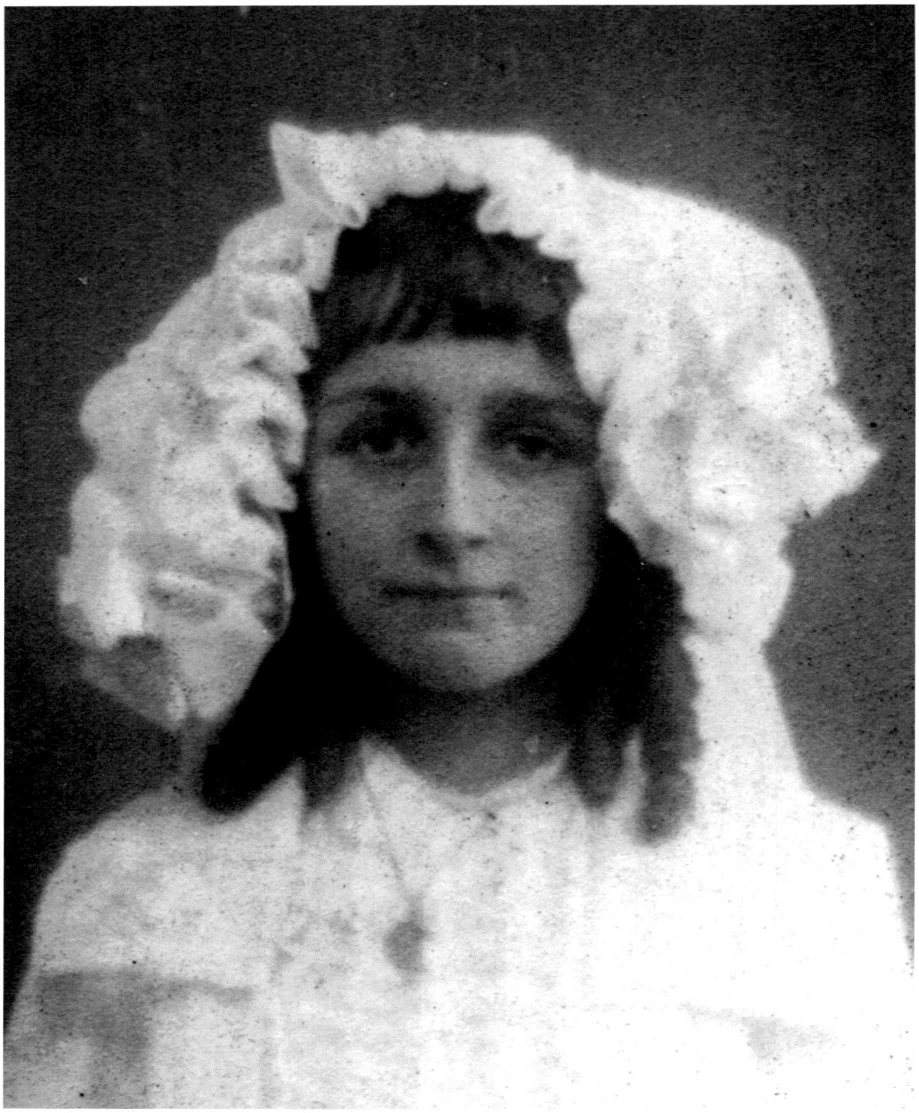

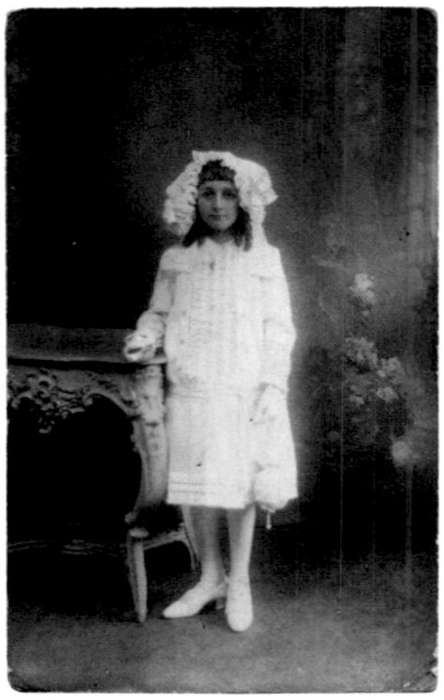

My dress, you know, wasn't as good as everyone else's. I felt sort of shabby. My shabby dress … my shabby dress was made by my mother who went for the simple look, which is exactly not what First Holy Communion is about. Everybody else had big floaty gowns, lots of frills and things. I had a very simple, sort of 1970s number. I remember actually, afterwards, when Princess Anne got married, I thought to myself, she's wearing my First Holy Communion dress, because they had the same sort of bell-sleeves. Just above the knee it came to, and then I had the white socks just up to the knee. Everyone else had lovely floaty, gauzy veils and I had the 'old Catholic maid' look veil, as if a piece of lace has just landed on my head. No fitted aspect, it was just a tablecloth thrown on your head. So you know, I felt a little bit shabby.

It was kind of like, I don't know, going to a party. Because it's a real dressing-up time – it sort of plugs into all that romantic dressing-up. And there's a slightly bridal thing, but also a sort of princess thing, you know, being special, being really special. If my dress was some other colour, it would have been an everyday dress – basically that was the problem I think. My mum thought it looked fab. You can see in the photo that I feel as if I look frumpy, you know what I mean? My shoulders are down and there's no pride.

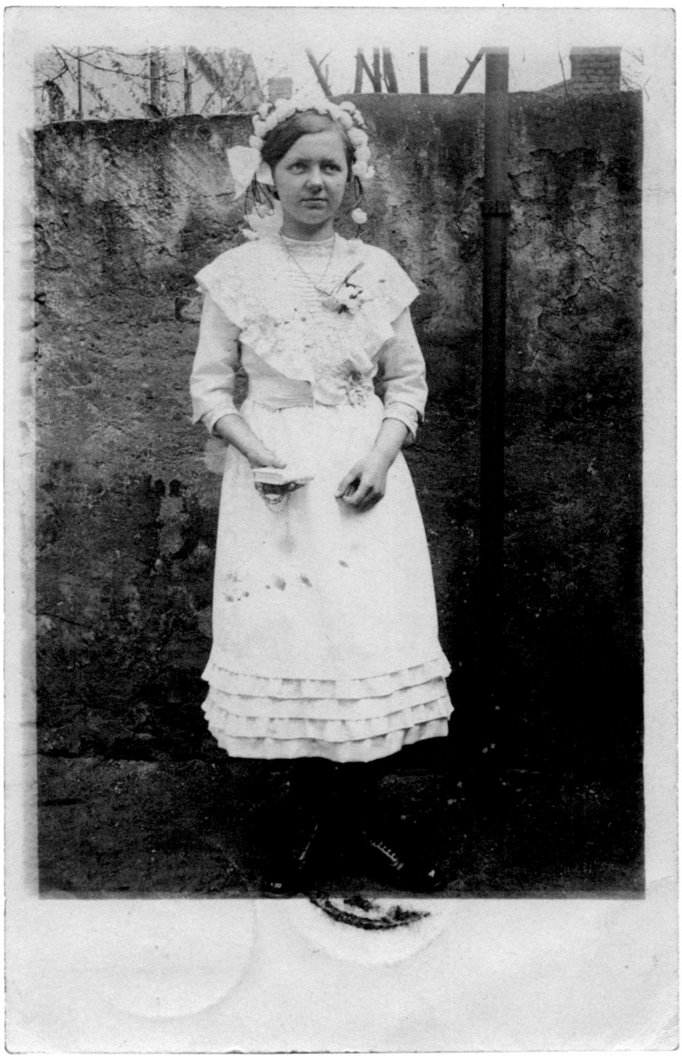

I remember it was the shoes I hated. I loved my shoes, but I hated them as well because I've got quite big feet. I've always had big feet. And all these girls in their little shoes, and I had these white patent shoes with flowers. I loved the shoes, but I just hated my feet in them. 'Cause they were about a size six, probably about a size five when I was eight. That's massive. I mean I've got size eight feet now. I remember just walking along and it was horrible, these big shoes.

Did the white draw attention to your feet?

Yeah, and I thought people would look at them and just think there's this nice dress and these massive skis at the bottom. I thought, oh if I just had small feet this would be perfect.

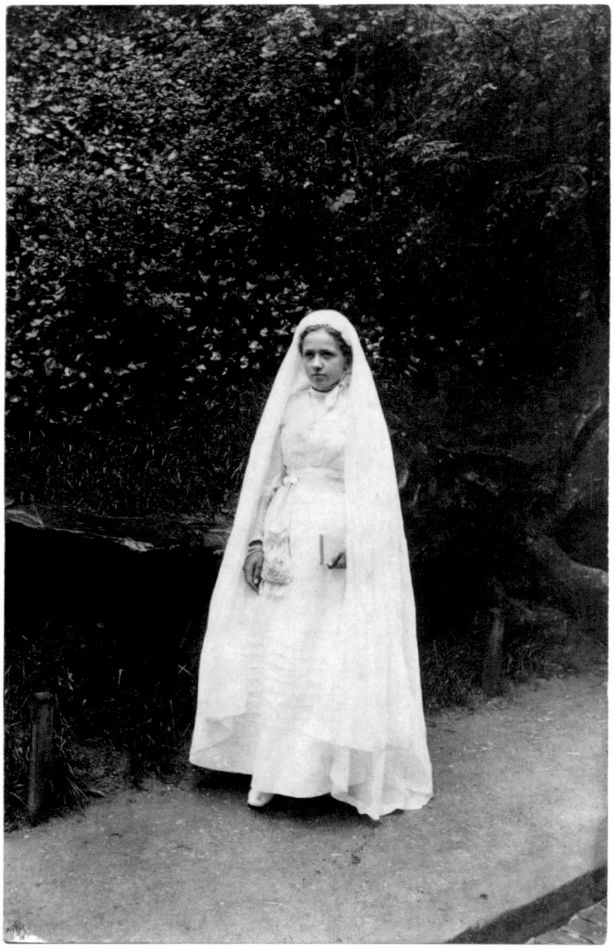

Did you have bobby socks?

No. I had to have a little garter-belt because you know, you had stockings – there were no tights. Pantyhose as they called them in America had not been invented. So we had these tiny little kind of garter-belt things. My mother had to teach me how to put the garters in and I had these little, slightly pinky-white stockings that went under the dress that were sold specially for First Holy Communions. The First Holy Communion Garter-belt Shop! I don't know where the devil it was.

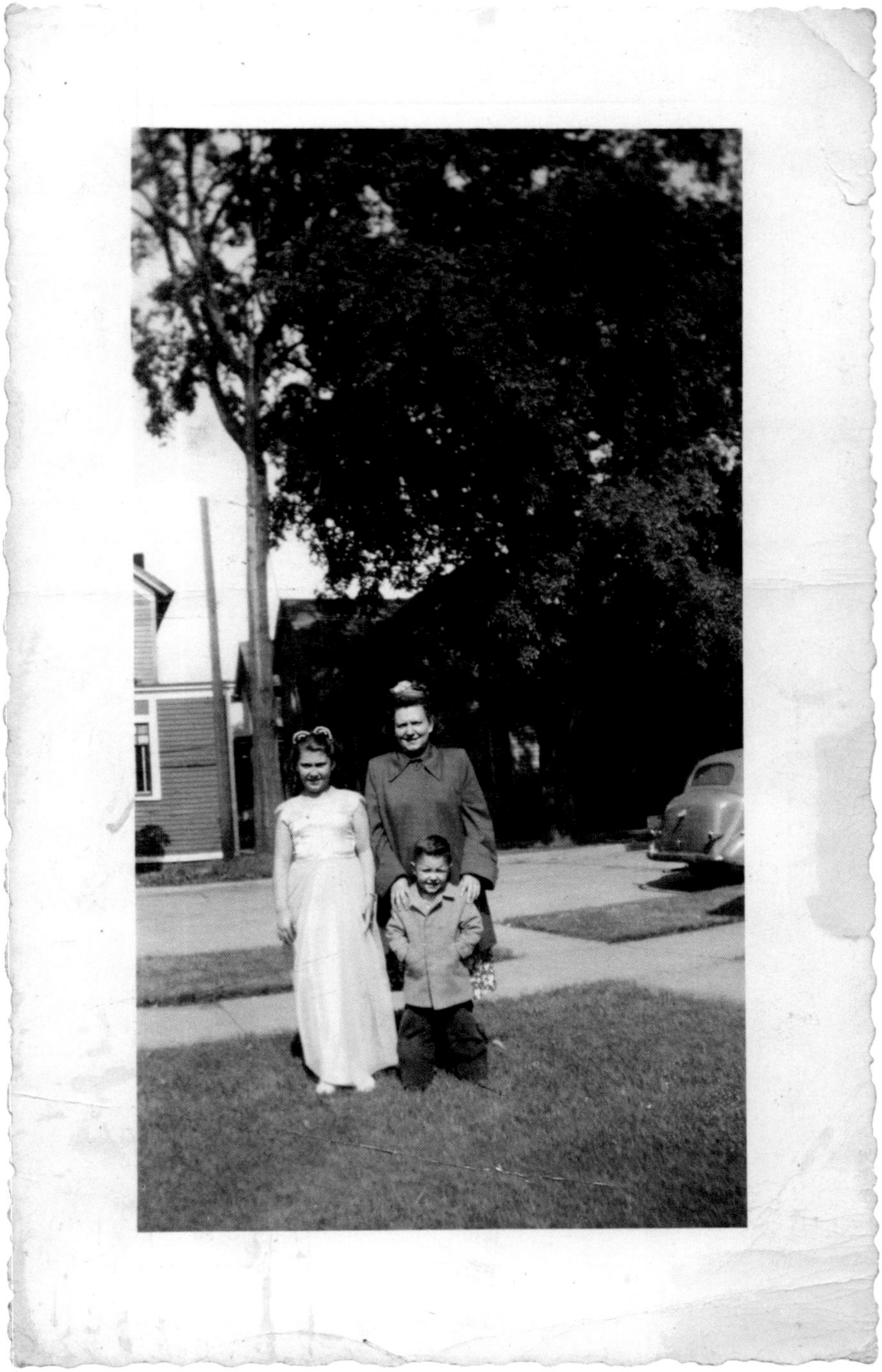

When I did my Holy Communion, I was eight. And I was really an early developer, and I had my period when I was eight and I got my boobs when I was eight. I used to go to the swimming club and my mum would, like, stretch down my top and say, 'Look she's got boobs.' I hated it. And she would be on the phone to her friends saying, 'Oh she's got her period' and I used to be crying all the time. My hormones were all over the place. Yeah, and the dress that we had to wear was all kind of tight. I really hated it, yeah, because it was quite tight at the top, so you could see my boobs and everything, and it was kind of short as well. And I remember on Holy Communion day we had to walk around the abbey, the ruins of an abbey, and it's outside and it's really beautiful. It must have been summer, but it was really, really windy. And my skirt was coming up and I was really, really embarrassed about that. Yeah, I remember my skirt coming up and trying to keep it down all the time, while holding my candle and trying to follow everyone.

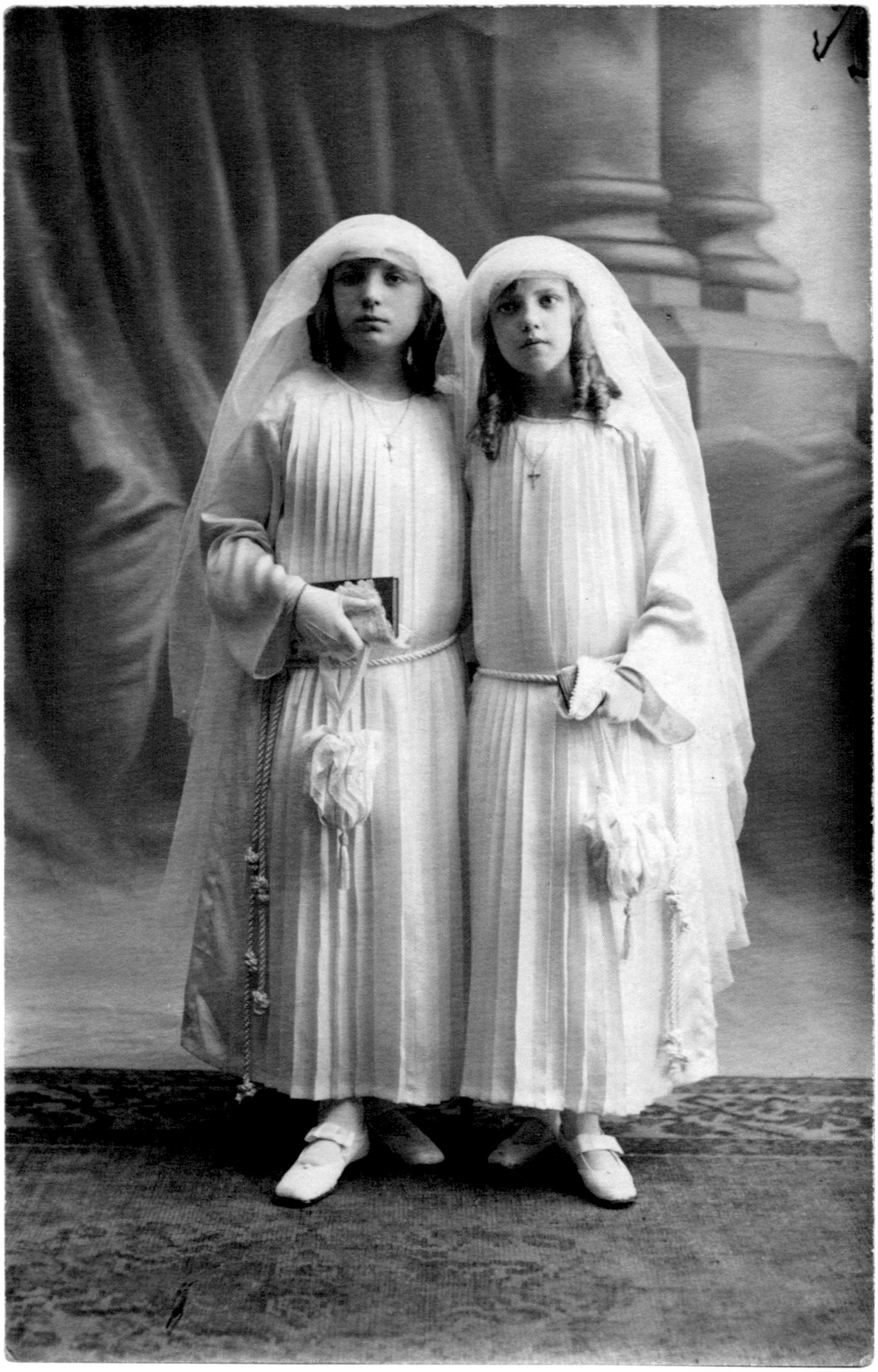

You learned to be too inhibited about your body, much too inhibited. I mean, to extremes where you can't let yourself go. When I first got married, I thought I had to be pure, just like Mary. I didn't think sex was part of marriage. I mean, that was my own hang-up, it doesn't carry through to all Catholic girls, but I wanted to be just like her. It was a great disappointment to my husband, you know. So I visited my family doctor and he explained to me what my responsibility was in this marriage. But I just thought because we were both Catholic he would understand. He had been in a seminary to become a priest at one time, so I thought that he would understand.

But he didn't?

No. It was hard to make that transition from abstinence into, you're married now, it's OK. You know, it's hard to make that jump. And I don't care what religion it is, children should be prepared in a different manner. They should be taught that it's something beautiful, not something awful, or dirty or, you know. Unfortunately, I didn't have a mother that could talk to me about something like that because she didn't have any experience.

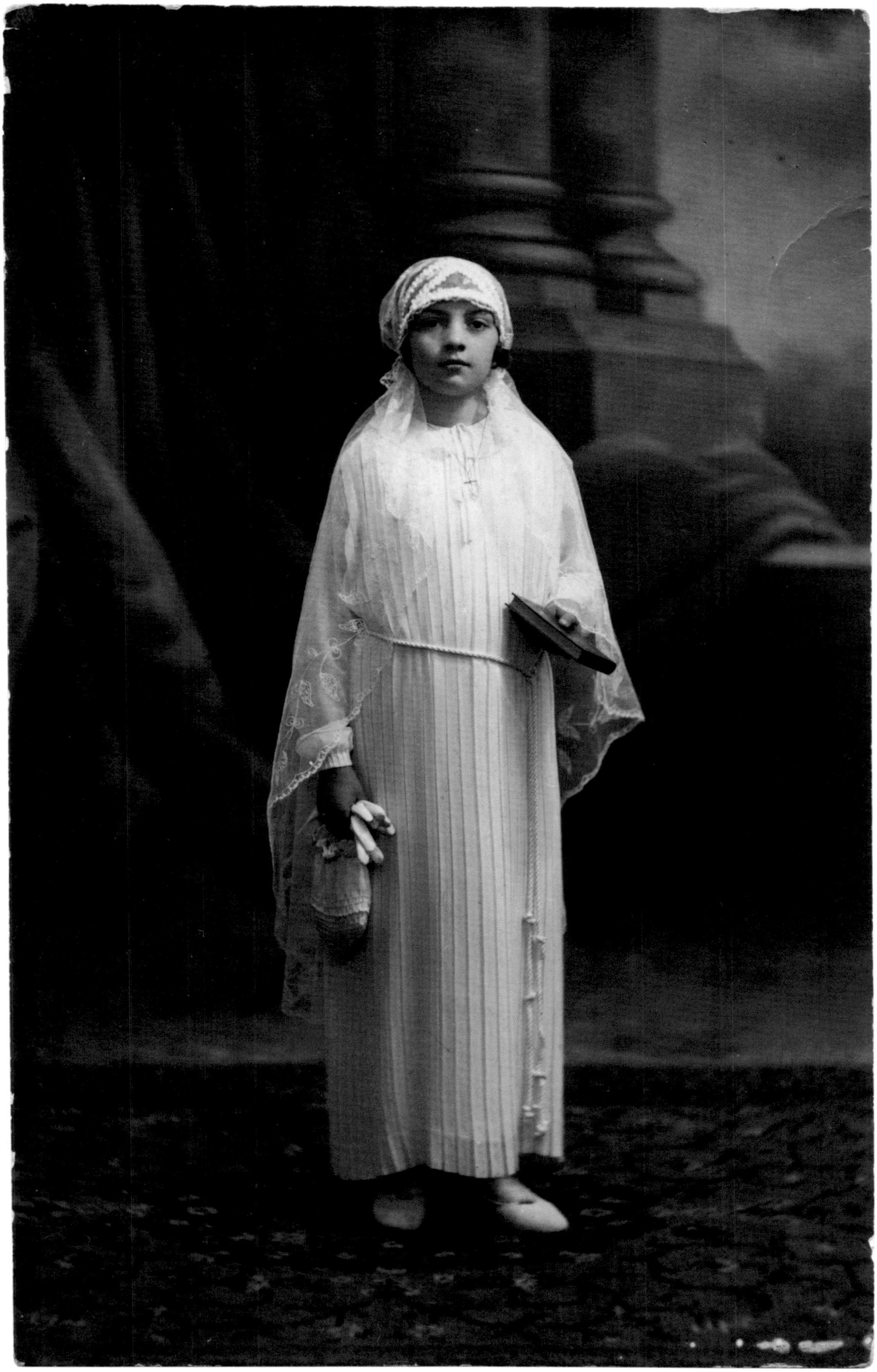

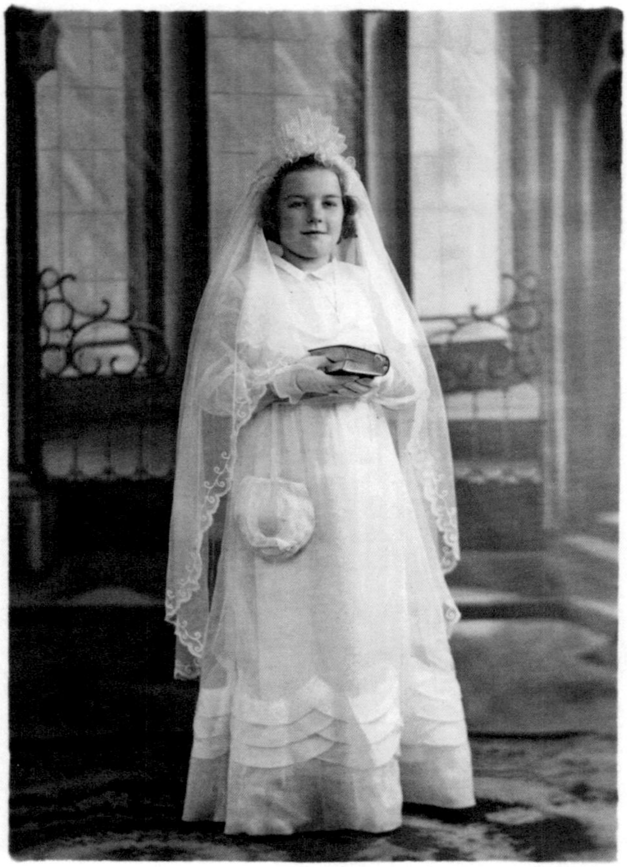

I felt all day like a doll, which has just been taken out of its box, with its beautiful white clothes; a bridal doll I suppose. So I had this feeling of being, I would say – starched, you know? As if I could scarcely bend in case I made a crease that became a crack.

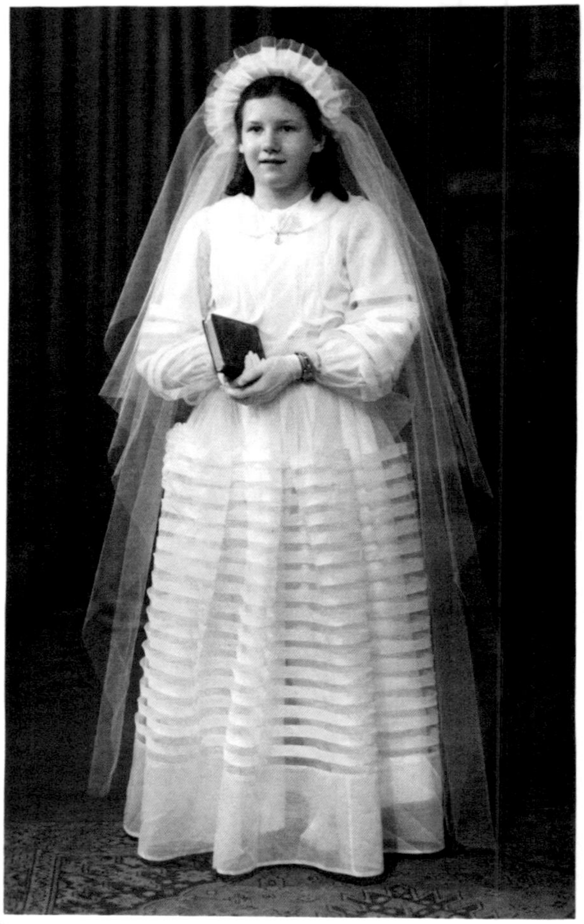

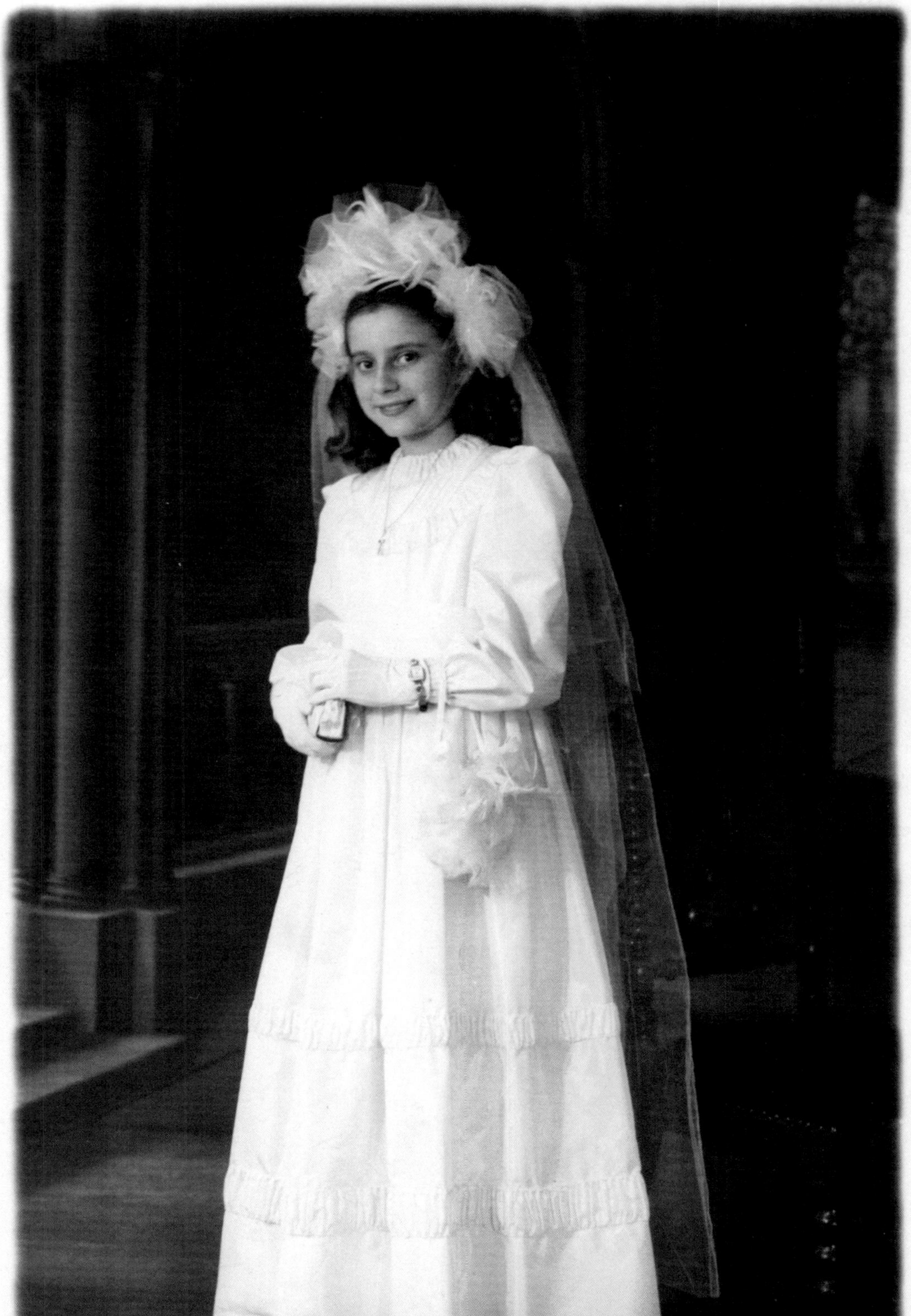

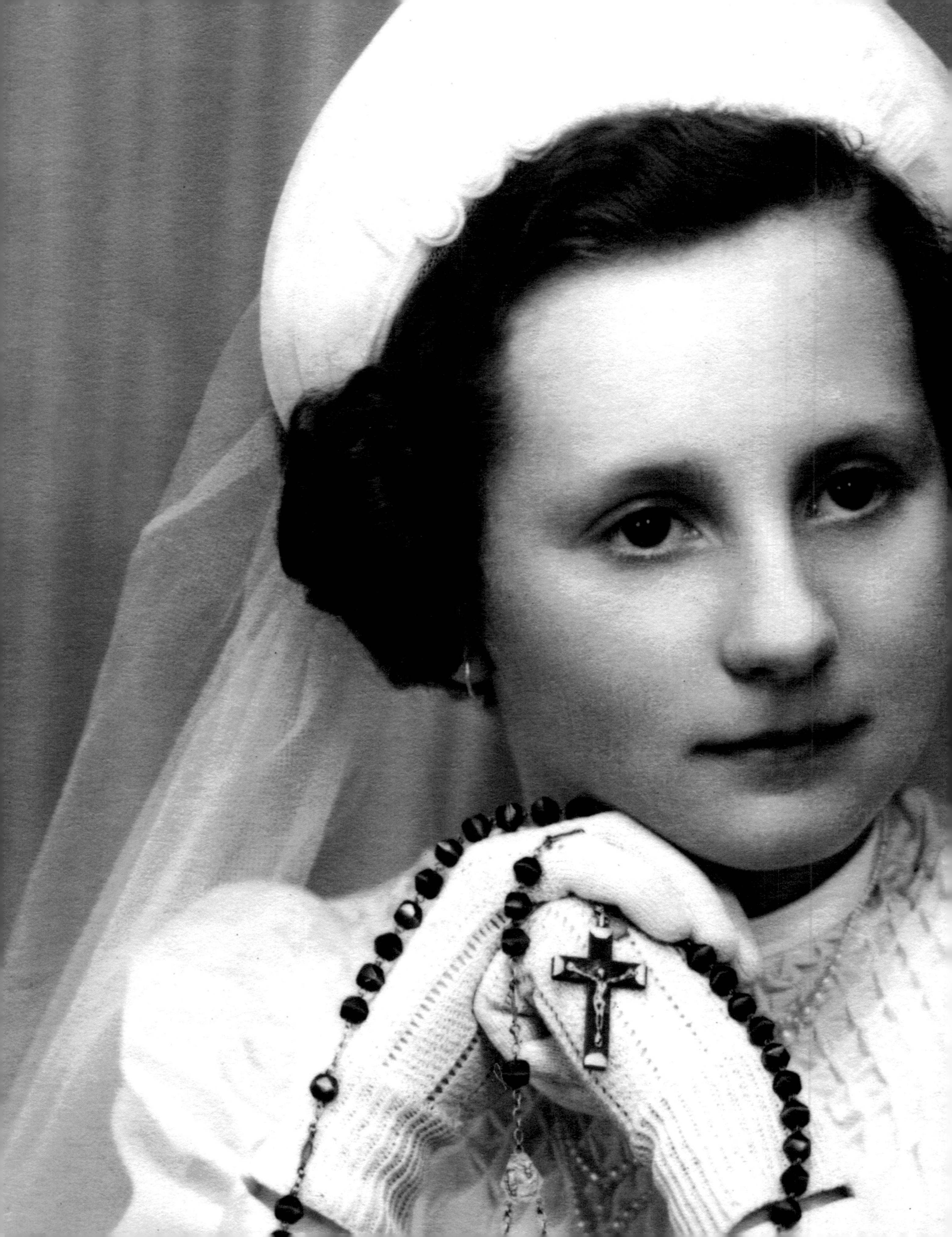

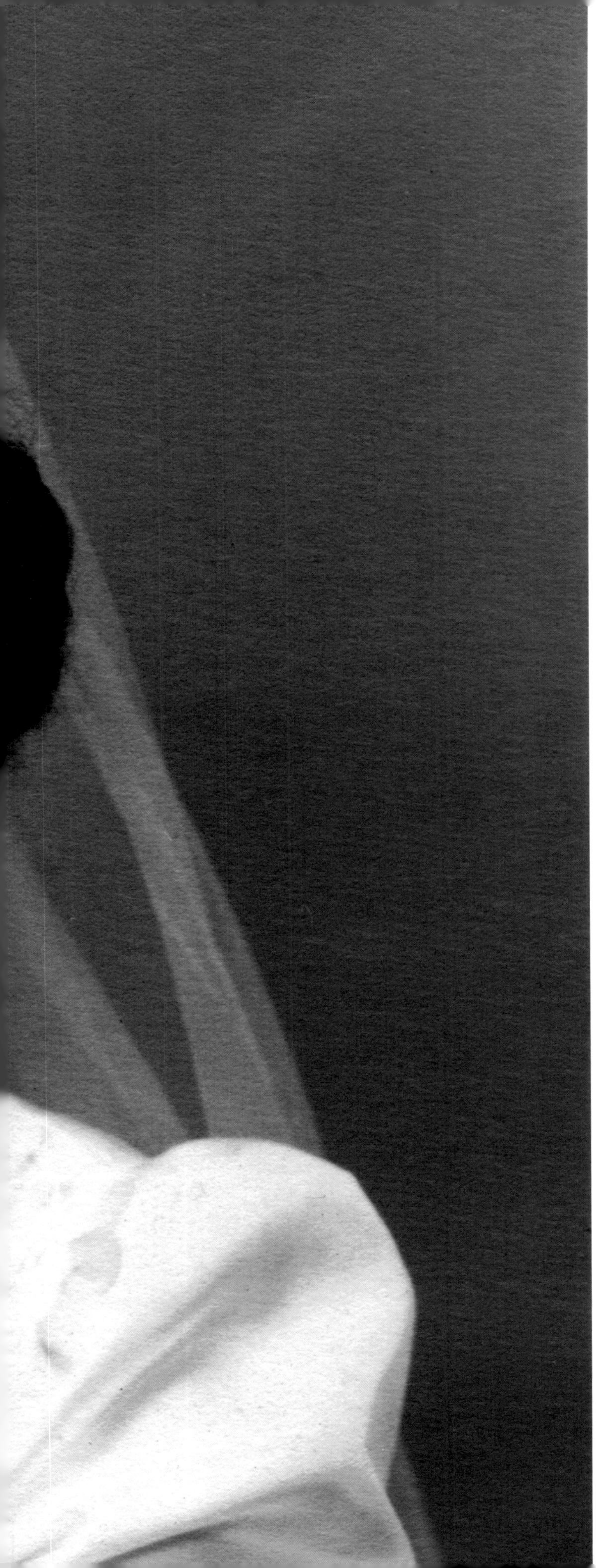

3

BLOT OUT MY INIQUITY

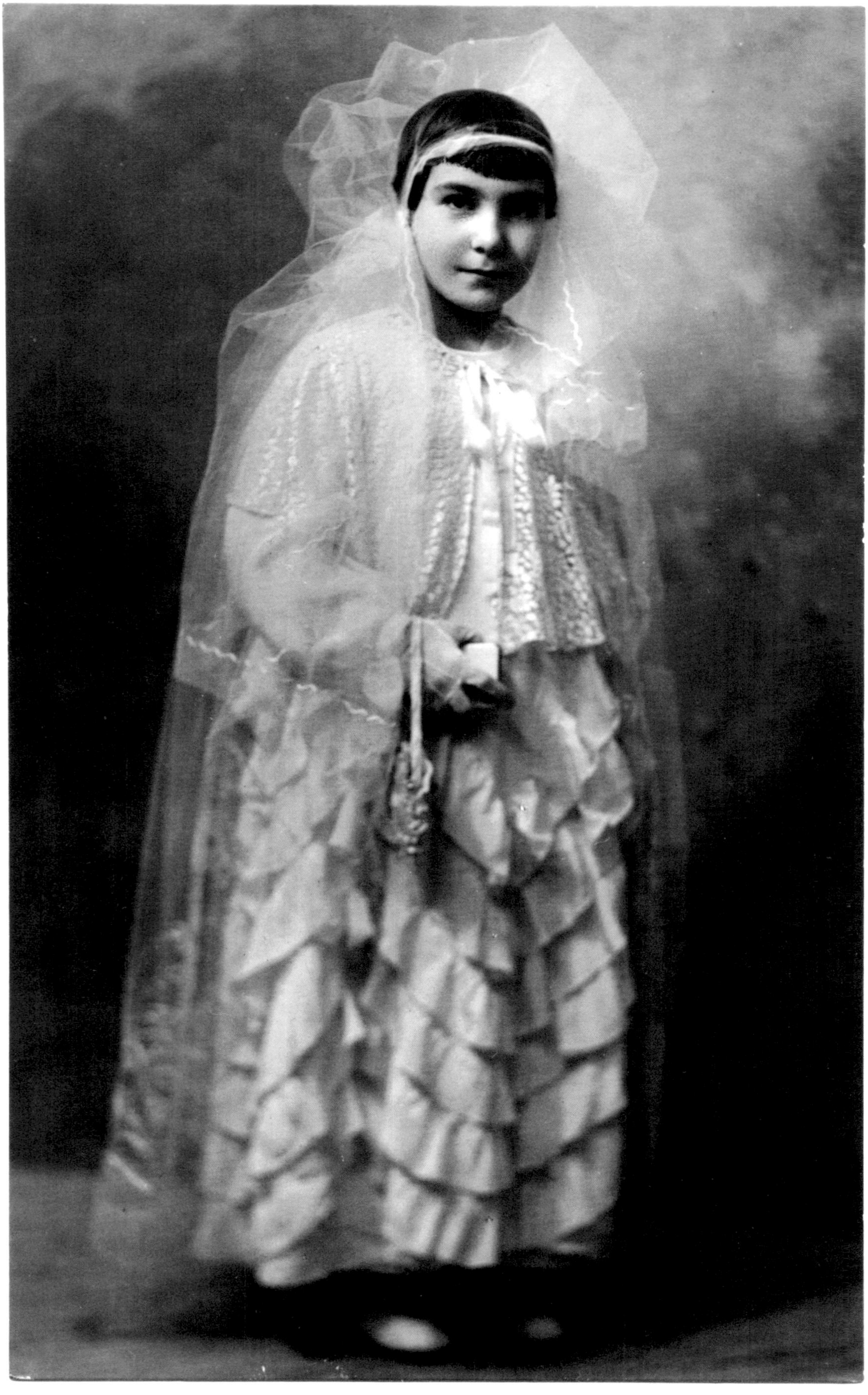

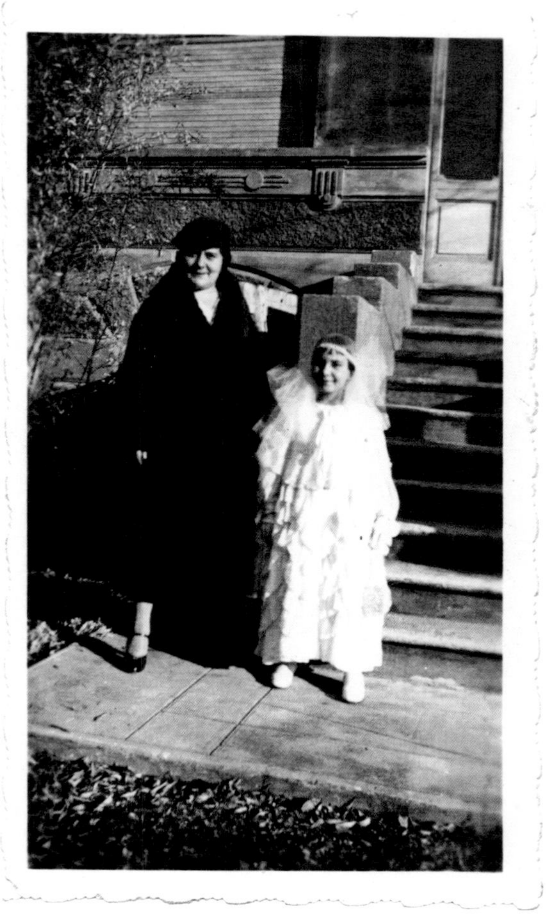

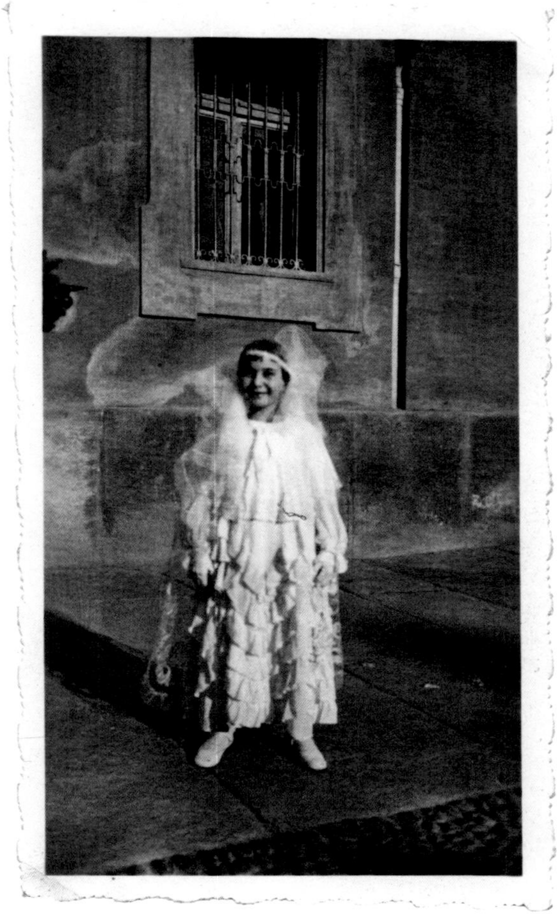

I think it's obvious that this is the age of reason – seven years old is set out as the age of reason. And preparing for the first confession is actually – you are encouraged to stand outside of your own activities. And the model that we used, of course, in my generation, was set by John Henry, Cardinal Newman's catechism. And that was shot through with Marcus Aurelius and the Roman Stoics … It's a funny affair this Communion thing because first of all you stand outside yourself and examine your conscience, as Marcus Aurelius did, like a Roman general, and then the next day you turn up like a Baroque marshmallow.

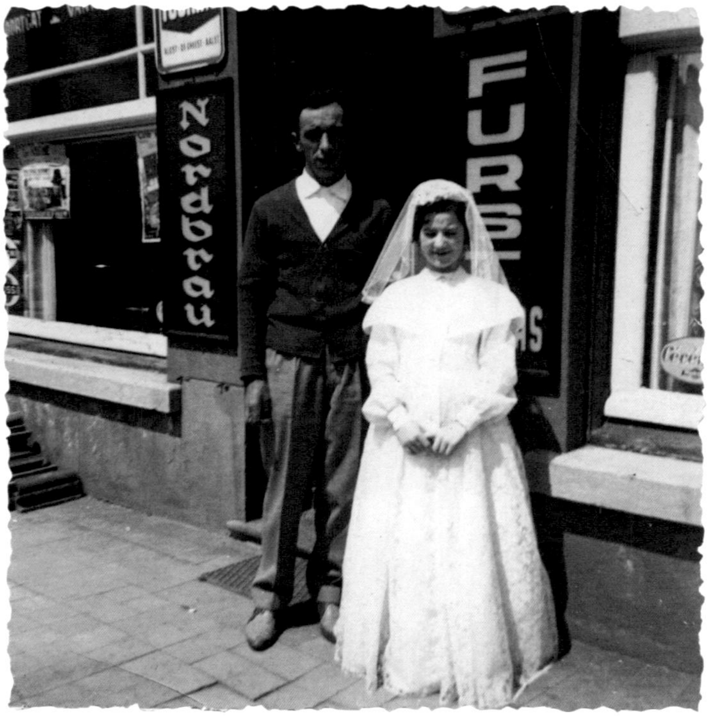

All I could think was, I'm not meant to be here, people are going to think I'm not meant to be here. My mum even pointed it out to me. She said, 'You know, this is something that you want to do because you think it's a party. Trust me, it's not.' And my father used to tell me stories about when he was growing up in the Catholic faith and the punishments they went through with the Christian Brothers. But I didn't care about that because it didn't affect me at all. It was mainly the fact that my friends were doing it and I wanted to do it too. That was the only reason.

You wanted to be part of the group.

Absolutely, yeah. But learning about Catholicism did scare the life out of me, I must admit.

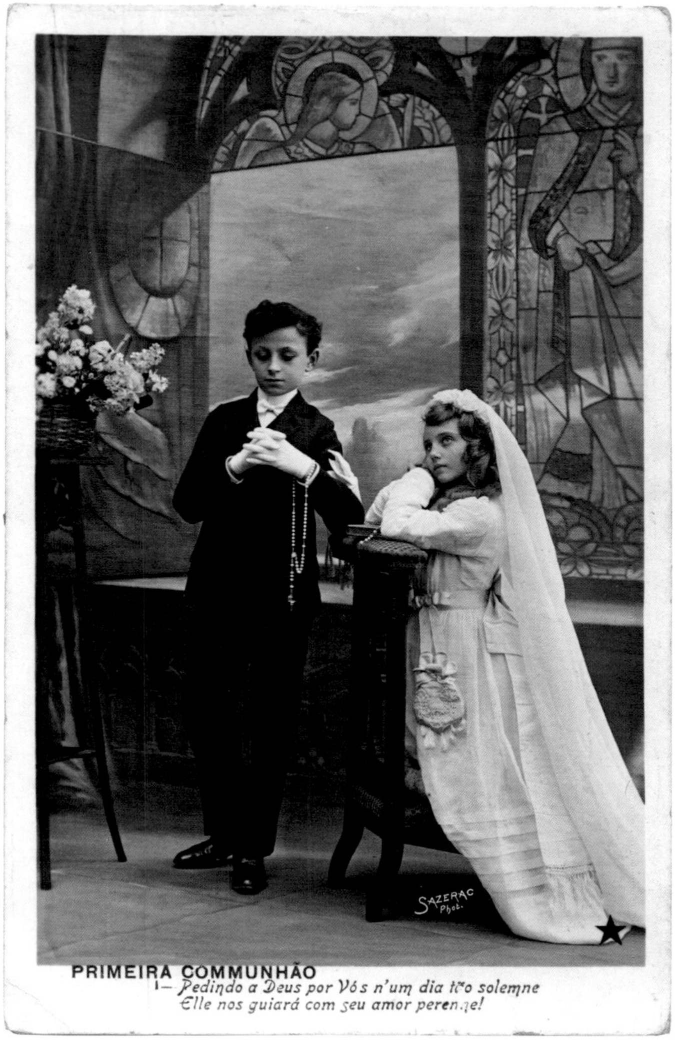

I used to have to go to school on my own, five miles away from where I lived 'cause the village had no Catholic school anywhere near it. So we had to travel for an hour on the bus, in and out every day. My brothers by that time were both at the grammar school, so I was on my own going in for an hour on the bus. So I'd get off the bus and then have about a ten-minute walk to school. I stepped out between two cars and a car was coming along fast and I nearly got knocked over. It screeched to a halt about ten feet away, but it seemed really close to me. And for the rest of the day I was shaken up. I kept thinking about it and every time I thought about how I'd shouted at my brother in the morning. And so, if I had been knocked down by the car, I'd have gone to Hell. That was a complete decision in my head, my mind was completely made up. I knew that if I'd been killed at that moment I would have gone to Hell and burned and I had very graphic images in my mind about what that would have been like.

Did that make you realise the importance of confession?

Yes. That happened after I'd made my First Communion so I understood the implications and why I had to go to confession. I took confession very seriously for a long time – I got anxious if I didn't go, until puberty kicked in. Somebody once said to me when I was in my twenties, 'Once a Catholic always a Catholic', and I remember being very angry. But now I know you are, because what you never lose is the sense that, you know, if I step out in front of a car having just had an argument with somebody, I could spend the rest of my life in Hell. And of course I don't believe that at all, but there's that sense that I have to put everything right. If something goes wrong I have to put it right.

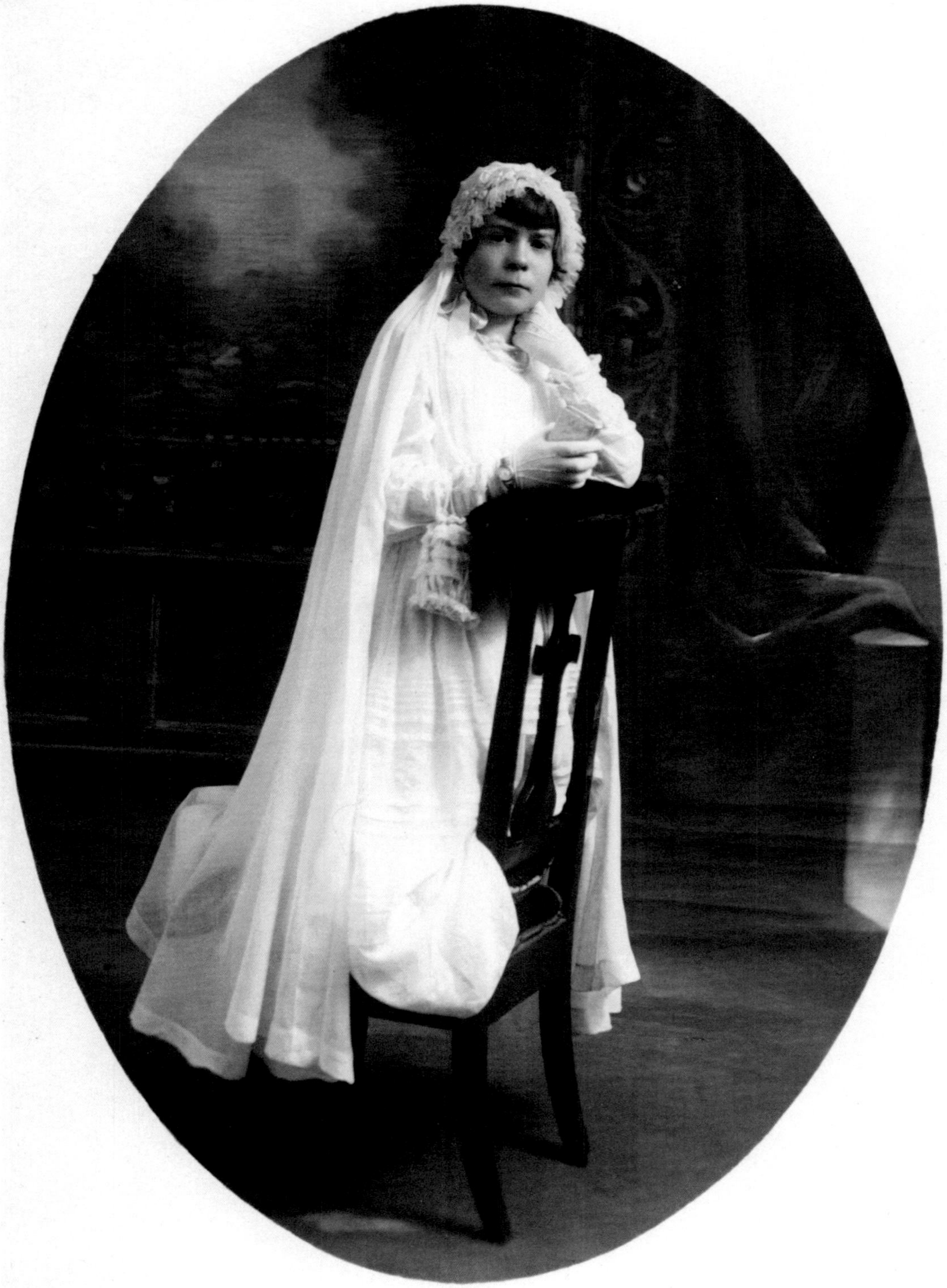

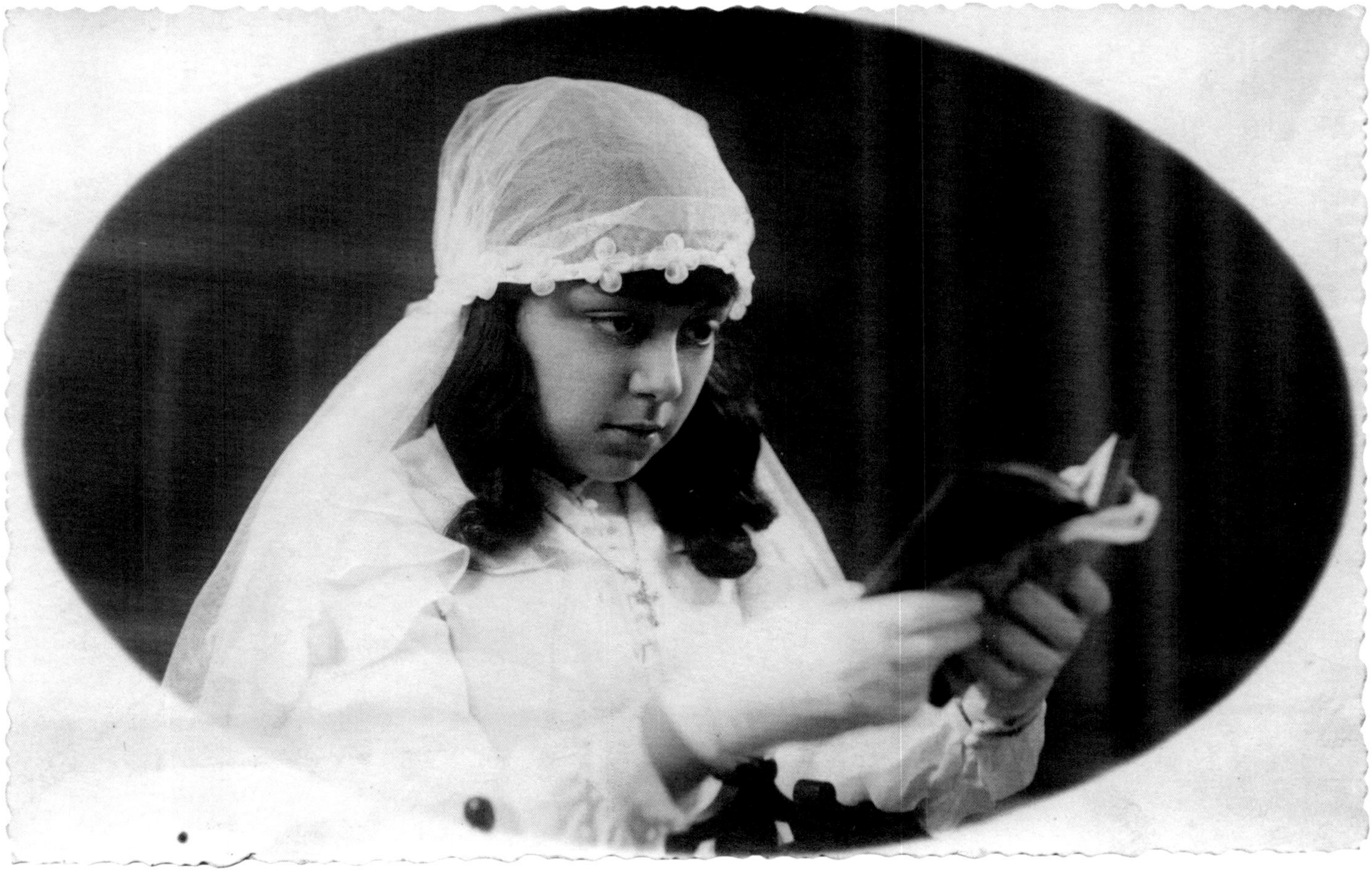

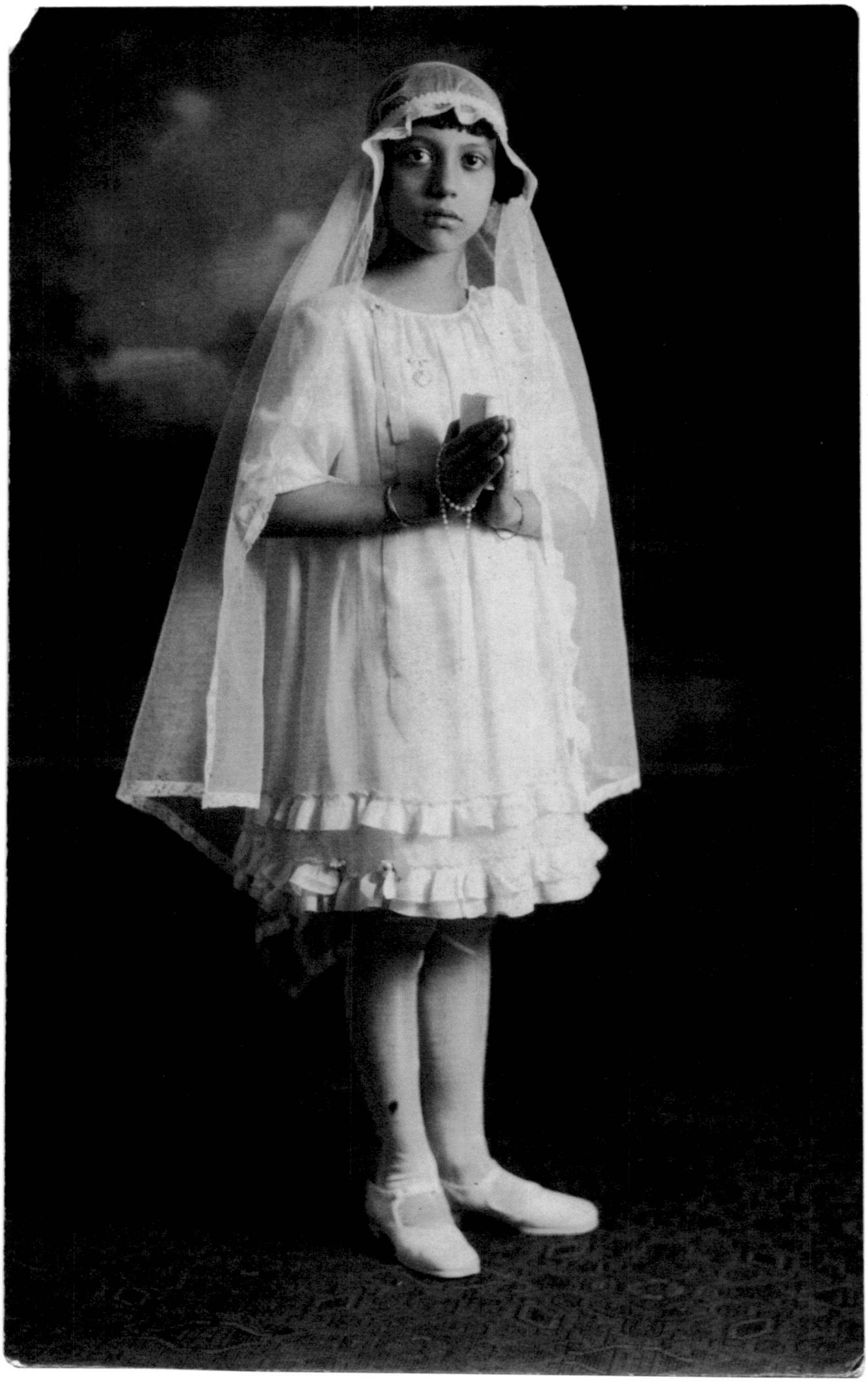

Getting seven-year-olds to examine their conscience must be kind of funny. You had a list of sins and you asked yourself whether you'd committed any of these. Of course you were horrified to find that, because the list had been specially prepared for seven-year-olds, you'd committed all of them.

What sort of things were on the list?

I hadn't fallen into the pit of stealing or swearing yet; anger, anger yes, that was one of the things; disobedience; violence towards my younger brother was probably the nearest thing to – of course that came under the murder commandment, so that was a pretty serious one, I mean, that was pretty rough; bearing false witness; lying; generally sort of lack of charity, you know – for a seven-year-old girl, lack of charity is more or less the universal characteristic; envy, envy of course, yes; jealousy; imprudence, you know, not acting prudently – a tough one to get your head around, that concept, but yeah.

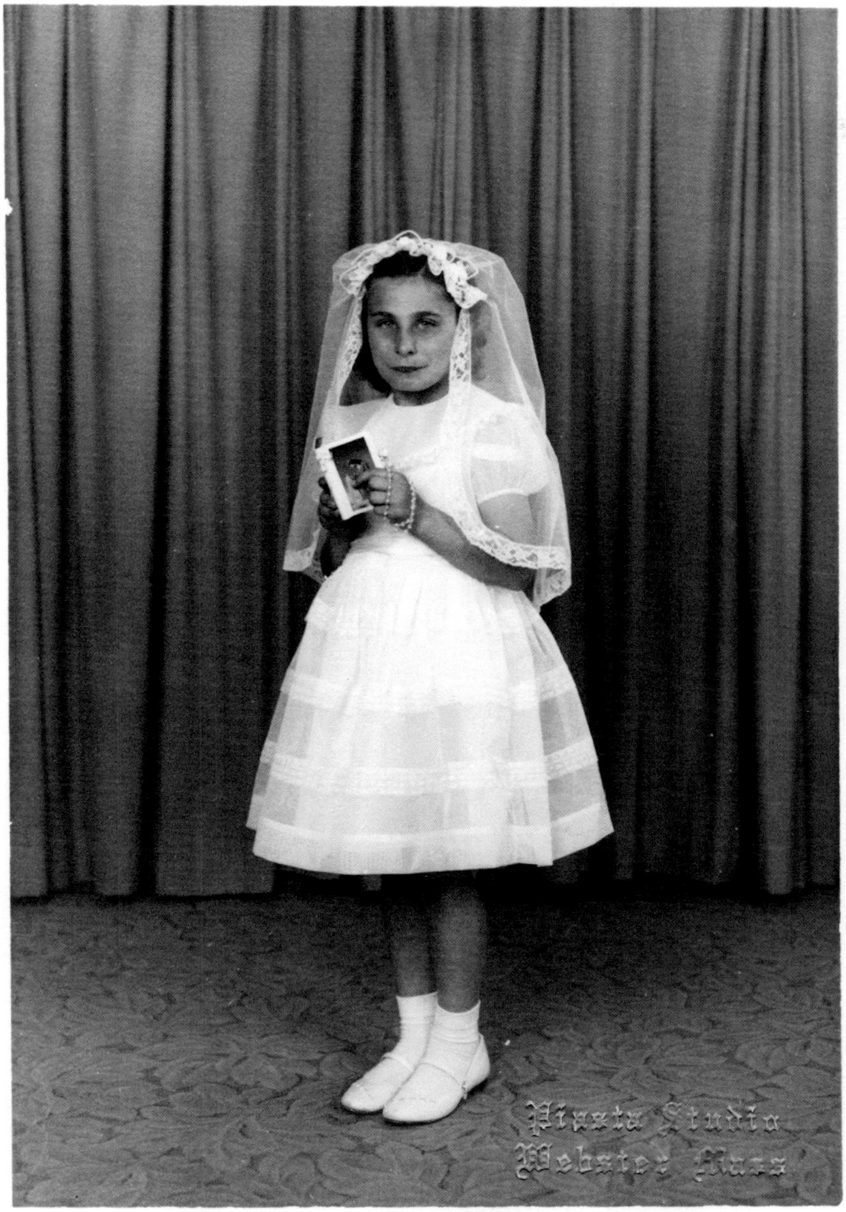

The confessional was dark and I remember being able to confess the things that I had done wrong. I remember taking some money out of someone's purse before I went to Catholic school. I took six cents to buy some apples and when I learned that stealing was an absolute sin, you know, I had to repent of that sin. And I remember that I was able to get rid of that. That was the big thing, getting rid of it. Taking that six cents, the apples were two cents a piece and I got three apples, or something, I think. I can't believe I did that, you know. I still remember bending down and taking the money out of her purse while we were playing jump rope.

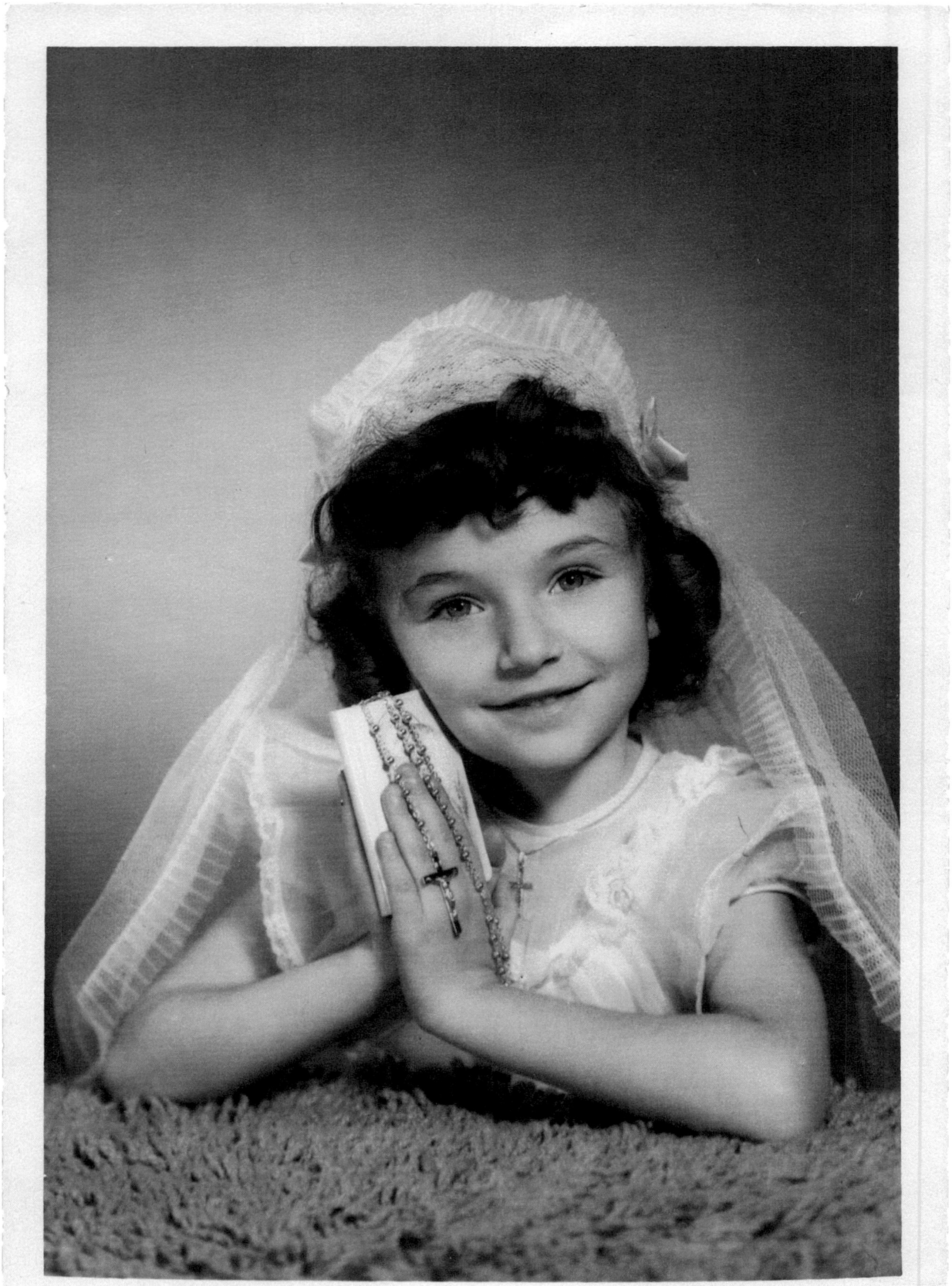

James was my second cousin and we were pretty much exactly the same age, and you know, bosom buddies, pals, like brother and sister. We had been told to come to school on Saturday morning at a certain time, let's say nine o'clock, and we were going to be given some things that were necessary for our First Communion. So, we arrived and were given boxes, and in these boxes were our prayer books. Maybe we knew this in advance, but I don't remember. We were told under no condition were we to open these boxes. We were to go straight home, give them to our mother or our parents, and then our parents, our mother, would give us the prayer book the next day, so that everything was pristine and clean. So off we go, and the first thing we do is go back to James's house, which is a grand old house with a massive old magnolia tree in the front garden, which at the time would have been blooming, so it would have been like climbing into paradise.

James and I spent a lot of time in this tree. So up we go into the tree with our boxes and to James's horror I say, 'Well, open it, open it, let's open it.' He's stunned and says 'Oh we can't do that, we're not supposed to do that.' 'What do you mean?' I say. So I talked him into opening it and we open our boxes and James's missal was slightly larger and this wonderful imitation black leather with gold tooling that said 'My First Missal', or whatever it said, 'My First Prayer Book' probably. And mine was smaller and it had one of those ugly, plastic mother-of-pearl covers. It was all ugly, ugly, ugly and I hated it and I lusted after his.

So you got the feminine version?

Exactly. Well boys were boys, and girls were girls and girls got the pretty things. Every boy, I suppose, was a potential priest, so it looked like a little priest's breviary – you know, black leather, severe. Although I do think it had gold edges, the way mine did. James was mortified that I had led him into temptation.

I retold this story to myself and thought, God, this is a real Adam-and-Eve story, you know; the little girl leading the little boy astray, and the tree of life. So, anyway, the deed was done and that afternoon we had to go back to make our first confession. James was terror-stricken. I mean, we thought we were in mortal sin and that we had done something absolutely terrible, that all the demons in Hell were after our souls and here we were, on the threshold of our First Communion and we had to be cleansed.

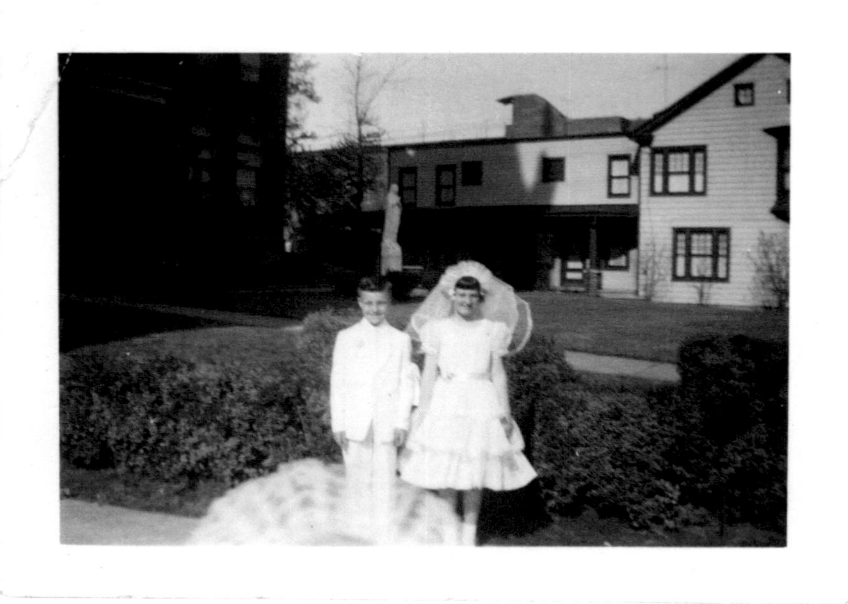

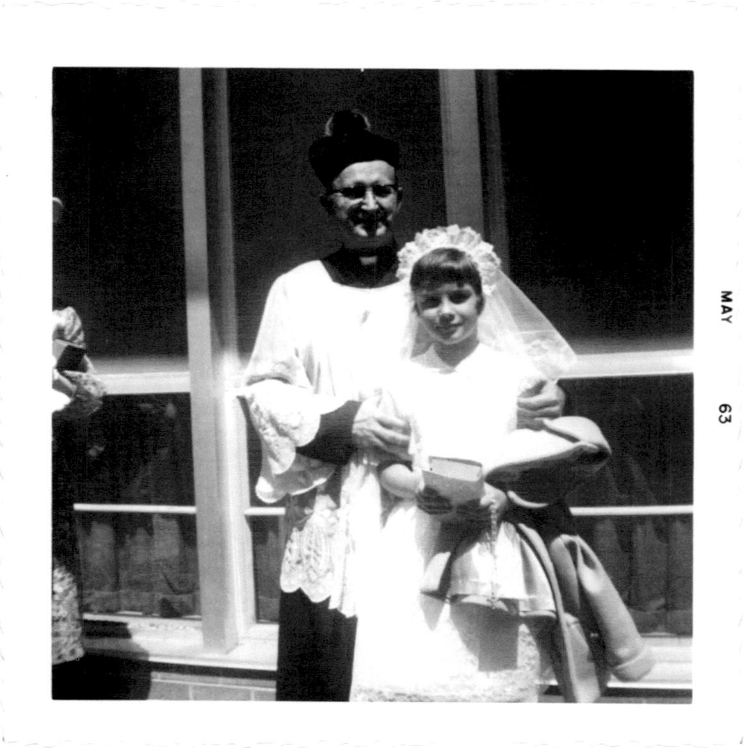

We would hold hands. I grew up at that stage. But at my school – this is something that will amuse you – they had a double yellow line down the playground, boys on one side, girls on the other, so you couldn't play together.

Seriously, a double yellow line?

I could show you the playground 'cause it's nearby.

And did you ever cross the line?

Yeah, of course. You'd hold hands at the line and everything – be a bit daring.

Who came out and separated you?

The dinner lady.

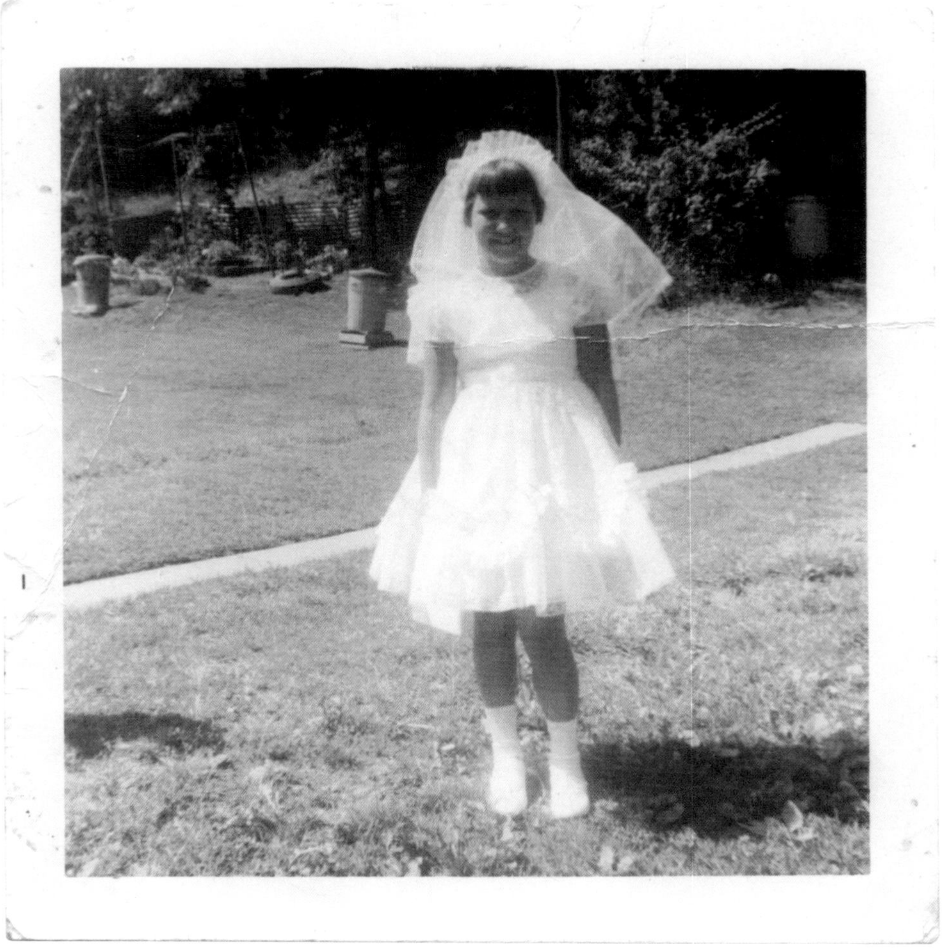

Do you remember anything
about the school?

Oh yes, yes. I was at Saint Maria Goretti, the raped saint of Sicily. Saint Maria Goretti was a poor little Sicilian girl who at the age of twelve was killed while she was raped. Her death was extremely mysterious to us because we had no idea what this very bad thing was that was going on. We were just told that she refused to engage in a very bad sin and so was killed by a bad man. So, we used to imagine, you know, that the bad man wanted her to kill her mother or steal the car or whatever. Because we had no idea at all about sex, of course. I can remember one confession. I remember confessing to adultery just to find out what it was. I was about eight then, and was told to confess to lies and given an extra five Hail Marys.

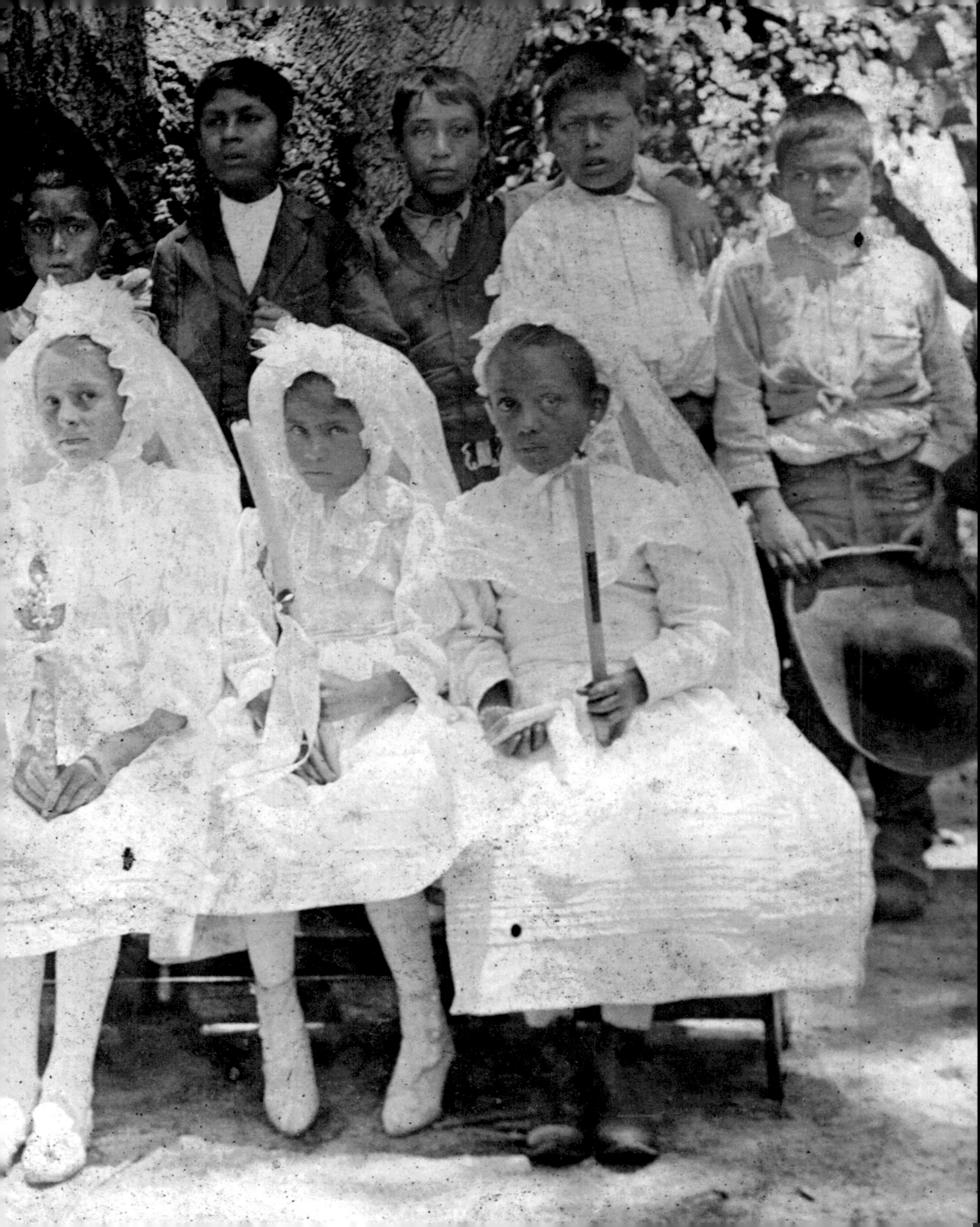

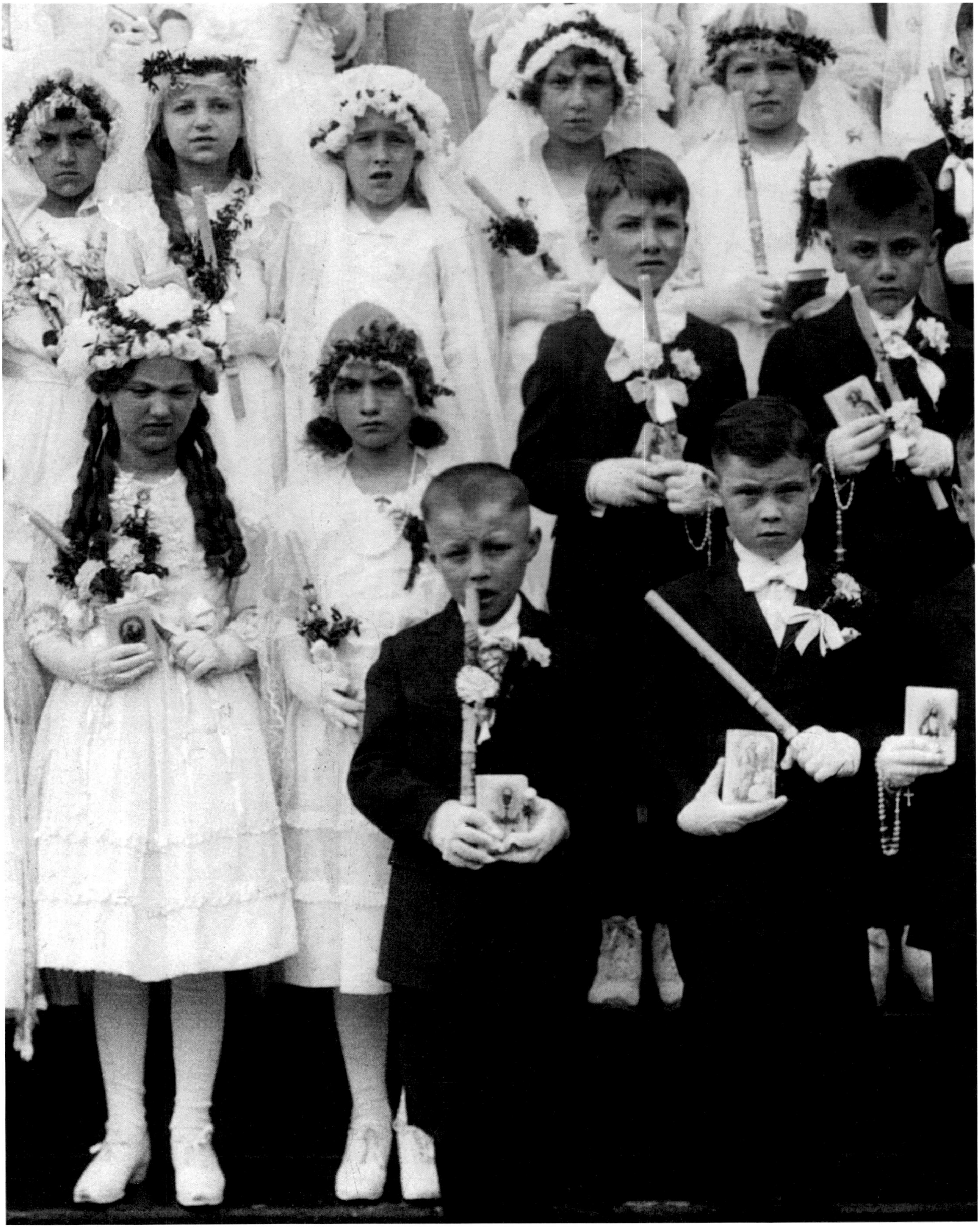

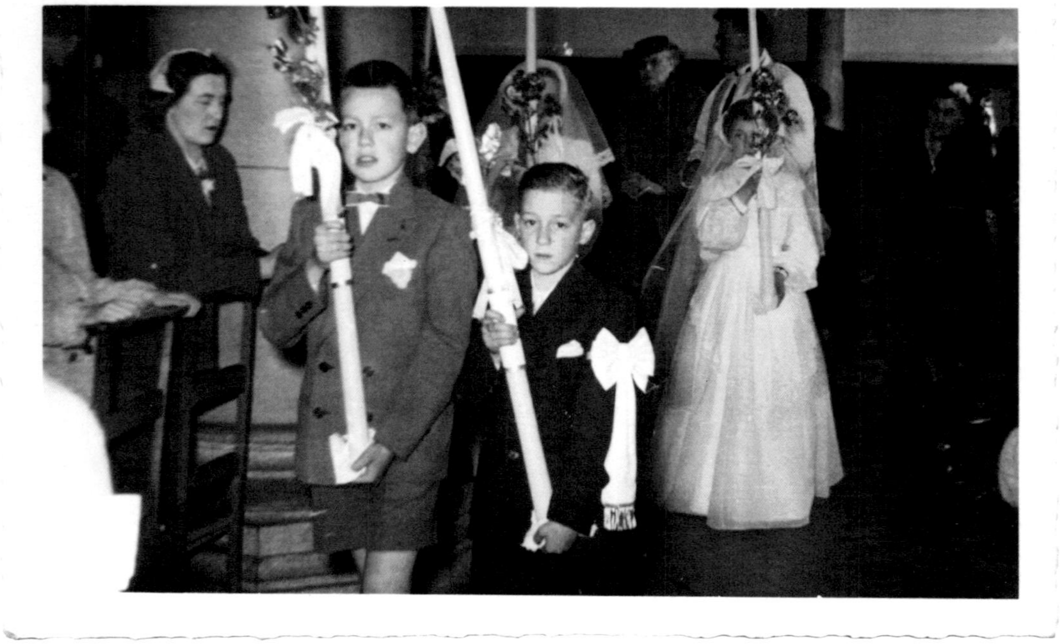

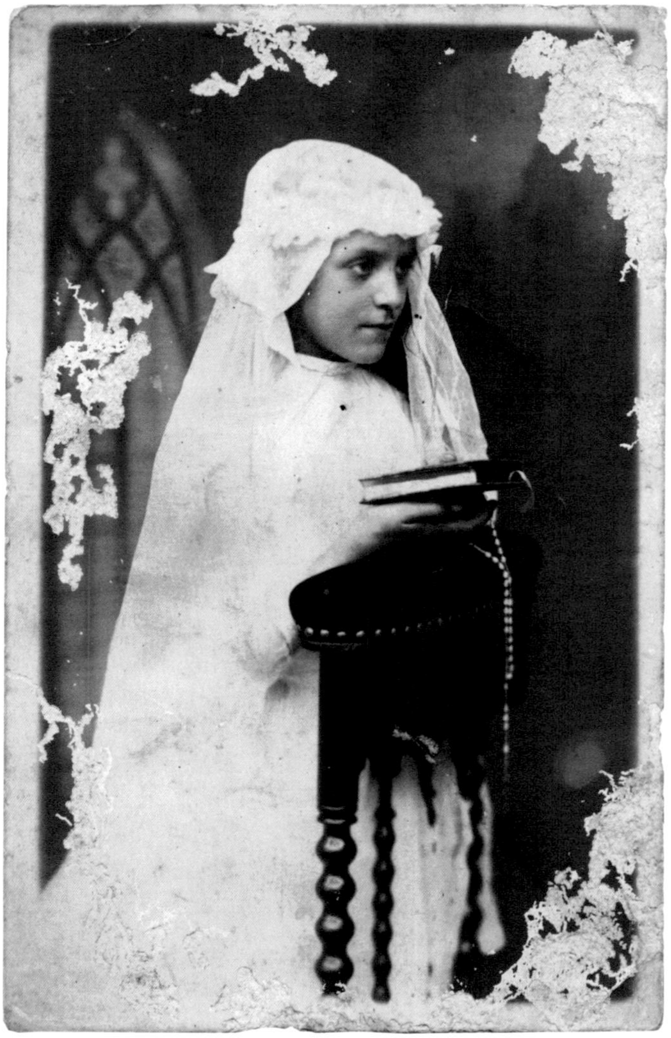

We started working out of these workbooks and we'd have to fill in what was supposed to have happened. Whatever – I never believed. I believe in evolution, kind of, a little bit. They started talking about Adam and Eve and all that stuff. Even now I don't exactly agree with that. Some of us, even at that age, knew about coming from monkeys – that's what we called it when we were little. They would correct you right away. I think one kid actually said, 'Oh, I thought we came from monkeys?' or something like that. She went into a whole lecture about how we did not come from monkeys.

So she didn't talk about it as a myth or story?

Oh no, she believed.

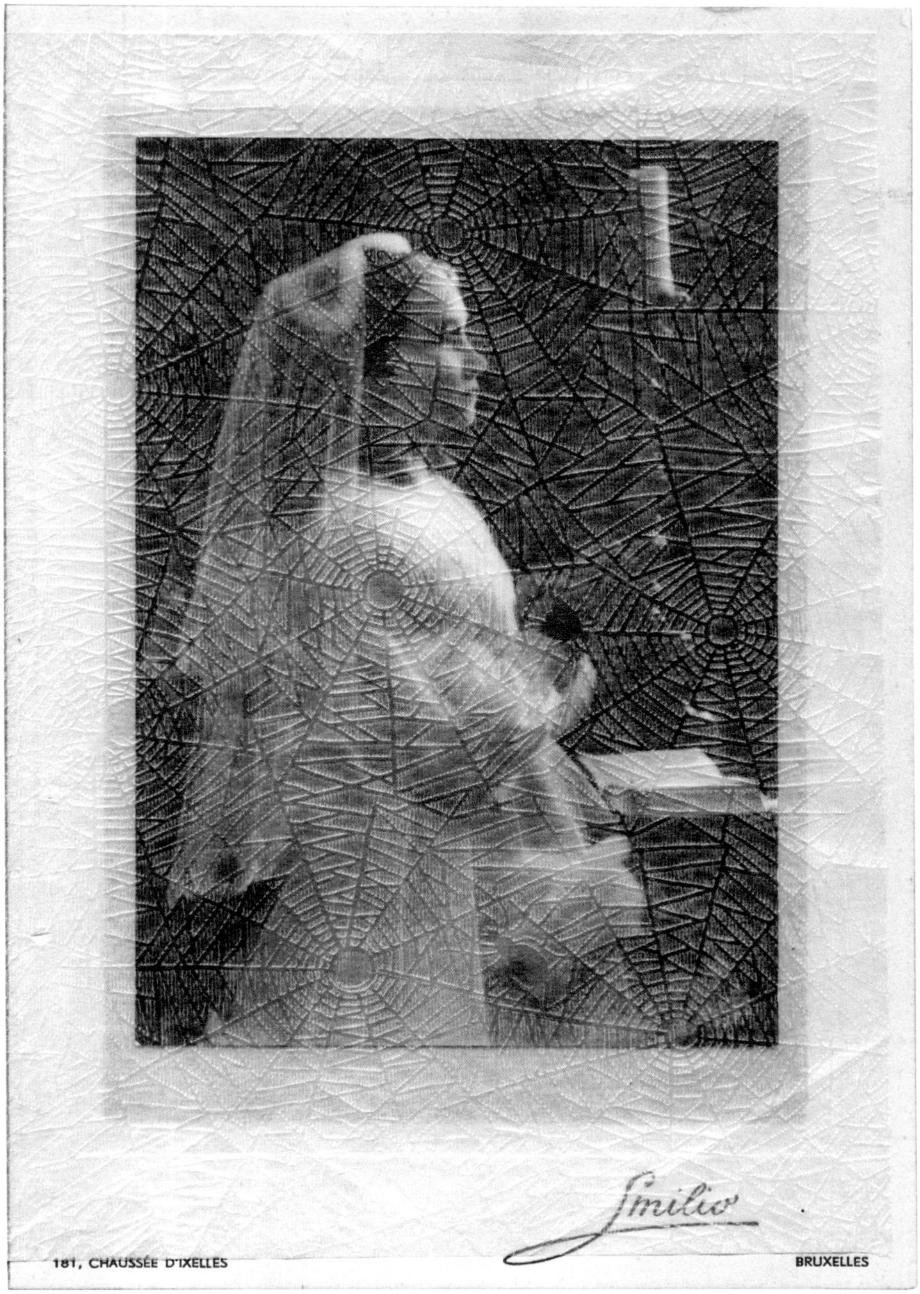

I used to spend quite a time – sometimes in the dark, or I would lie under a fruit tree looking at the sky, I was quite isolated at times – trying to get my head round notions of eternity and infinity, and the relationship between the two. The notion … They would talk about fires that consume your flesh and constant torment and so on. And then there were images that I'd seen, like Hieronymus Bosch and things like that, and they would all register and from a very, very early age. I certainly had a very visual imagination from an early age.

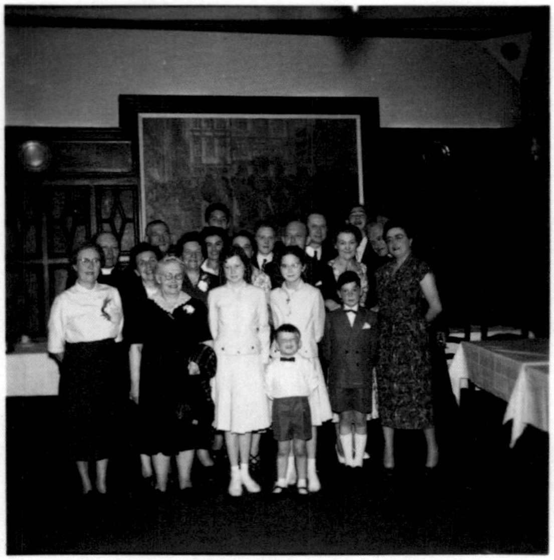

I would say my parents were quite devout in an undemonstrative, unimposing kind of way. Like, I remember my mother saying more than once in the course of my childhood, your faith is the most important thing you have. And she definitely believed that – that is the most important thing.

And my father too, yes. I would say he was deeply devout in a very quiet sort of way. He used to read the *Imitation of Christ* when he was depressed. So when we saw this little gold book, we knew that it was a very, very bad sign.

If you didn't show up to confession on Saturday mornings, somebody would go, oh what's going on here? But if you came from a really good household where you were, like, perfect, you probably didn't have to go but every two weeks. Even if you didn't have anything to confess, you still went because it was part of that process of who's in confession and who's not. And then, if you stayed too long in the confessional – oohhh. And if you had to make all these Acts of Contrition afterwards, it was like, you know, either you were a slow learner and you didn't know the prayers, or what did you do? I mean, think about it, if you grow up in an area where everything is very religious and somebody breaks away and does something different, it makes it, well, let's face it, who wants to hear about somebody leading a clean life?

So when you grow up in a small community, you know what's going on in somebody's life by going to confession. Who shows up for Communion, who shows up for church: it's a report card for your lifestyle.

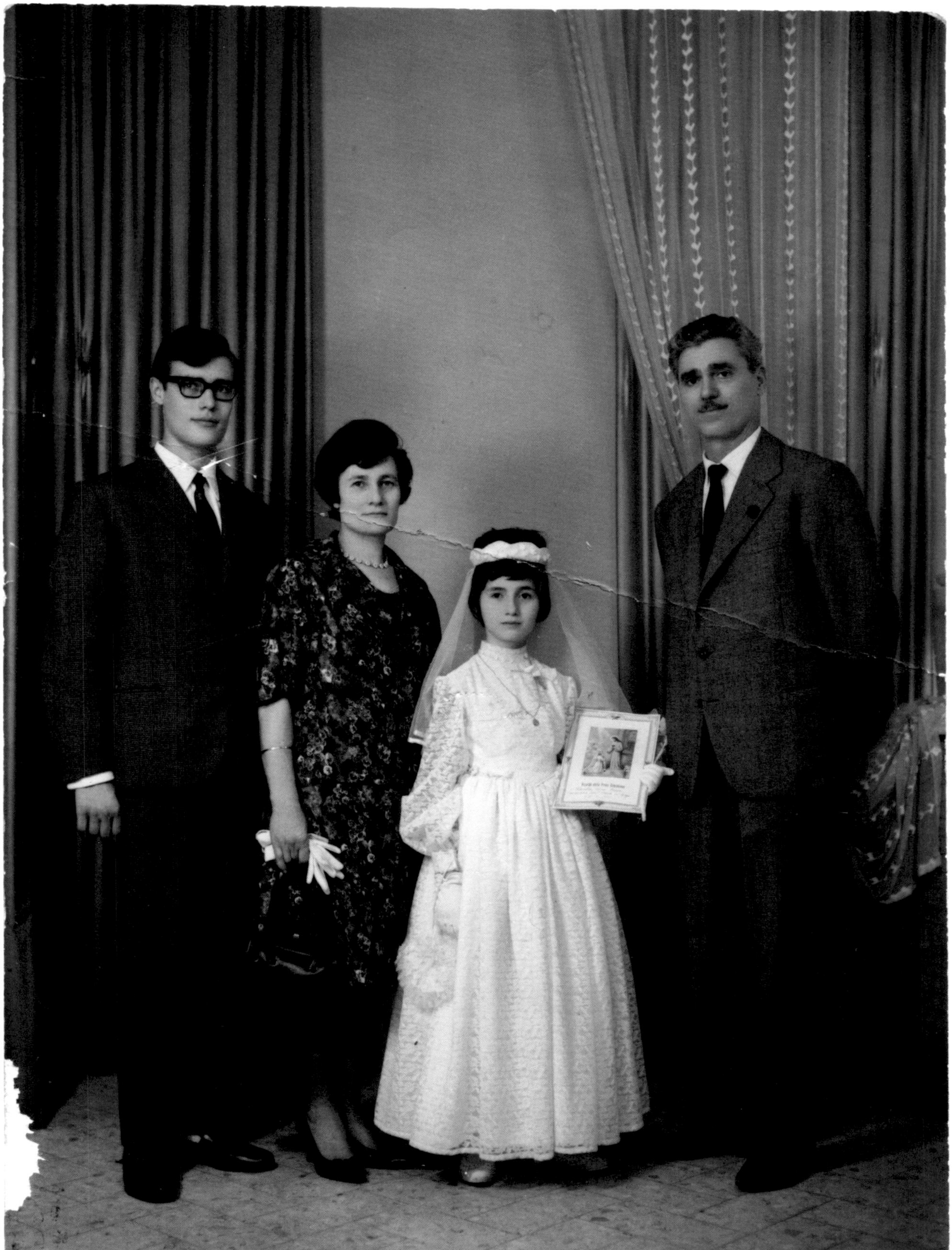

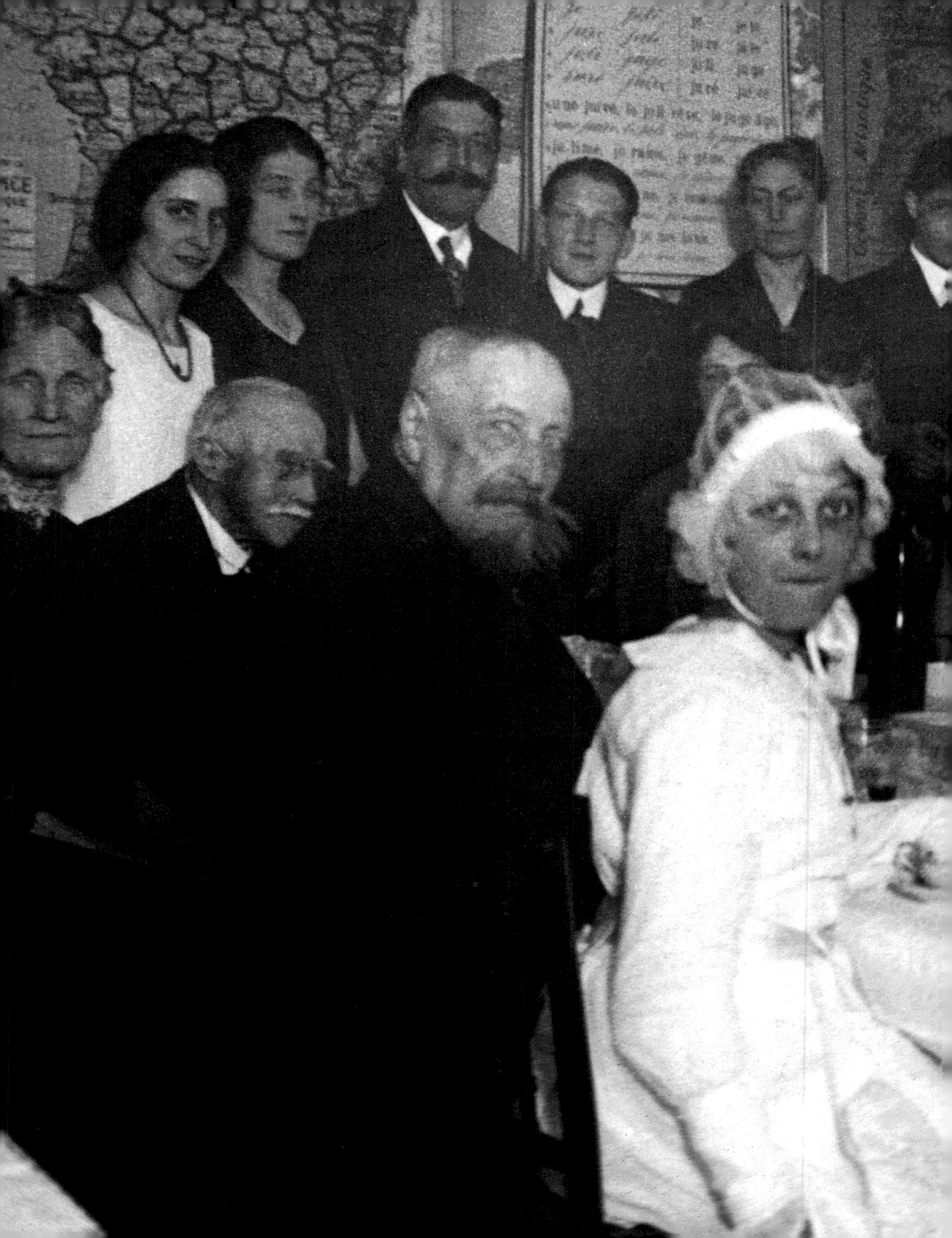

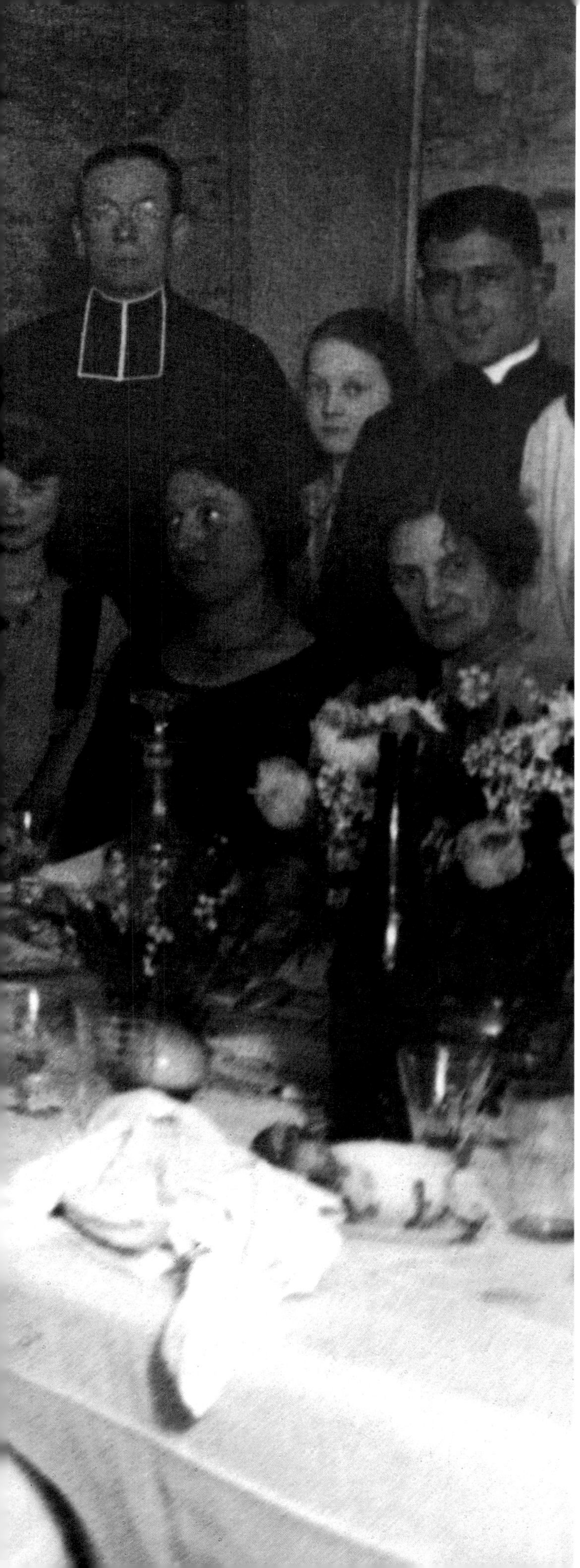

4

HAVE A FORETASTE OF HEAVEN

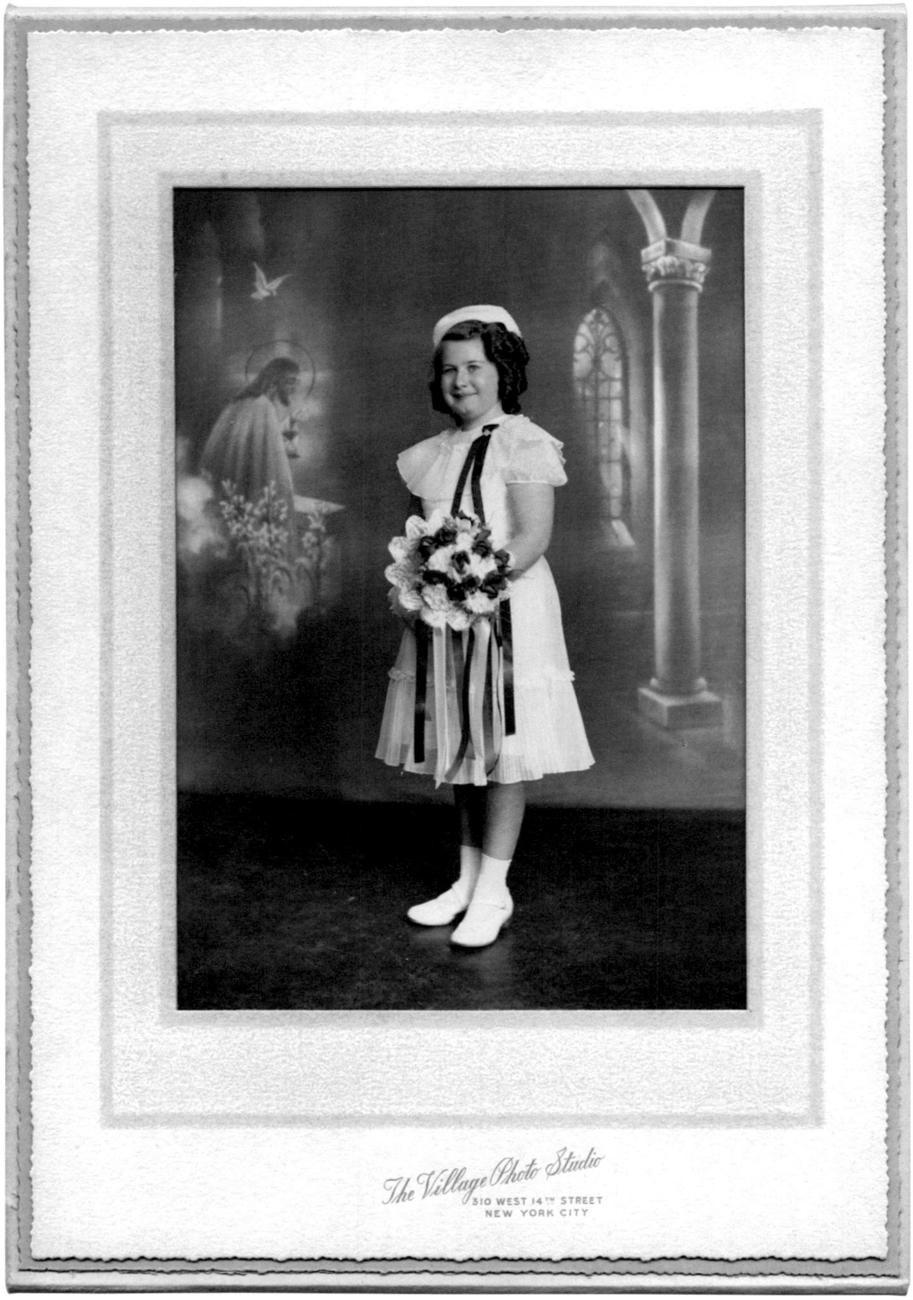

I said 'It tastes absolutely glorious,' which is such a ridiculous thing to say about food. I remember thinking at the time, why did I say that? Yeah, I can remember a really smug expression on the teacher's face when she thought, 'Ah yes, yes, that's exactly it.' But I can remember being astonished by the fact that I'd said that and for a long time I thought it was some kind of weird miracle, that God had put these words into my mouth, which I didn't really believe. Yes, so obviously I did like the taste.

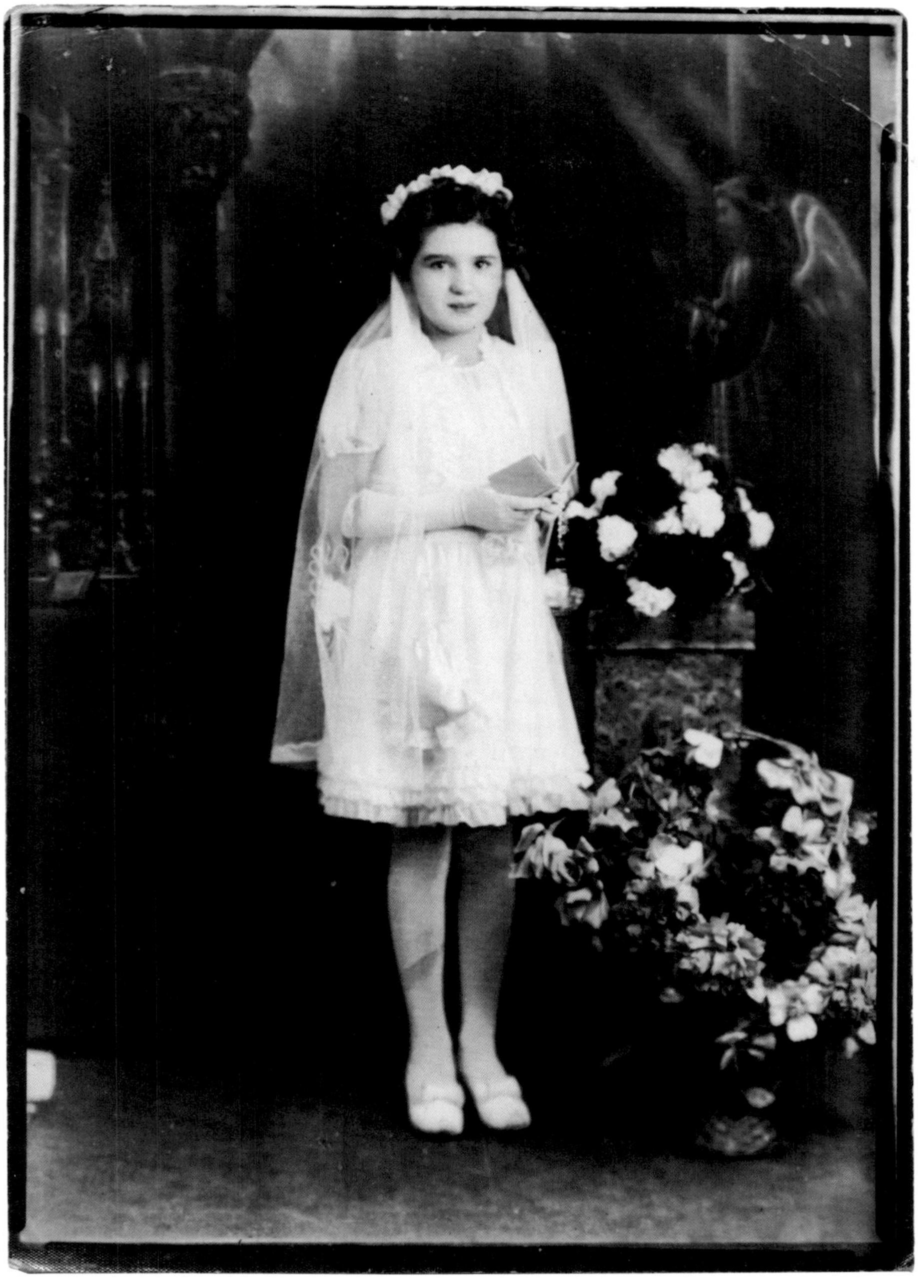

I couldn't understand transubstantiation when I was a little kid. I thought that the priest was a magician. I didn't understand how he could do his little prayer, cover it up with the little card and the fabric and then drink the wine. But then why is it that when he comes to give you Communion, they're just wafers? You don't figure out till you're older that they buy the wafers at a holy religious store – they buy them in gross form and somehow somebody sneaks them underneath the altar. It's maintaining the mystery that keeps people in faith and hope.

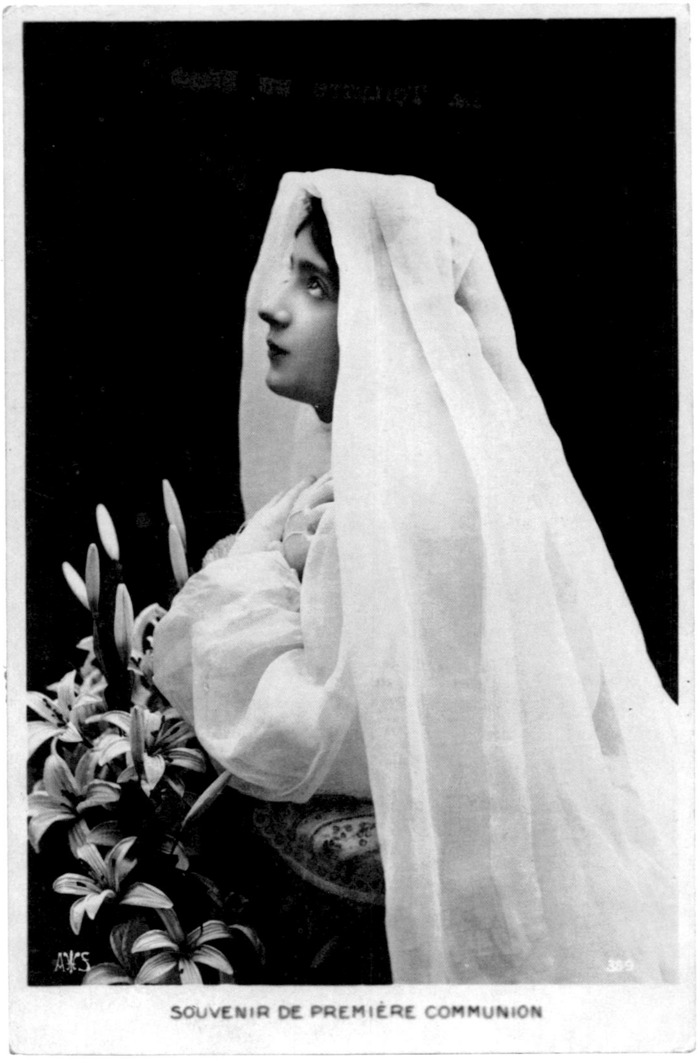

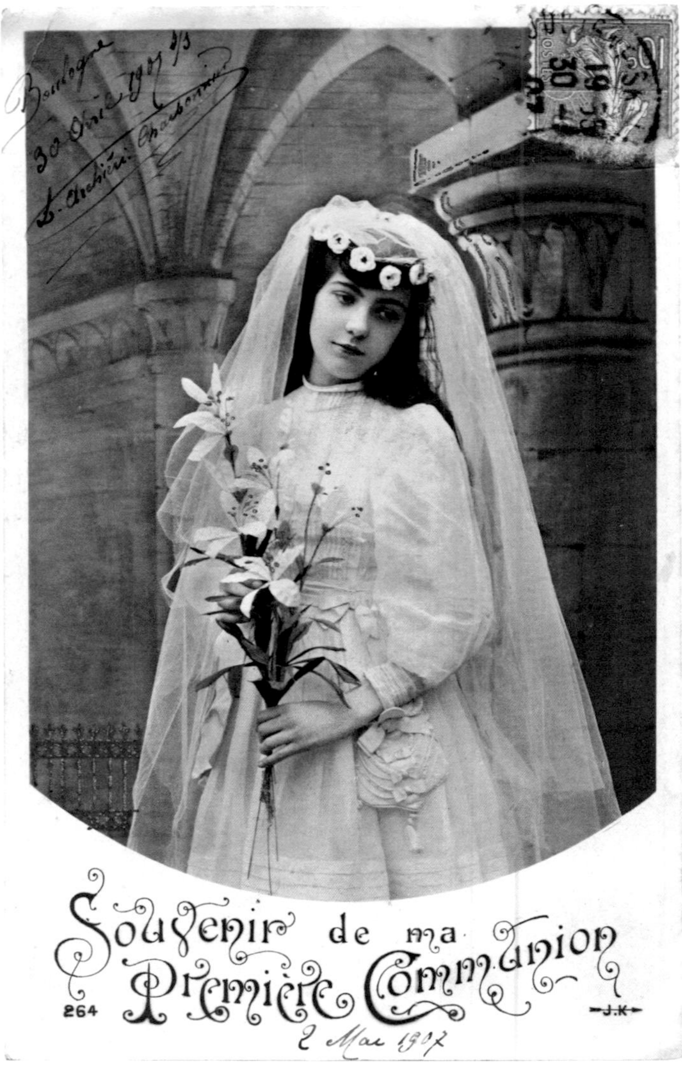

You want to gag and it tastes like fish food. Have you ever tasted that powdered fish food? No, I never tasted – I don't like fish – but it's like that texture. Like, if your hands are damp and you go and get the fish food and it sticks and you can't get it off. It's the same process.

So you used your tongue?

Oh you bet I used my tongue. I was told, oh no, you just don't do that, you're not supposed to break it, you're not supposed to chew it. And I just thought, who's going to know except the big guy upstairs?

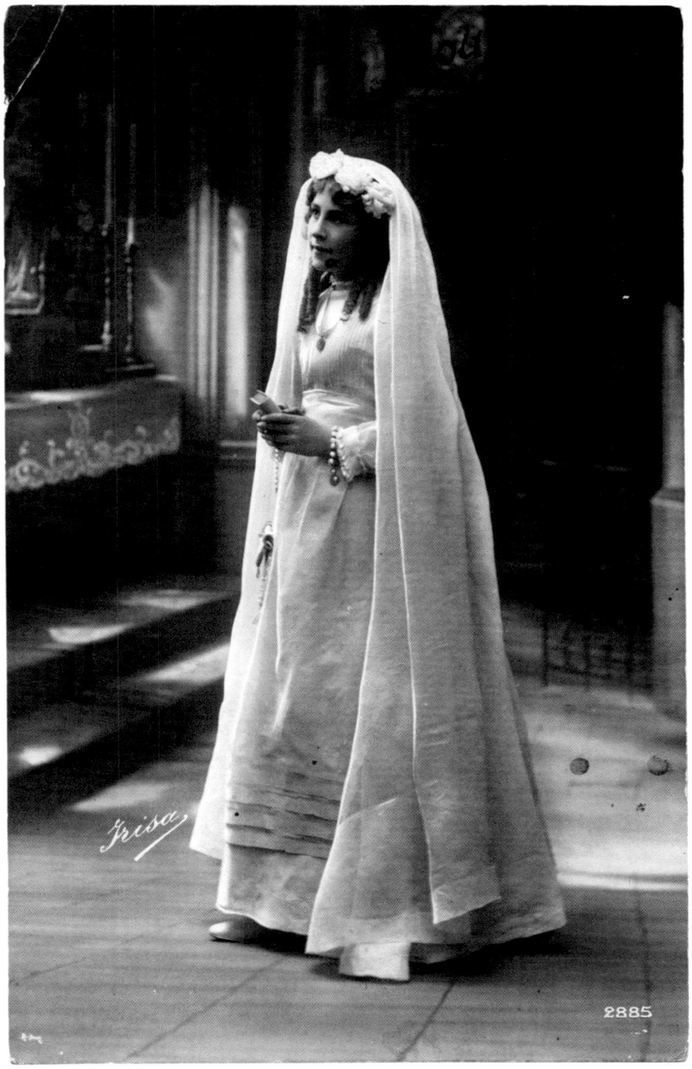

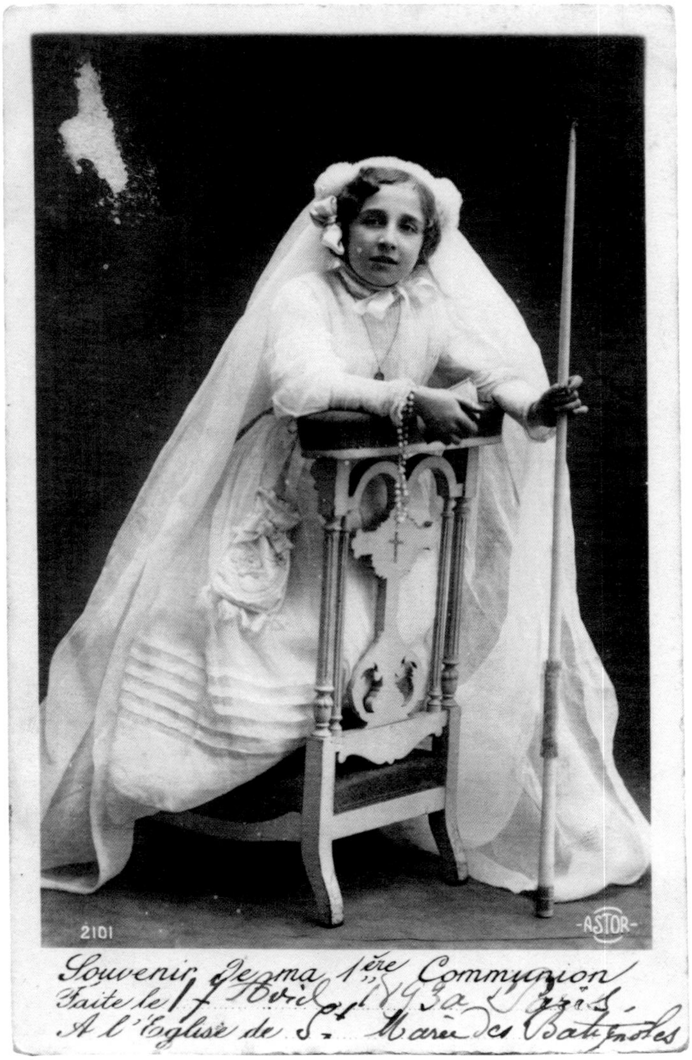

I remember thinking that when you drank the wine, that everyone else has had their mouth on that cup. Now that was quite gross. I didn't like the wine, 'cause it's horrible. It was really kind of strong and fermented – horrible. It's not like Lambrini, kind of bubbly and cidery.

You know the red light?

No.

If you go to a Catholic church, then the altar where the Blessed Sacrament is kept – the wafers, the Holy Communion wafers – will be indicated by a red light, which is a little like a votive candle, but it's red. You won't see red on the other altars. Although sometimes Our Lady's Chapel will have a blue light. So it's like, 'He's in, the red light's on, He's in. That's where He is', that's an indicator. That has always struck me. 'He's in, we're here. Yeah, we're in business.'

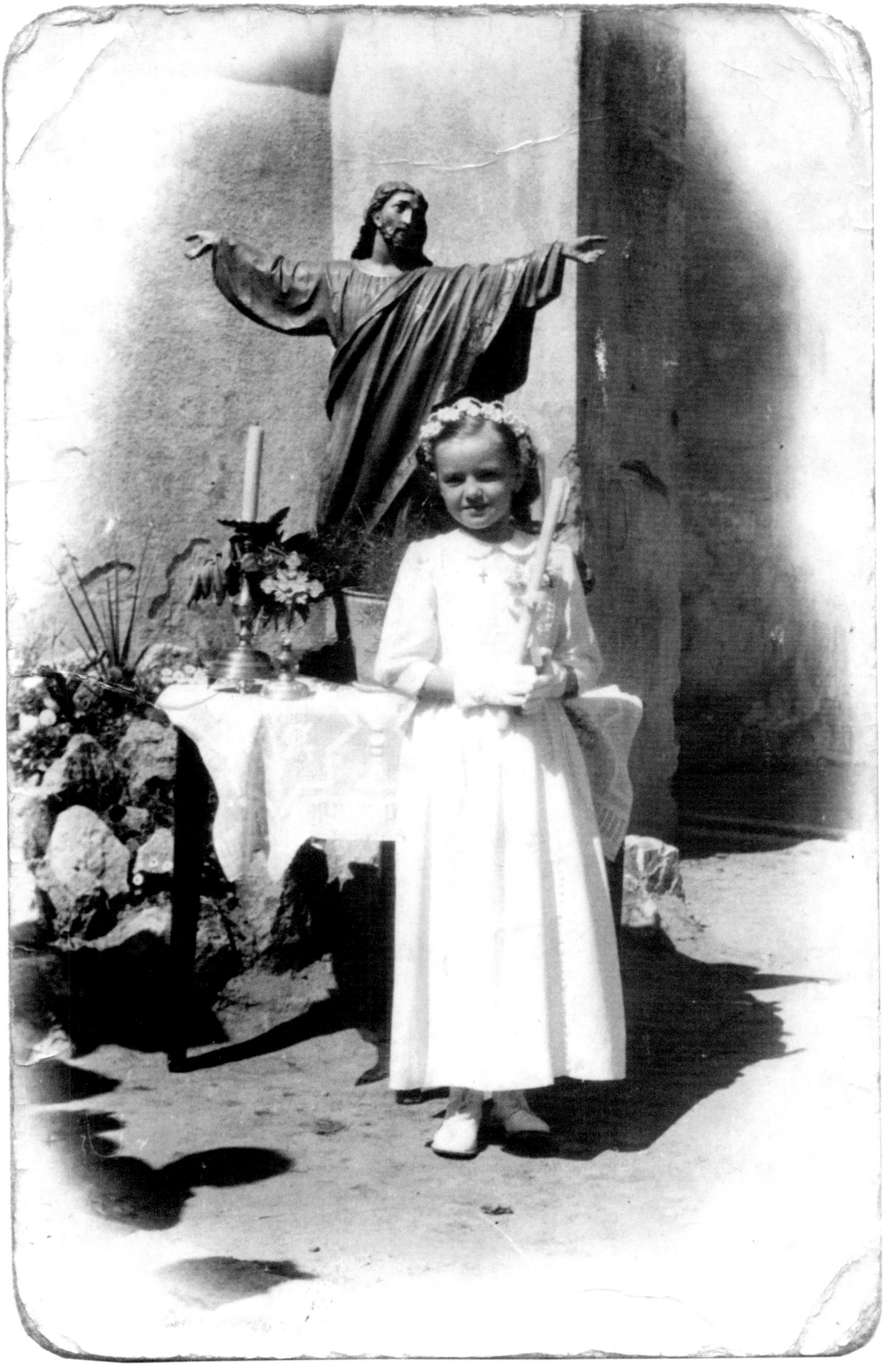

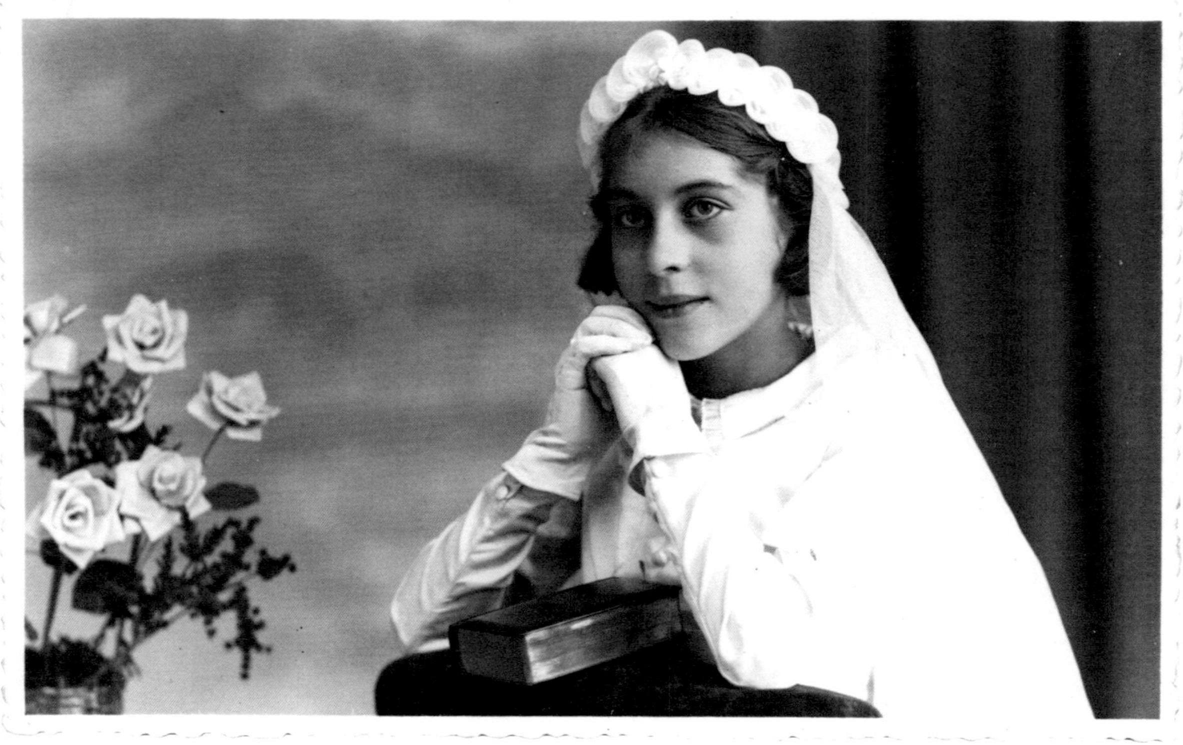

Well, you had your eyes closed you know. You had to close your eyes – I can still feel the Host going on my tongue, 'Oh, Dear Lord, you're here' – I remember it.

You felt that at such a young age?

Oh yes, it was 'Dear Lord, you're here' and I pressed my heart.

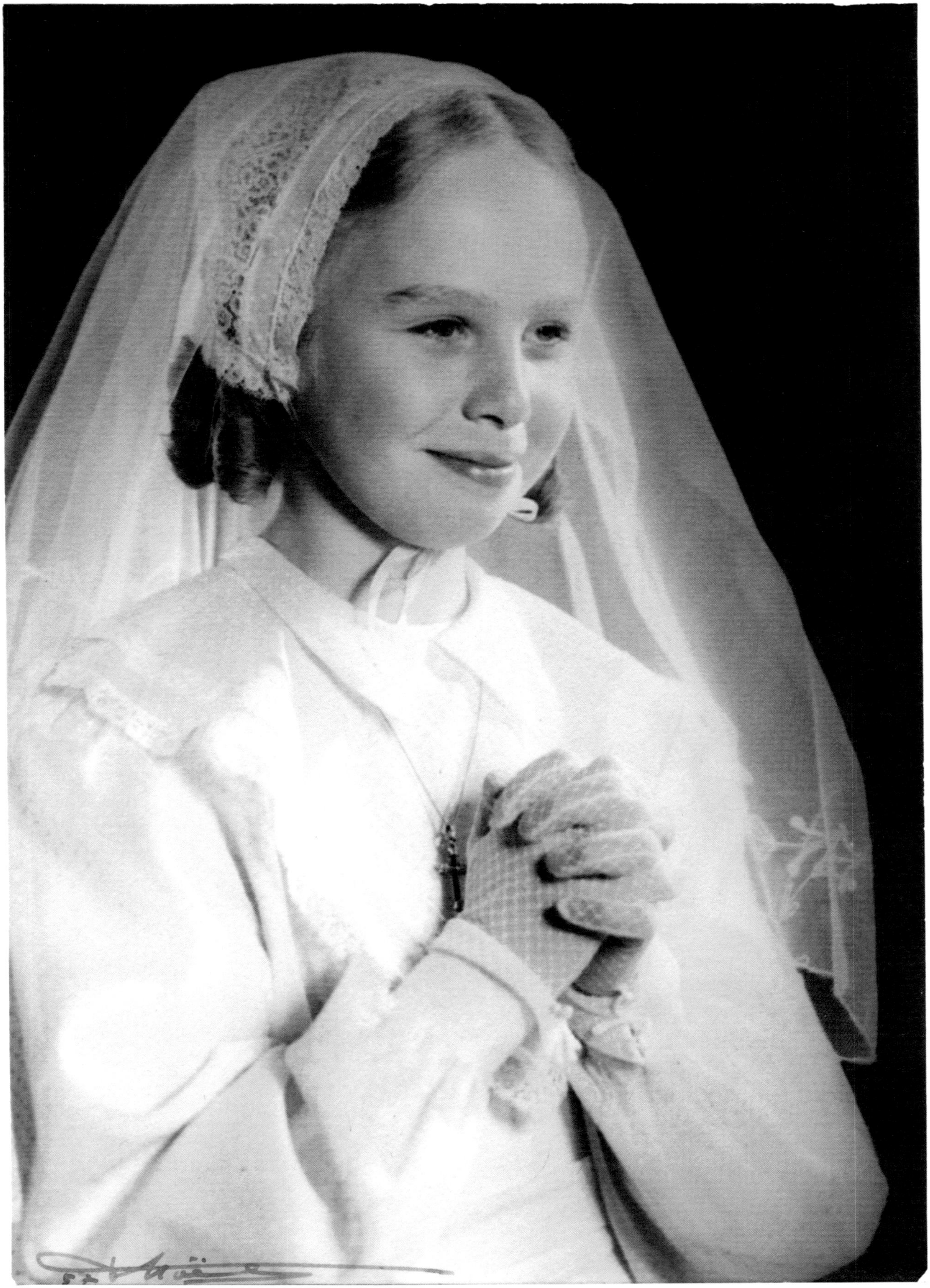

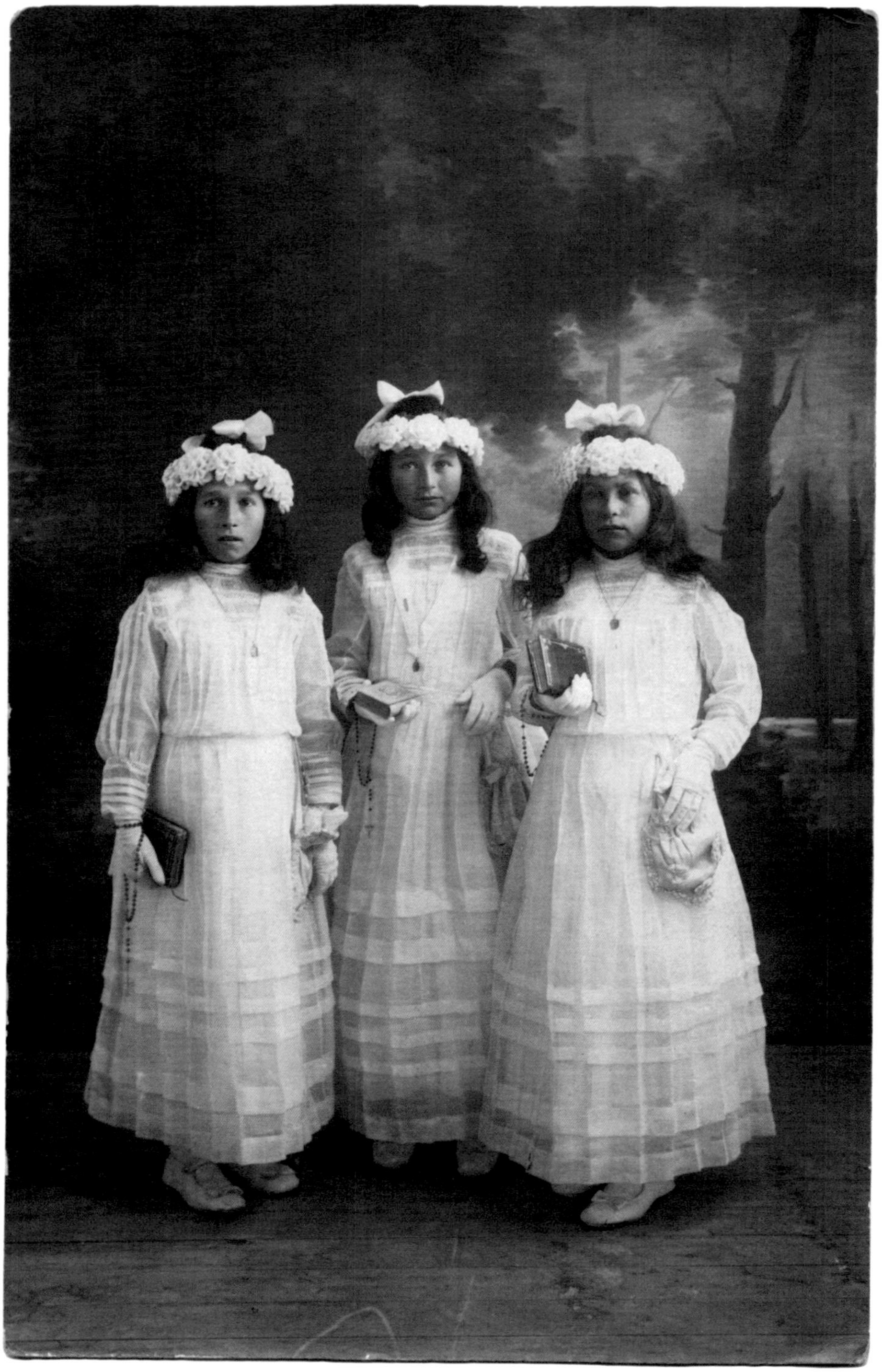

What do I remember about the Communion itself? Well, sort of mind-blowing to try to wrap your brain around, that God was actually three persons – and that is quite literally how it was explained, not three entities or three energy forms or three manifestations but three persons: God the Father, God the Son and God the Holy Spirit. So, Communion, the wafer, the Host, the piece of bread, was about God the Son, but it was also indirectly about the Holy Spirit because the Holy Spirit is the power, it's the mover and the shaker, the invisible one. In those days it was a white dove; a white dove signified the power of the Holy Spirit, meaning that during all of these prayers and offerings and rituals, by the power of the Holy Spirit, the bread would turn into, symbolically and energetically, the body of Christ.

> I can't imagine that you would think of it in those terms as a six-year-old.

No, so I can't back up to being that age. But I do remember the three persons and all of that and just trying to, trying to grasp the concept of the Trinity. It blew the sockets in my brain. It was too big for me to understand, so you just sort of had to accept it.

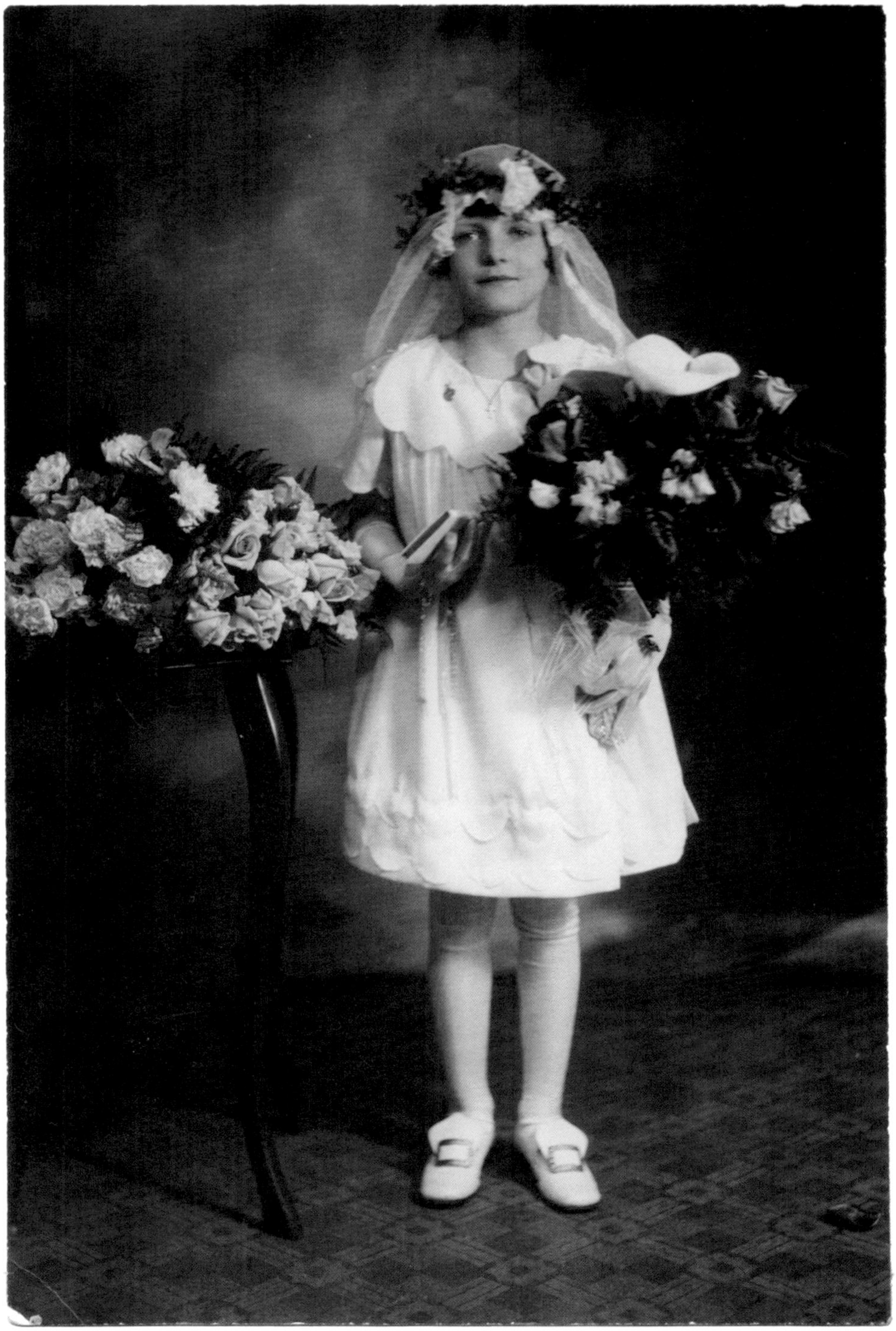

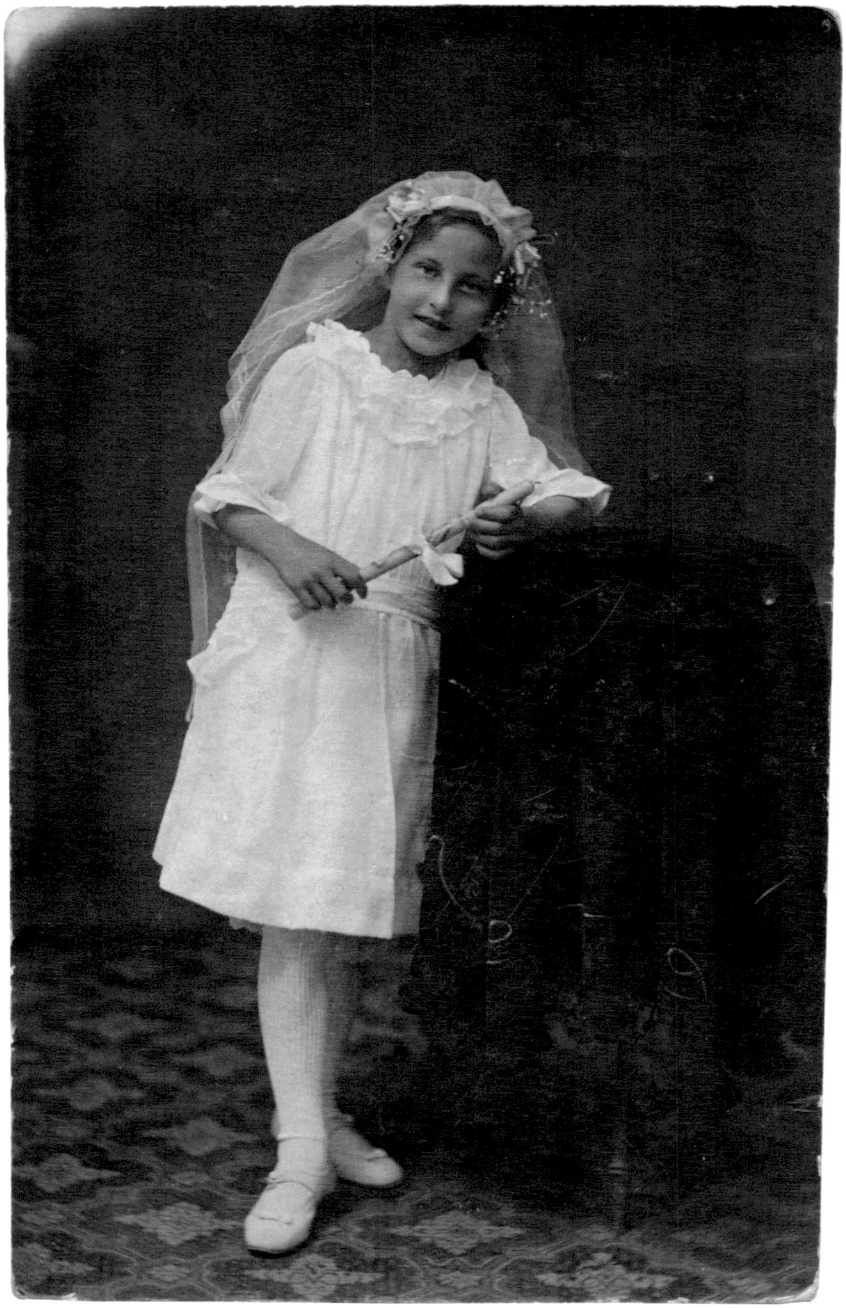

The priest said, 'When I say Body of Christ, don't think you're actually going to eat Jesus Christ's little finger,' and that image has stayed with me forever. He was trying not to make that image in my mind. He was trying to say, you know, don't think that you're actually going to be a cannibal if you have Holy Communion, but of course, if you say that to someone – I was only five, it's usually sort of seven – if you say that to little children they go 'Ugh.' The prospect of eating Jesus Christ's little finger, it was very strange to me. You just wouldn't say that to a kid. I was completely OK with the symbolism before he tried to dismantle it and then he sort of … Ugh.

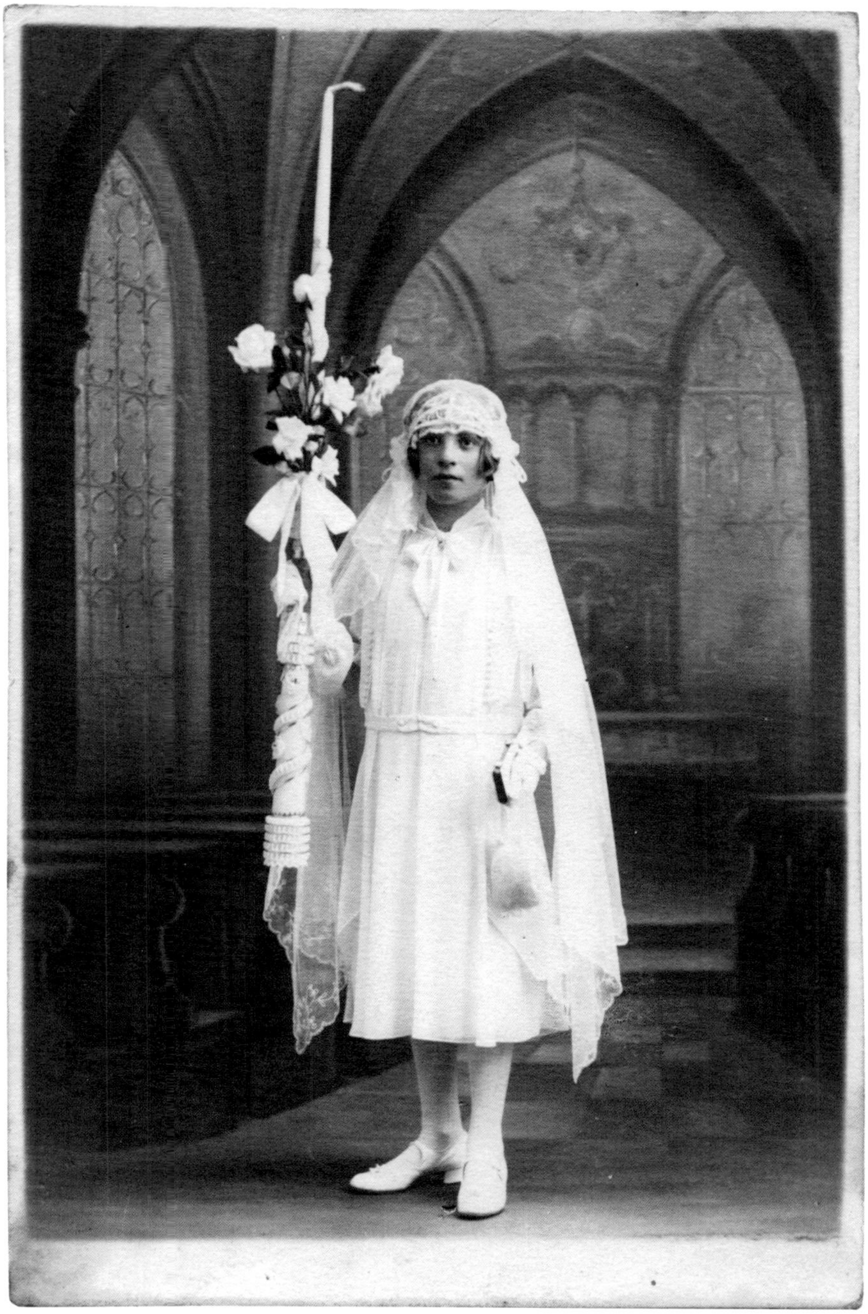

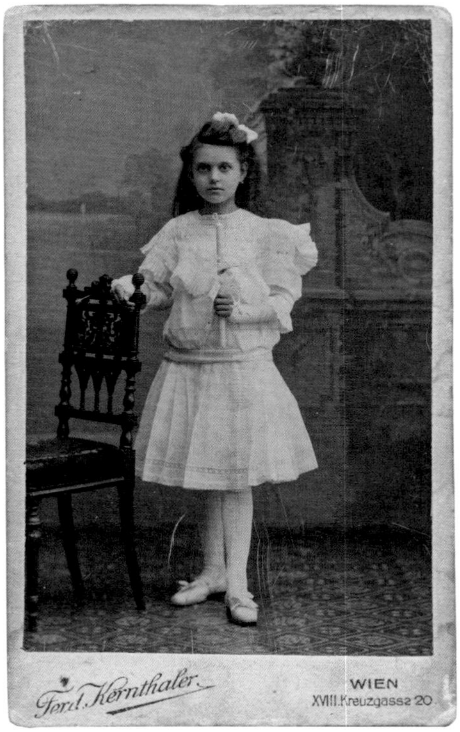

The other thing is grappling with transubstantiation, because of course you're not allowed to make your Communion unless you can actually sincerely say you believe in it.

And did you?

Oh absolutely, yes. I mean I was desperate to do so. But in fact, the kind of psychomachia, the mind drama, is something that children of that age do find incredibly easy to get hold of and to engage with. I mean, you know, their stories are shot through with it and of course with the saints' lives. The stories that we'd been brought upon are shot through with all sorts of great successes in this kind of struggle. You know, in the psychomachic struggle between good and evil.

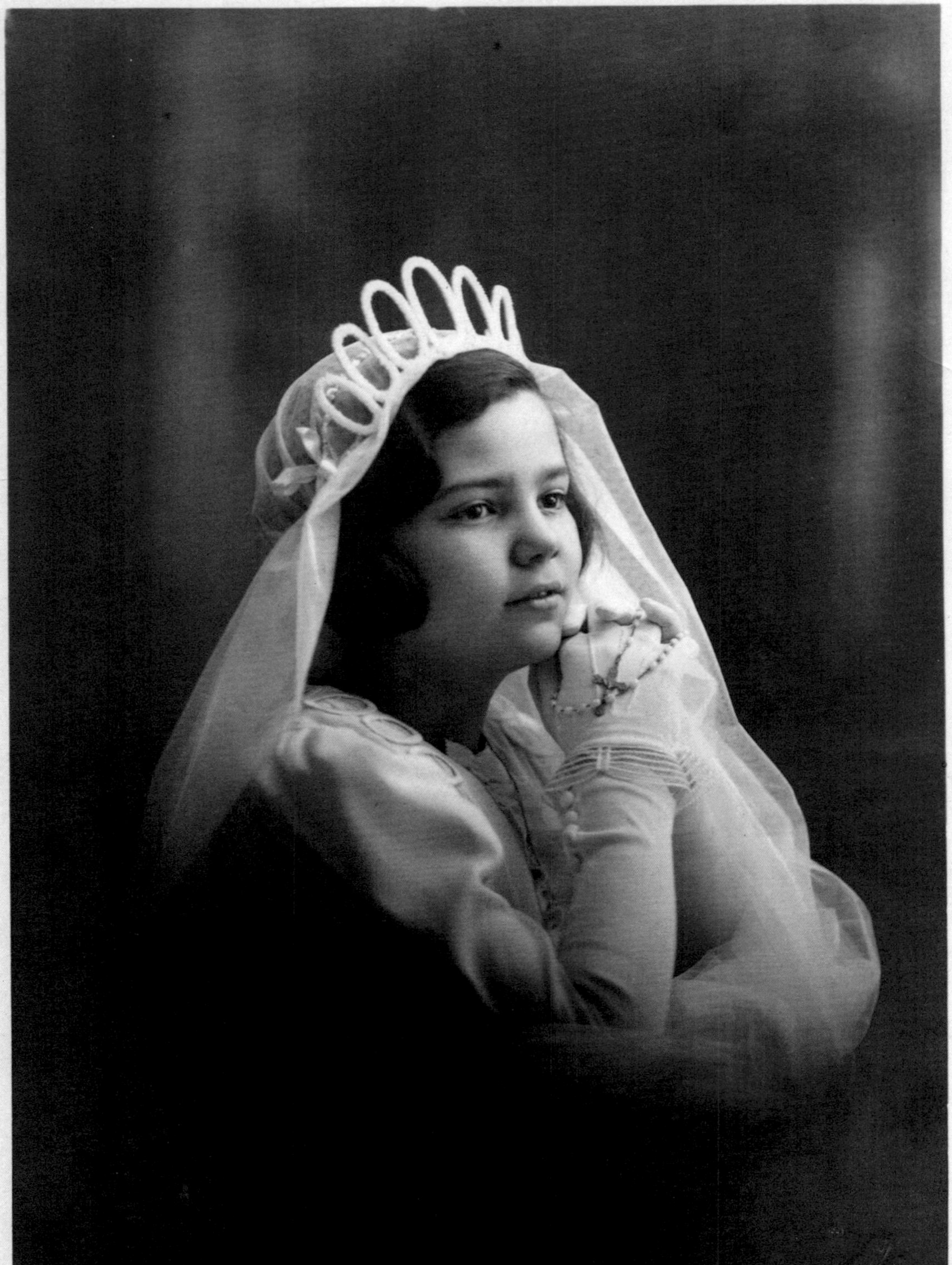

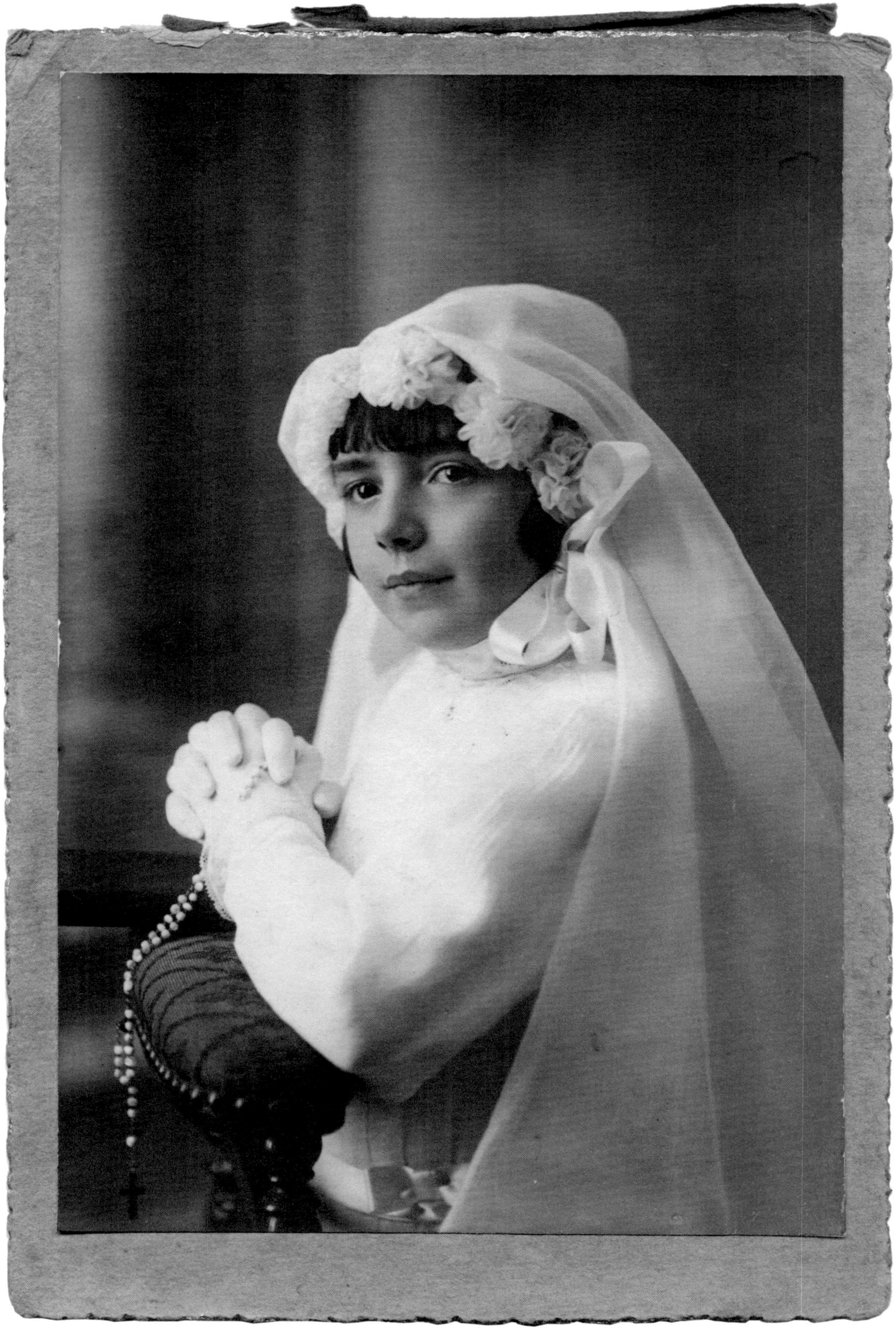

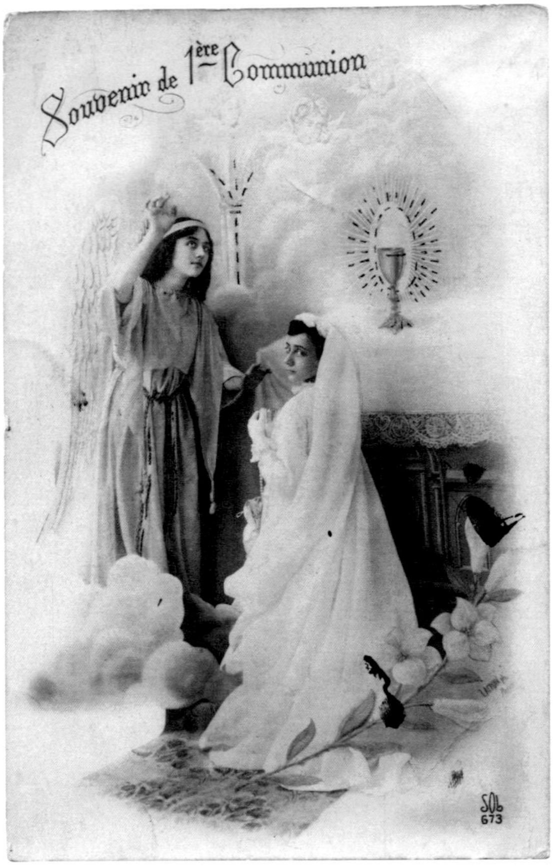

You had to practise feeling holy and worthy – and practise having your whole life changed and becoming a totally different entity. Because after all, you'd been taught about transubstantiation and so it wasn't only the Host that was changing. I mean, a sacrament is an outward sign of an inward change and so you were preparing to be irrevocably something else.

And of course, around the Host there is all this kind of Counter-Reformation popular literature that gets fed to children at this stage of their lives – the desecration of the Host, what happens to people who desecrate the Host. And this Counter-Reformation literature had in fact been revived during the Second World War so there were all of these stories about Nazis coming into churches and stamping on the Host with their jackboot and blood spurting out of the Host, because it's really the body and blood of Christ and all this kind of stuff.

It seemed to me, more emphasis was put on what would happen if the Host fell than if … than on religious things. So the nun would be asking questions, and it was very much a question-and-answer thing, but like every third question she'd surprise you with 'And if the Host falls?'

> Were you afraid that the Host would drop?

No, I was waiting for them to drop the Host so I could point to it. 'I'm not touching it, see' … I would be the hero, you know? And so, I think there was a slight disappointment because nothing went wrong. I remember being disappointed. I do remember that. Because she would describe this thing, you know, if the Host falls, they come and they have special, you know, the priests have to pick it up and then they've got to bring a special holy cleaner. So, I do think that I was really hoping there would be this big dramatic moment when I received it, you know? I wanted the drama, the heroic moment.

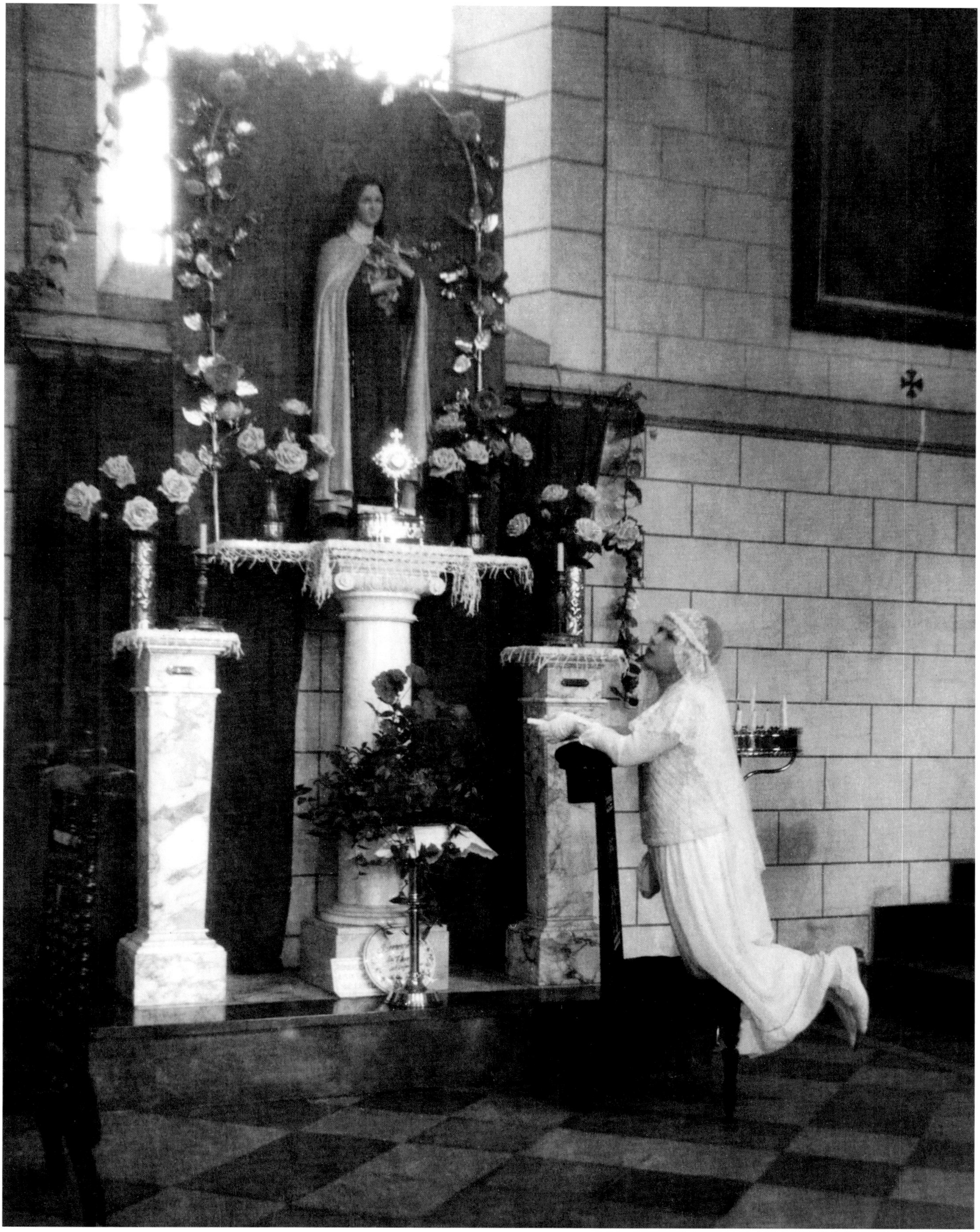

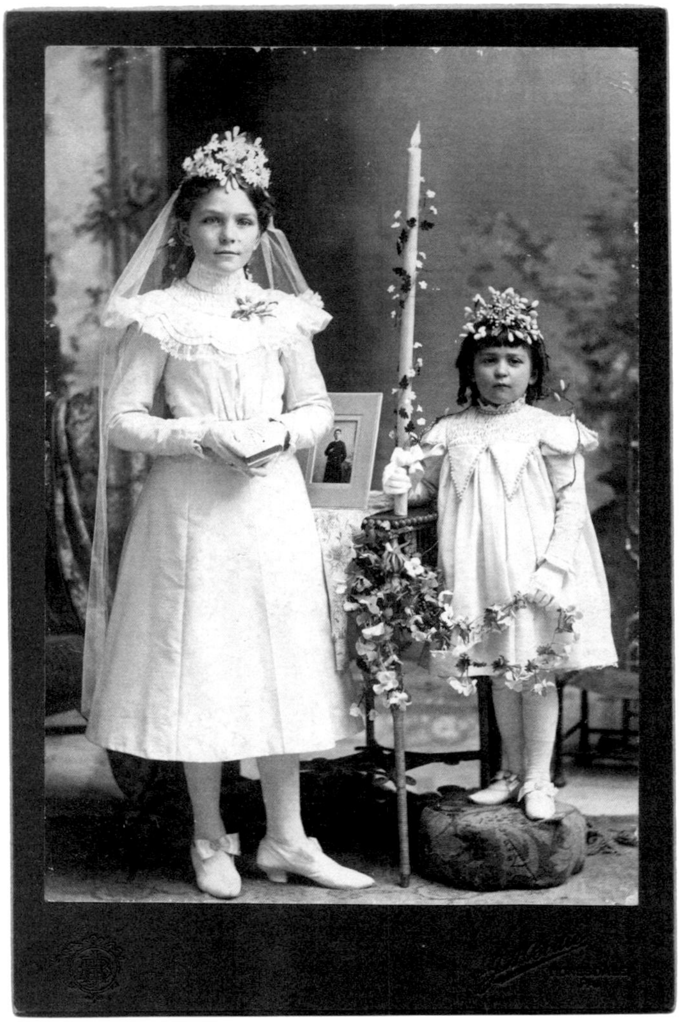

It's supposed to be the first time you take the body of Christ or whatever. Just a few months before that, we had been staying down in Cork with my mum's friends. Her daughter was my age and though we only saw each other once a year, we were best friends. The uncle was a priest and he lived in the house and he used to give Mass in their house every Sunday. So after he gave Mass one day when we were there, she, like, waited until everyone was gone and locked the doors. She took us in and had a pretend First Communion with us and gave us the proper Communion bread and wine. Yeah, her uncle was a priest, so she did the whole ceremony thing with us.

We didn't tell anyone at all, we didn't tell a soul. But then she actually died about a year later in a car crash. She and her mum and her brother were going to collect her uncle, the priest, from a train station, and they got squashed between two lorries and a car. Then we told my mum about the Communion. It was like, oh my God.

> So you were given your First Communion by a girl.

Yeah, it was really special. It was kind of against the religiousness of her family, I think. She was like, I'm going to give this to you.

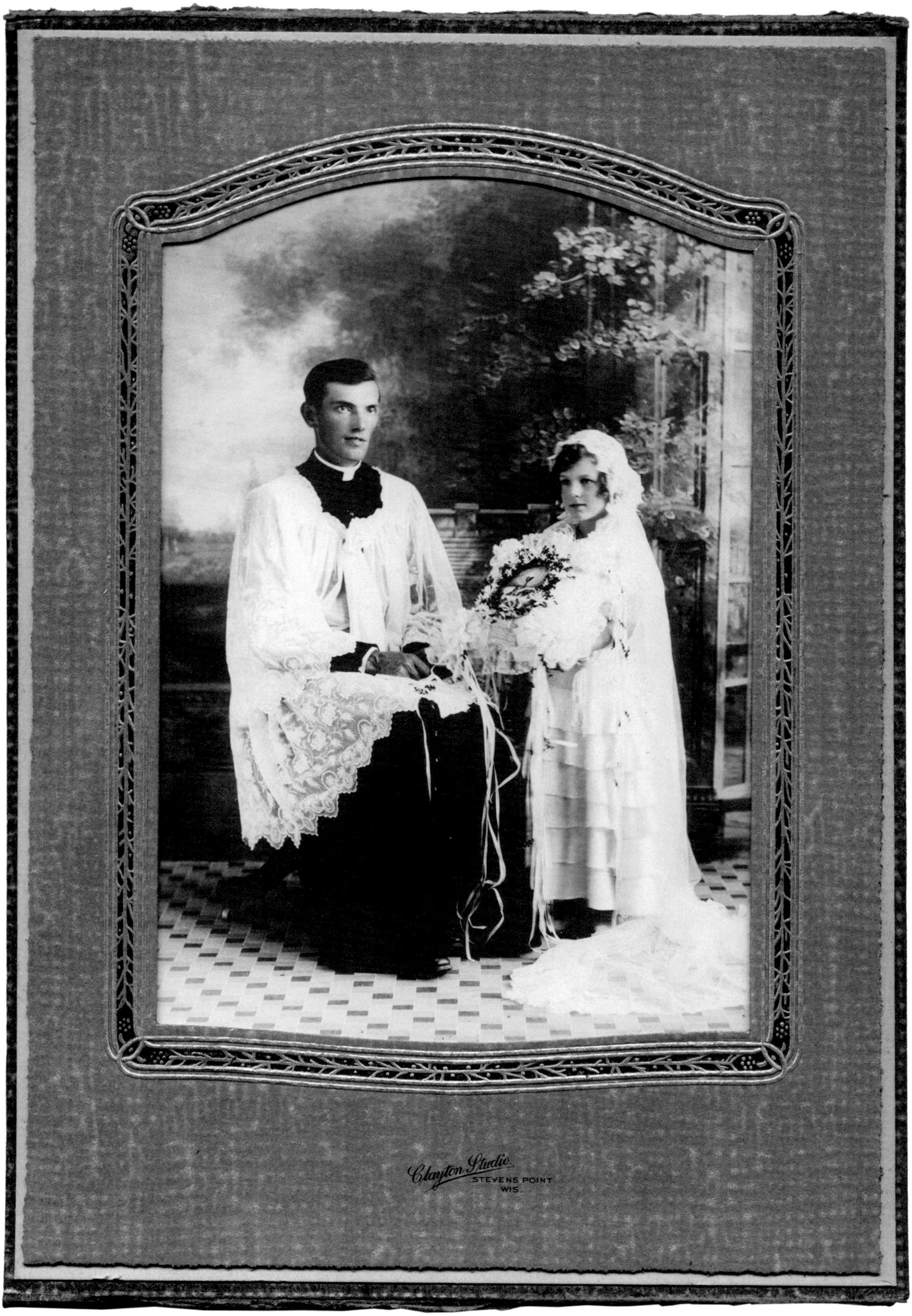
Clayton Studio
STEVENS POINT
WIS.

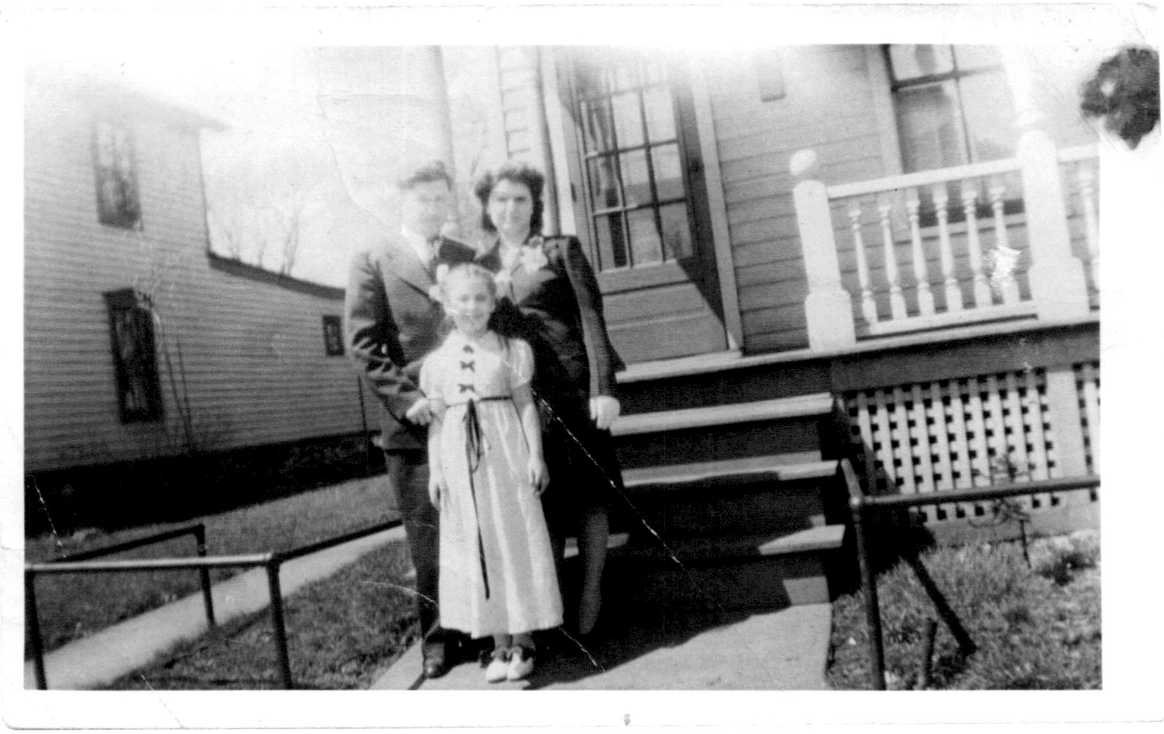

He was a really nice priest, and he was down-to-earth, British and had a little bulldog. He wouldn't mince his words, so he wasn't a hypocrite. When he was angry he was very direct, and once he upset my mum, because he told her that she should spend less time in the church and more time at home being a mother and a wife. They had a big row.

Was your mother a housewife?

No, she was a teacher and she used to commute up to London every day. Just imagine: four children and having to get a train up to London, come home, get the tea and look after the children. But the thing is, she would come home and she would go to Mass. And frequently my dad would ask 'Where's Mum?' and would go into church and get her out, wanting to know where his dinner was. I suppose the priest thought, well you know, it might be important that she should compromise somewhat. Back then you know, you didn't get the new man that would come home from an exhausting day and start feeding the kids. And there was Mum across the road receiving Mass.

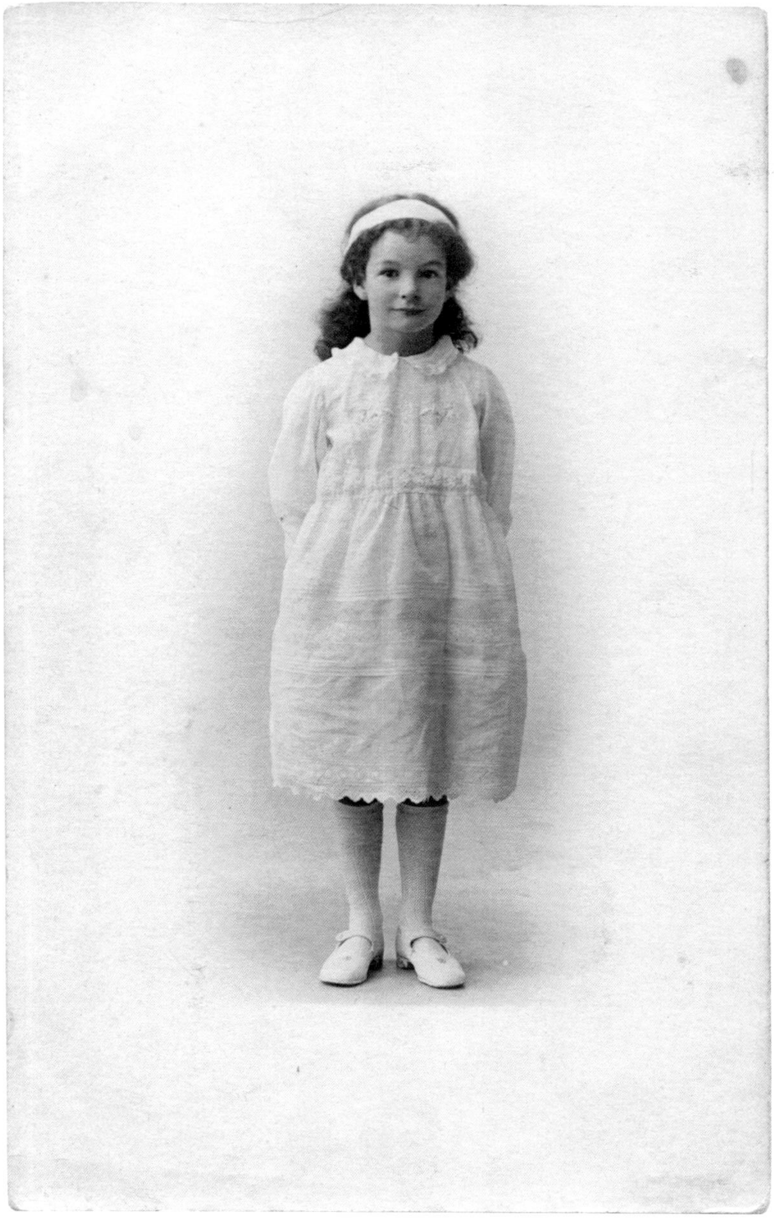

I can remember thinking what would 'grace' be like? The whole idea of 'grace', because you hadn't had any 'grace' before, except when you're a baby and you're baptised, so this concept of some kind of petrol that you were given by taking the sacrament, you know, well what was it? Was it a light or was it a nutrition or was it? What exactly would it feel like? And I suppose, if you do any meditation, it's something close to that idea. Some kind of quiet space. And that was, I guess, my nearest thing to it, of what you might feel like; that you'd cleared your mind. But it's all part of the very intricate ritual of Mass. And to miss out on that part is to miss the whole point in a way – the whole lead-up, the repenting, the preparing and then feeling peaceful. And there are parallels to be drawn with other forms of spiritual ritual, as I said, like a meditation where you have to empty your room, empty your mind, then hope for something else. Yes, hope for something else to come in.

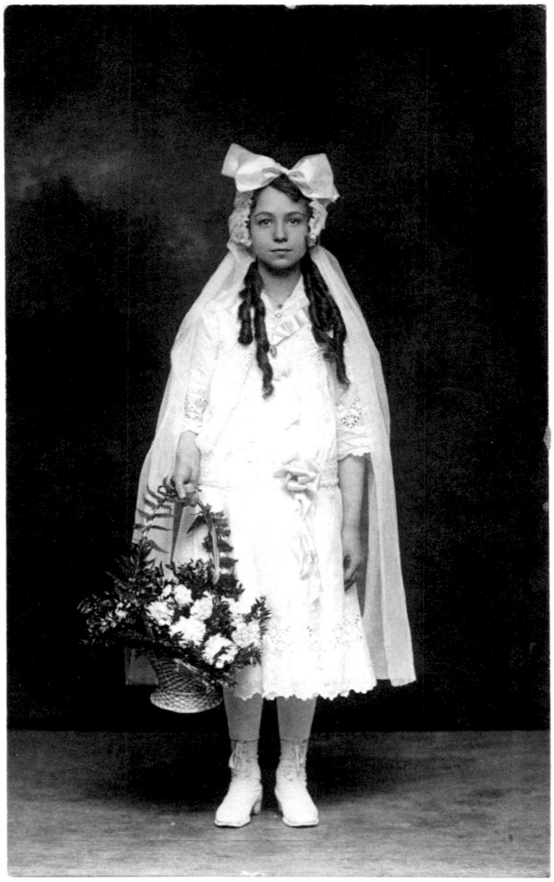
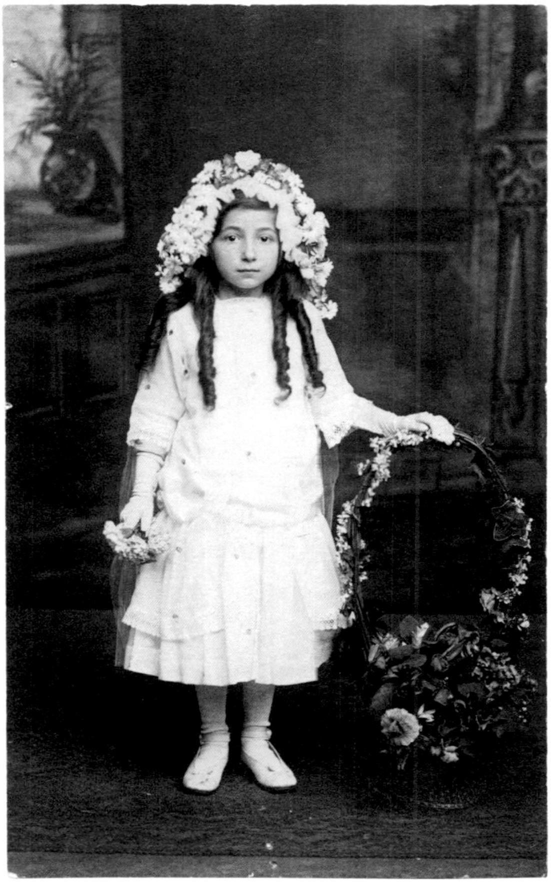
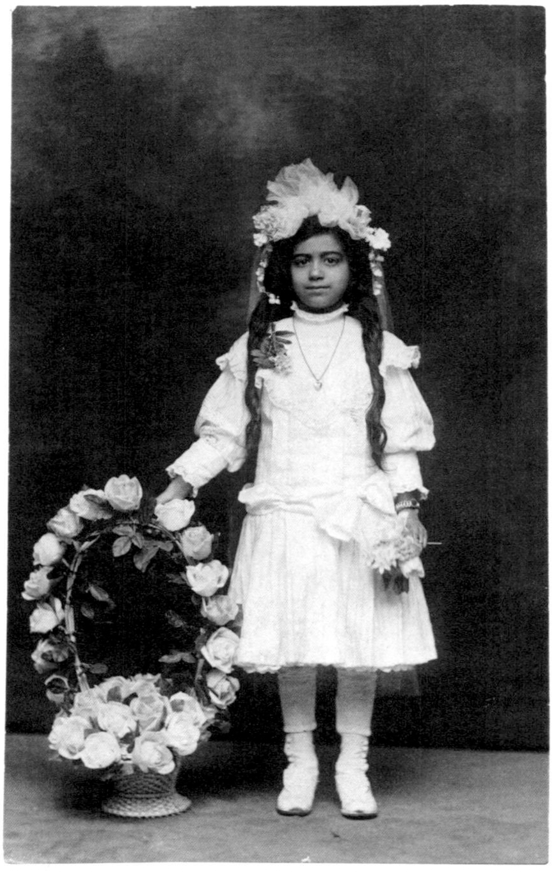
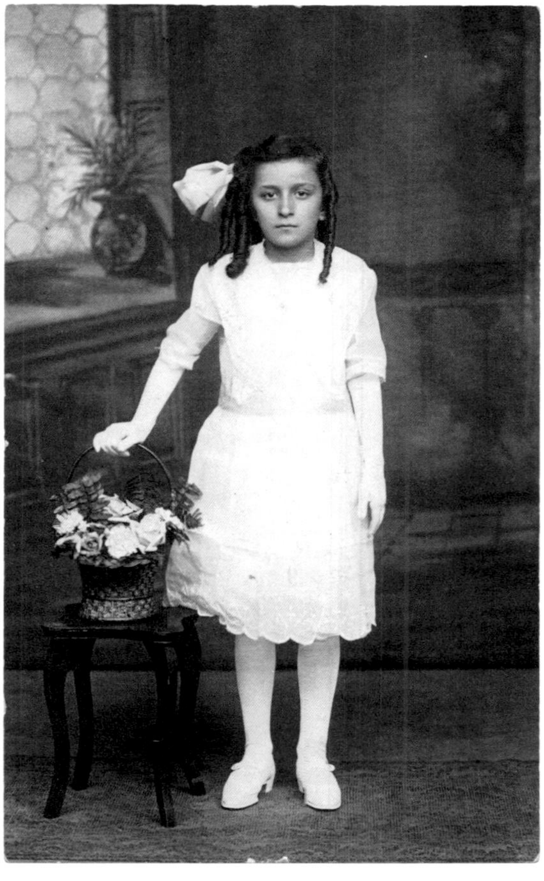

In New Mexico I had my Confirmation before my First Communion. I was somewhere between four and five years old – really small. I know this because I found photographs of the goat and me and I'm very tiny.

Anyway, I was so excited. I remember getting these little gold shoes from Spain – they were gold leather – like patina, you know, not flashy gold. My little shoes came from *Los Niños*, which is no longer around, which is a shame, because it would be like walking into a shop in Paris or in a special part of London. And I was so excited, I was so proud. So I ran out to the backyard to show my little *cabraito* – my grandmother had chickens and she had this little goat for me – and he was not there. But the rope was still there. So I thought – well, he ran away. But no, he didn't run away.

And then I came in and asked one of the elderly women, 'Where's my *cabraito*?' And they said, 'Oh, we have to tell you something.' And I said, 'OK', and they said, 'Sit down.' And I said, 'OK', and they said, 'Well, in order for you to get your name, the honour of having your name, something has to be sacrificed' – and I went, 'Oh?' but not understanding 'sacrifice'. So they said, 'In order for you to get your name, we had to do something because we're going to have this' – You know, they have this big family celebration on Sunday. Now we're talking a long table with all, you know, the head of the family, the patriarchal person and the grandmother, and then it's all the ages until you get all the way down to the youngest, yeah?

And so she says, 'Well, get your favourite chair', a little itsy-bitsy chair, and she put it right in front of the stove. And then she said, 'Well, you can still show the shoes to your *cabraito* but he had to die for you in order for you to get your name.' So she says, 'You can still show them to him.'

It's tradition to have the head of the goat in the oven roasting.

You eat the head?

Yeah, the head is like a real big ritual. My grandfather was a cook at one of the restaurants in Santa Fe, a chef of some sort. And he always liked to use the leaves from celery, parsley and onions. He clipped them – they came out of the garden, you know all that foliage like – who's that painter?

Arcimboldo.

Yeah, so instead of it being this horrifying thing, she said, 'Well, go ahead and tell the little *cabraito* about your shoes – show him your gold shoes.' And so I said, 'OK', and I sat down on the chair and she opened up the oven door and here is this gorgeous head filled with all these wonderful – you know, what to me looked like flowers. It was nothing more than the little leaves of the vegetables. I'm sitting there saying, 'Look at my nice shoes – I get to wear them to the' – and 'I'm sorry that you had to die in order for me to get my name, but that must be really, really important or big that this had to happen.'

I've always loved my name. I was named after my grandmother and my aunt, you know. So, it wasn't frightening. They did it in such a sensitive manner for me that I wasn't scared. But you see, one of the things which you learn in the Hispanic culture is that the minute a child is born, someone has died also – somewhere.

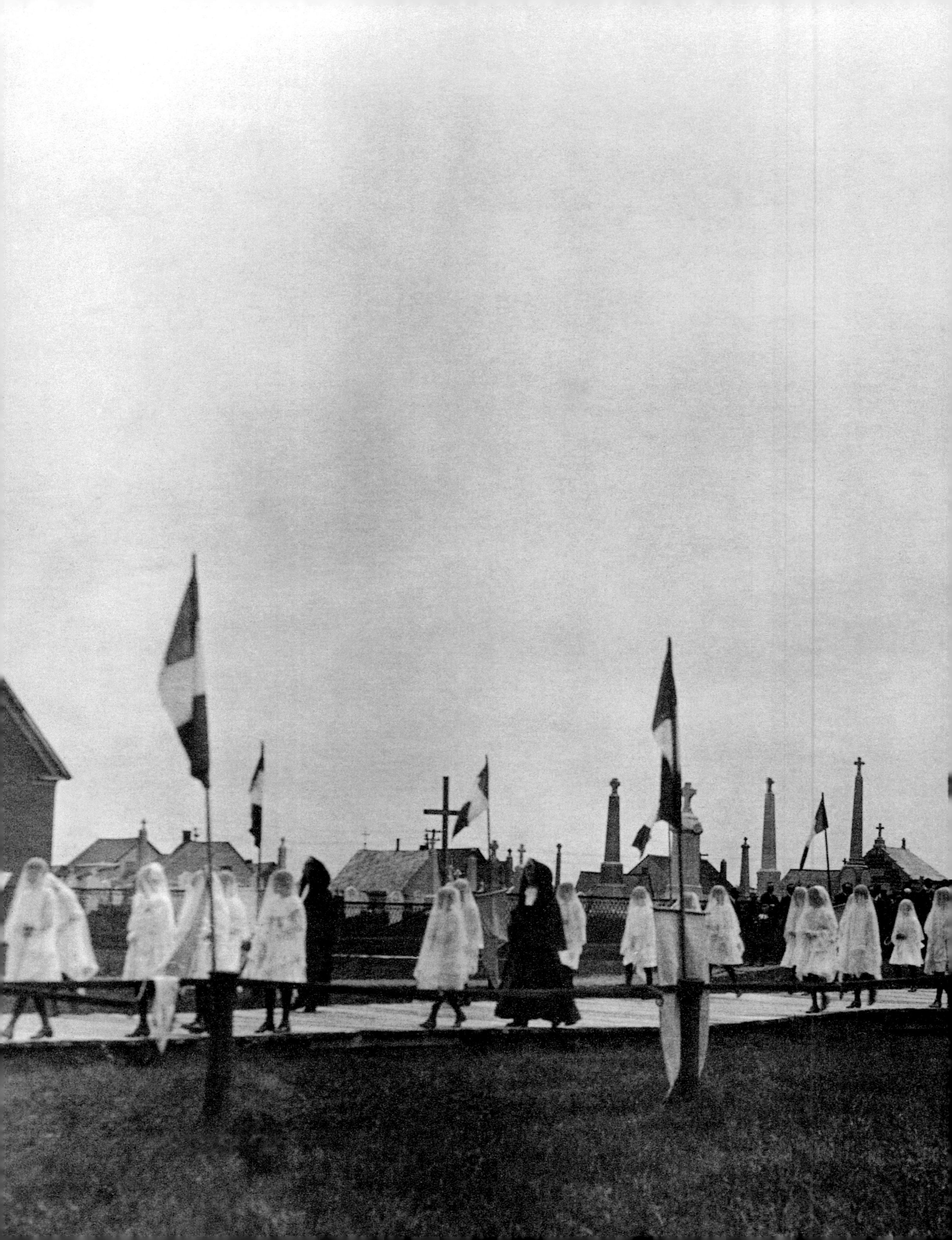

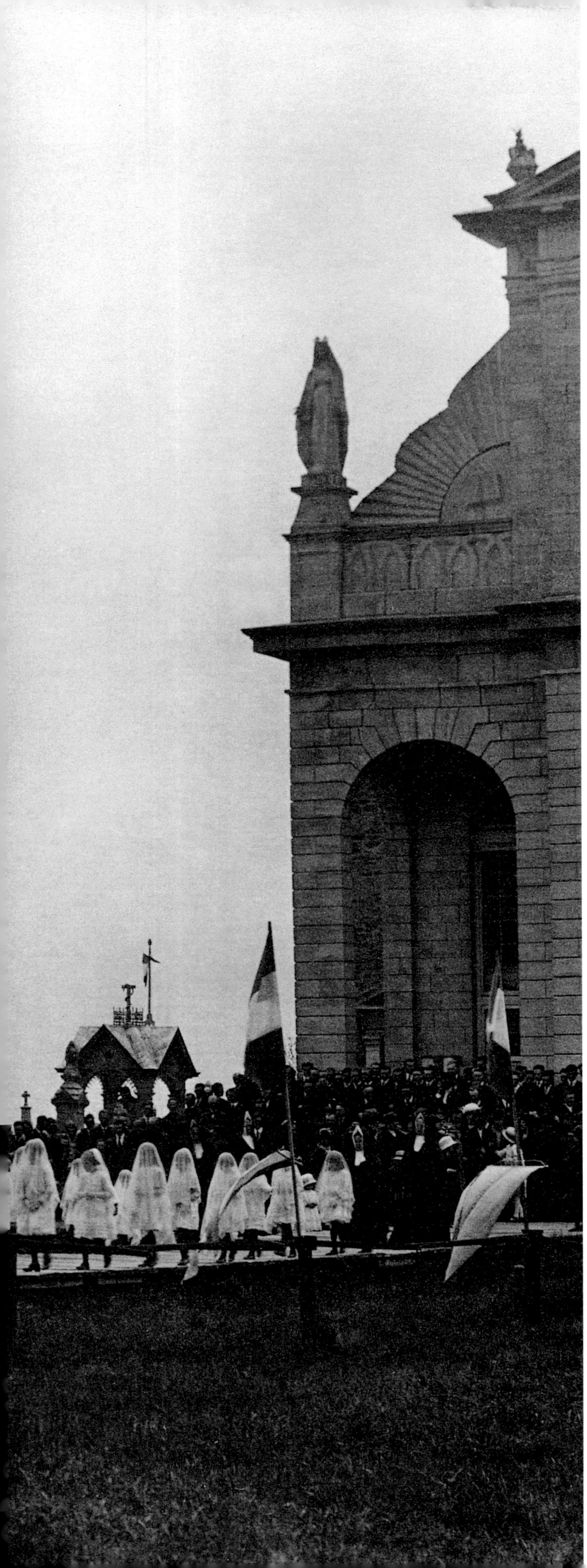

5

FROM THE ABYSS OF MY NOTHINGNESS I ADORE THEE

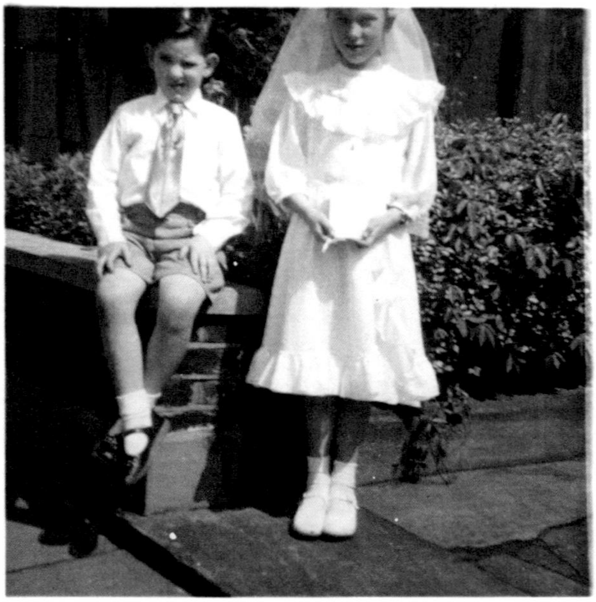

It was funny to see. These were classes of fifty-five to fifty-six kids, but we were two classes so there were over a hundred kids. And, you know, fifty-some girls in these little lacy white dresses and veils and fifty-some boys in their little suits and bow ties – it was quite the event.

So you were brides and they were –

Grooms I guess, 'cause to me, in our class, the boys and the girls look liked a set. A little bride and groom ... if you're going to look at it from a distance.

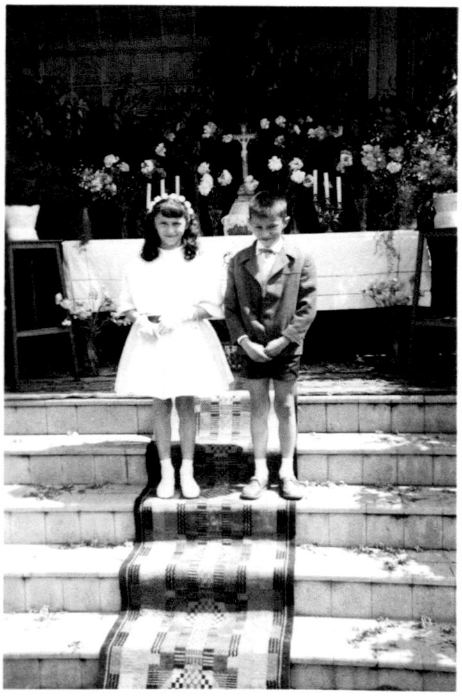

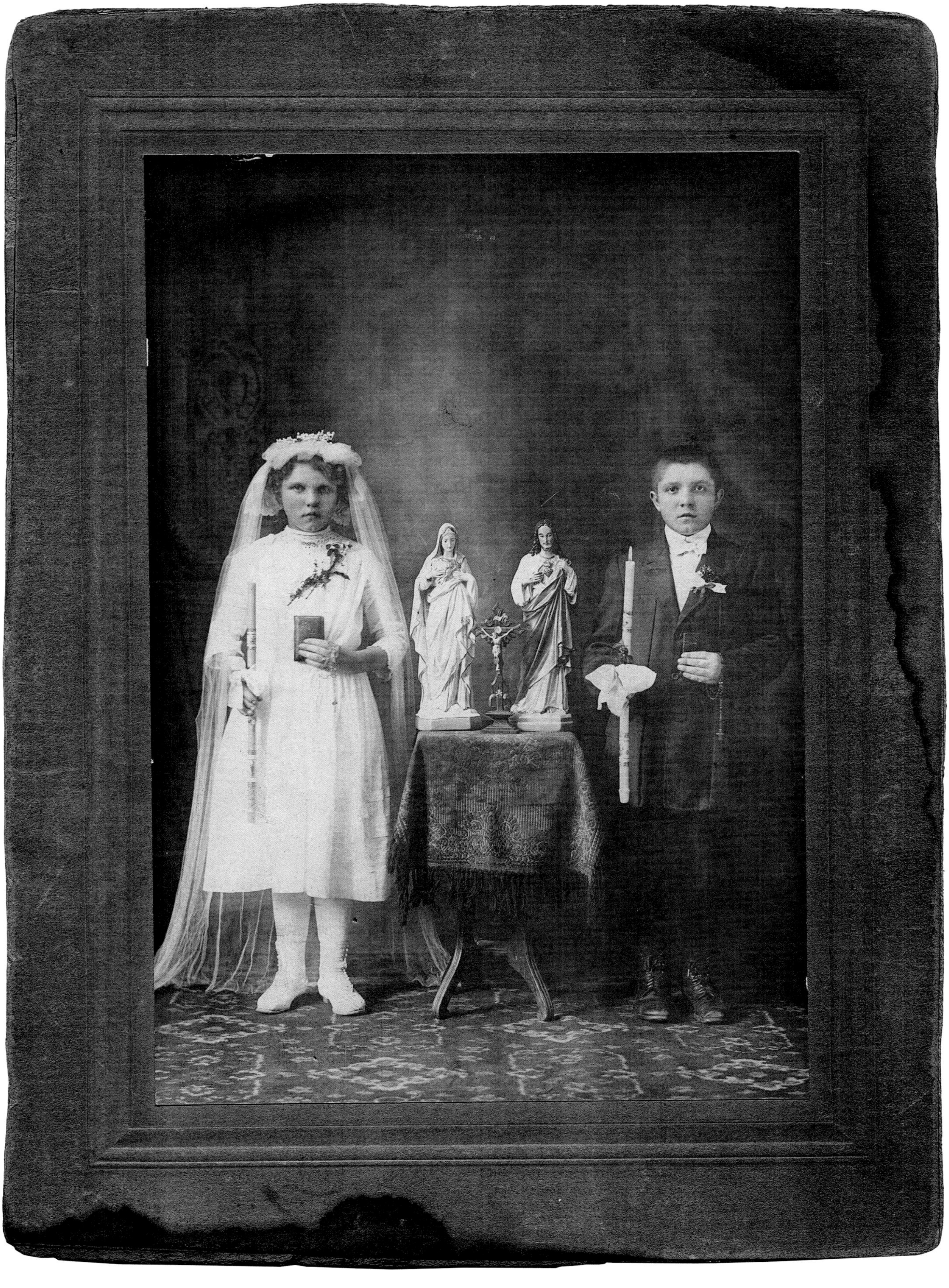

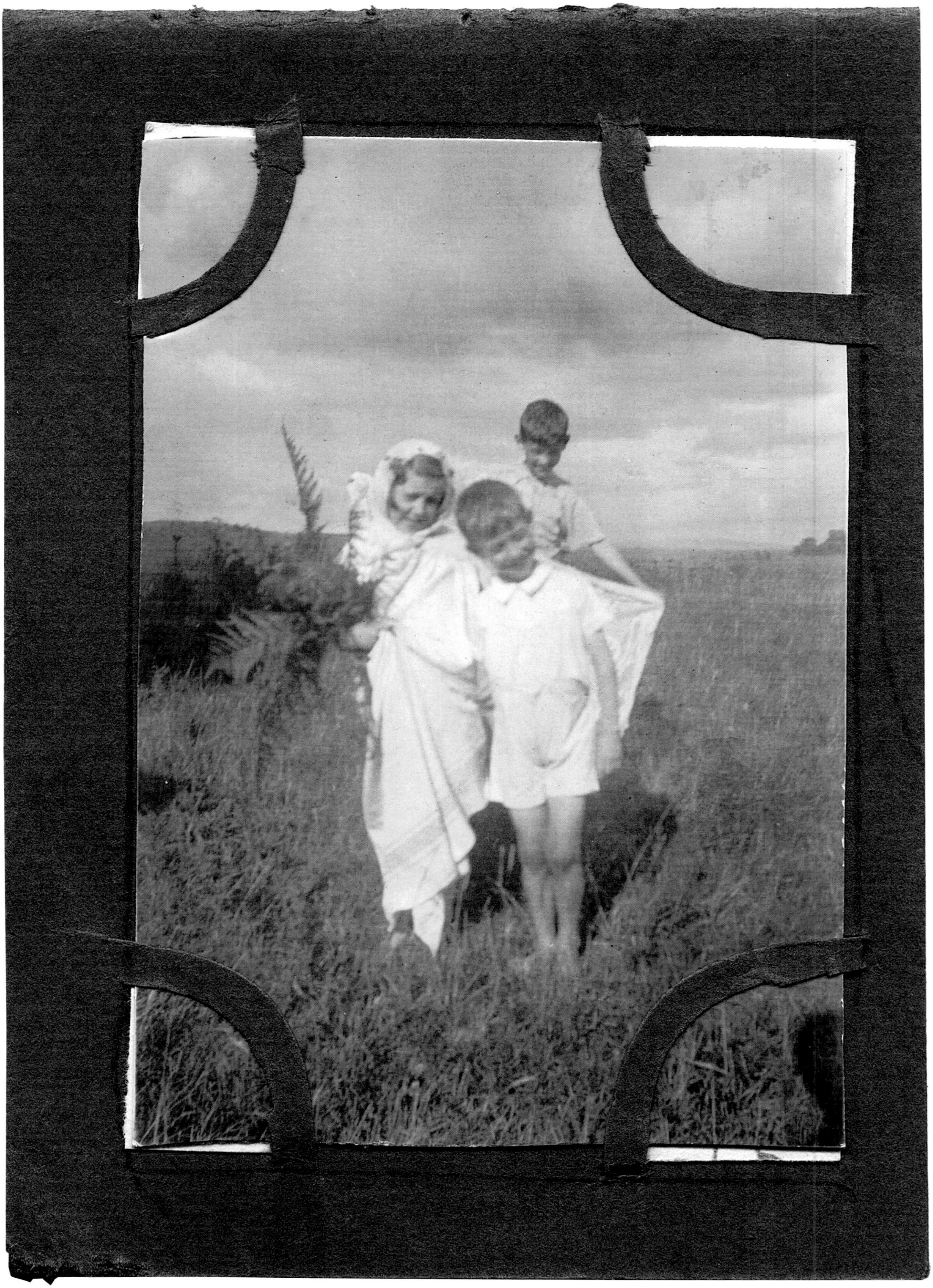

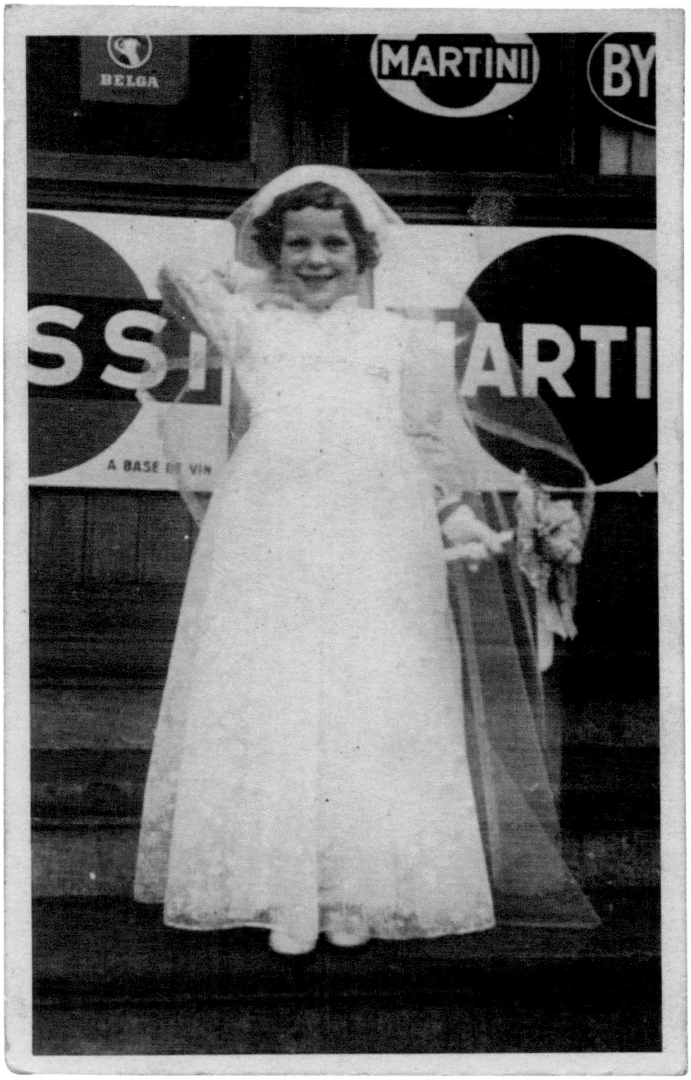

Probably the most exciting aspect was the veil. It was pretty intriguing as a kid. It's a big deal going to a special store to get it, picking out the one you want – even though they're basically the same, there were some that were a little bit more ornate than others. I got to pick out the one I wanted. It was like a fitted veil, but it didn't come forward at all – it was just on the back. From the time you're young, you put on towels and you pretend. You practised between being a nun and a bride, you know, when you went to Catholic School.

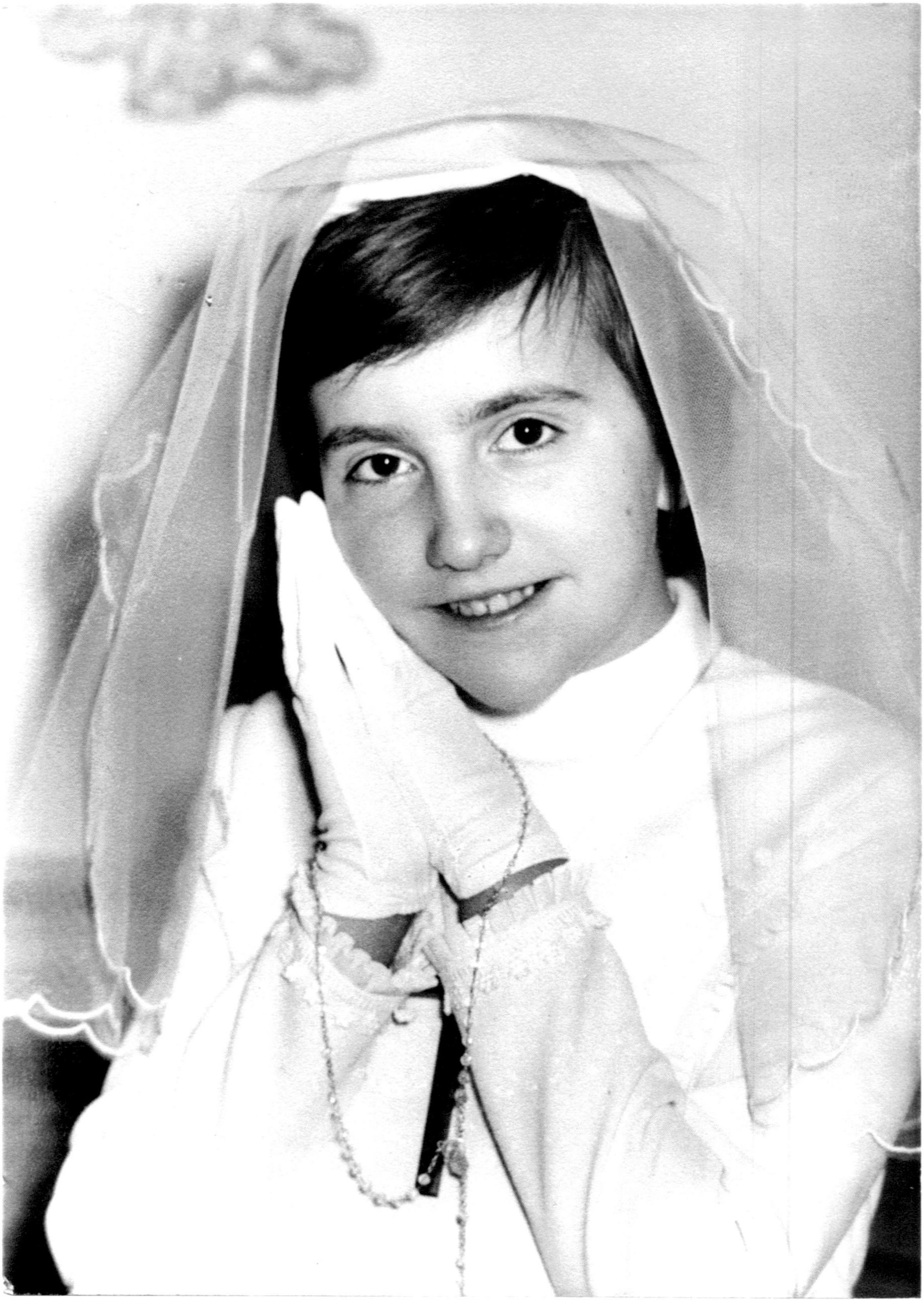

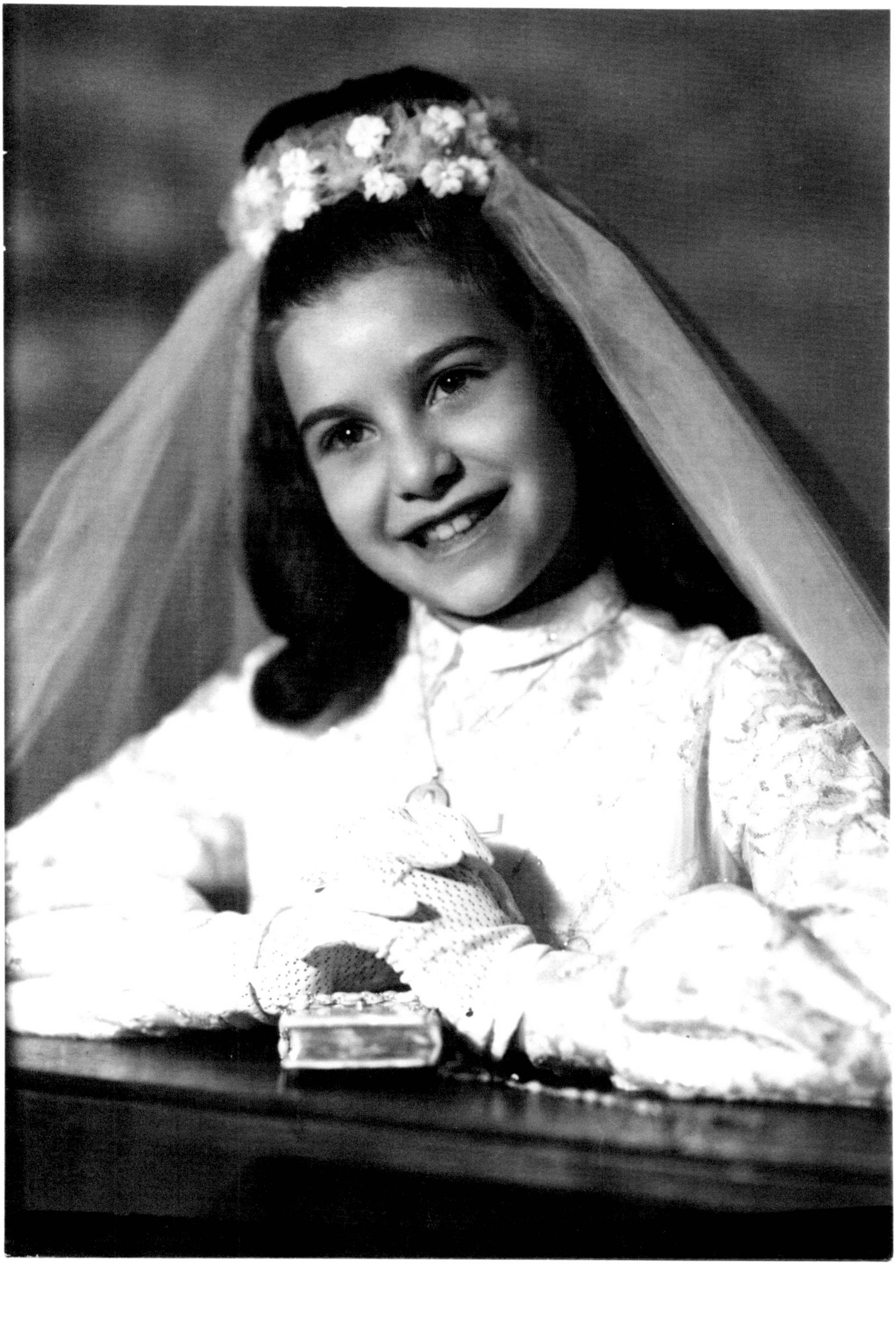

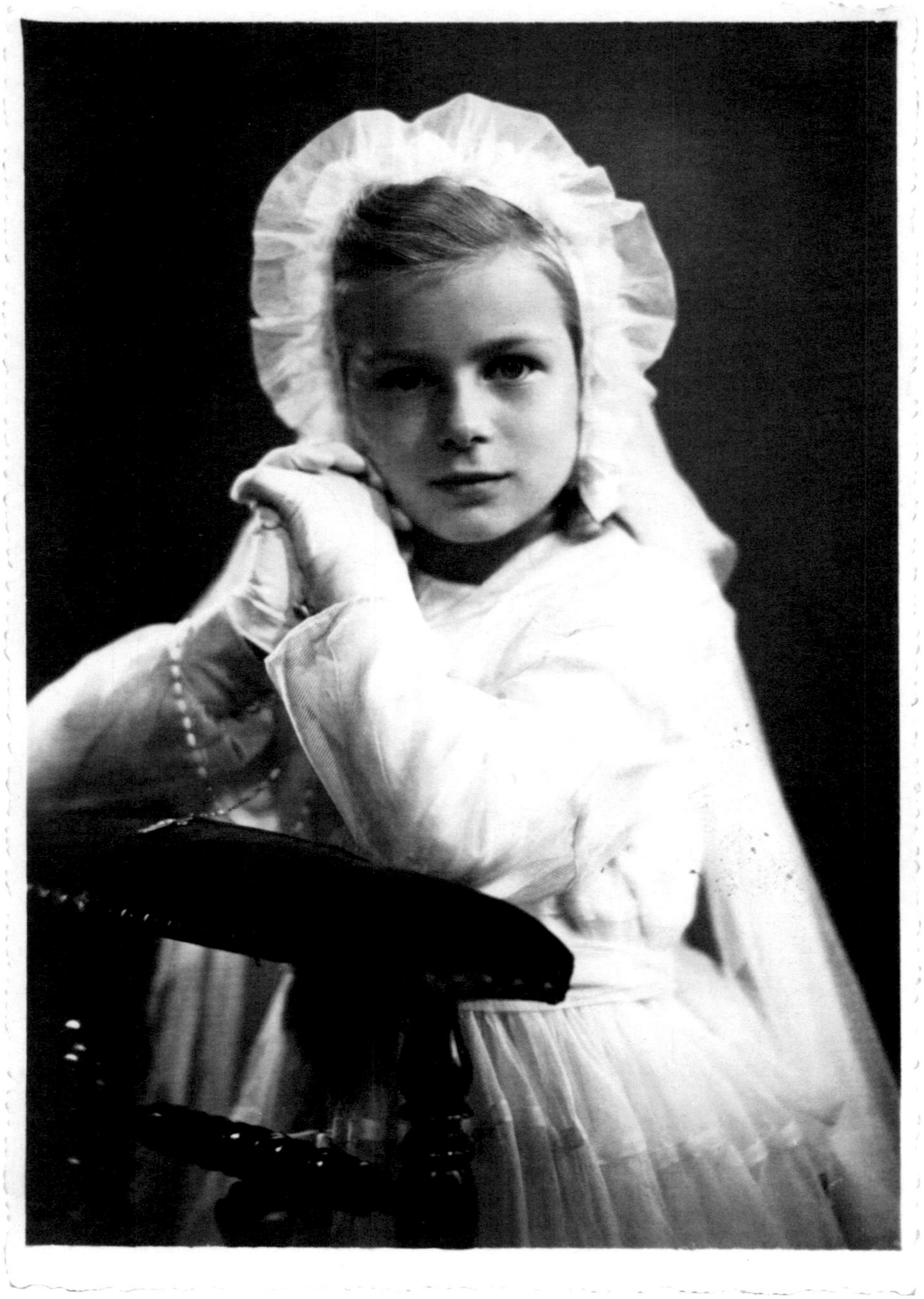

Oh yes, well, I mean, you were an angel, a flower, all the things that are in ... You know, there's an awful lot of poetry around the event. And in our case, of course, it was largely Franciscan poetry, the poetry of the late Franciscan saints. So the flowers falling from the heavens and the lilies and the roses and, of course, all the poetry that goes along with the celebrations of Mary in May, which are really sort of pagan spring rituals, all of that stuff is associated with you and your dress.

Add to that, the fact that little girls do tend to sort of walk around in some kind of wonderland, you know, walking into lampposts dreaming of themselves as princesses, at the age of seven anyway. I mean, my own daughter did even though she wasn't raised as a Catholic.

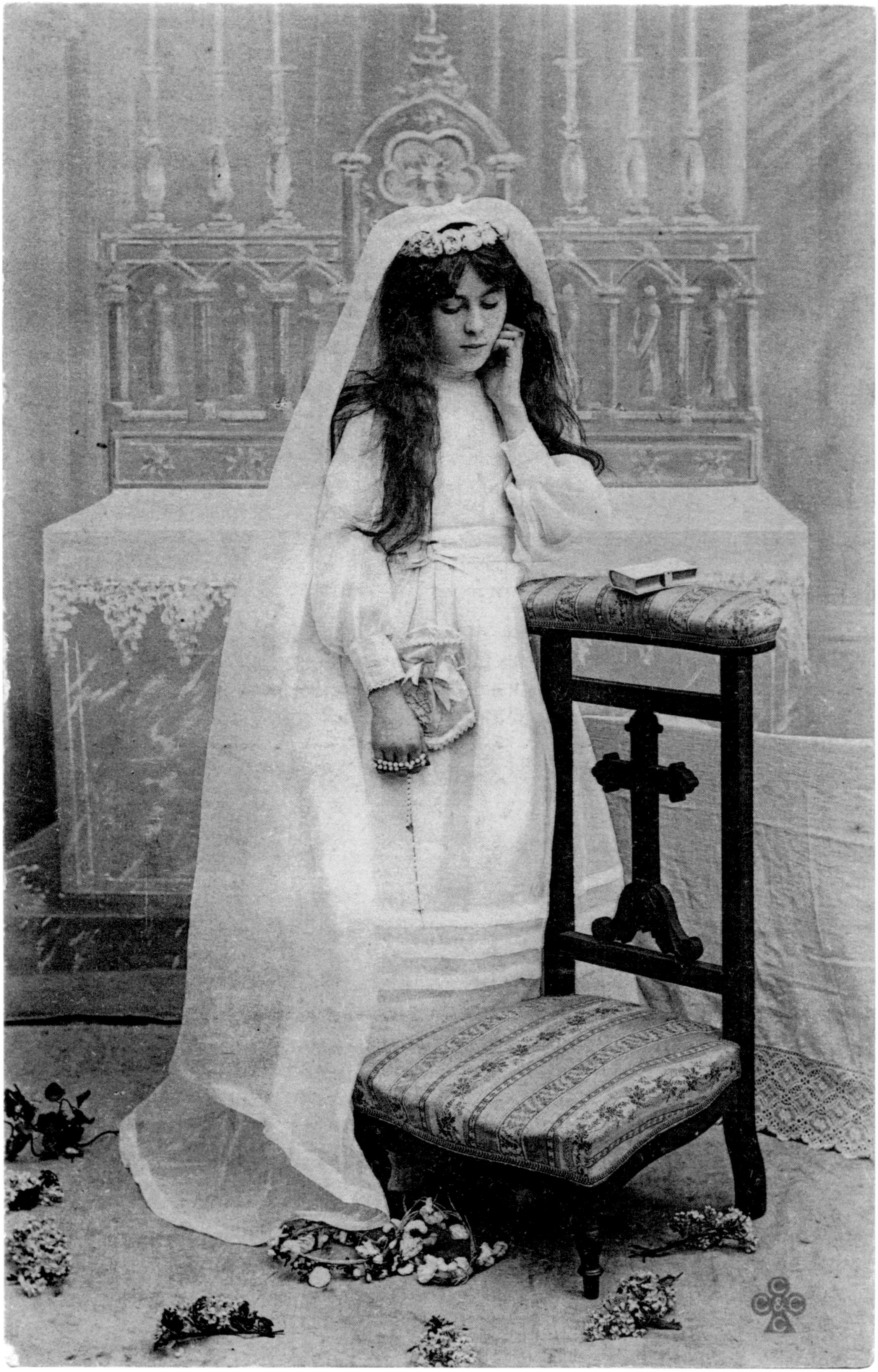

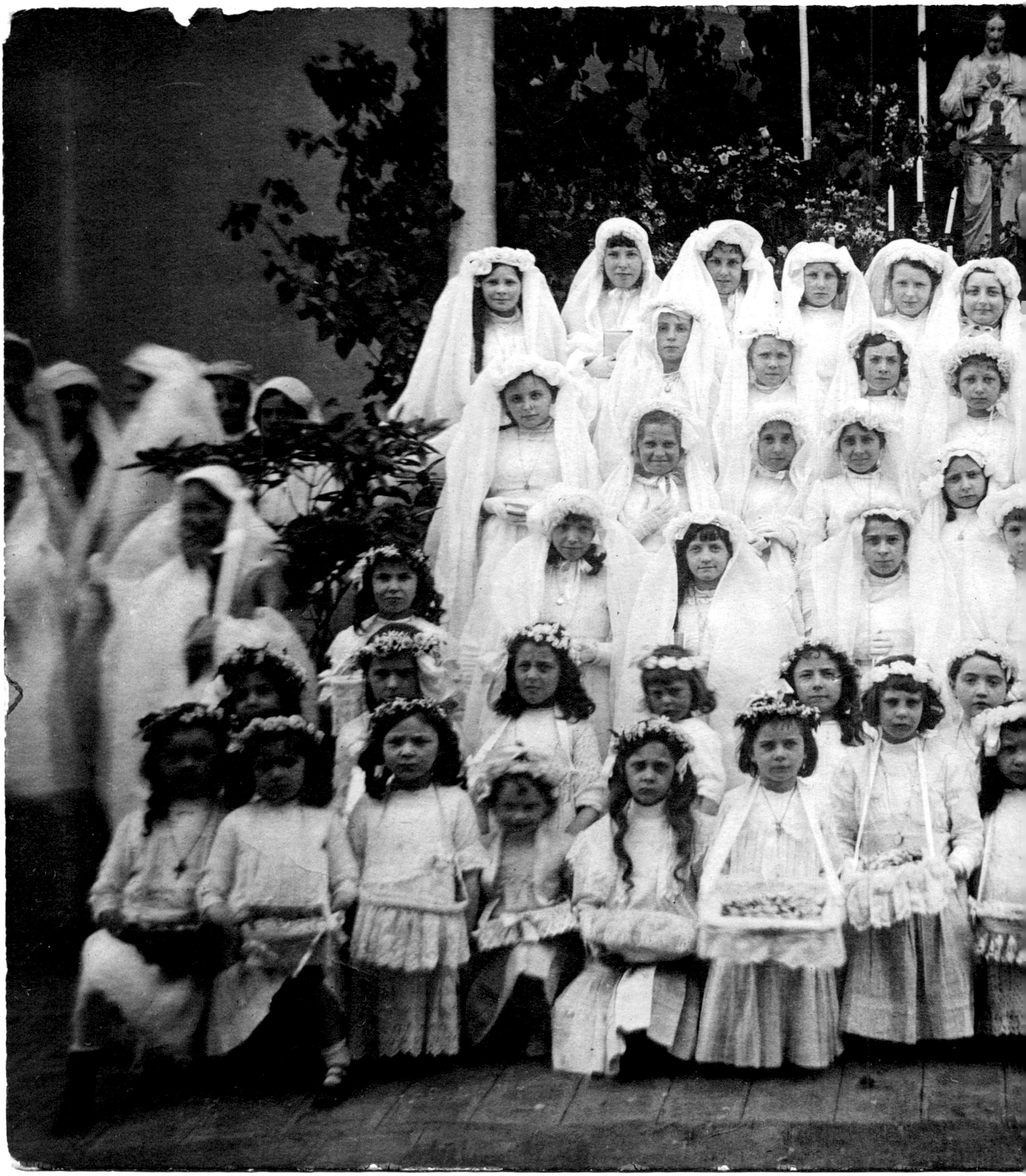

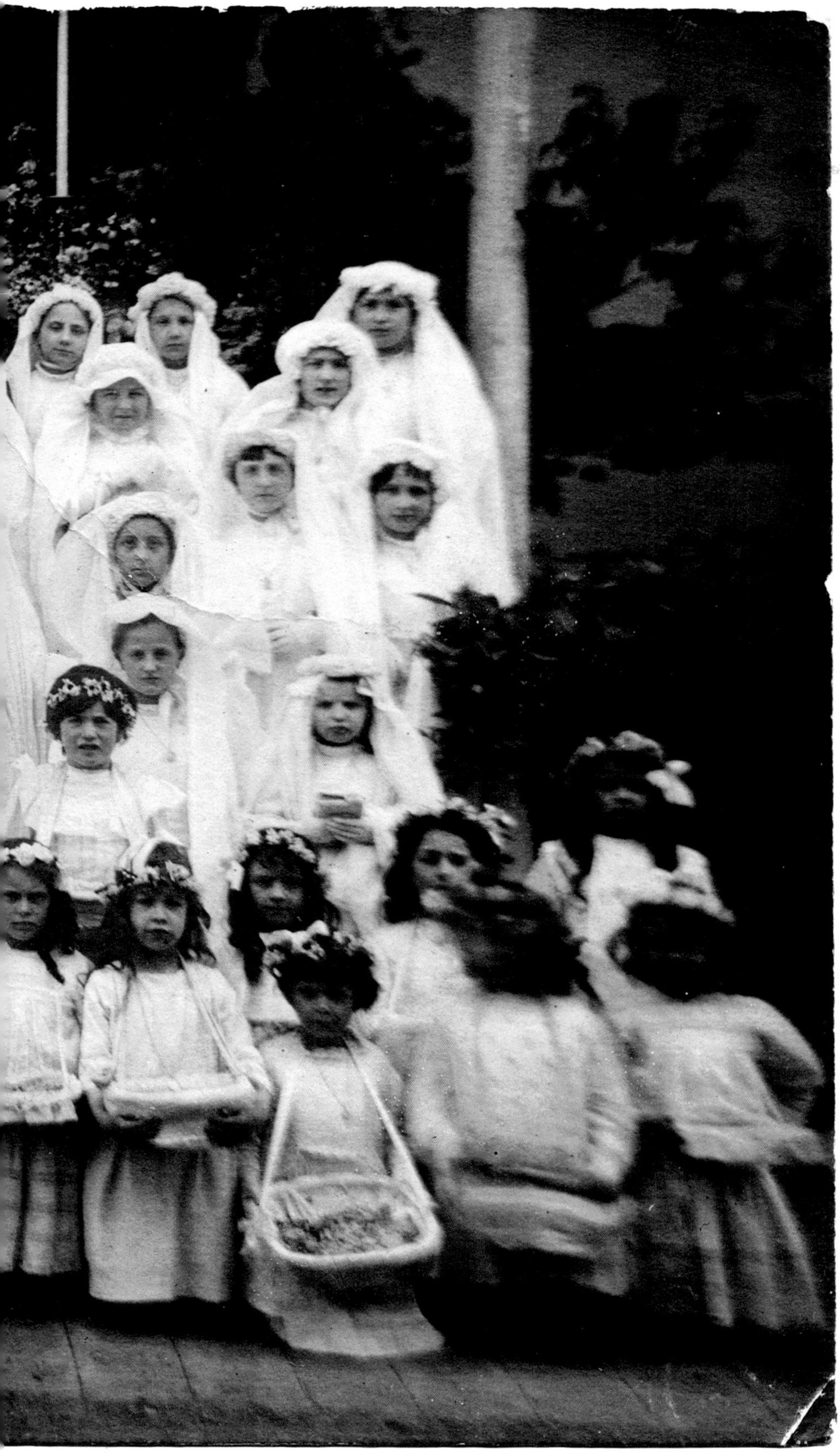

The thing about the Holy Communion dress of course is, it's not the first time that girls have worn it in those days, that kind of bridal outfit, because we wore them on the May procession. I mean, I'd always had a very disturbing time in the May procession because of my allergies. Where most of the girls were there with great handfuls of blossom, you know, from baskets, that they were chucking about all over the place and singing 'Oh Mary we crown thee with blossoms today', I had to be well back and out of the way, behind the grannies, because of my hay fever.

So you couldn't hold the flowers?

No, and so I always had the dress and I was in church with everyone else, but in the procession I had to walk away from the other girls which was quite upsetting. I was always apart from them. So the first time I actually walked up in the procession was at my First Holy Communion.

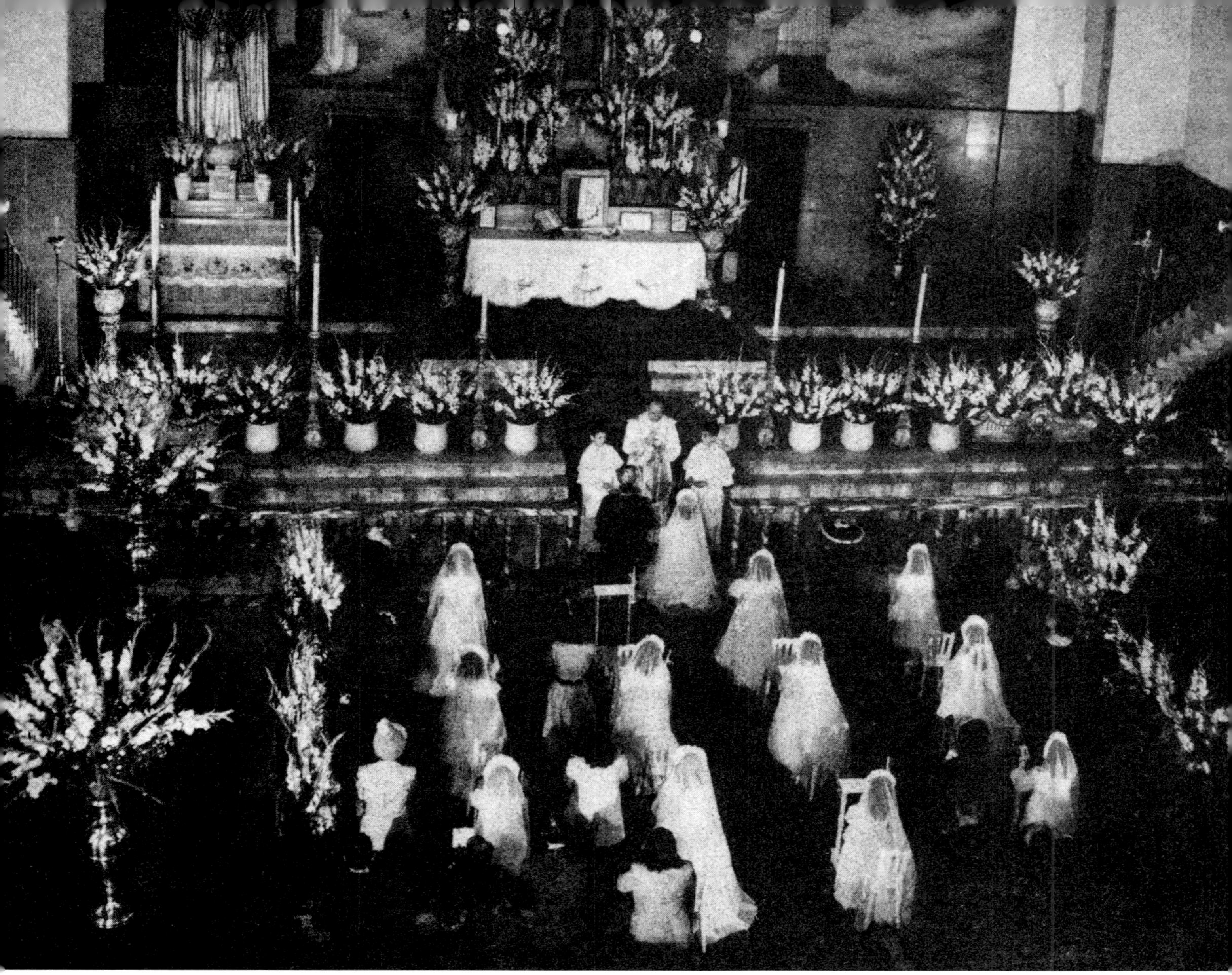

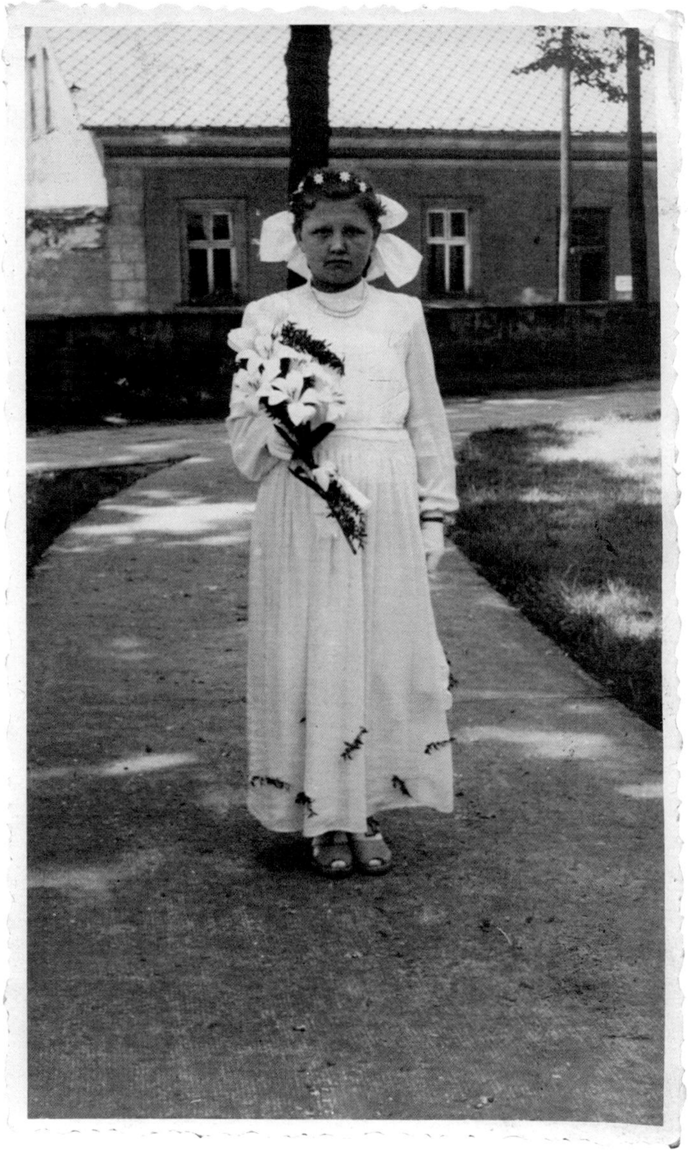

The funny thing was that my mother was late, so my mom and dad, and I guess my whole family, were late to the church and the procession had already passed. The church was packed, everybody was up there, you know. In South America, churches are very long from the entrance to the altar. It was a large church, and I guess when I was seven years old or eight it looked longer. So it seemed like I was walking forever to reach the procession, by myself. Yeah, I walked in, they gave me my flowers and the teacher kind of pushed me forwards.

So you walked down the aisle solo, like a bride?

Like a bride, yeah. I was so nervous – everybody was looking at me, you know.

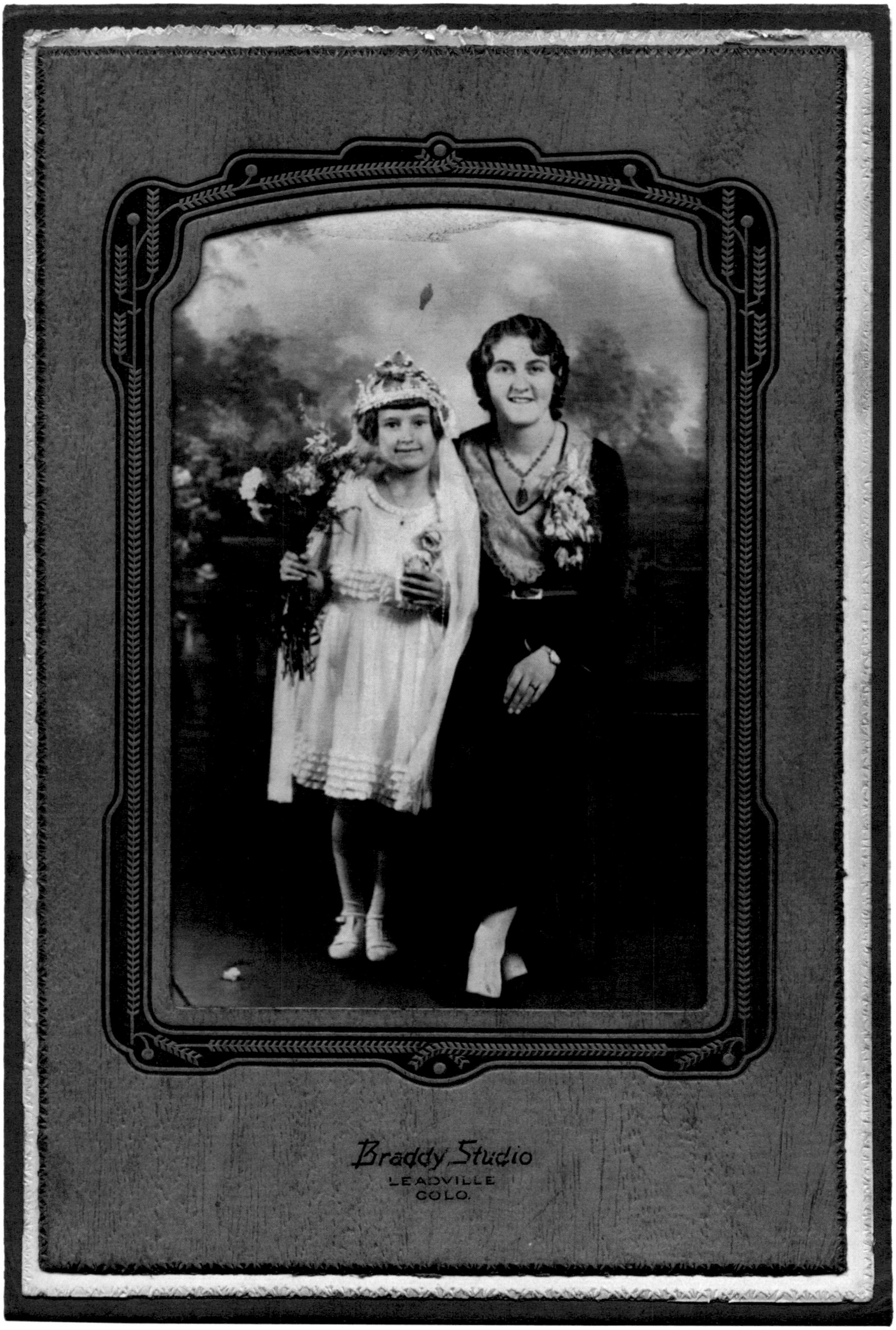
Braddy Studio
LEADVILLE
COLO.

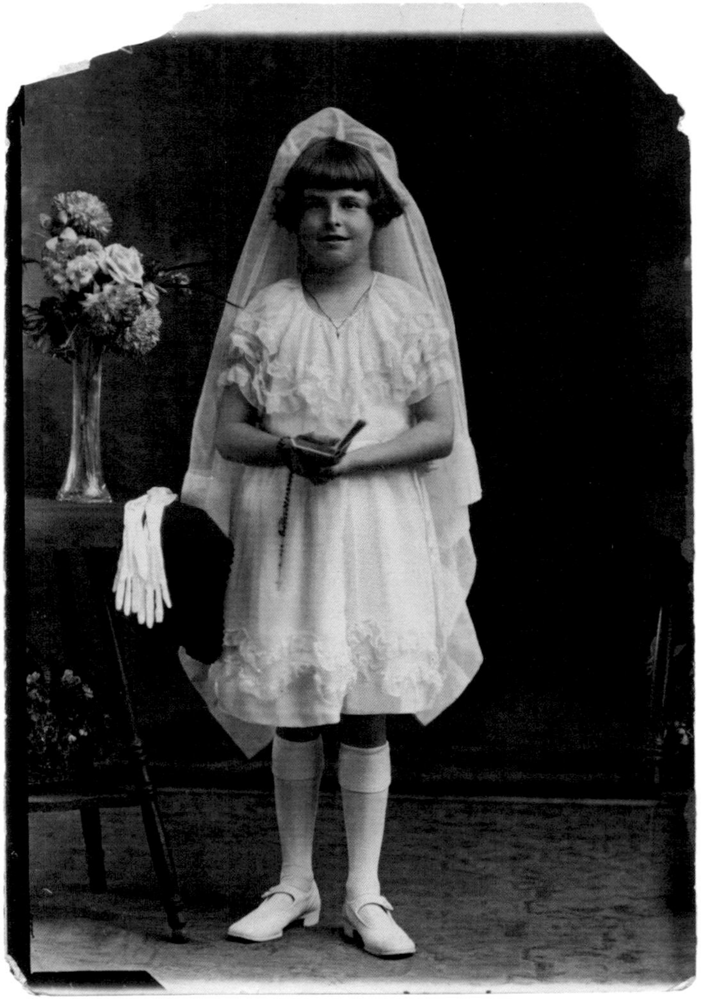

I remember my mother singing – she had such a bad voice and you know how kids get embarrassed. You'd just put your head in your hands and think, oh God, let it be over. Whatever songs they were singing, she was joining in with gusto. Yeah, lusty gusto.

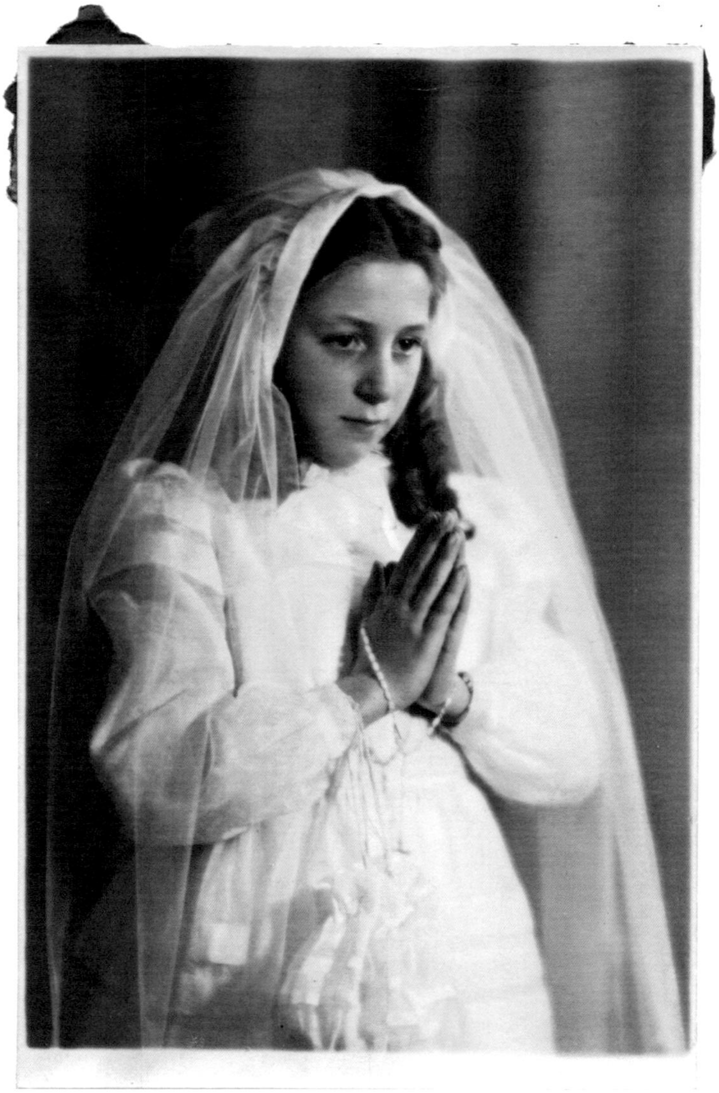

What we had to do was to walk down the aisle with our hands folded, pointed up to Heaven. Because you're taught that if you turn your hands downward, the prayers go to Hell. But when your hands are extended upward that means the prayers are going to Heaven. You had to be in the most reverent position.

I just remember resentment, not really resentment, but I felt like I was sort of letting the side down by not being floaty. I remember looking round and seeing this row of little girls in their pretty, frilly stuff. And you know, when I say I'm jealous of the other girls, it's that particular image of looking round and seeing this row of very pretty little brides. I felt really jealous because they looked so good in that dark, ecclesiastical kind of way. It's partly, you know, the bridal thing, but it's also a sacrificial lamb thing as well, because lambs are white and fluffy and you're going up to eat the Lamb of God. It's all tied in with the pastoral thing too. But you know, there is that kind of slightly sado-erotic-y sexual thing of a woman in white in a dark, dark space. Strange.

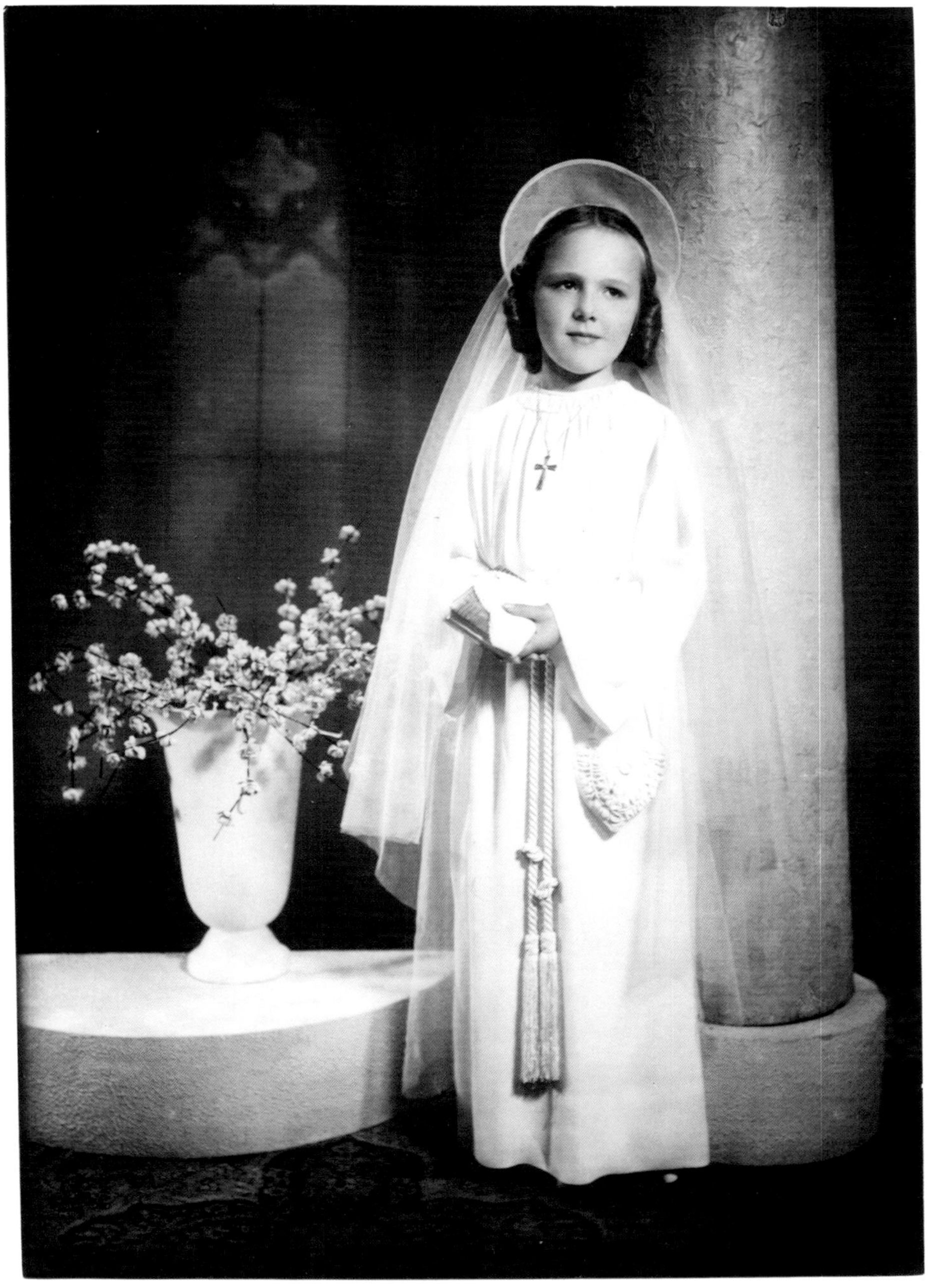

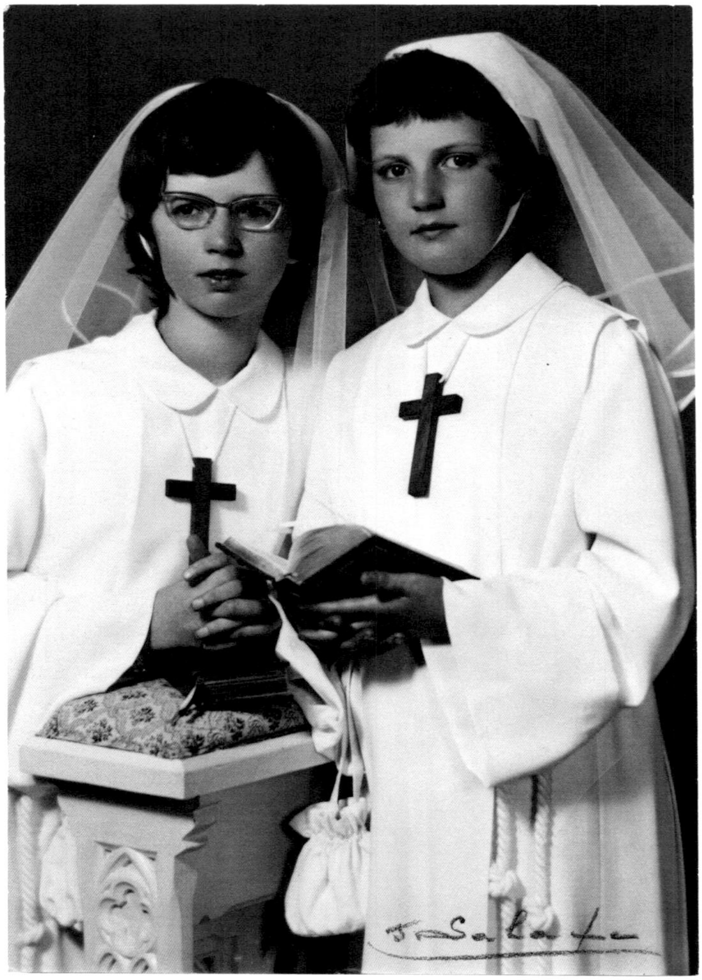

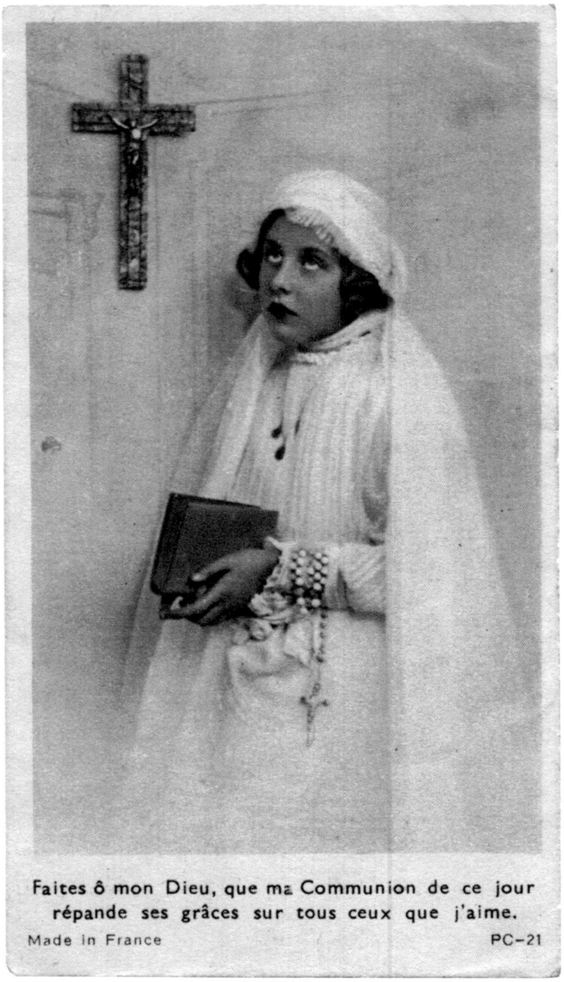

There's something erotic in terms
of the look – the gaze.

It could be articulated through the language of the *Song of Songs*, or Saint Bernard – it's picked up through the whole history of the Catholic Church. I mean, all through the medieval period, it wasn't just Bernard … Many of those virgin mystics talk about being betrothed to Jesus. Jesus comes in a dream or in some kind of vision, like to Catherine of Siena, or Teresa of Avila in the 1500s with her breast pierced by a shaft of the burning love sent by the bridegroom. So all of that, in that sense, it is erotic.

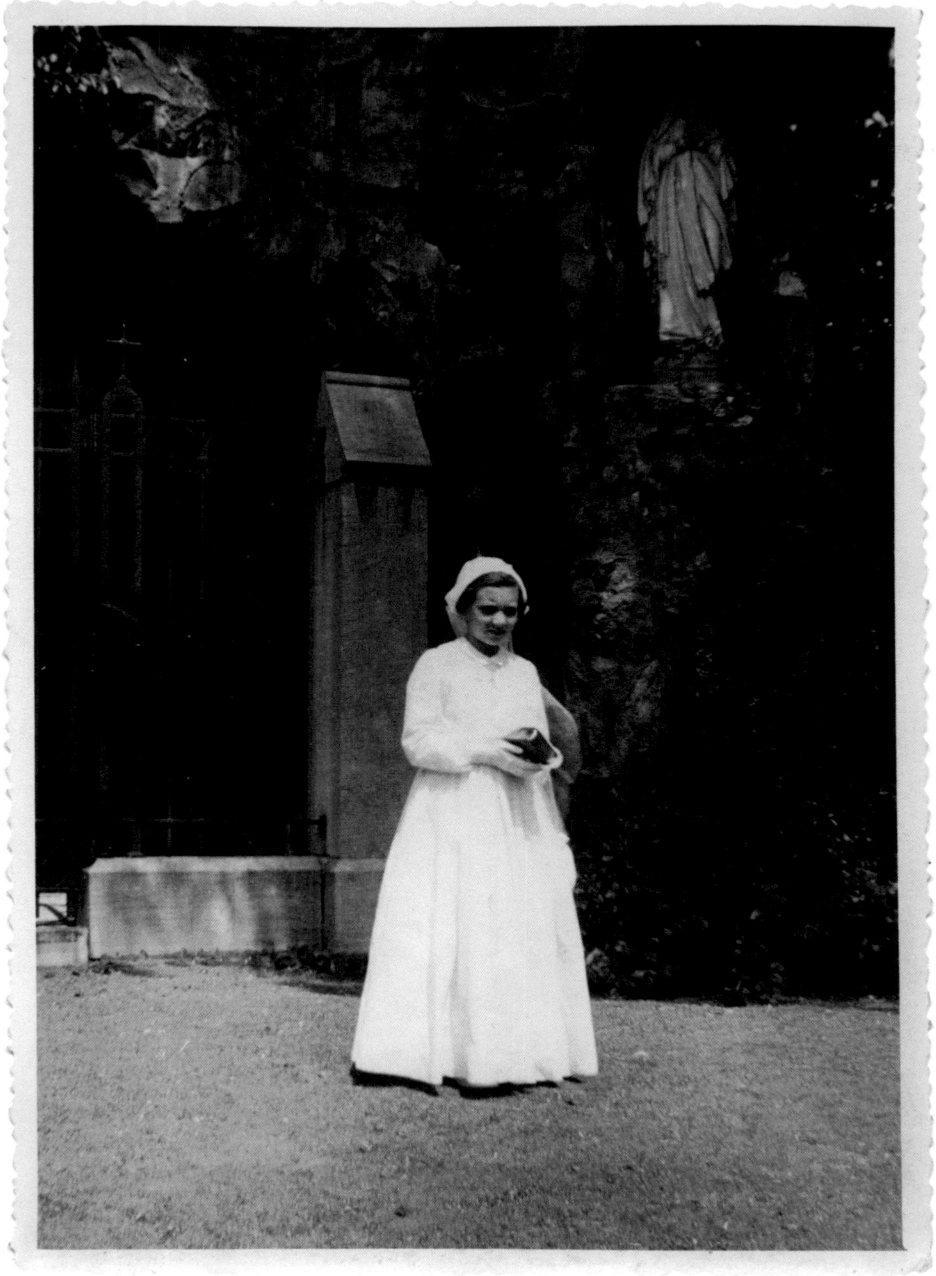

A Jesuit listened to me. We sat in the Piazza Navona, I remember, on a very cold, windy day, and talked. And he said I should get a notebook and write down, you know, the thoughts that occurred to me every day for the next ten days, and pray about whether I should be a nun or not. And then after the ten days – it actually took me through Holy Week into Easter Monday – on Easter Monday, I went to see him again and I said, 'This is what I've written.' And he demanded to read it and I was terribly embarrassed. I remember looking up at this plasterwork ceiling just wishing the earth would open and swallow me up. When he read all that I'd written, he said, 'It seems to me you've got a generous heart. I think you should try it.' And I said, 'I'm terrified.' And he said, 'You'd be a fool if you weren't.'

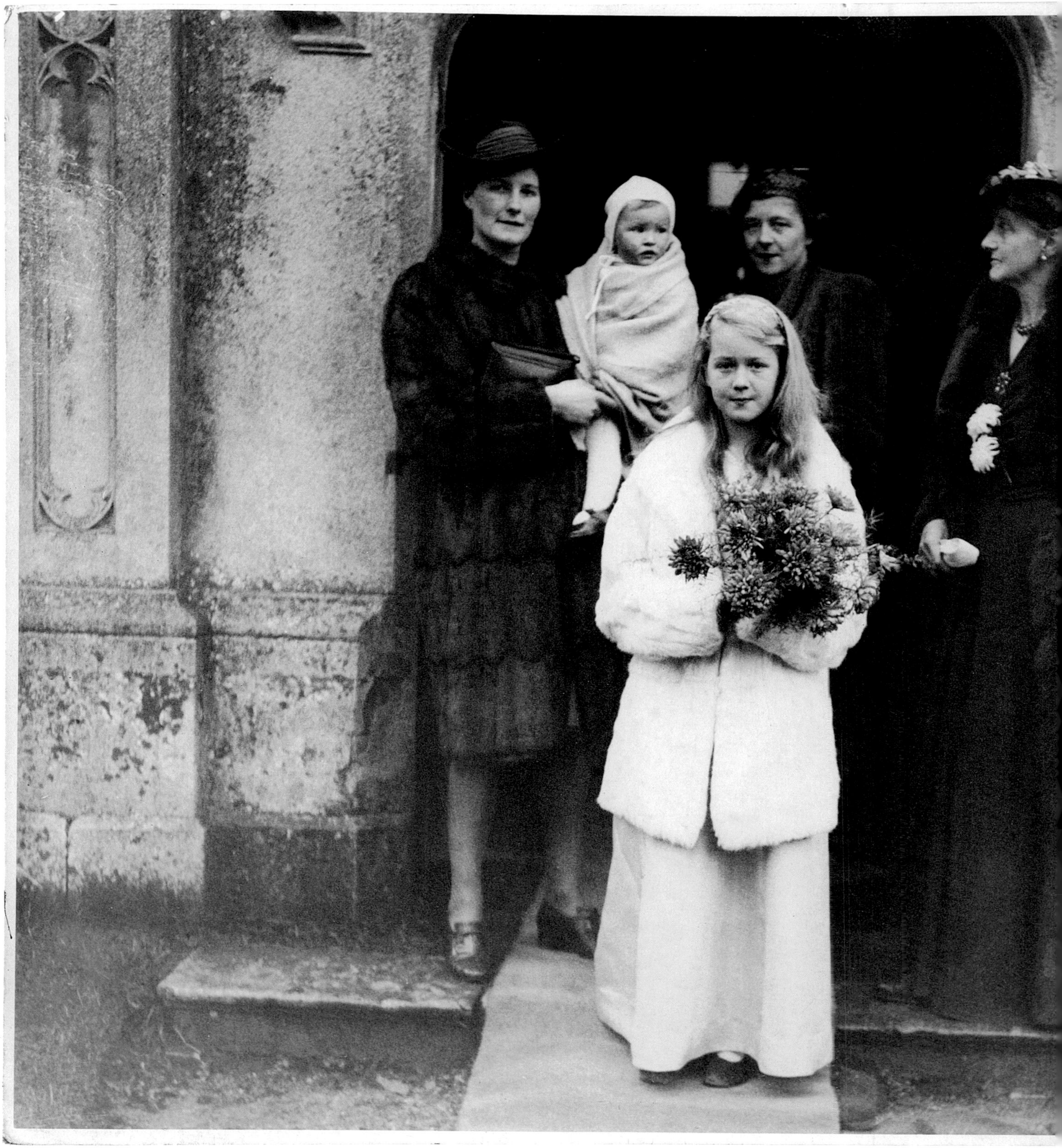

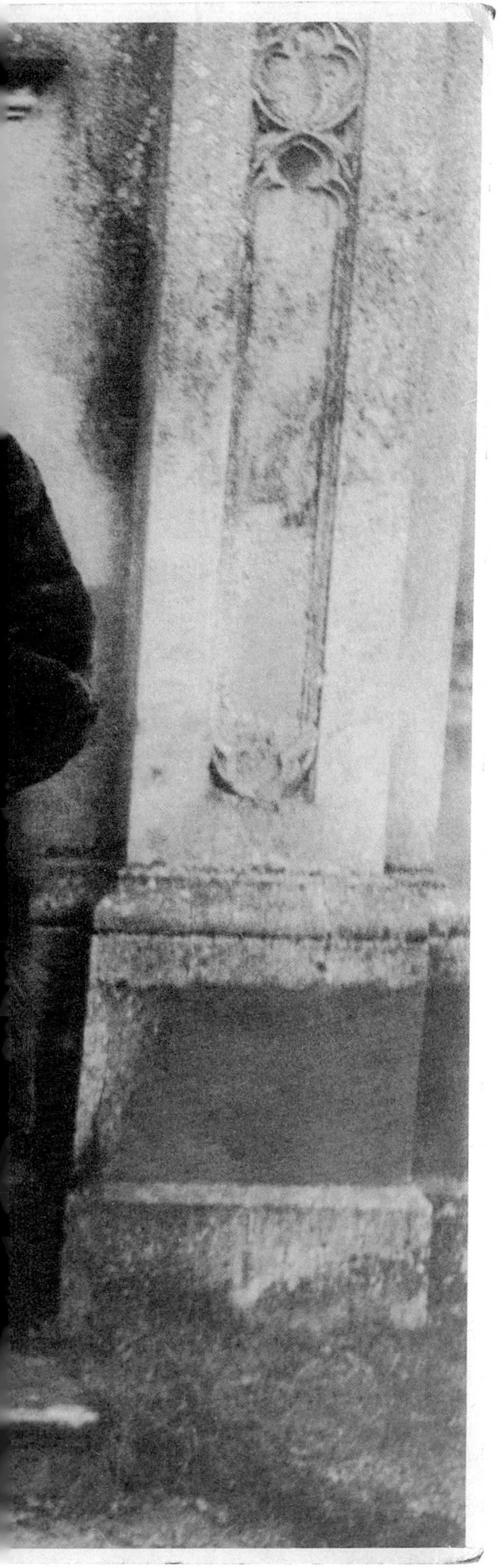

I don't think it's bridal in the sense of matrimonial bridal. I think it's bridal in the sense of the relationship to nuns when they enter a convent or monastery and take vows. And one of the vows they take is a vow of celibacy, in other words keeping oneself for oneself – or in this case, in Catholicism, keeping oneself for Jesus; the spouse and the spousa. So the little girl is the archetypal spousa, or even, in a way, the image of the purity of the soul.

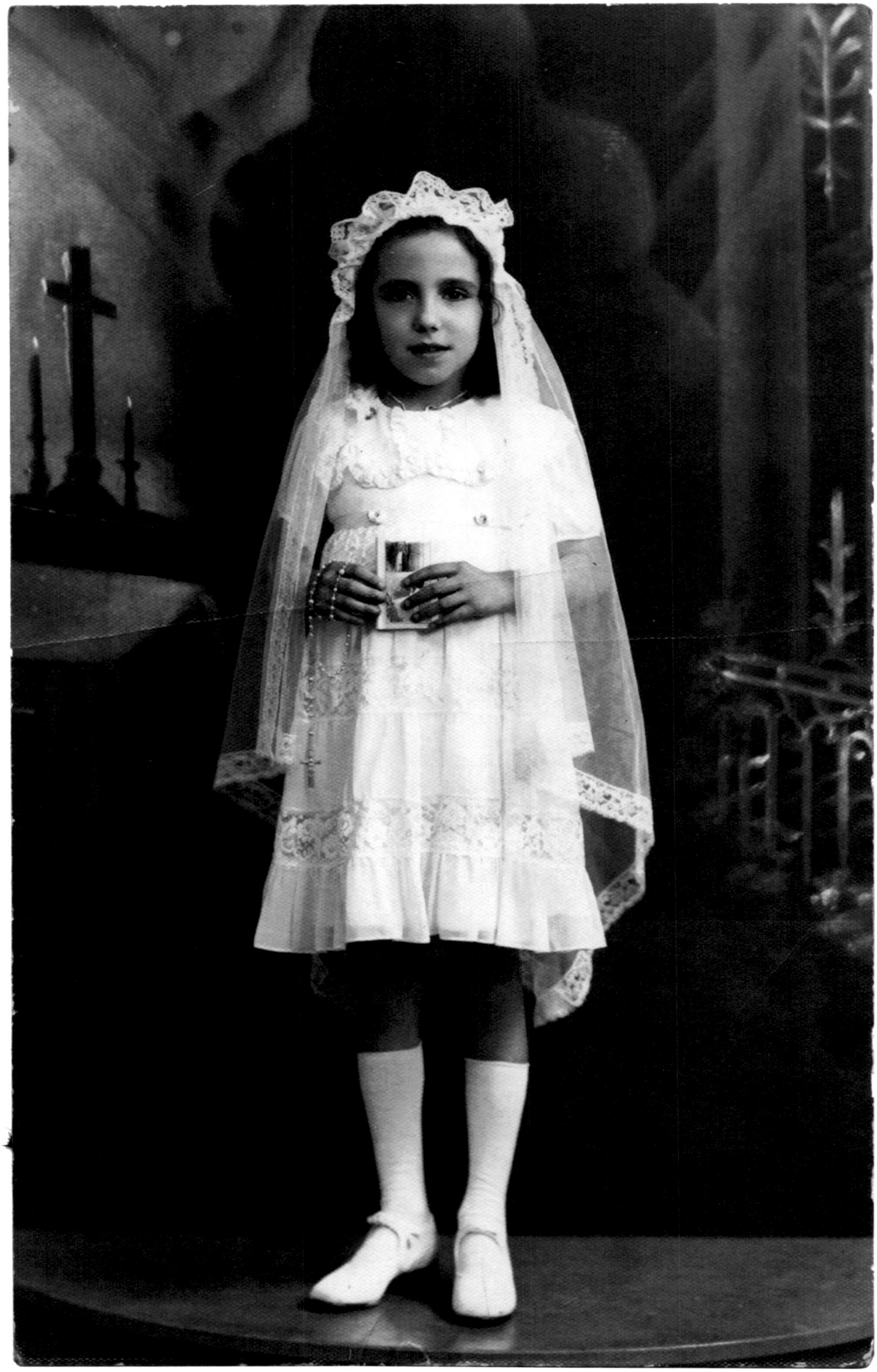

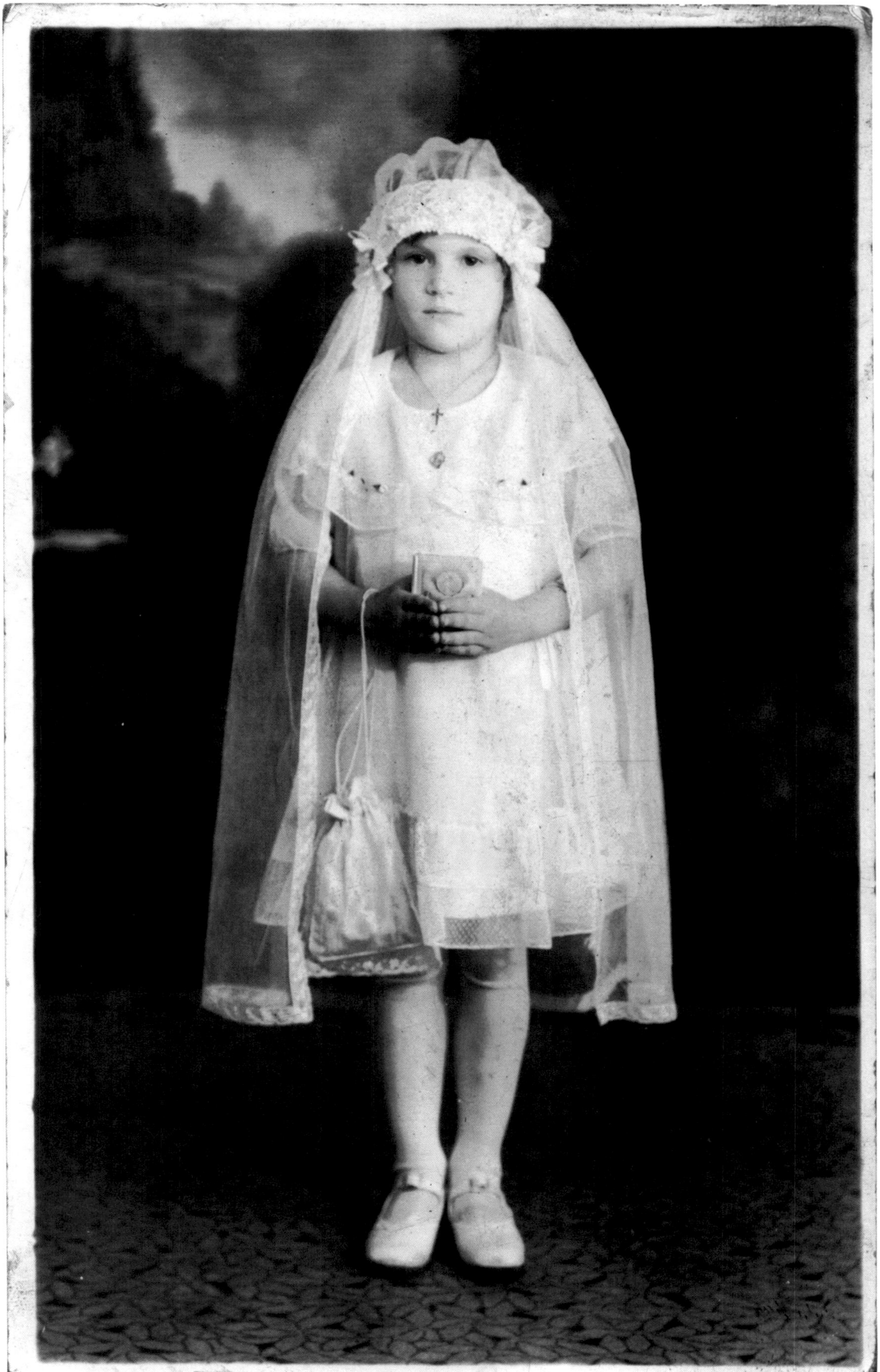

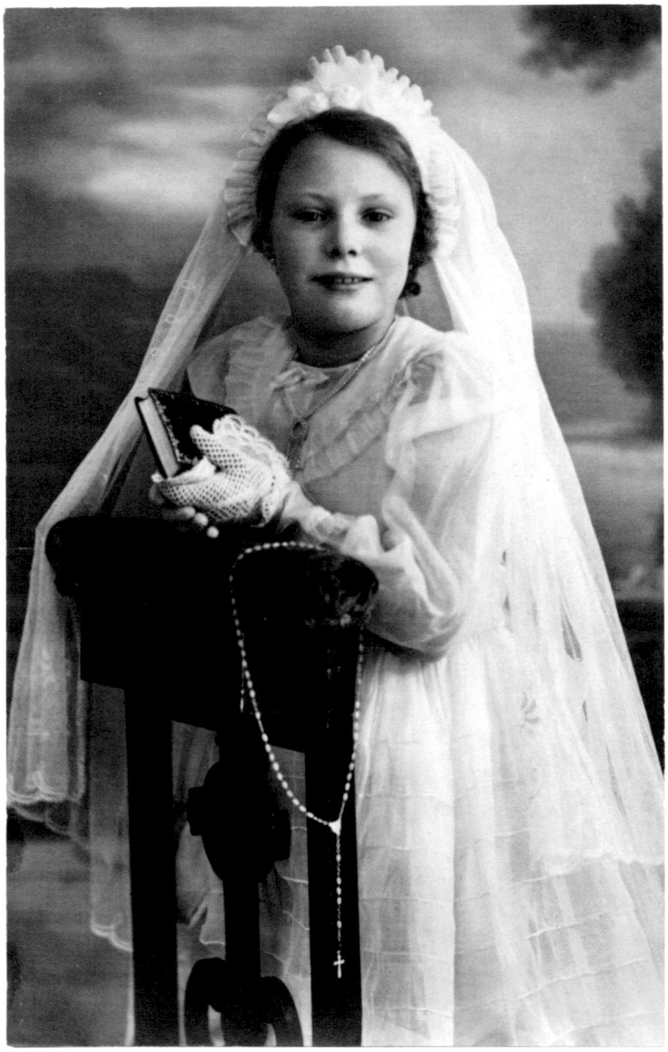

I miss the continuity, the seasonal changes, the Church's seasons fitting in . . In the same way that I wouldn't want an eternal spring or summer and enjoy autumn storms and icy winters. I enjoyed linking the Church's calendar with those other things and the continuity, the ancient continuity, perhaps beyond Catholicism, touching base with all kinds of other things. You know, the spring rituals, the fiery sermons at particular times of the year and then something would come around – a psalm or a gospel that you would remember from another time and another place in your life. The older you got, there was a kind of ritual to it, which is very attractive. And some of the poetry within the psalms is absolutely exquisite, you know, the gates of paradise, pillars of ivory … and the symbolism is something I wouldn't have missed out on. Yeah, it messes you up in some ways, but it's something you react to.

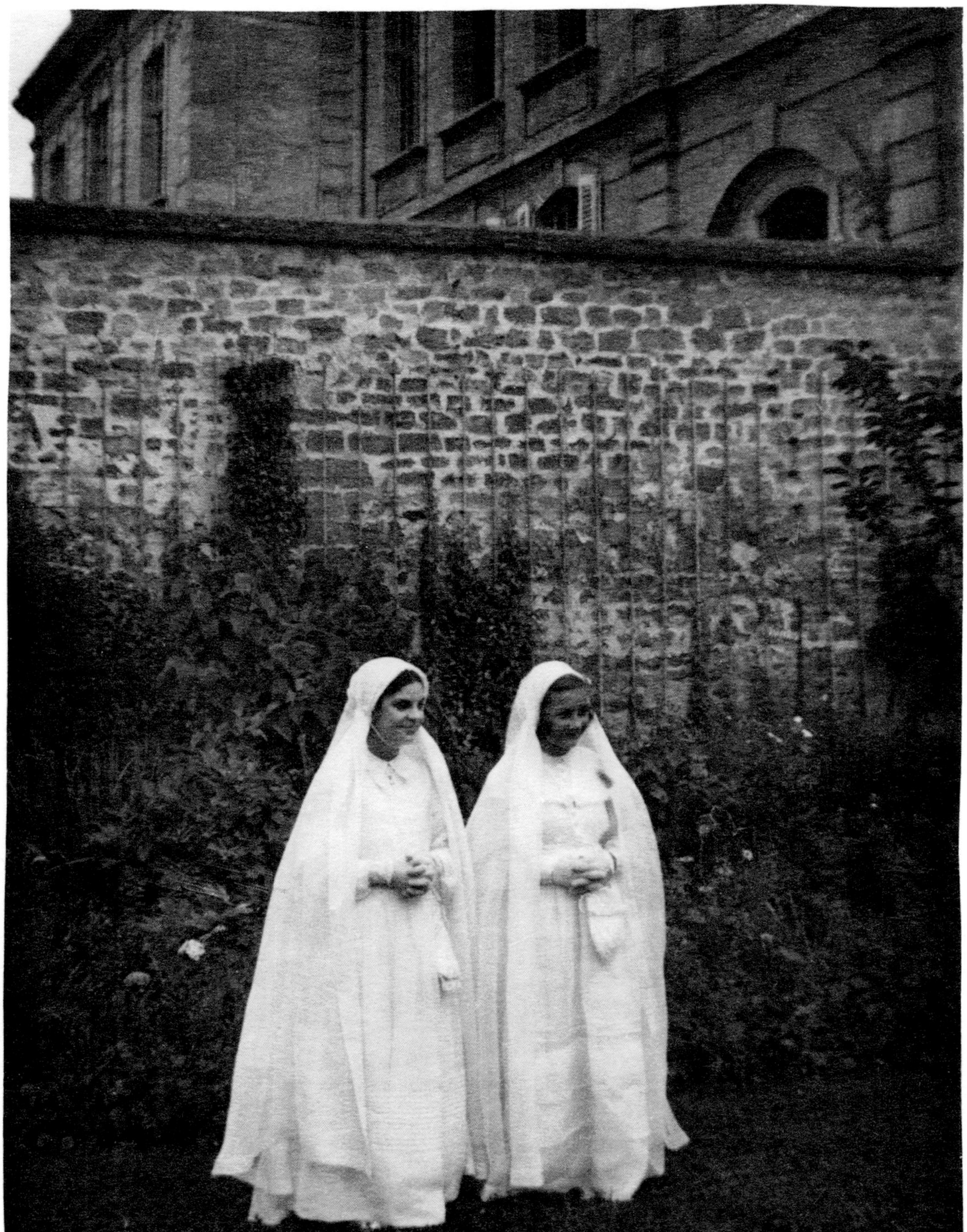

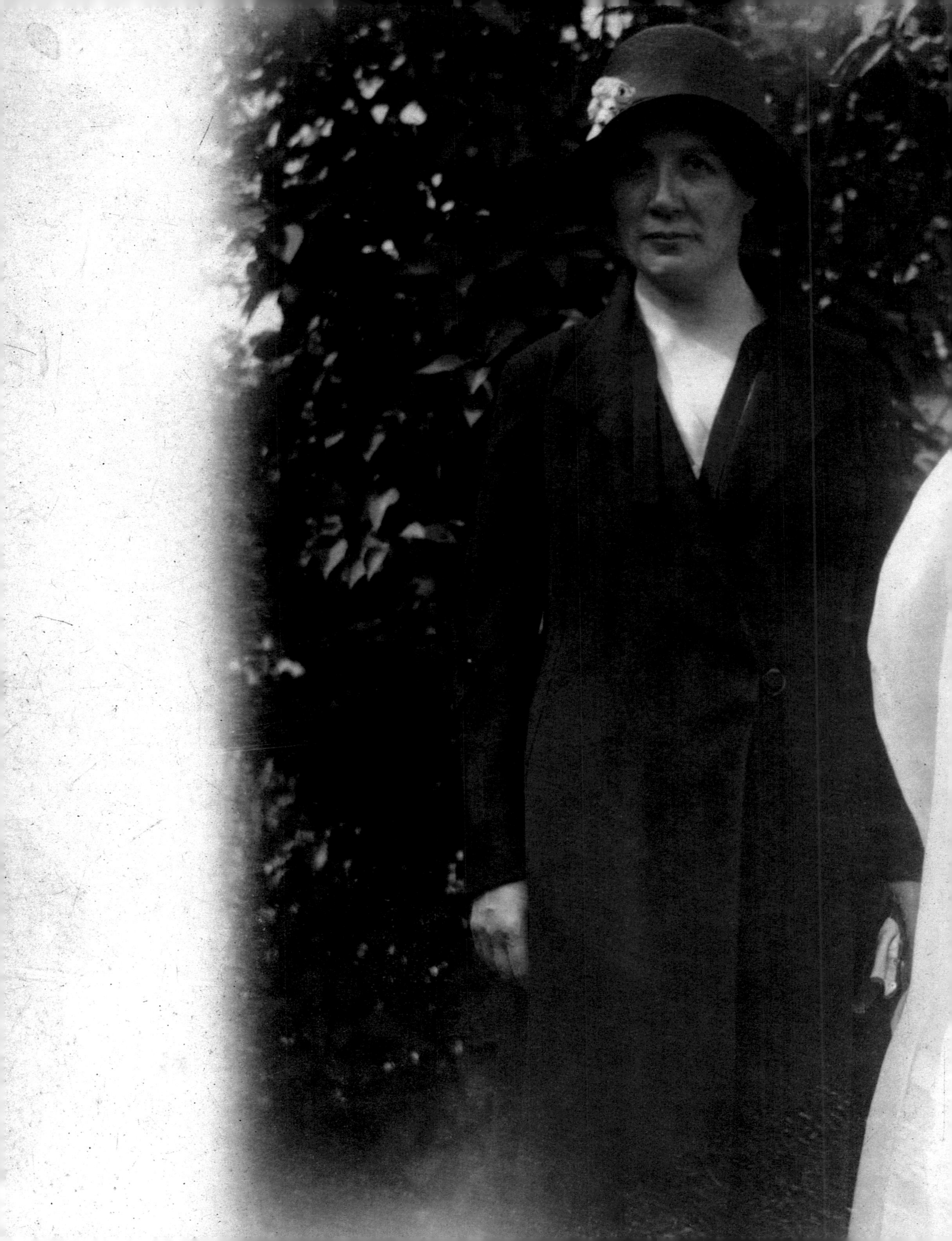

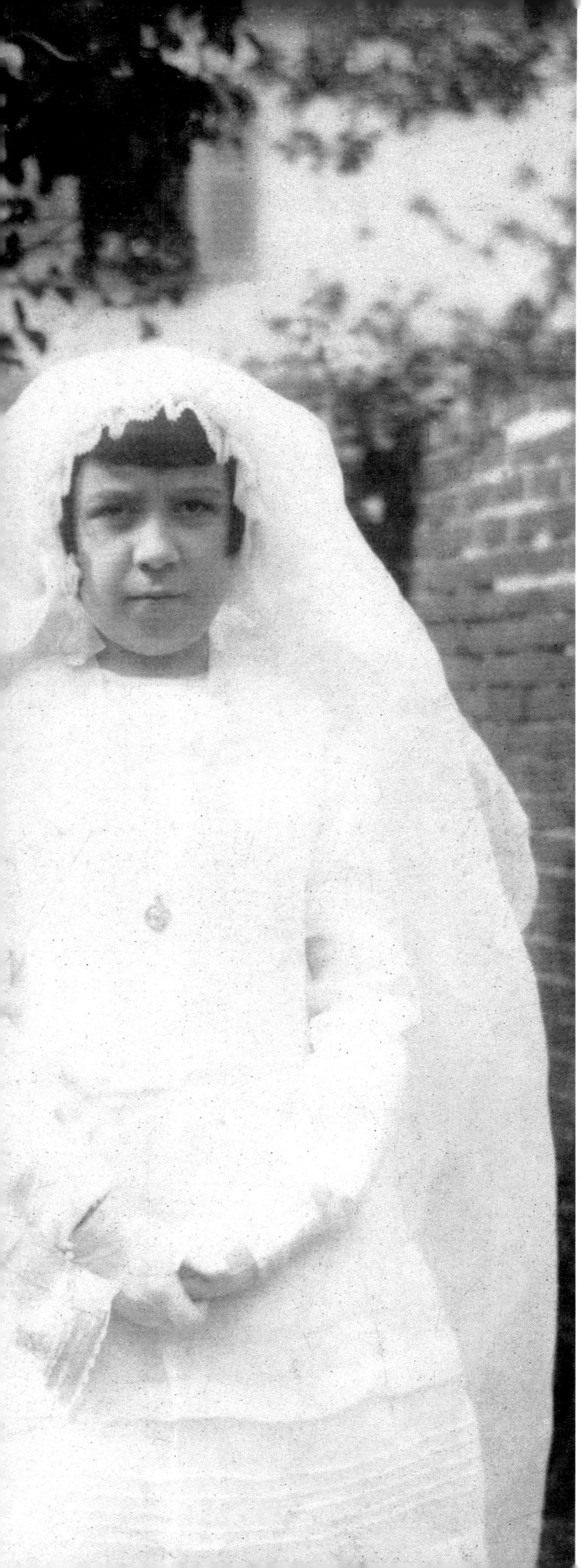

6

PRINT DEEP IN MY SOUL THE MEMORY OF THY BITTER PAINS

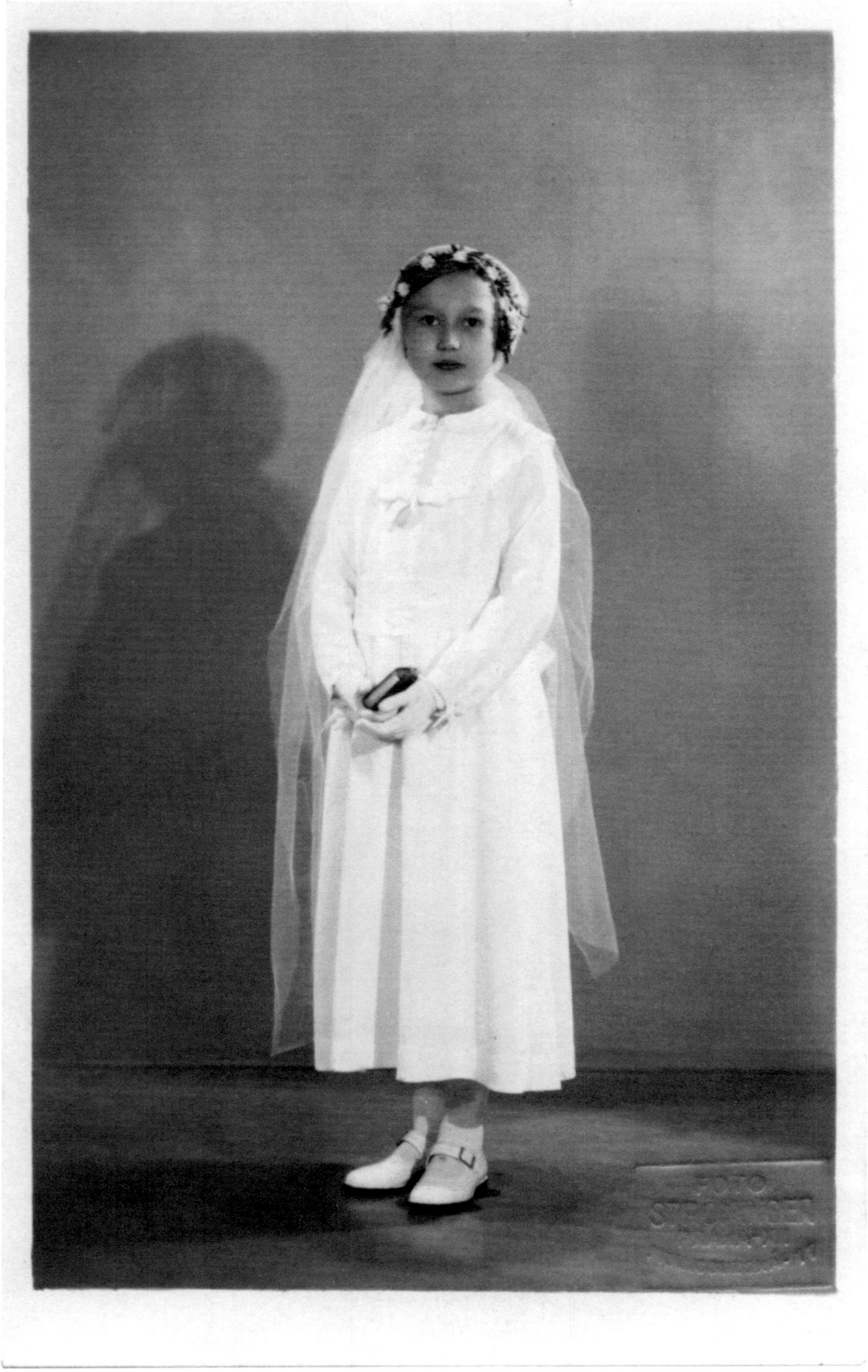

I was conscious, you know, that God was observing me. But I don't think I ever felt that that was a constraint, really. It was much more of a problem being observed by people.

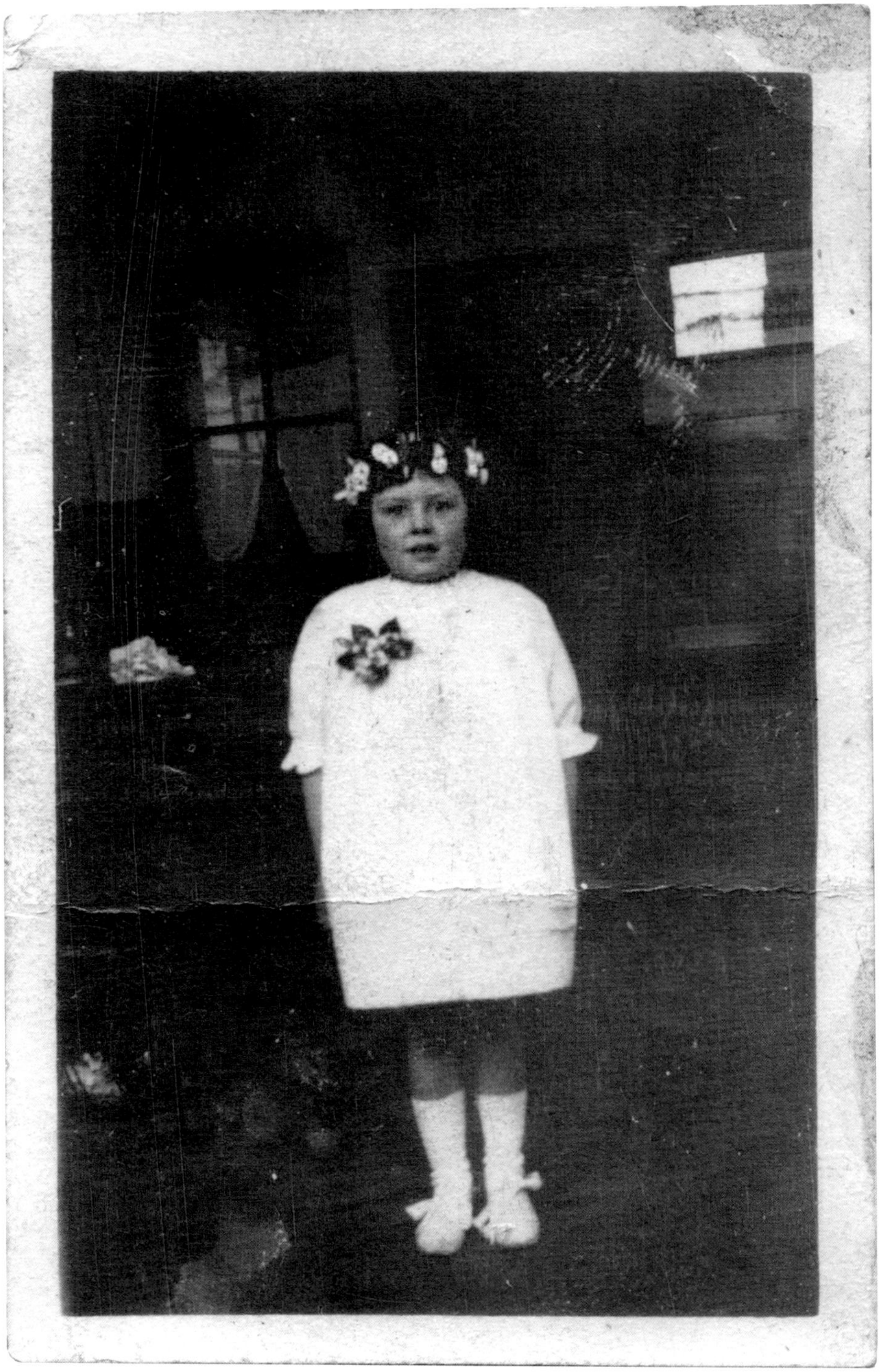

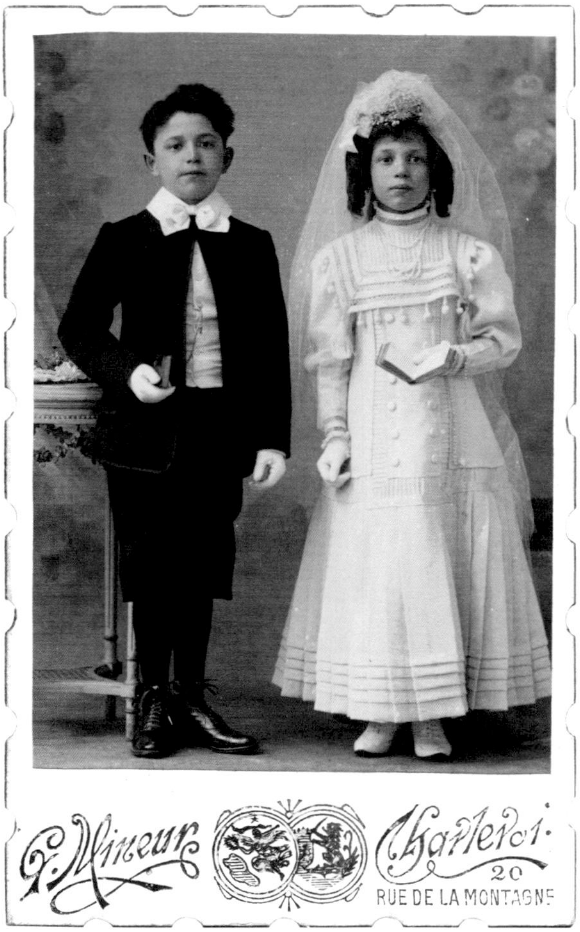

You see, I was younger than everyone else in my class, so I couldn't make my Communion at the same time as everyone else. So they did all the preparation for it, and I did too, but mine didn't happen when theirs did. It happened later. And there was me and this other boy called Harry, who was younger as well. So, he and I made our First Communions together, just the two of us. So, instead of having a whole gang of people, at least I think this is what happened, there was just me and Harry walking down. I do remember we had to hold hands, either for a photograph or walking down the aisle and I really didn't want to hold Harry's hand, nor he mine.

They used to dress us the same but in different colours. I'd always have red and she would have emerald green. It's so that people wouldn't get us mixed up. They'd have to tell from the colour that I was wearing that it was me. For the Communion my mum got her friend to make us dresses. The only difference was that I think my dress had plain cuffs and hers had little frilly kind of cuffs. That was the difference between our dresses. Yeah, we were in white, the exact same, but different cuffs and that was it. There's one really nice snapshot. We're both stood with our heads turned round like that to the camera – so you'd have the back of the dress with the bow on it and we're in the prayer position. Our elbows are kind of like that, so you can tell. But because the cuffs are at the front, and because the picture's from behind, I don't know who I am in the picture. It's really strange.

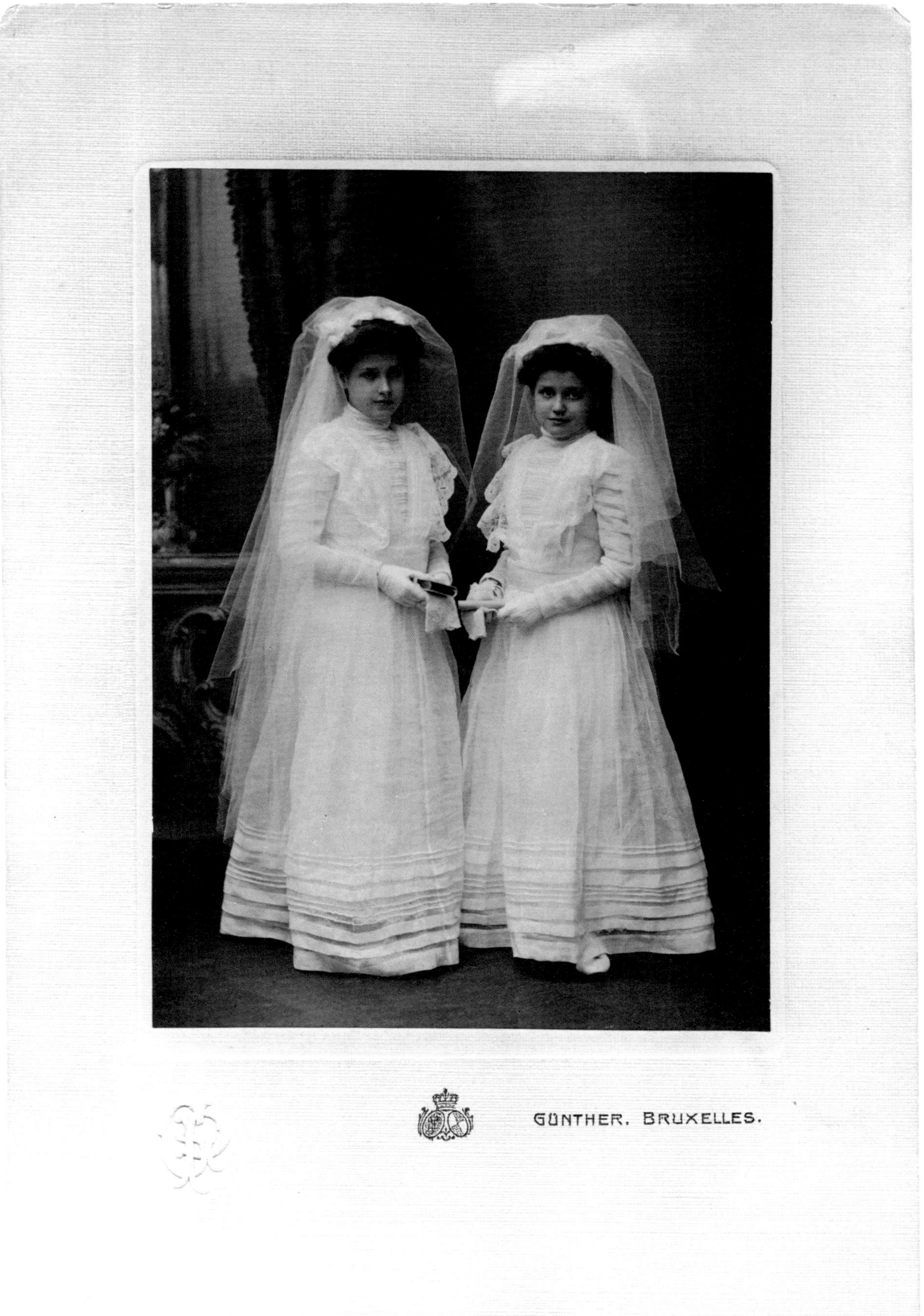
GÜNTHER. BRUXELLES.

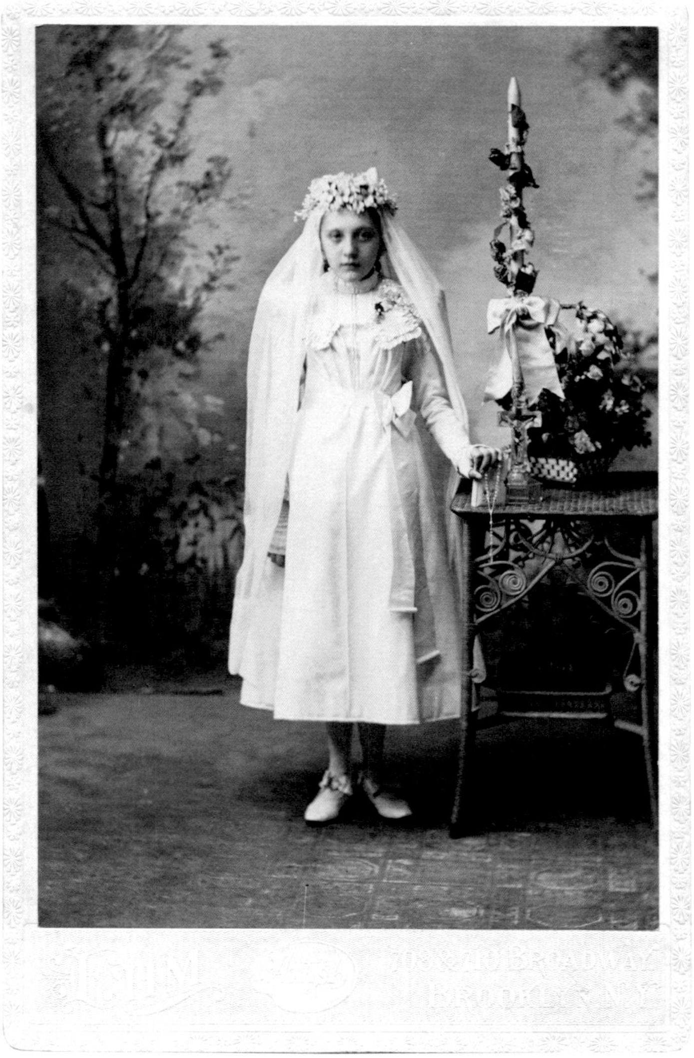

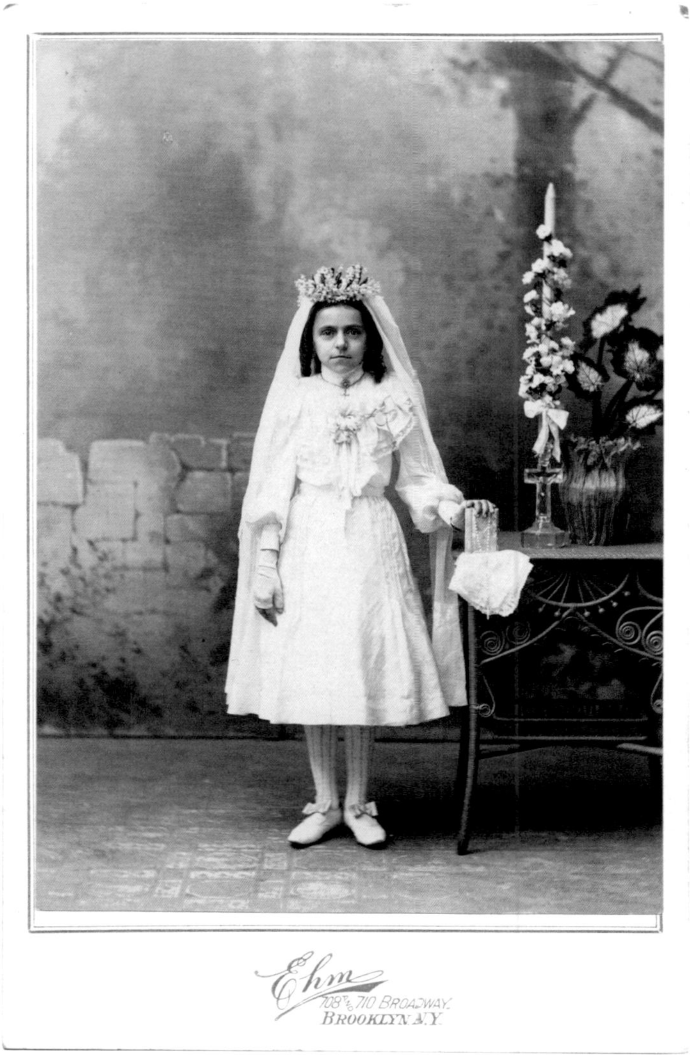
Ehm
708 & 710 BROADWAY.
BROOKLYN N.Y.

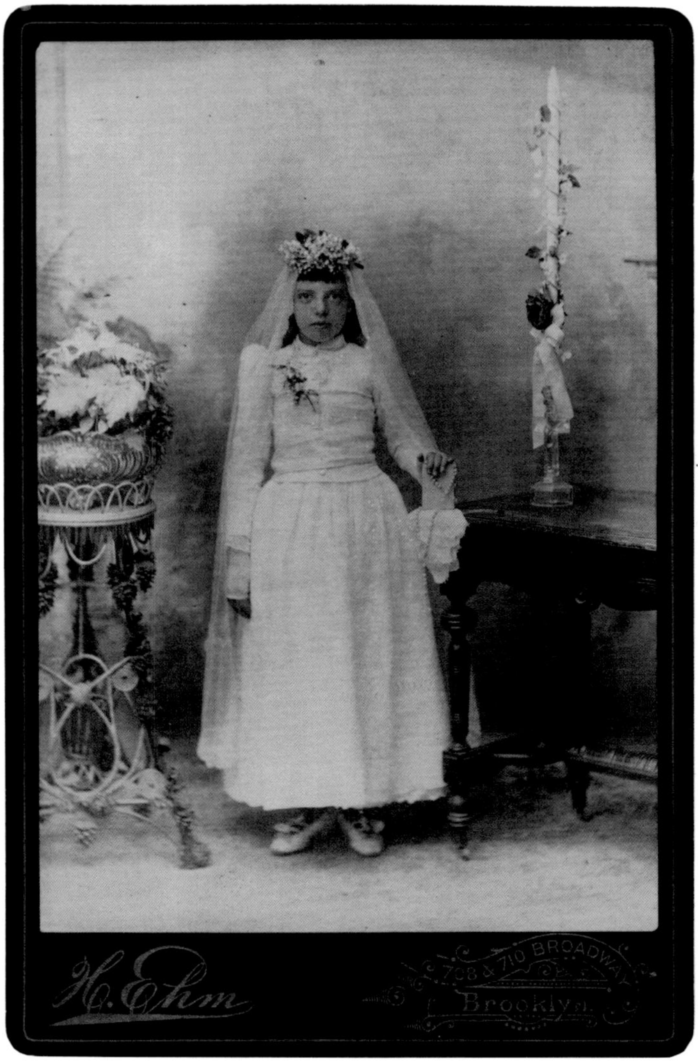
H. Ehm
708 & 710 BROADWAY
Brooklyn

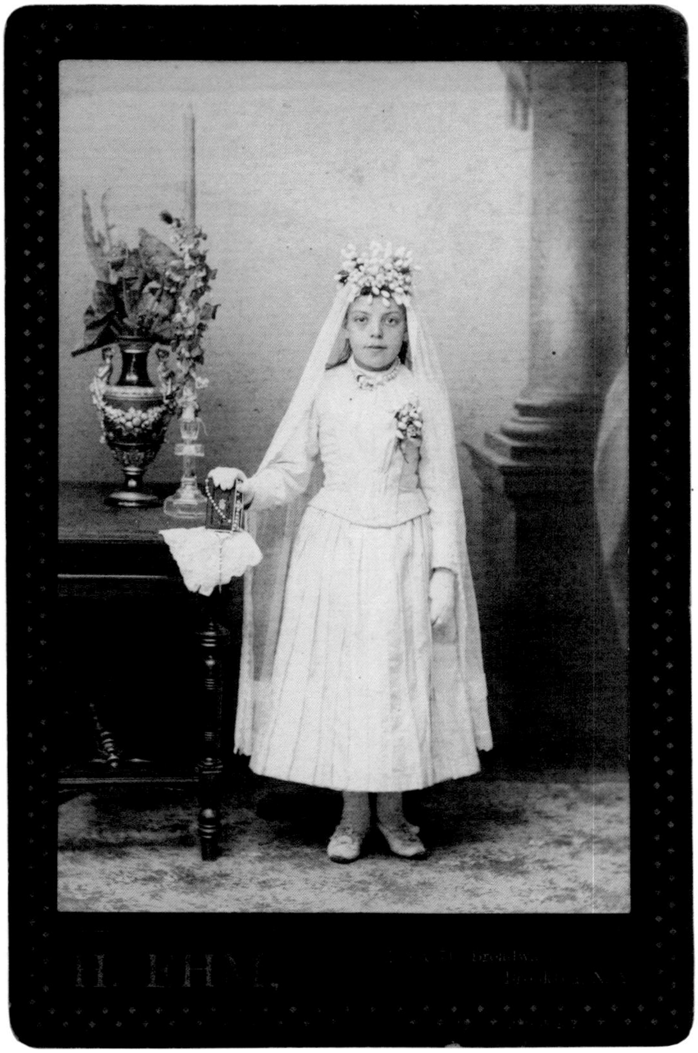

Children now are always being photographed, but growing up in the early fifties, people didn't have the money for film. I mean, I remember we had a Box Brownie camera but we probably didn't have any money left by the time they bought my First Communion dress. I came from quite a poor family, so I don't recall it being an issue. Presumably nobody else had photos either, because I don't have any memory of other people taking photos and my not having them. I don't think it occurred to anyone.

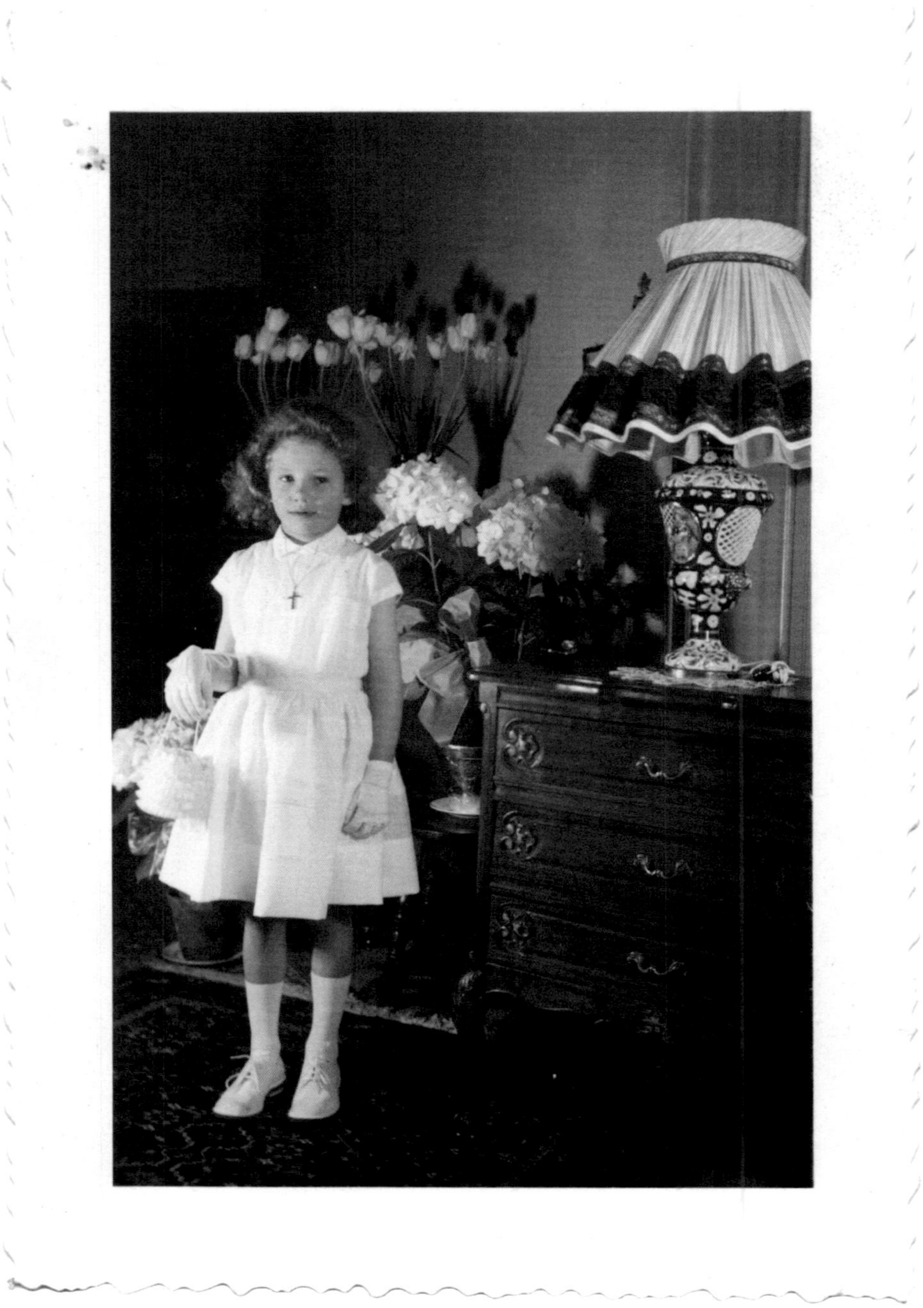

It was a formal portrait with a photographer and we were arranged by height.

So it was a group, you didn't have an individual one?

No.

No family snapshots?

I've never seen one if they did. So, that says something, doesn't it?

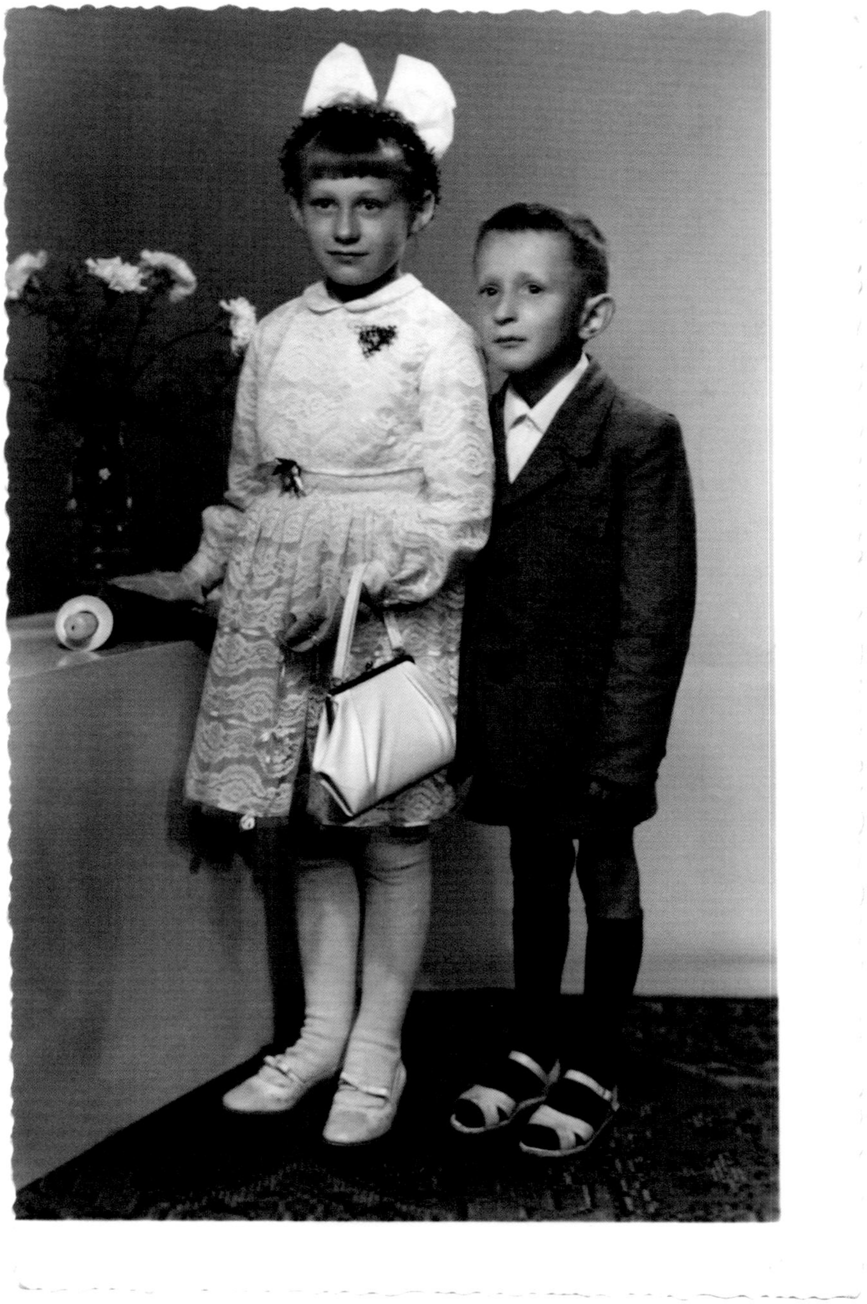

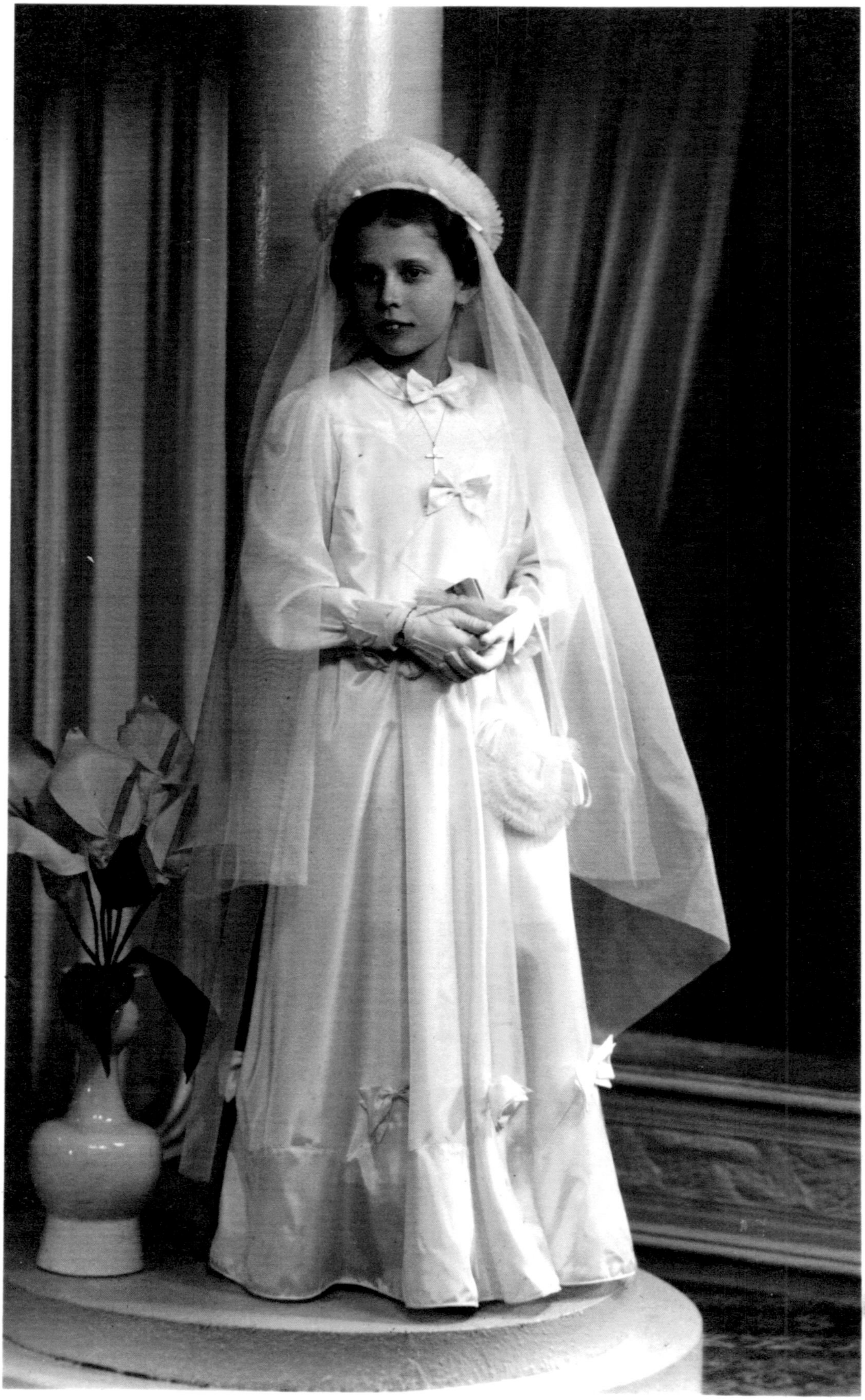

I'm standing there in my Communion dress and I'd lost – one of my front teeth had come out. So, the photographer touched it in.

You were smiling?

Yes, with this gleaming white mark where he'd touched in the front tooth.

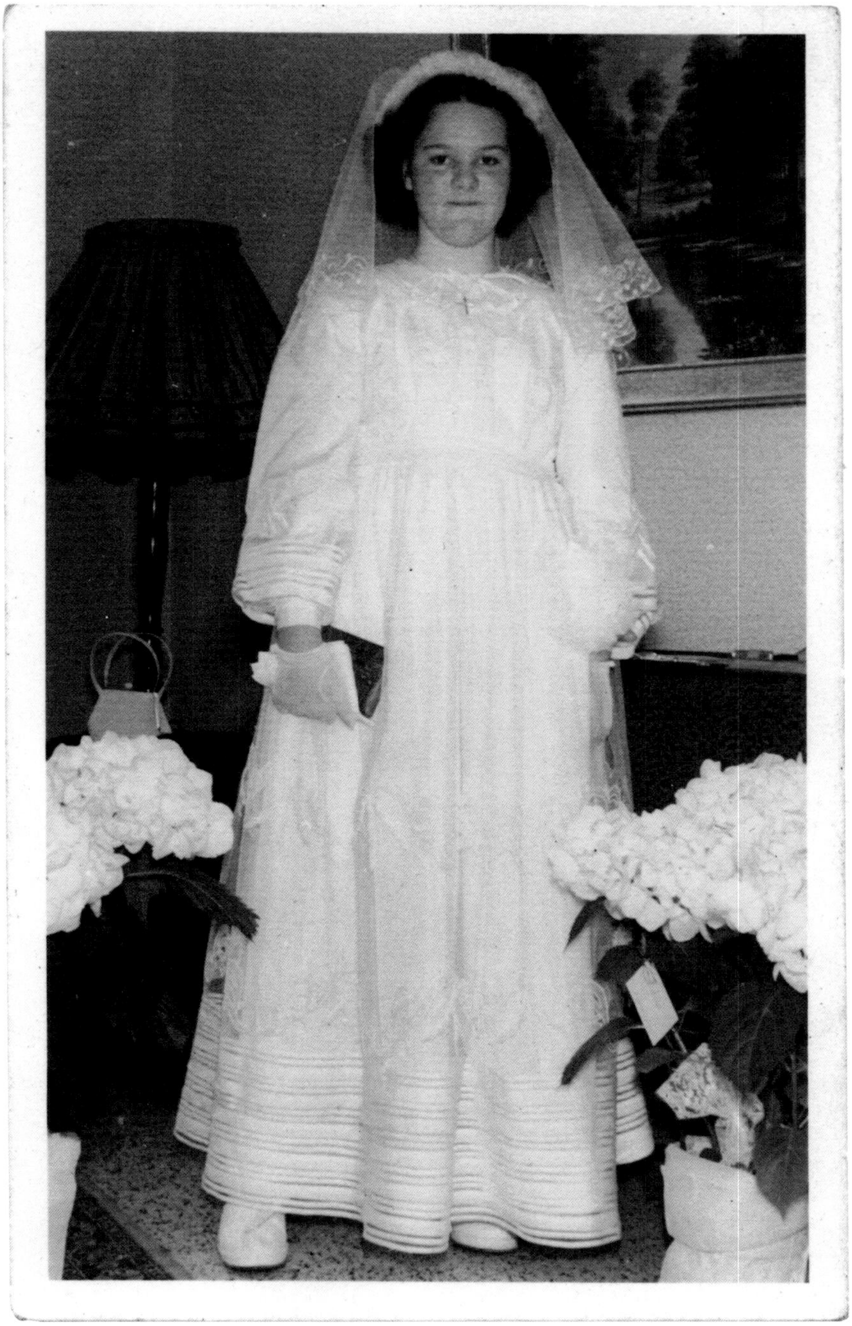

I think my mum and dad were taking pictures of us all. And then in the afternoon, it was a really hot day, we had a barbecue out in the garden and all my friends from school came over. Yeah, the whole family was there; I can remember my brother and my dad were out in the garden with the hosepipe, just spraying people and having fun with it. Oh, and I remember being quite shocked because the priest showed up at the party in the afternoon. Apparently he was a good friend of the family.

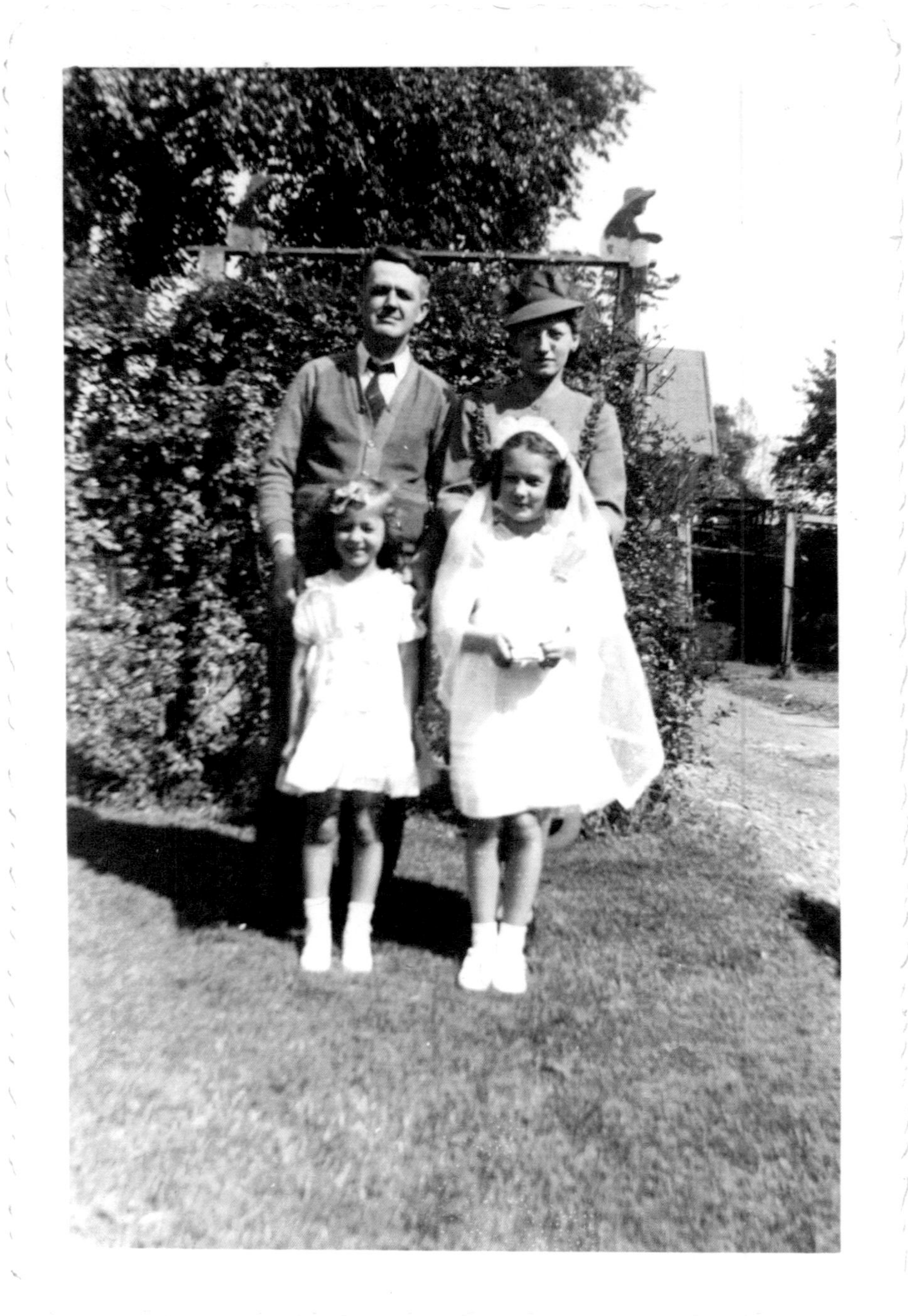

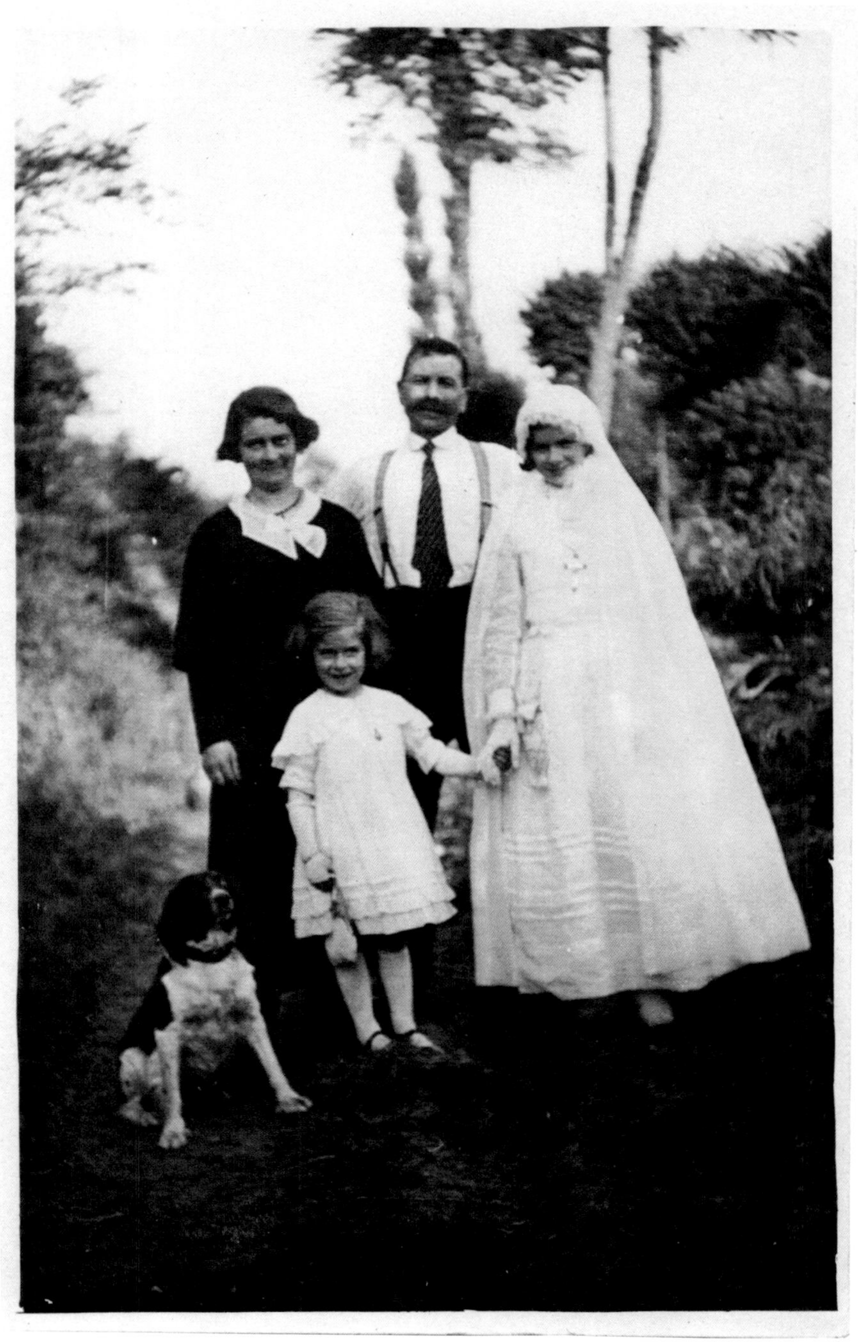

One of my brother's friends must have taken the picture. There are five of us, my mum and dad and my dog, Lady. She was a mixture of quite a few things, Jack Russell mainly. We had just gotten her actually and she had already bitten us all a few times. There's us in the picture, I think my brother's holding the dog. But we all look really … no one's smiling.

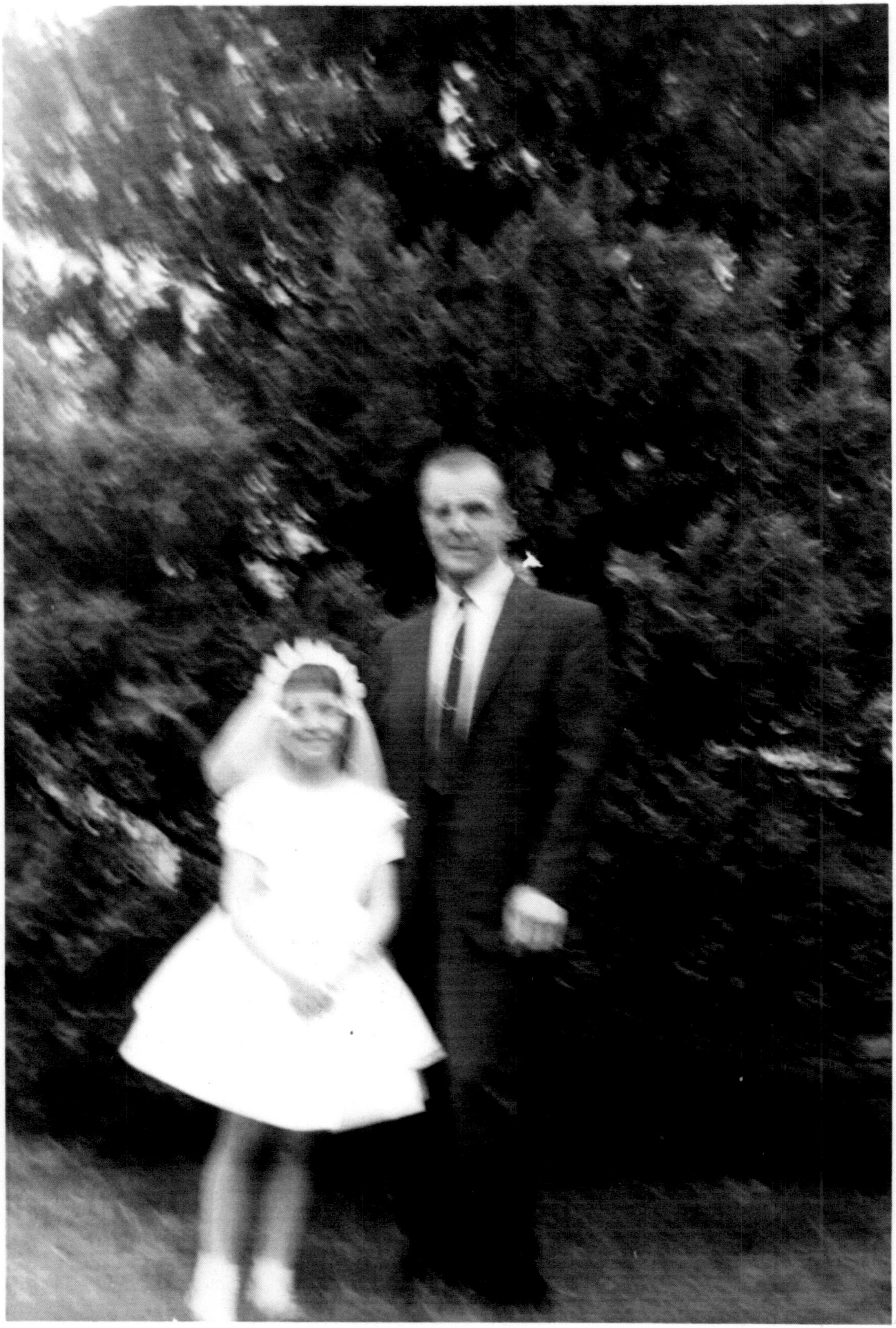

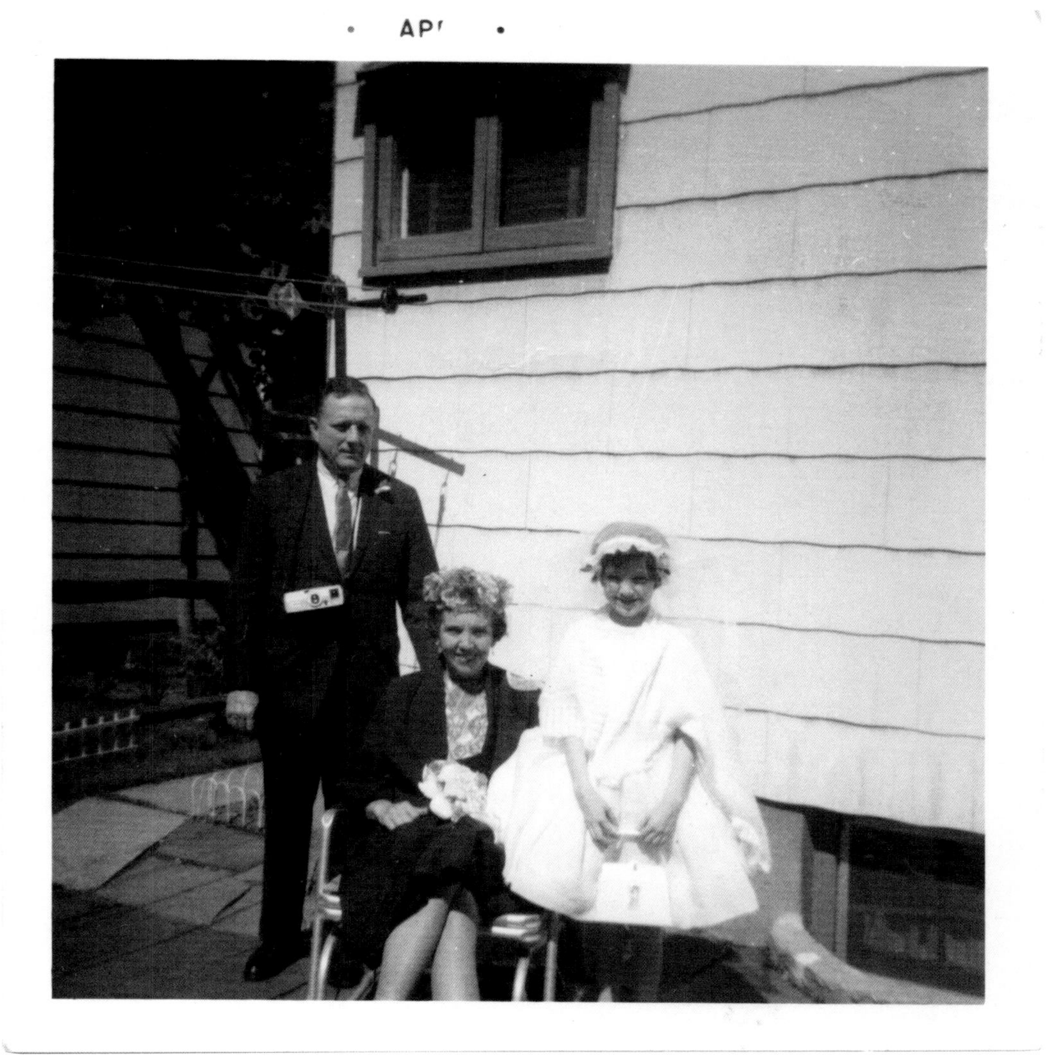

My father fashioned himself quite a photographer. Well, the funniest thing was, I think he was usually, you know, so drunk that they would all be blurry. And he always had these really expensive cameras and you'd stand there and – I mean, he was never a stumbling drunk, I never even knew my father was an alcoholic till way later – but most of them came out blurry. So he'd have these rolls and rolls of film and I'd think, well, this must be kind of difficult. So when I finally got my first camera I'm thinking, how the heck am I going to use this, you know? Pictures never come out …

Were your First Communion pictures blurry?

Well, some of them. Most of them.

I thought I had a veil, but I had no veil.

Gloves?

No gloves.

A little bag – any accessories?

None.

Did you hold flowers? Did you have a candle?

Nothing.

Were you given any gifts for your Communion?

Nothing.

Jewellery, a rosary, little Bible?

Nothing.

Boy, you were stripped down.

Yeah, very minimal. And I said to my mom today, 'So we don't have any pictures or anything?' and she said, 'No.' My dad was really against that; he felt that it was completely unnecessary to take pictures.

Not even snapshots?

Nothing.

Do you remember the day, or when you had to get dressed up, or when you had to go down the aisle?

No.

You don't remember it at all?

No.

Do you have photographs of the day?

Yes.

You do? But when you look at those photographs, do you remember it?

No.

Really? How old were you? Were you really young?

Seven.

So you don't remember anything? Nothing?

Nothing.

I wonder why?

Sorry.

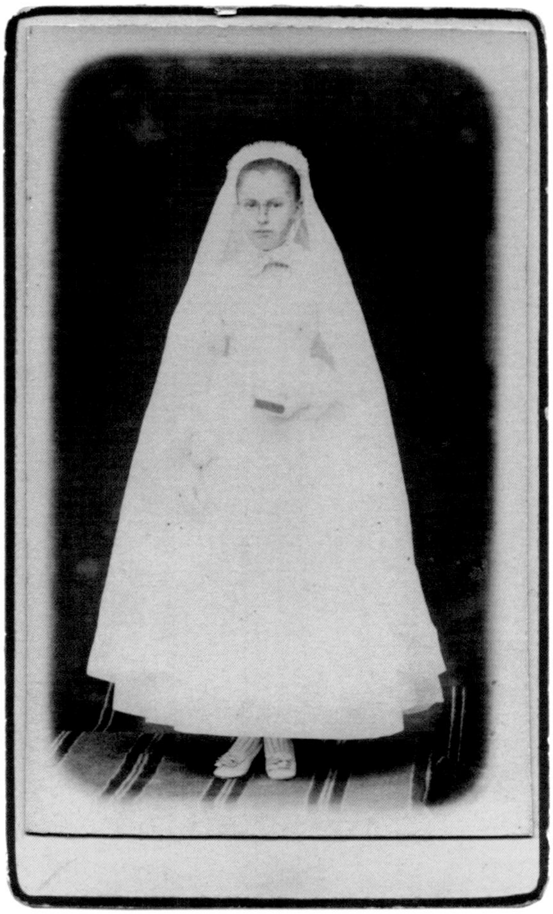

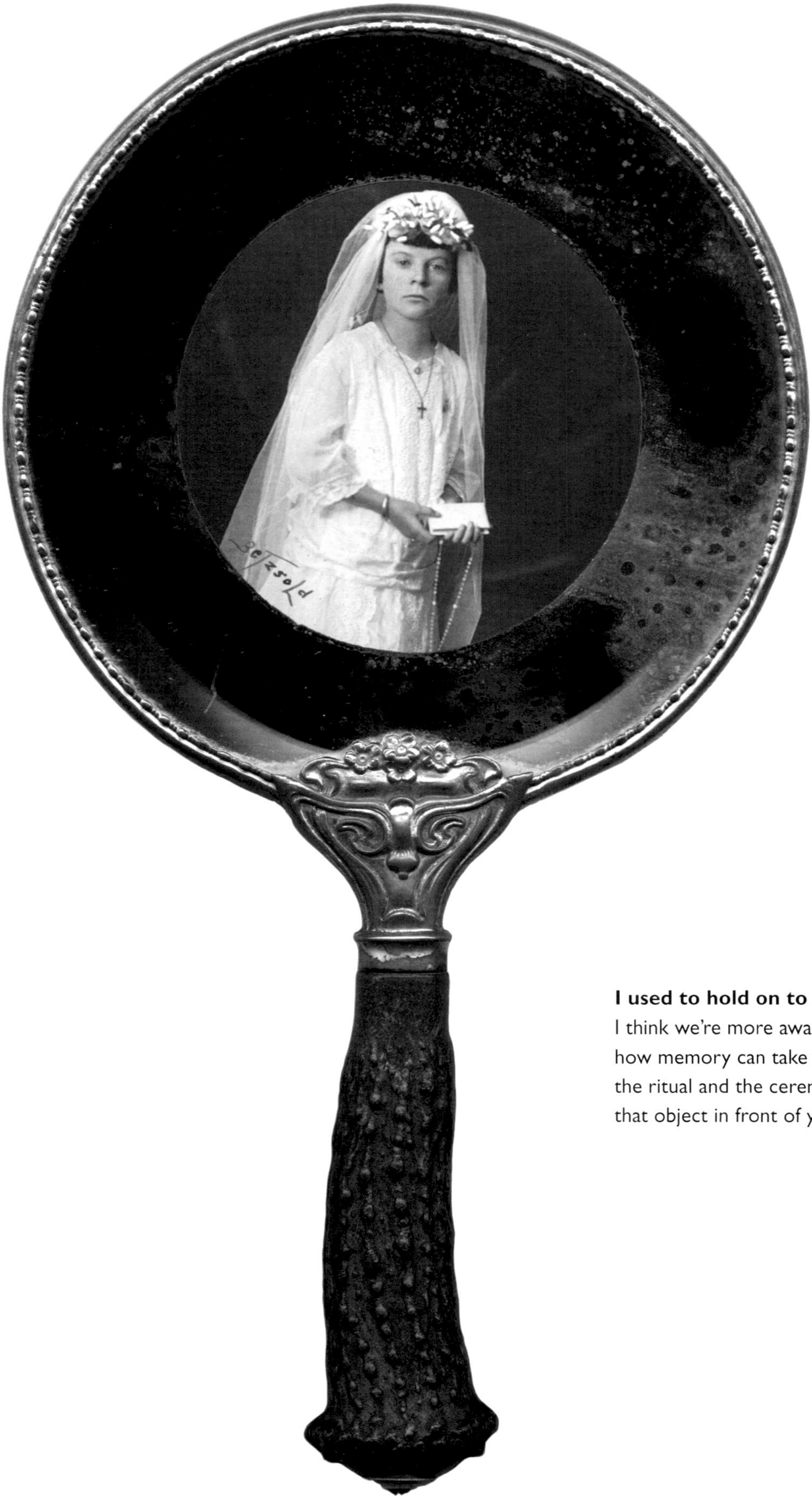

I used to hold on to a lot of things.
I think we're more aware, more sensitive to how memory can take you back in time to the ritual and the ceremony if you have that object in front of you.

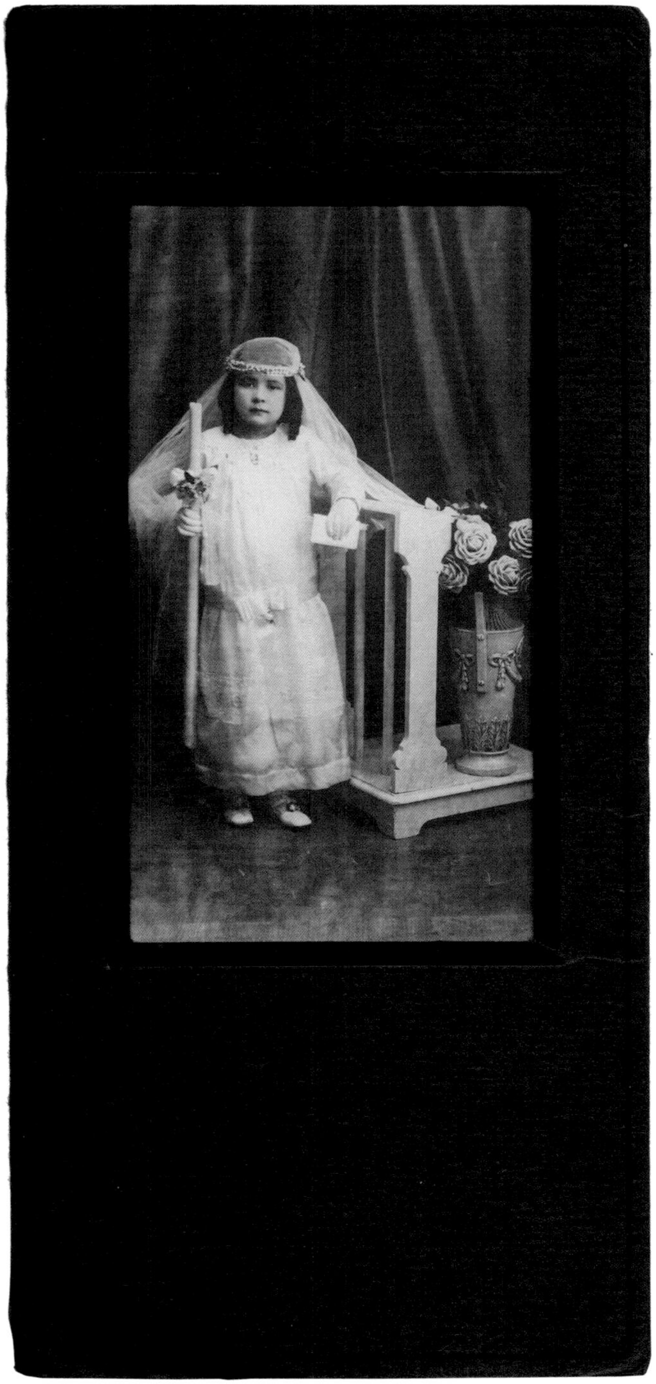

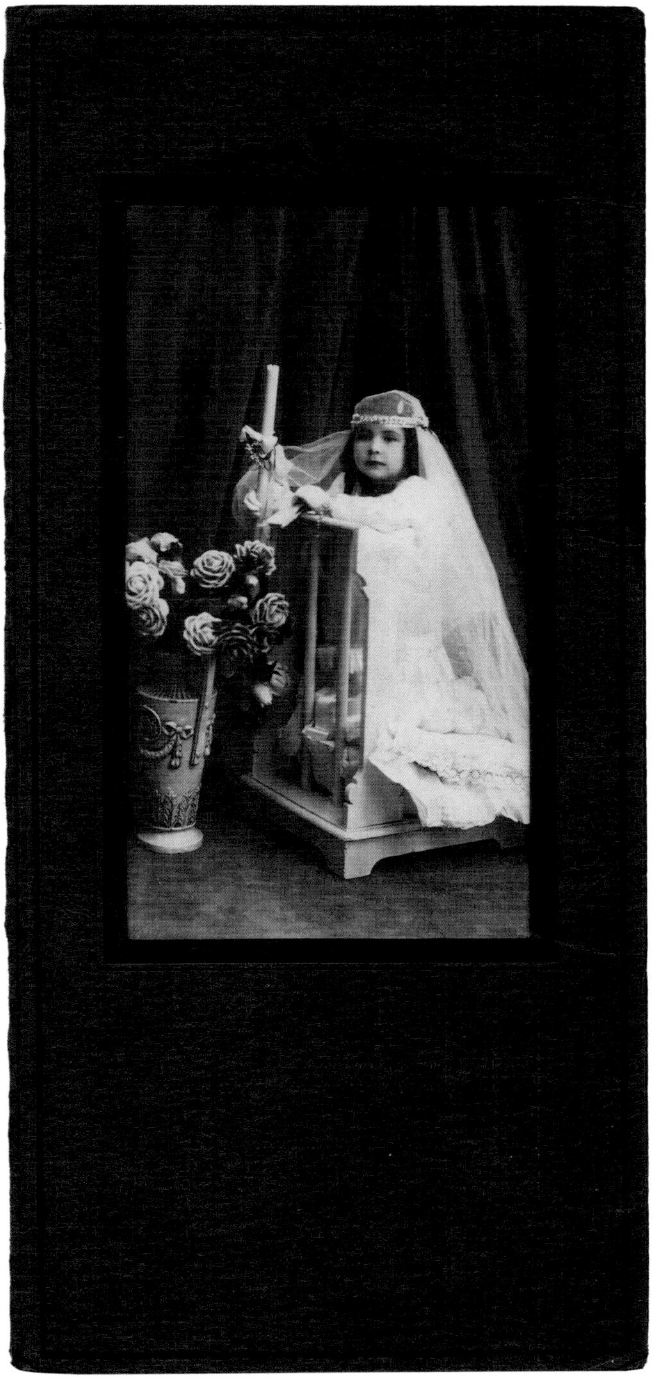

I remember one weird thing from my sister's Communion. They took a photo of her and she was standing in front of this tree and in the photo there's this glow from behind her. It's really strange. She's wearing white and she's got a white veil and she was just glowing. It looks like there was some kind of big light, like a sense of God or something.

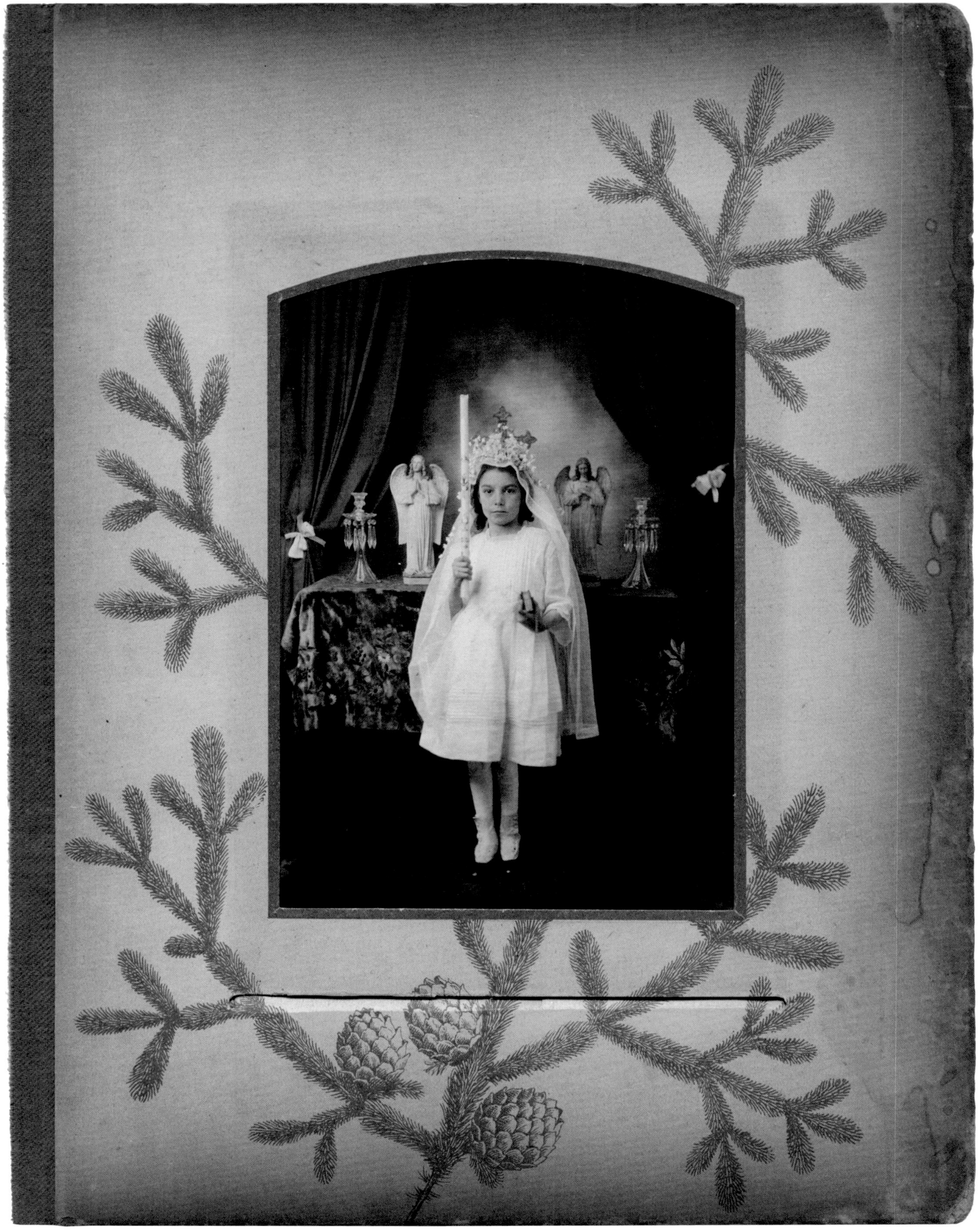

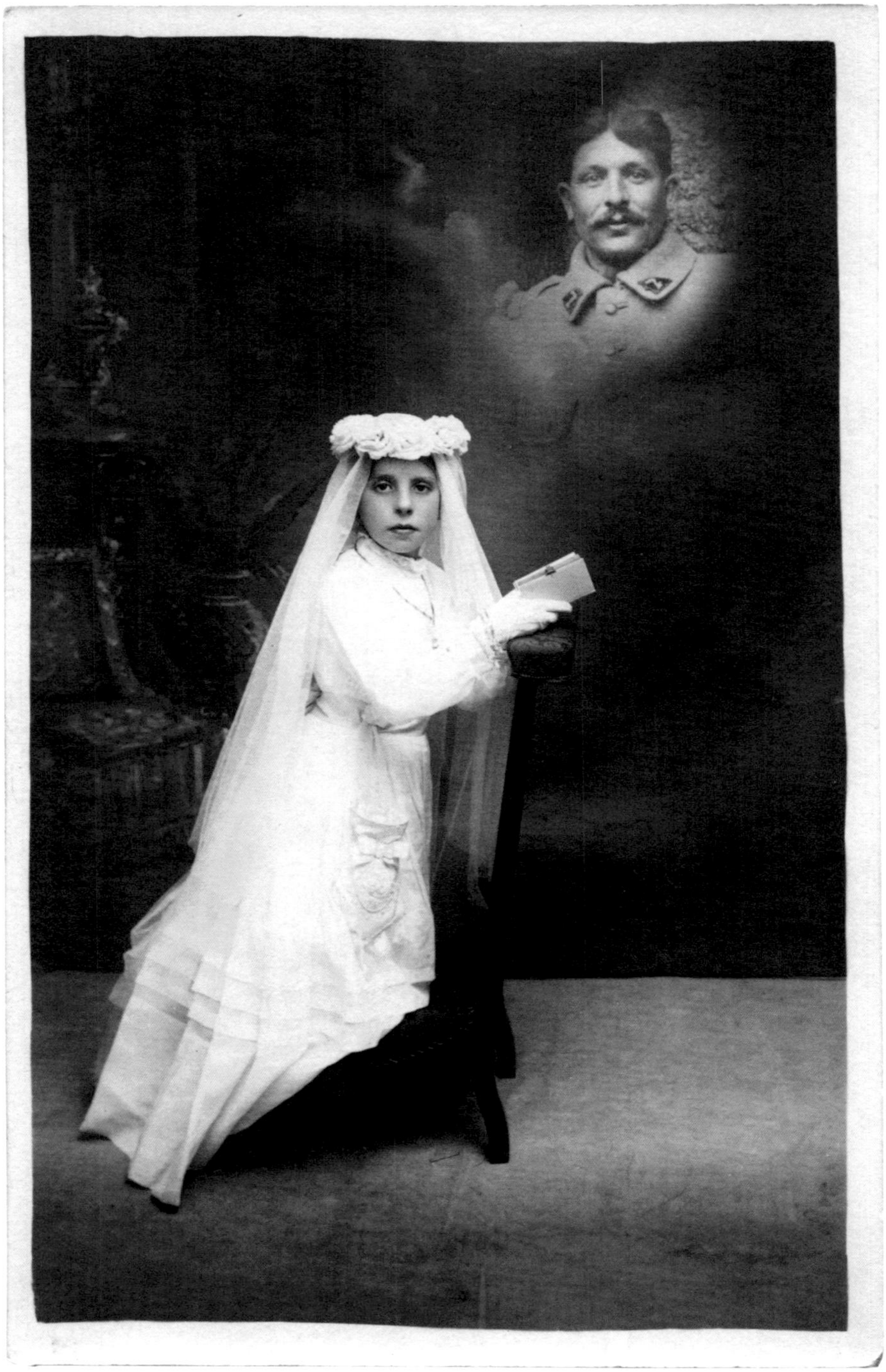

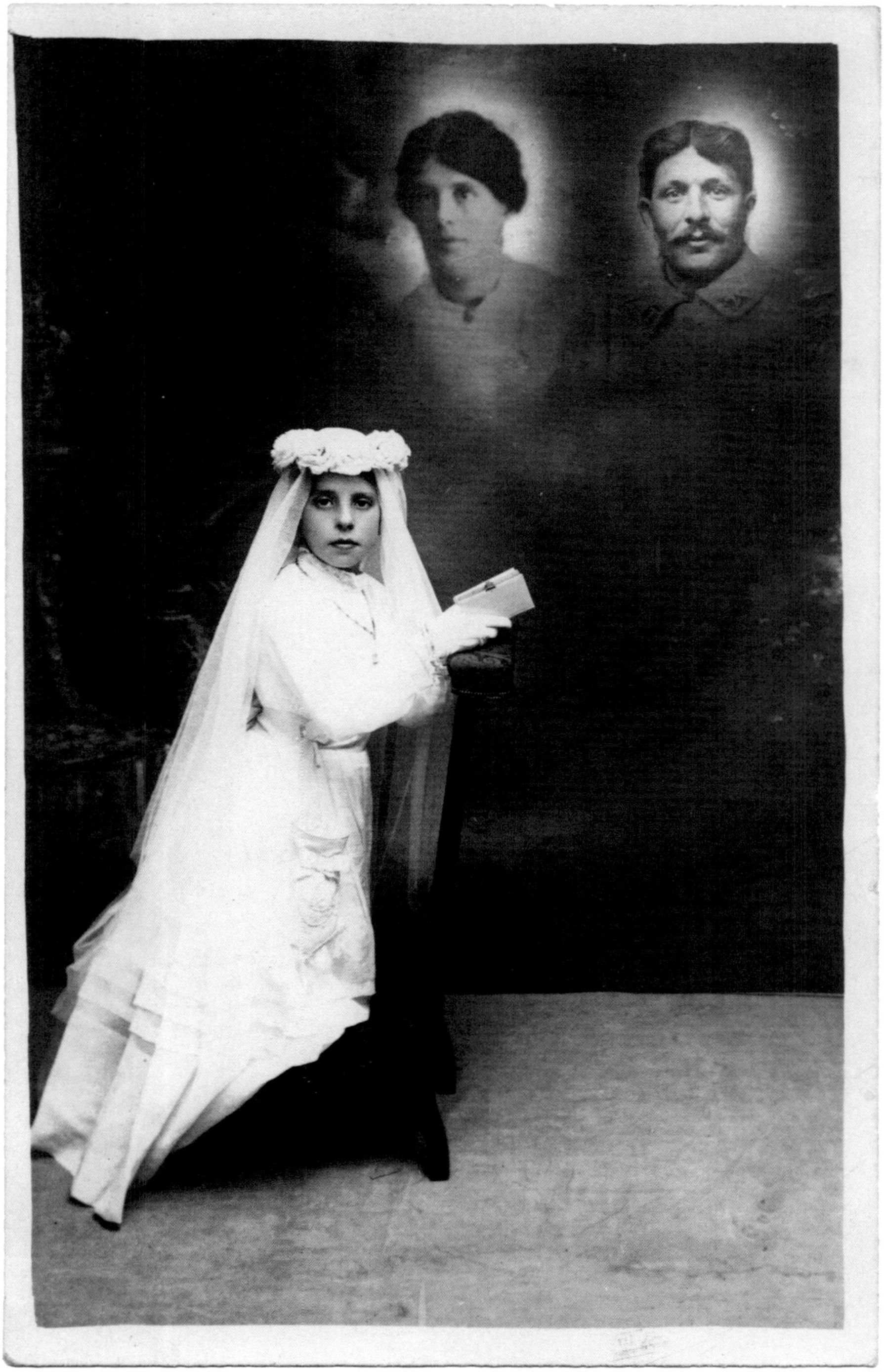

My mother was a very practical woman. She'd have a few snapshots and that would be fine, a record of the day, that's all. She wouldn't want big things up on the wall; we only had the Sacred Heart on the wall. But, you know, my mother never had photos up around the place. She wasn't a photo sort of person. Though later on in life she put up photos of her parents. I think as she came nearer to her death, photos began to appear.

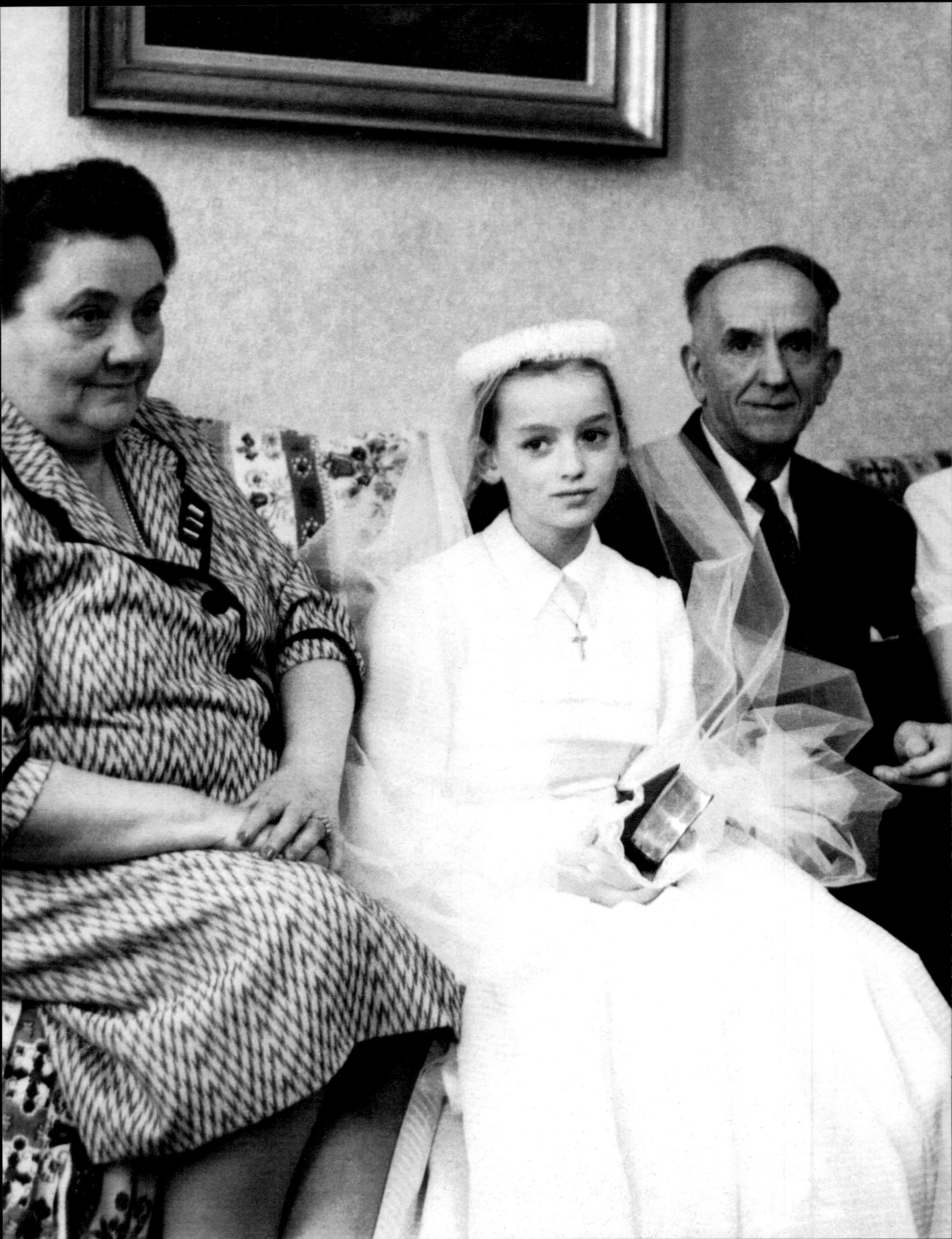

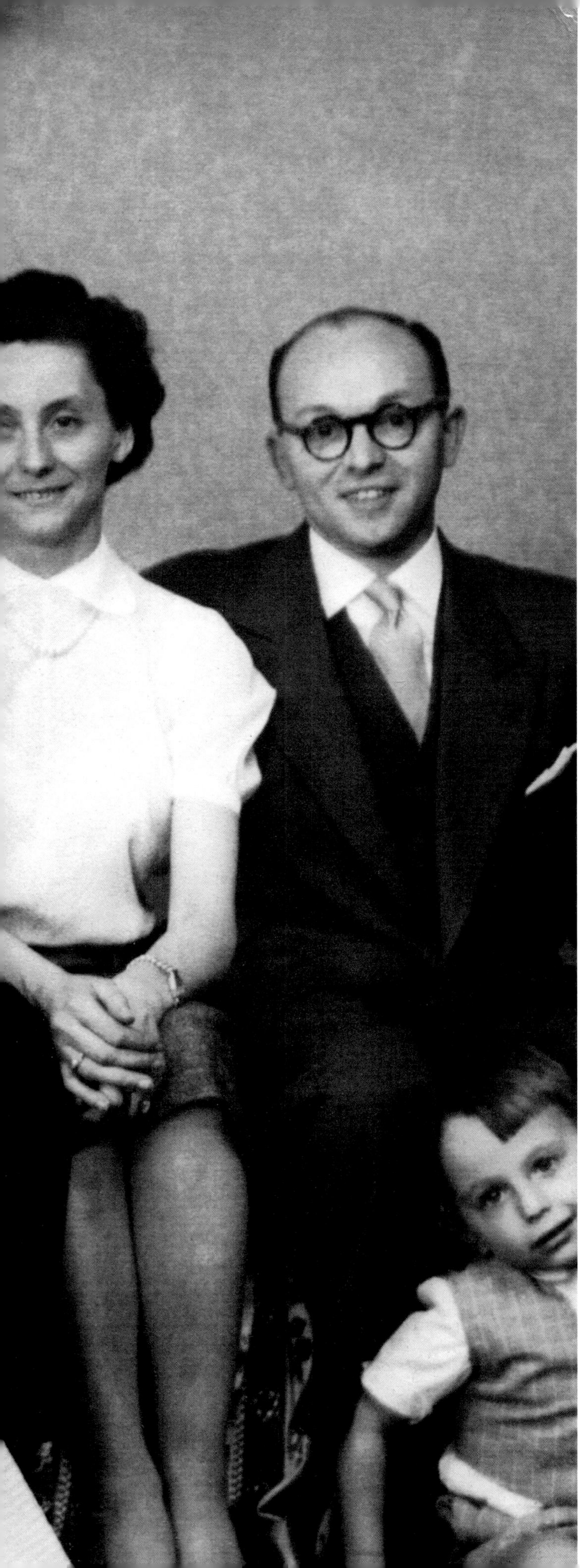

7

THE FRUIT OF EACH MYSTERY

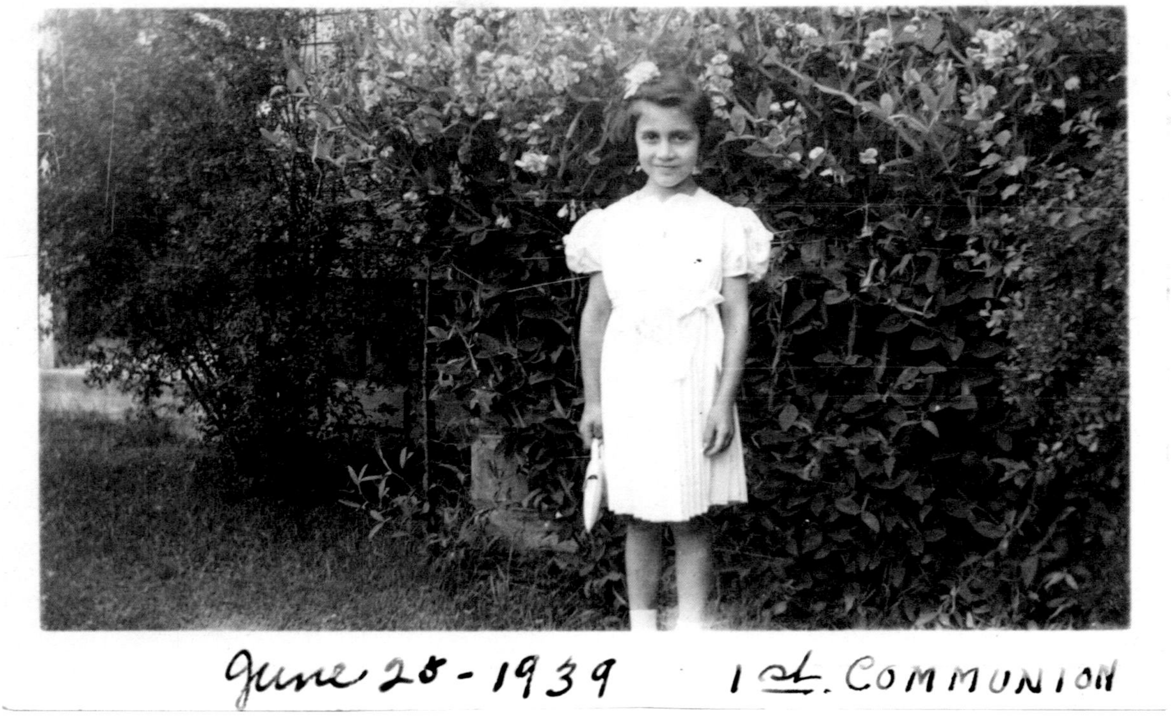

I remember being quite confused as to why I was so special on that day – because that's how you're made to feel. We got presents, and I found that really strange. Why am I getting presents for going to church? The funniest one was an alarm clock. I also got the obvious things like rosaries and crosses. I also got a Bible for my First Communion, a gold-leaf one. They were obviously significant presents. But the thing that sticks in my mind is that alarm clock for some reason.

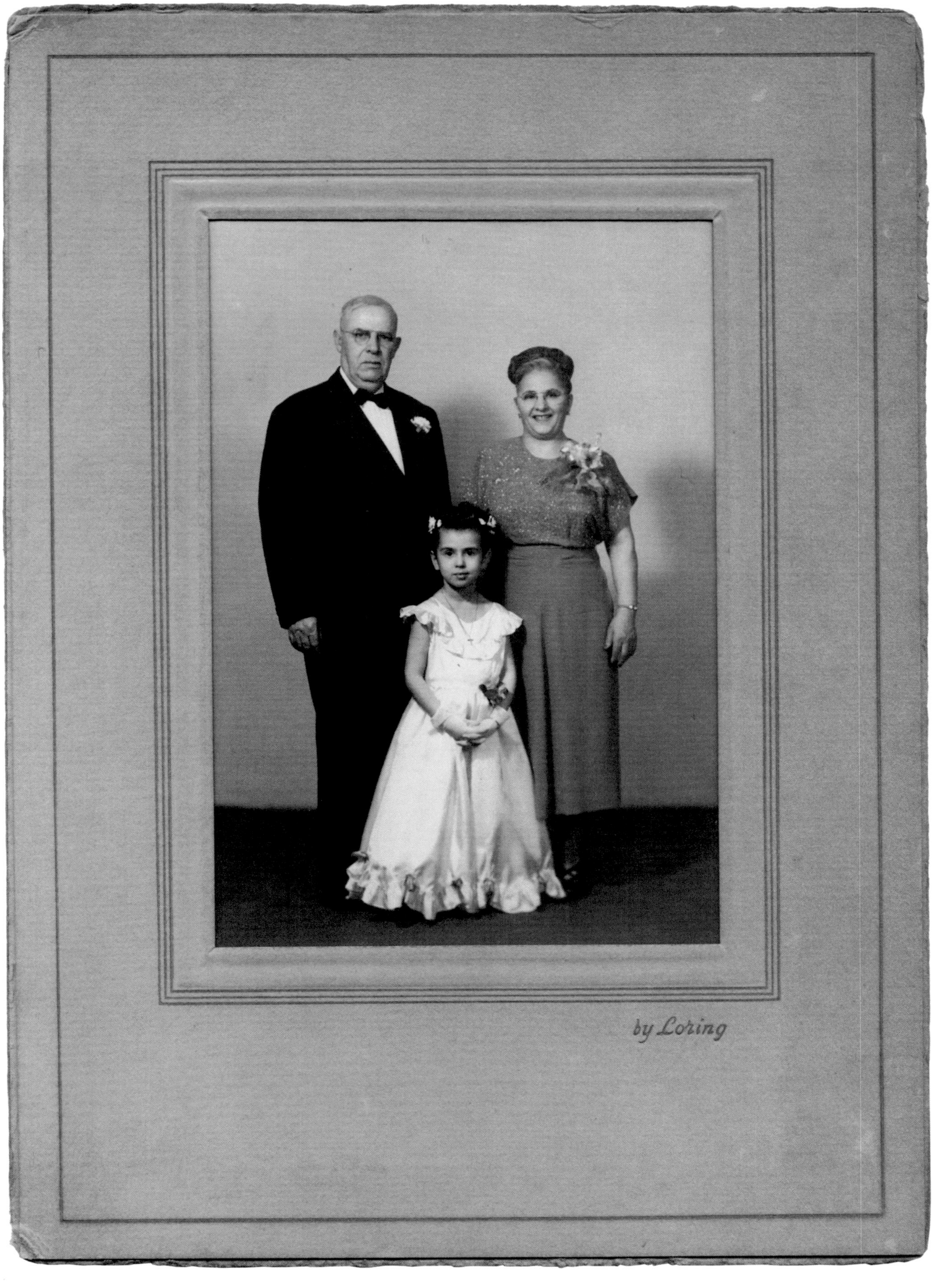
by Loring

Oh it was a lovely prayer book.
I remember being absolutely thrilled. It was a white sort of pearl type – it had little, very, very fine pages. And I used to just love the feeling of turning over those tiny, fine, almost tissue-paper pages, you know. And they would crackle as you turned them over because they didn't quite sit in the book and it was just gorgeous. I remember holding it between my hands 'cause it was curved and beautiful and it was a lovely thing.

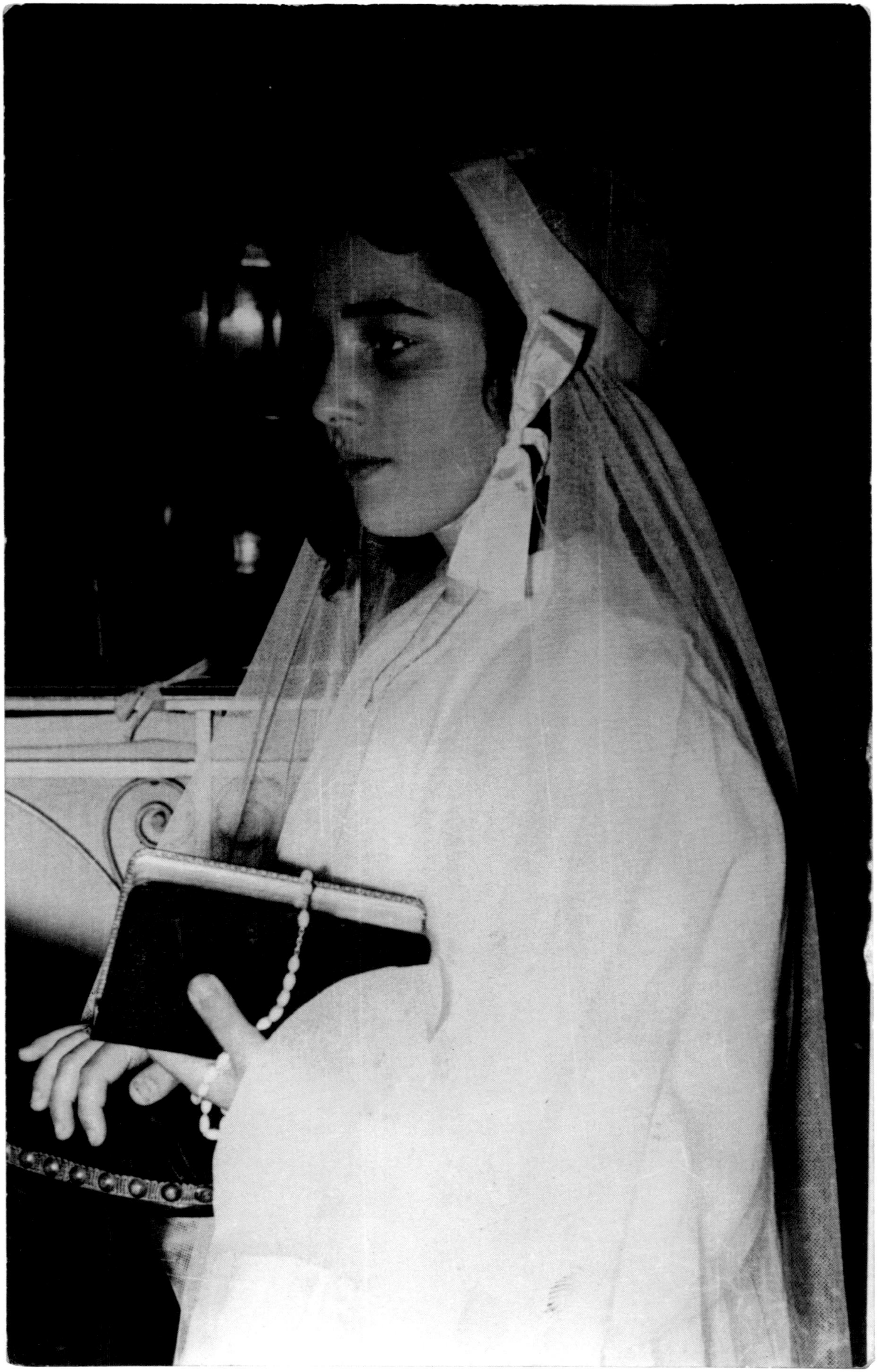

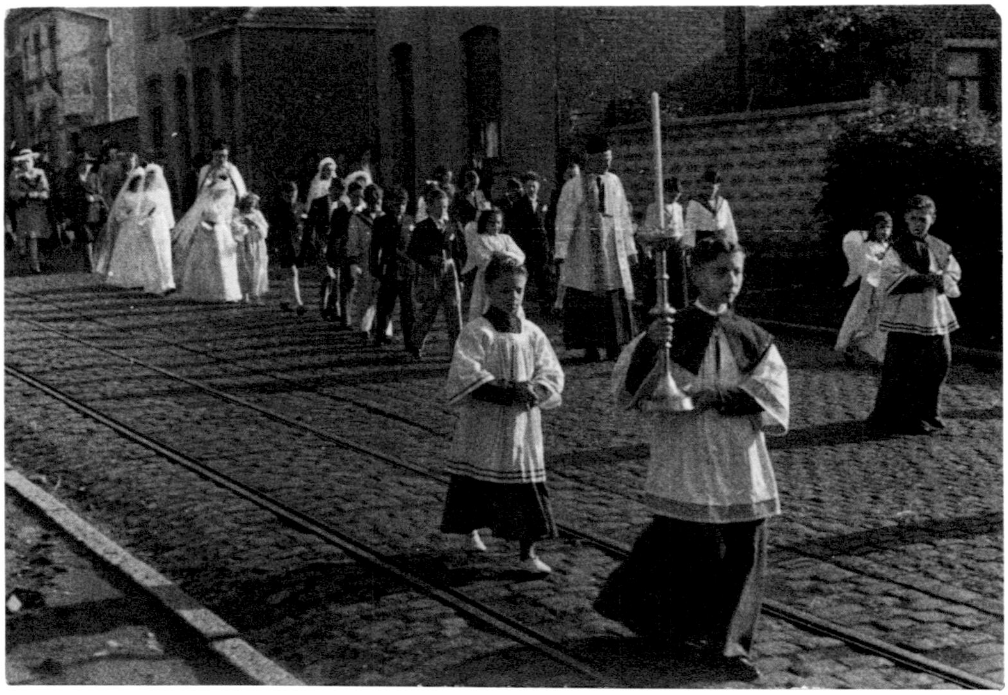

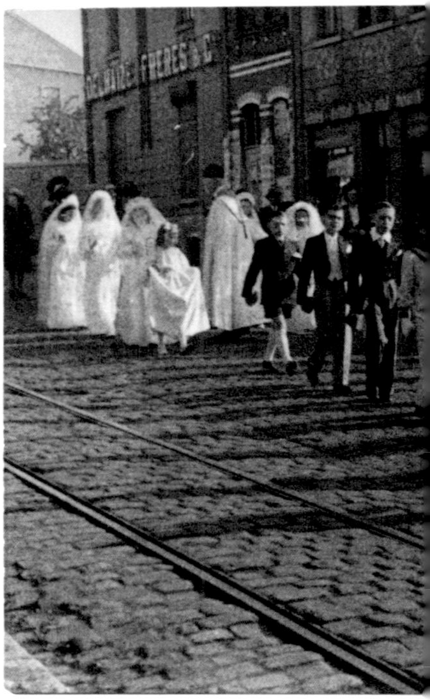

I remember my favourite gift, which was from my mom's best friend. She gave me a bathing suit from the US. It was a big thing to get presents from the US in those days – still is. It was in a terry-cloth bag, matching the bathing suit, just like the bikini. Yeah, I got a bikini and that was my favourite gift. Because I remember that it matched the bag. When I went to the swimming club, I had the bag, the towel and the thing.

What did it look like?

It was yellow. I have a picture of it somewhere. Yellow and white with little daisies or something, you know? Very simple, I mean – at that age. But I don't remember getting, which a lot of people do, a medal, cross or rosary. I don't remember any of that – just the bikini.

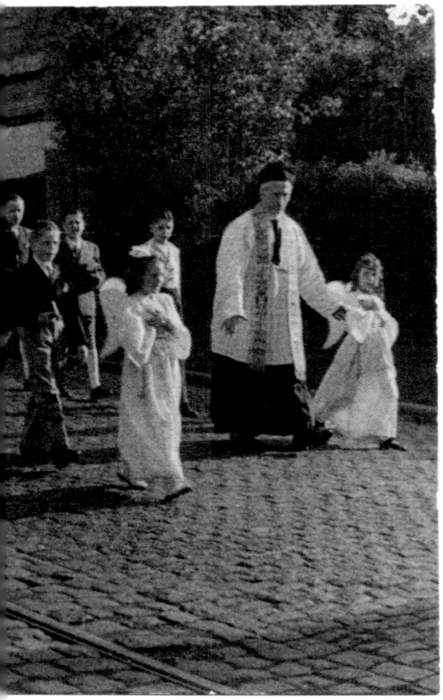

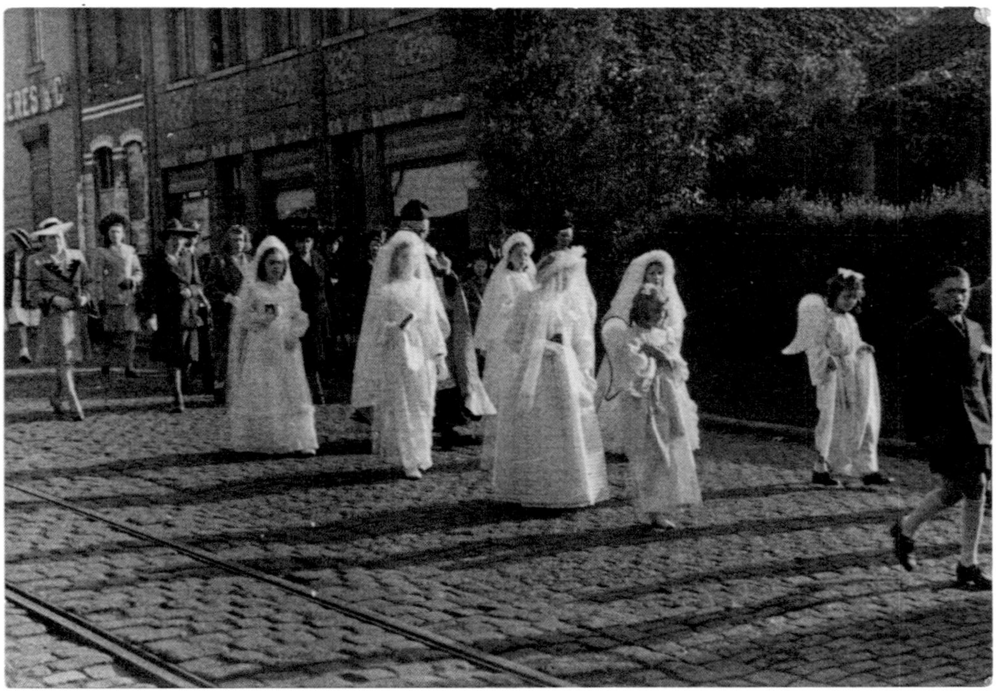

I got two Communion cards, like proper cards, obviously bought from a religious shop, kind of big, in a box. You like take the lid off the box and then take the card out and it had a cross on it saying 'On your First Communion, loads of love from' … I had one from my mum and my dad and I had one from my sister as well – I only just remembered that. And I had a rosary from my nan, which I've still got in a little silk bag; a white rosary with beads which I've never learned how to use. You're supposed to use each bead for each prayer. But there's so many beads! How could you do that many prayers? When you do your sins they say to do twenty and you count twenty beads up from the bottom bit, don't you? My nan bought it more because it was important to her. She had a wooden rosary that her mum gave to her. She said when she died, she wanted it put in her coffin. So I put her wooden rosary next to her body in the coffin. I put it in there with a photo of me and my sister and a poem I wrote her.

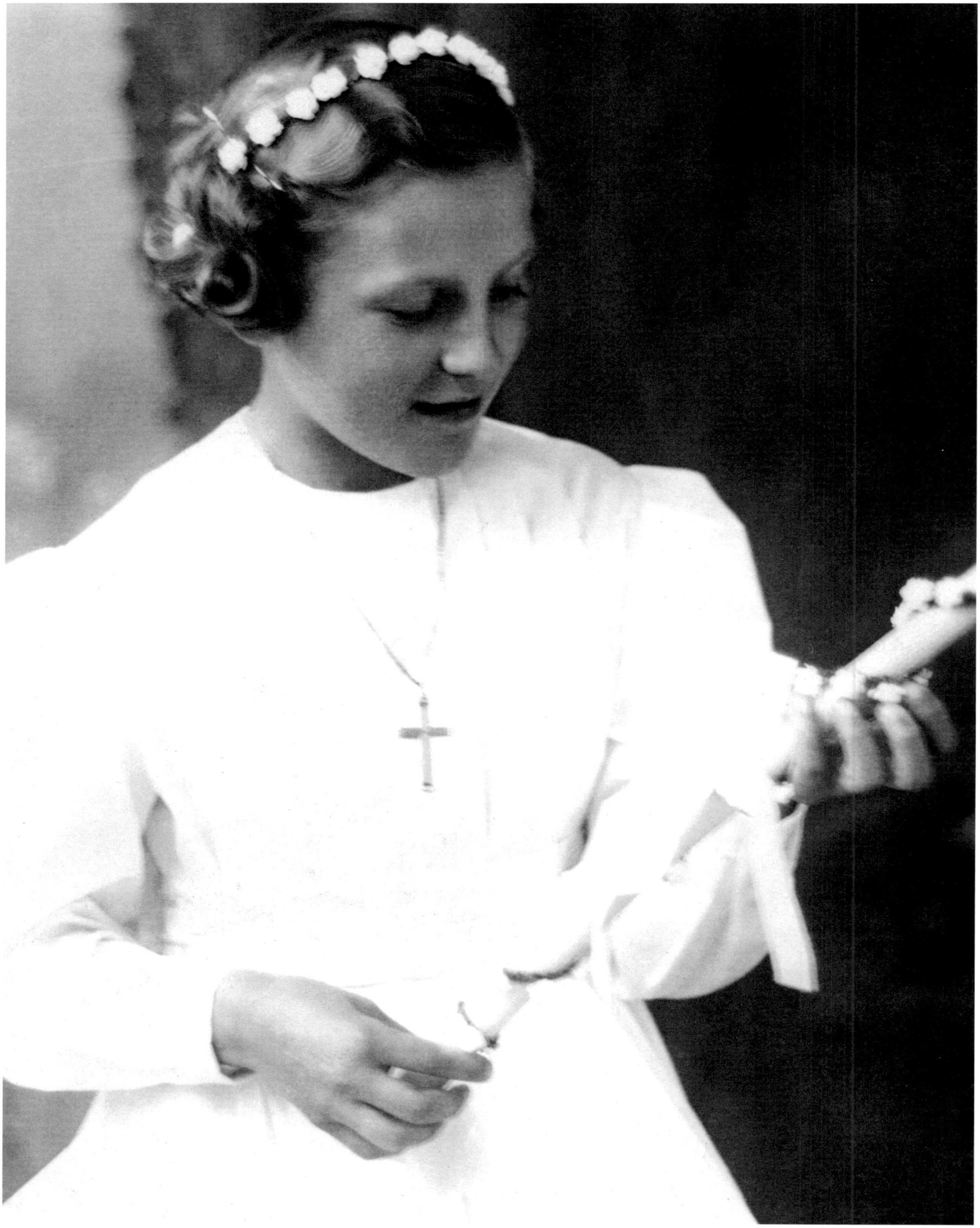

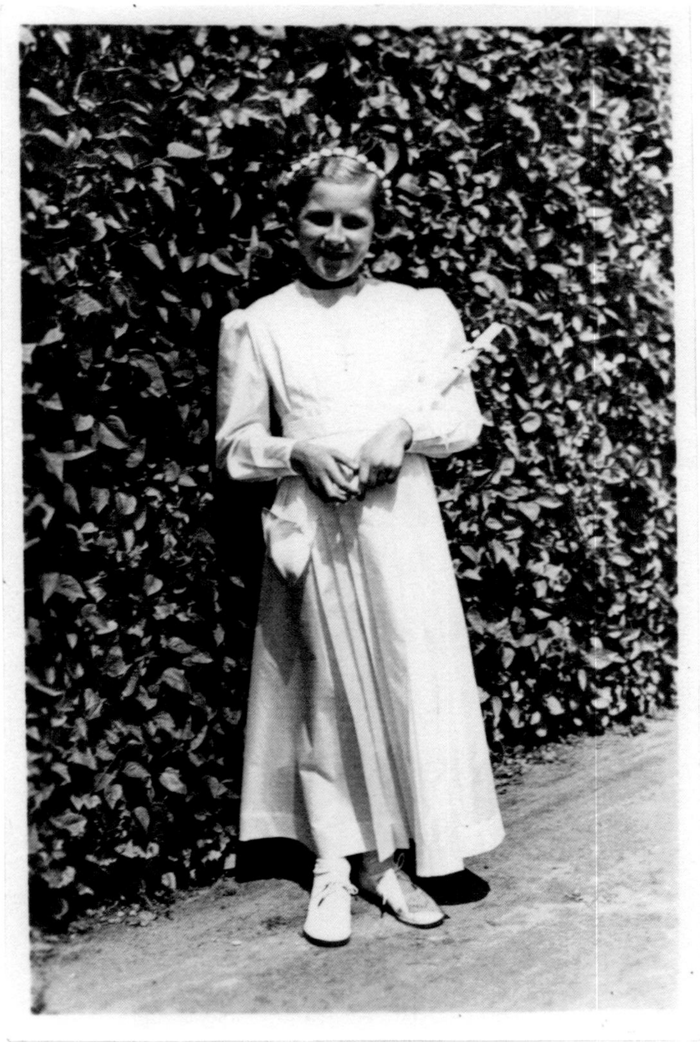

Oh yes, the candle. Actually the candle is given to you when you're baptised. Your godparents buy you a big candle and you carry it for the Communion as well. And you are supposed to keep it – I mean, this candle symbolises life and it has to be with you all your life. And the last time you light it is when you are dying.

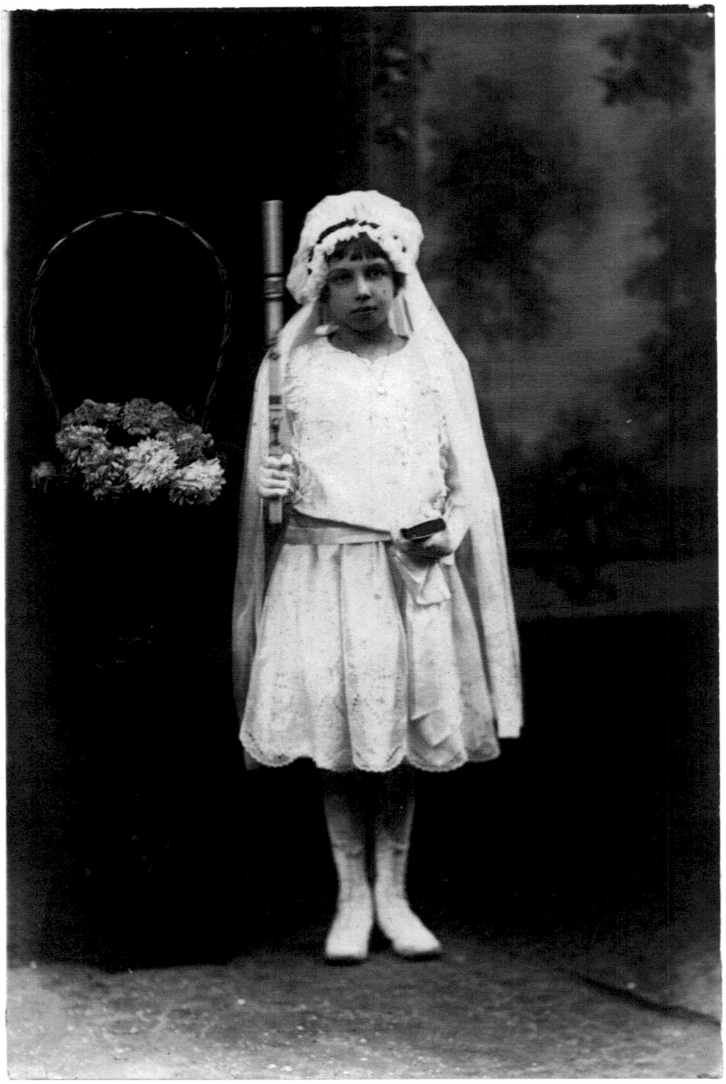

It was the Feast of Christ the King, which in those days, was a bit different from what it is now. I think it was October 25th. Anyway, on Guy Fawkes Day, either that year, or a couple of years later – possibly even that year – we had lots of fireworks. And at some point, goodness knows why, a candle was needed. Anyway the thing was that my special candle was used – it was deeply inappropriate. It was just convenient, you know? I mean there was no other candle at hand. I have this impression – it was dark, fireworks going off, it was all a bit confused, and this candle burning down. I don't suppose the whole candle was used on this occasion, but after that I felt that the candle was messed up. It was no longer the Holy candle.

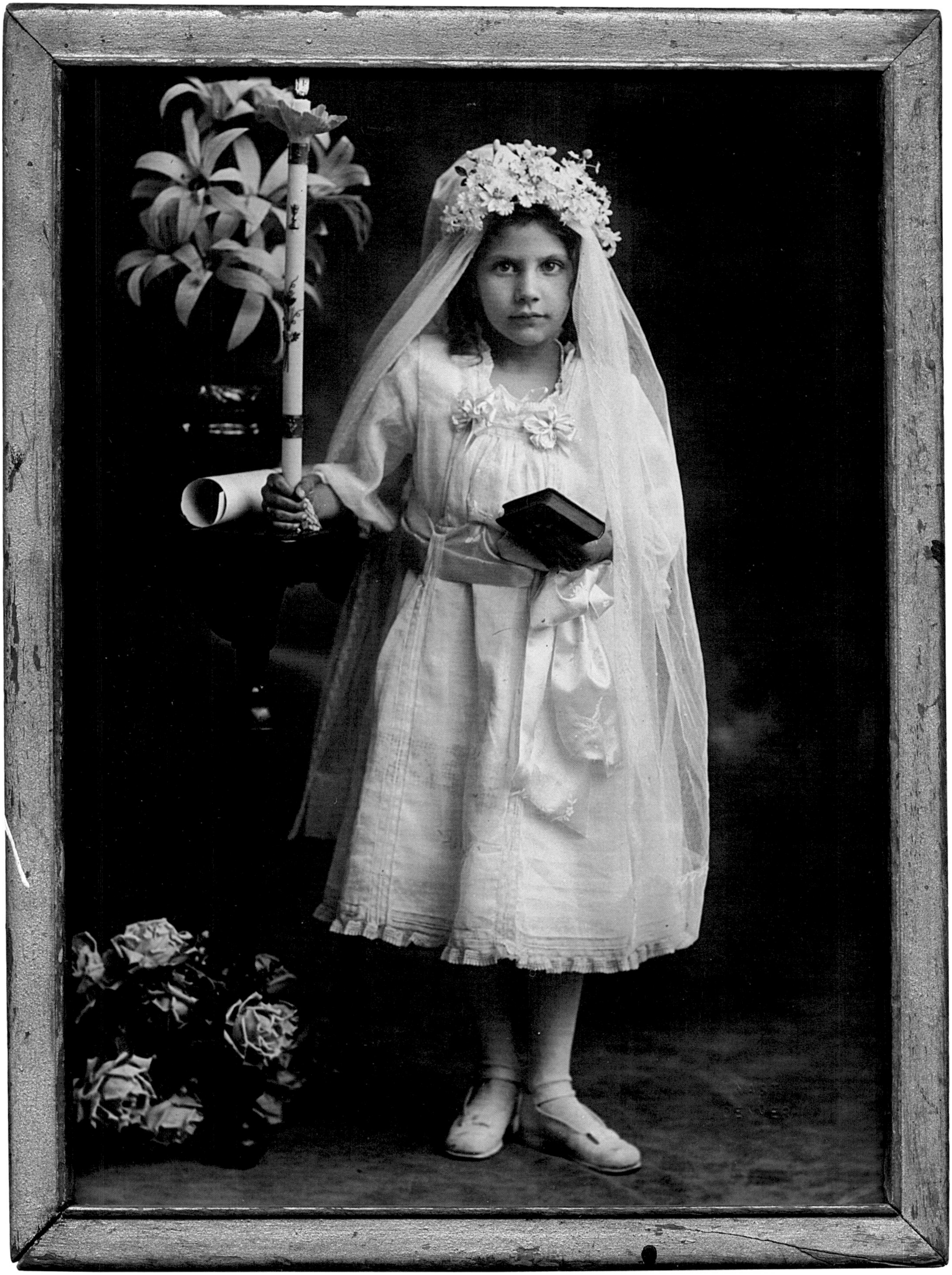

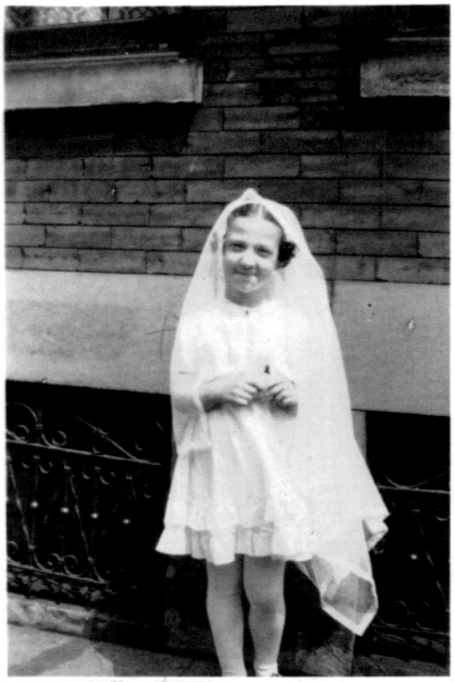

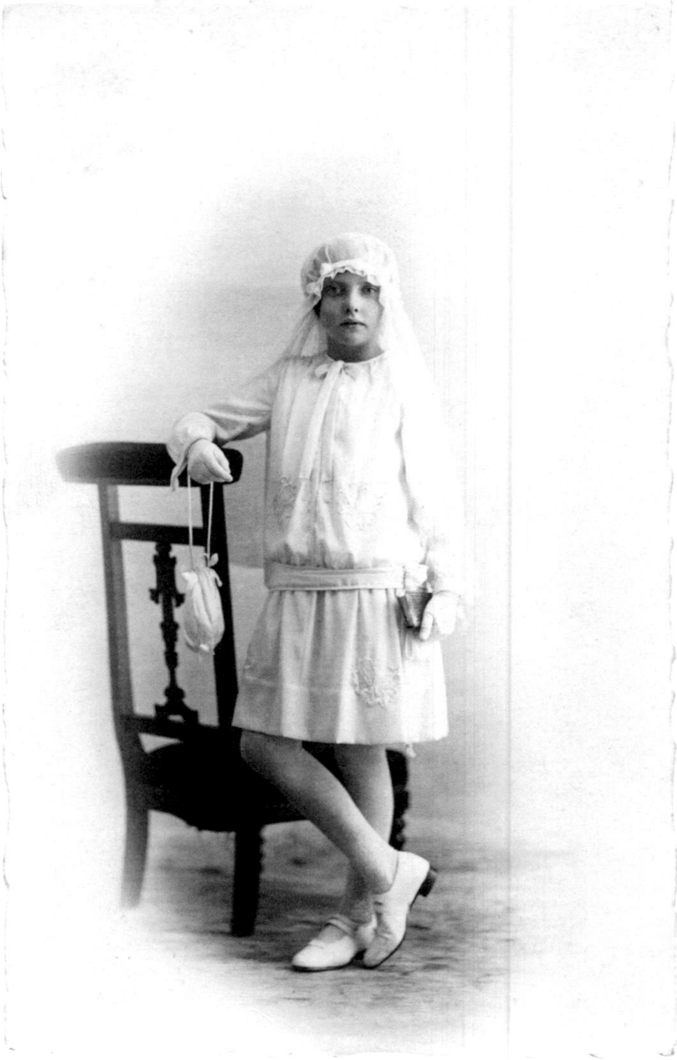

I got my own, my first bank account.
I remember that because I got money given to me as well, and all that money went straight into that account. I didn't get any in my hand. I think I got about £40–50 in cash, which was a hell of a lot of money back then, yeah '77. If I hadn't have done the Communion, I don't think I would have got an account that early. I've still got it. It's not something I use. But that initial money is still there. I have never used it, no. It's blessed as far as I'm concerned.

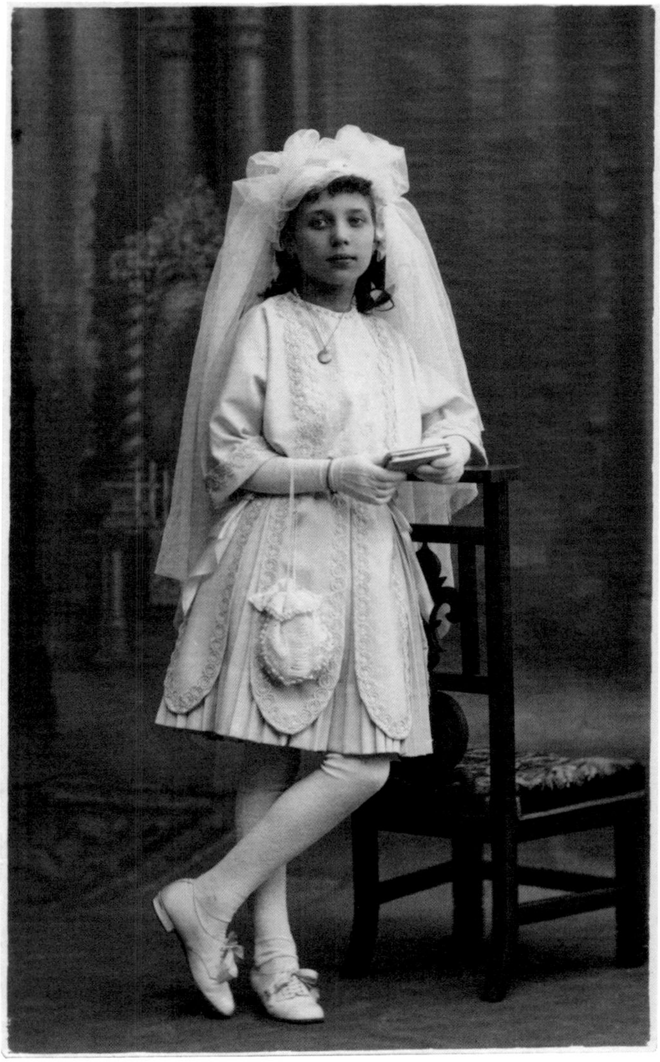

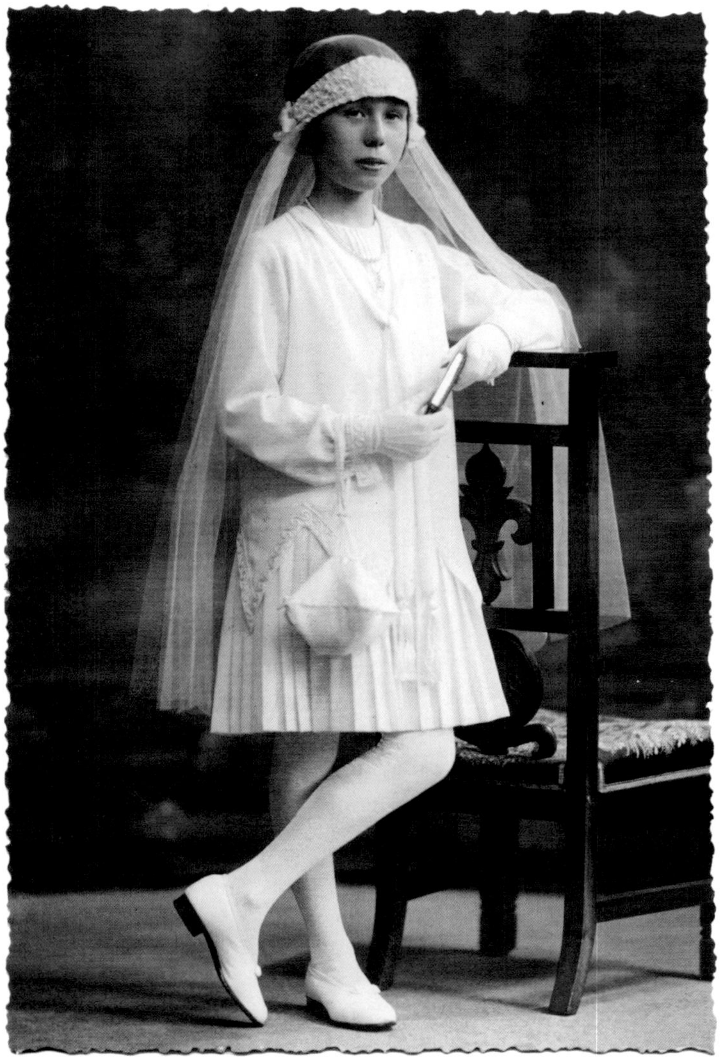

It was after lunch. We'd had our lunch and dessert was coming and the coffee and everything and that's when I started counting up the money. And my uncle, the priest, who was always there – actually he was the one who chastised me about counting up the money.

Do you remember what he said?

Oh I think he just thought it was not appropriate or, I suppose, the right way to behave. I felt stung. I felt really bad actually. It sort of ruined it. And then I remember feeling very resentful for about an hour afterwards. Then I probably got over it.

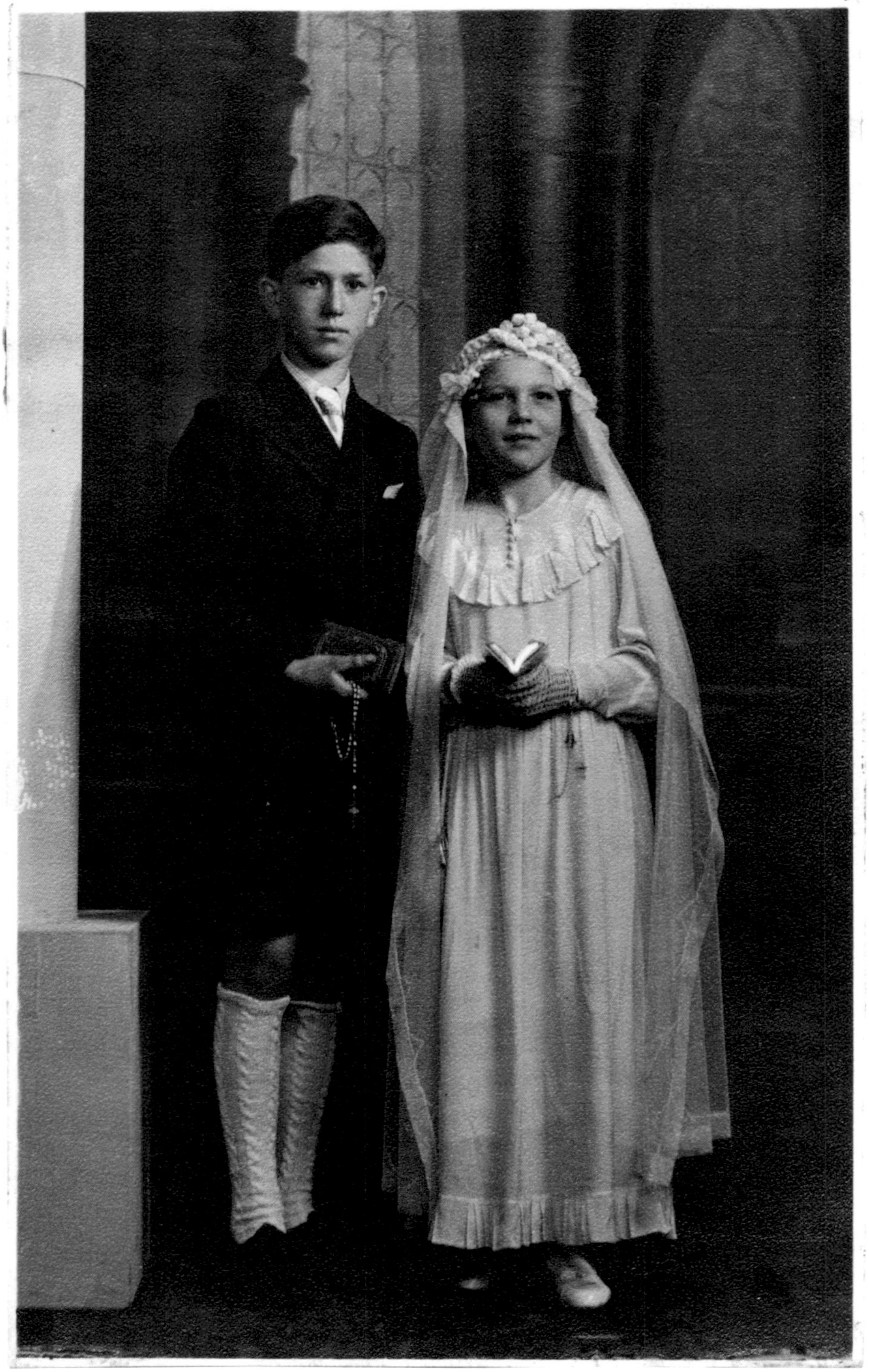

We had relatives come. We always visited our relatives, they never came to us. And they had to drive three hours and there was quite a big to-do made out of it. Actually, I thought it was odd because nobody ever came to visit us. Wherever we lived, it was always us visiting them. My father or my mother must have said to them, 'For God's sake, you never come over.' It was just about them fulfilling an obligation to visit. 'Cause we would haul across wherever, you know, across a state, or a couple of states, to visit them. But they came to our Communion.

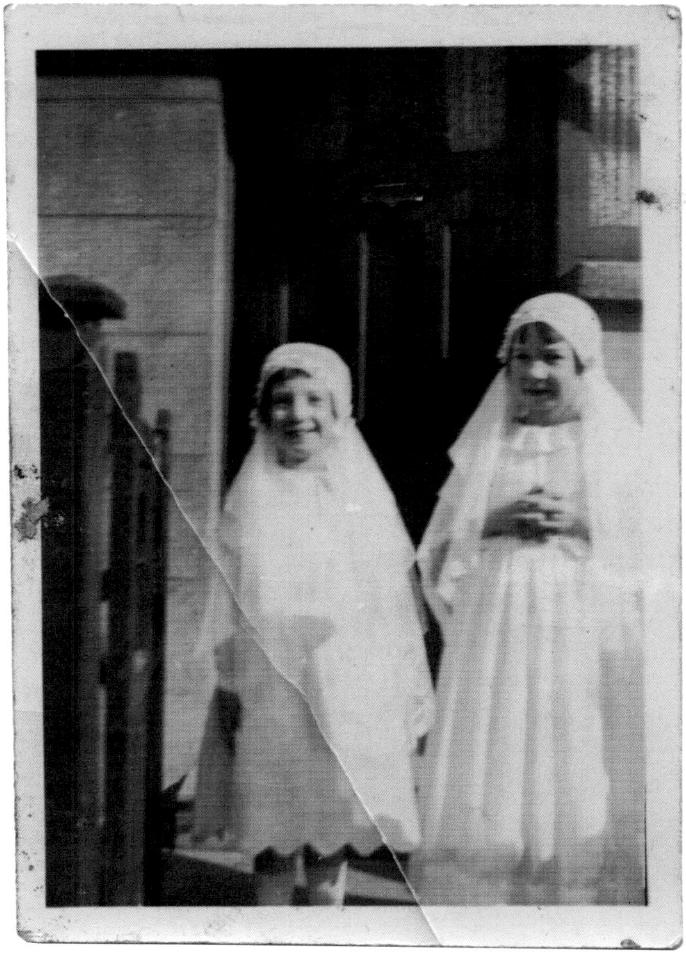

There wasn't a place where we could all celebrate together, like a local hall, so most people just went to their separate parties. We headed off to Shenley Berry Hospital, which was quite a way away. It's actually a hospital for mental people, but they have a hall that we rented out.

You had your party in a psychiatric hospital?

I think because my dad and mum worked there and stuff, I was quite used to it. But yeah, it was kind of strange, especially since you had to be careful, I suppose. You'd see the odd patient walking about and stuff. Actually they tried to get into the hall but we shut and locked the door.

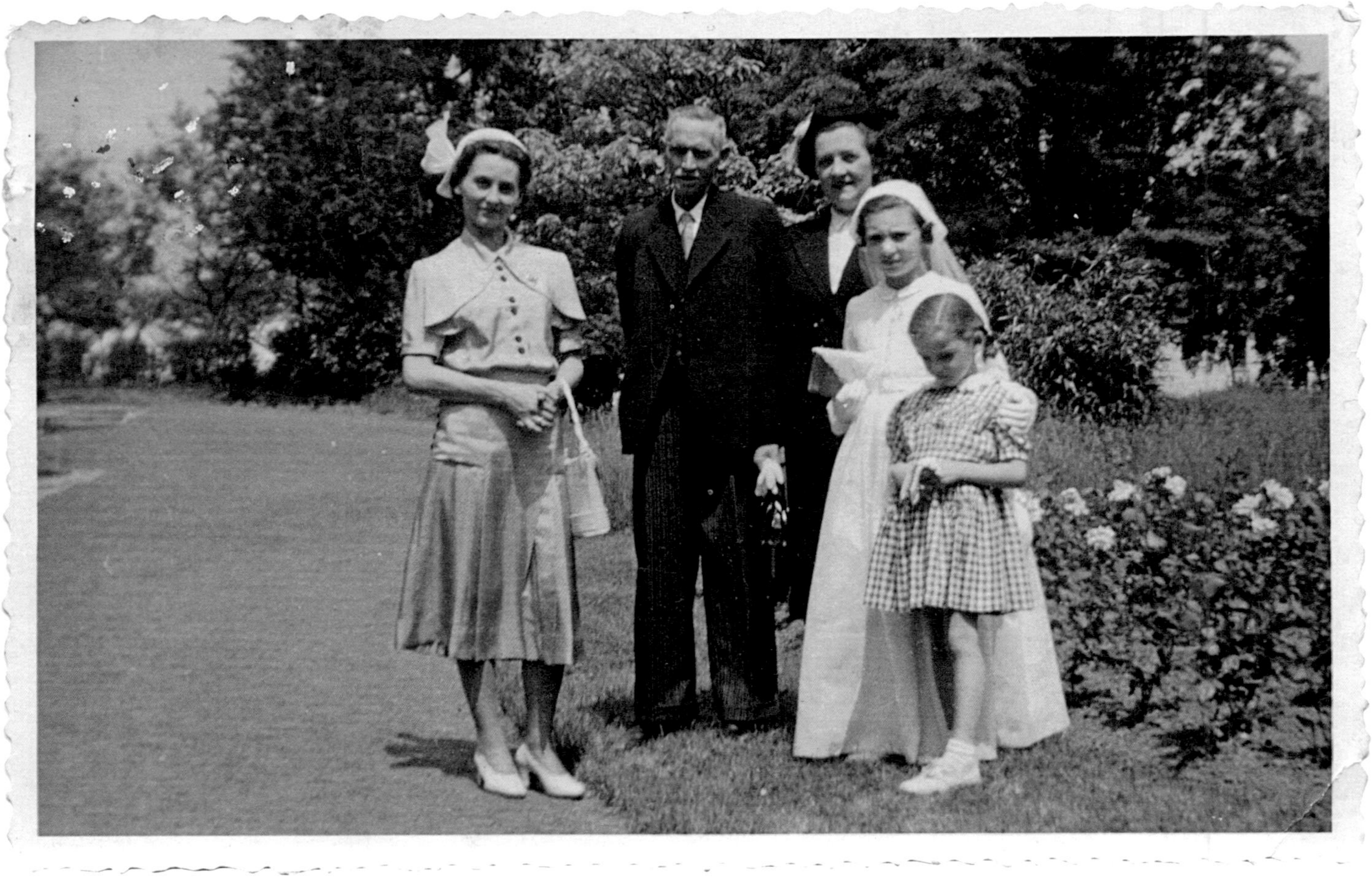

My mother was the ultimate centre-of-attention needer – so I had pretty much got used to being in the background. And you know, I think probably I was the centre of attention for only half the day. It was all very fleeting, you know. I don't think it lasted, as I said, beyond one o'clock. Things went back to normal, which meant get the hell out of the house and take that dress off.

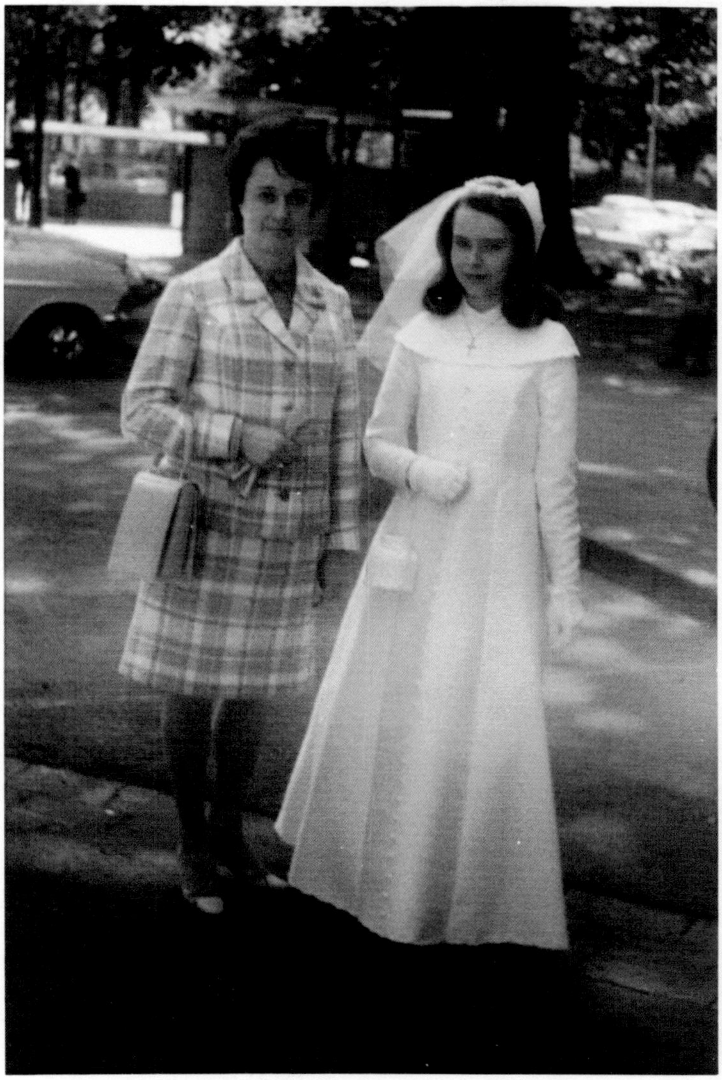

You got your 'after' outfit to wear. That was a blue crimplene dress-suit.

What, like a honeymoon outfit?

Exactly. Yes, because you see you wouldn't want to be wearing the white dress 'cause you'd damage it, you see. It would be sent down through the family, because there's no point in wasting money and buying another dress.

Was the dress-suit a hand-me-down too?

Oh no, you'd get that brand new – and a little funny peaked hat, white peaked cap. It wasn't like your peaked cap today, but it was a peaked cap. And it was all, I guess, polyester, as that sort of stuff was 'in'. I mean when you think of crimplene, what is it? It's just a kind of polyester. But I suppose that was fashionable at that time. Yes, so I remember my little turquoise dress-suit.

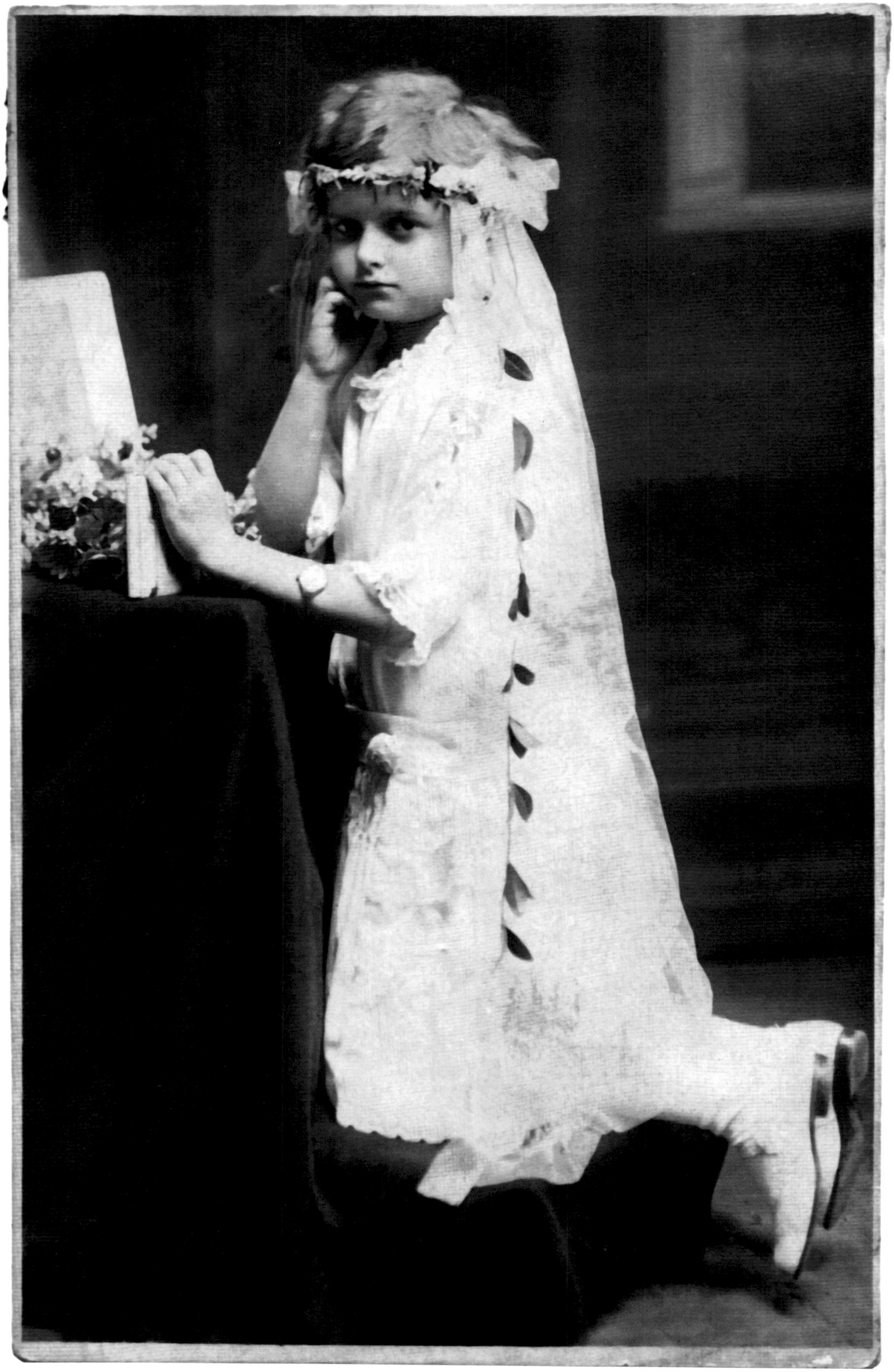

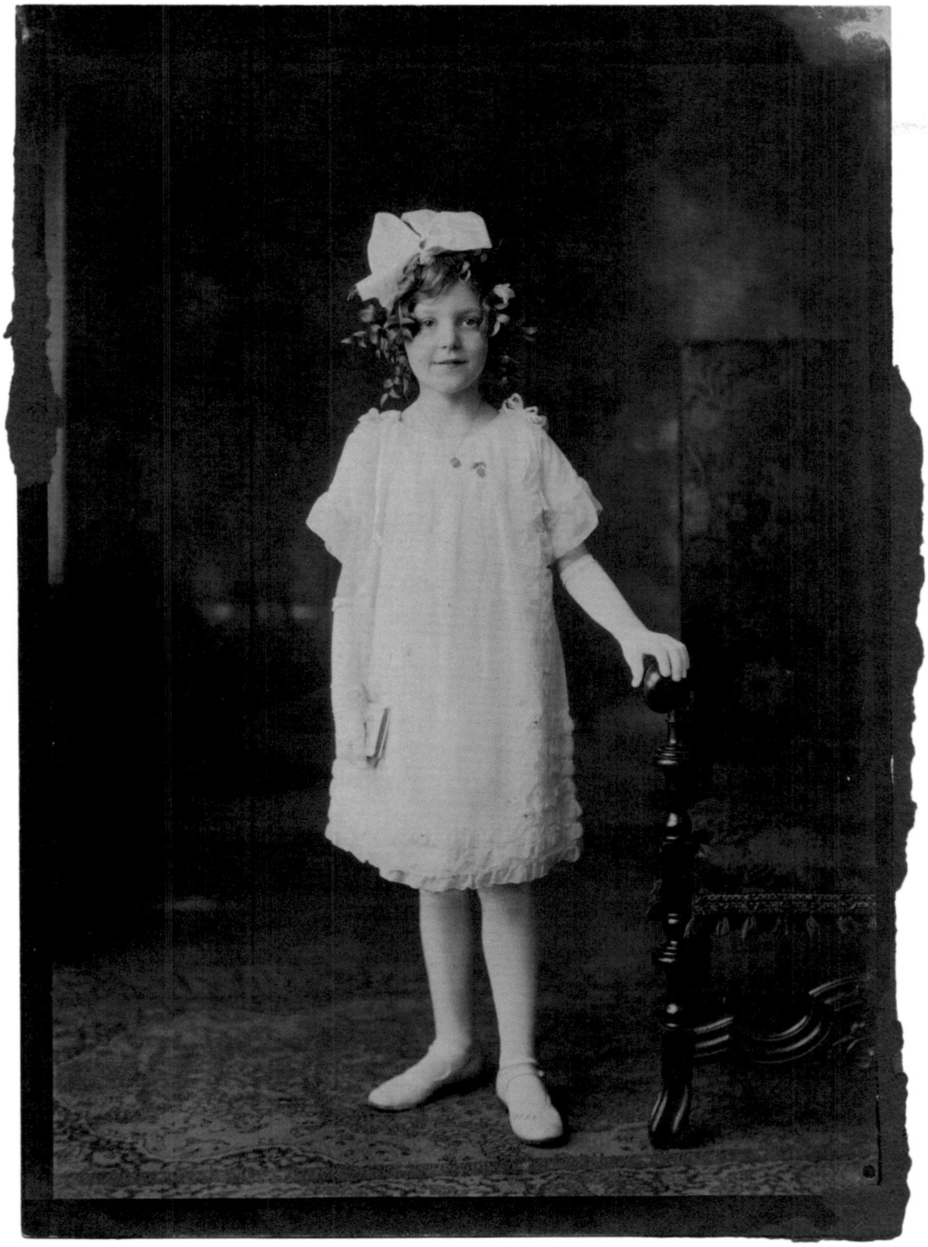

I felt very important 'cause when we came back from the church for the party, I had a special seat. My Grandmother brought this very odd, big, huge chair that was sitting at the head of the table. Everybody else was sitting on normal chairs on both sides, I can't remember in what order, but there were parents on one side and godparents and grandparents on the other, in some special order, and I was at the top.

Like a queen.

Oh yes, it was a high seat, it was big. It was decorated all in white fabric and then green stuff, ivy or whatever. Green is important because, remember when Jesus died, on his head there was the crown? Well, this symbolises the crown.

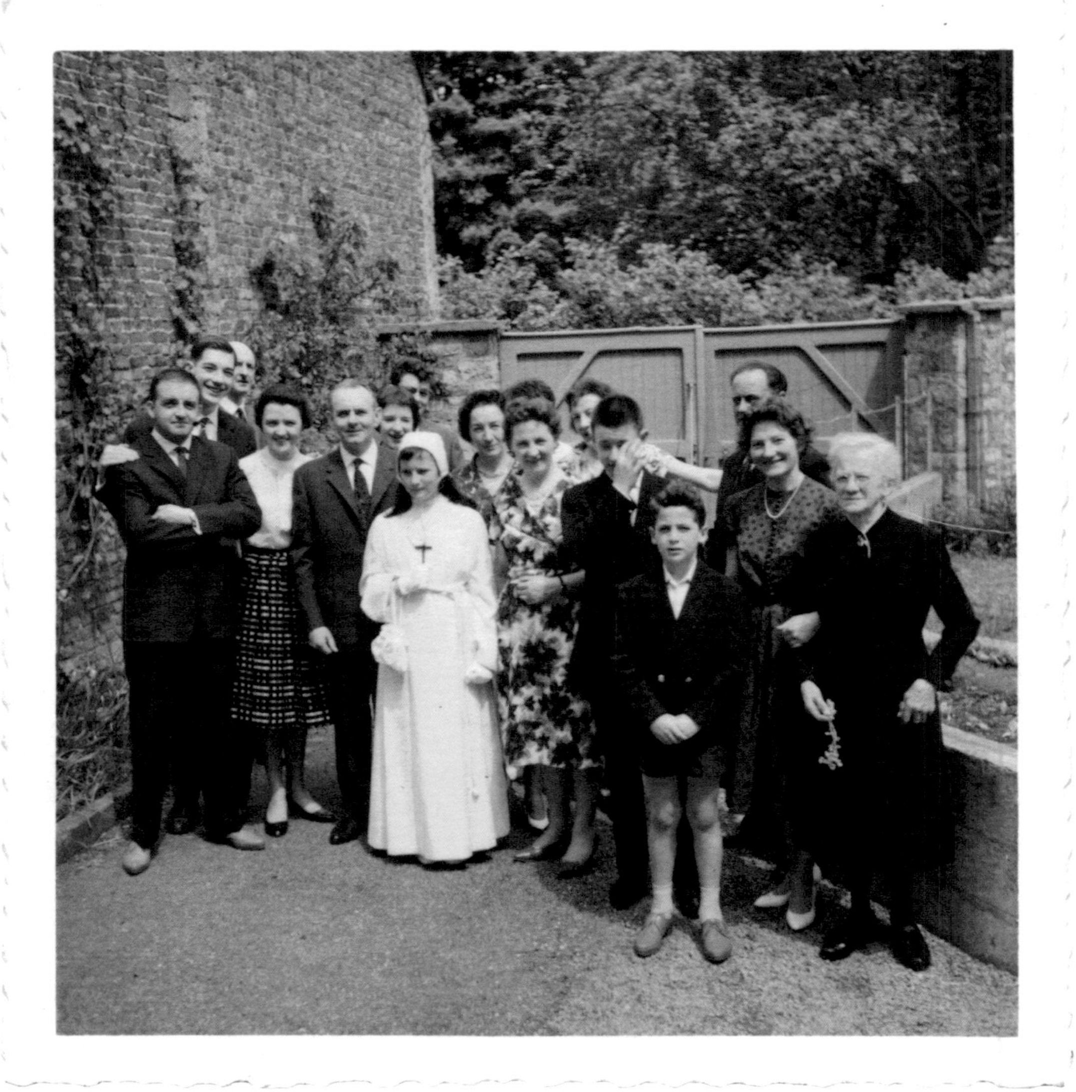

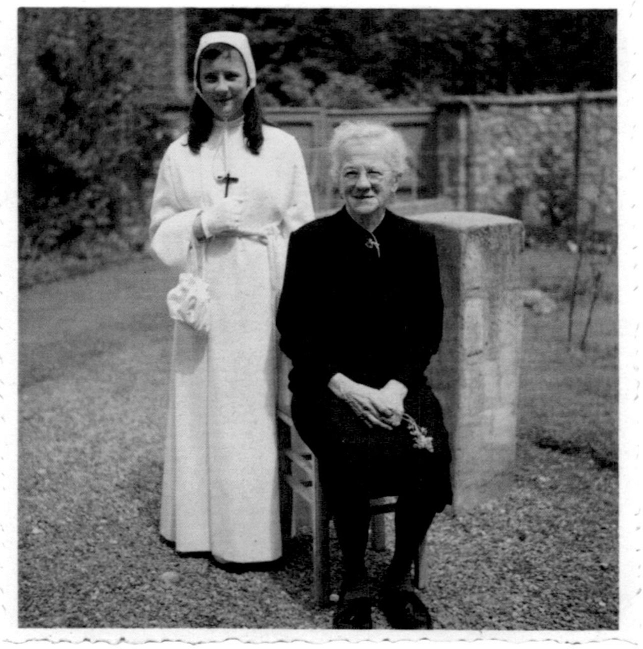

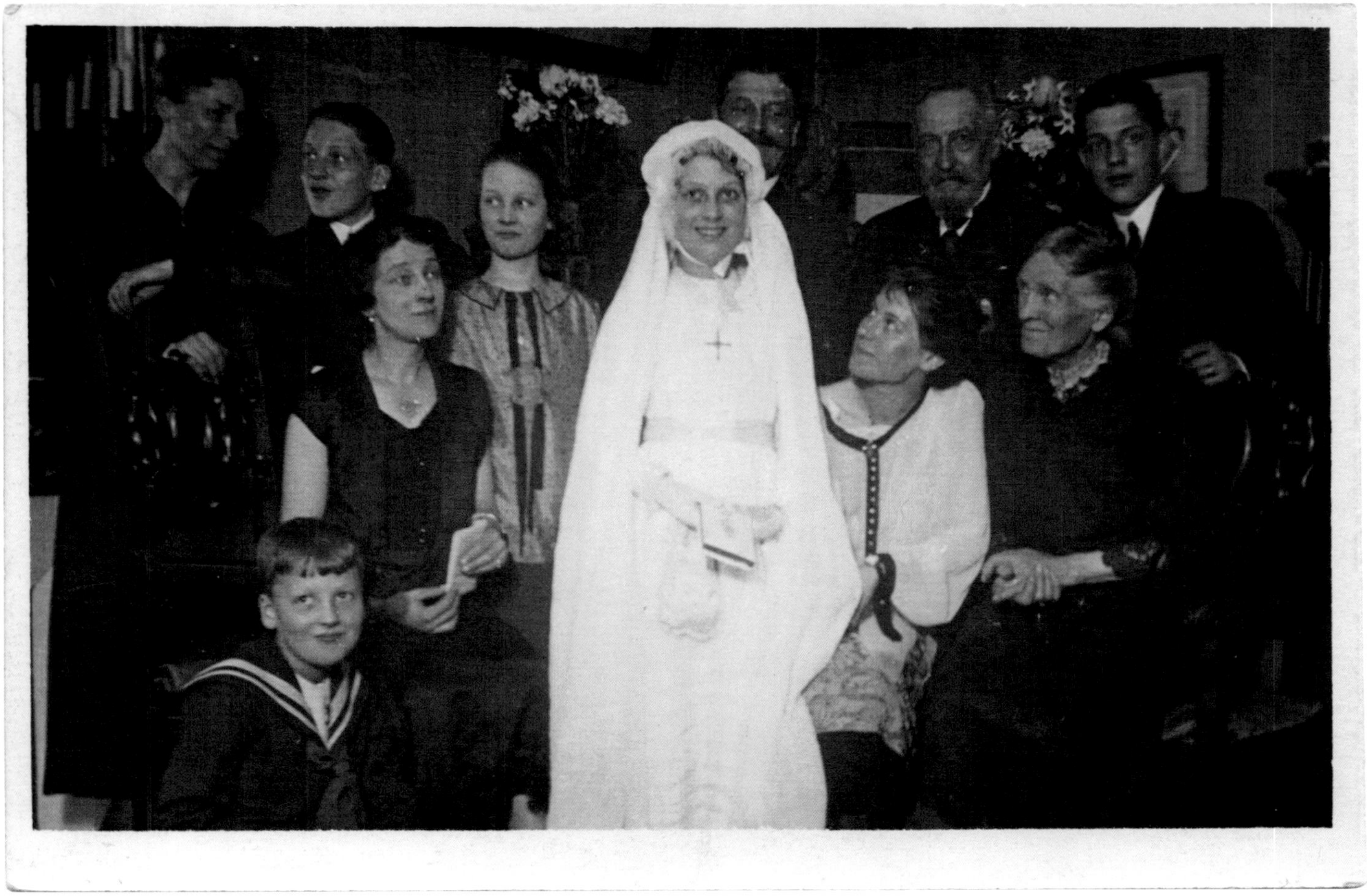

My grandmothers used to make all these coconut things, you know, and the coconut was not like today, all stibbly – it was really beautiful and long, yeah. It's like the woolly stuff that you would get when you pet a lamb. And it was like – wow! You'd think – a cake? What significance is a cake? But it's still in bread form; it's flour, which if you go back many years, anything that one partakes of has some kind of flour in it, 'cause it's part of life, you know? And so, to me, that little episode was just so powerful, to see that dessert because, you know, how often did you see a lamb cake?

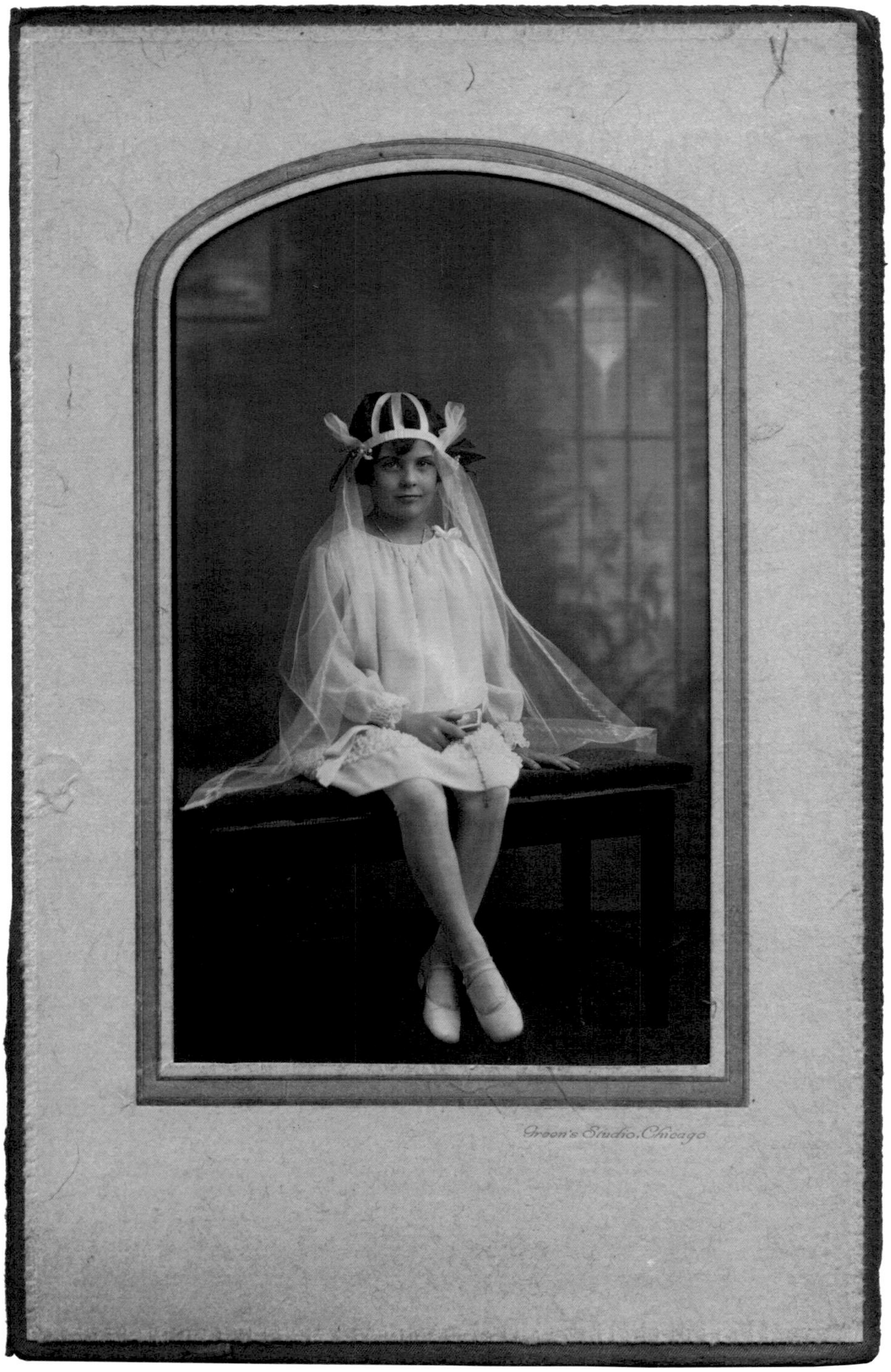

Oh my cake was beautiful, because she got the best lady known to decorate it. In Colombia we have a cake that only very few people here know how to make. It's called the wedding cake. It's not even called cake, it's called *ponque*. It's brown and it has a lot of raisins and, I don't know, it's almost like a fruit cake. They have to leave the raisins and – what do you call those little green fruits? You know, those things they have in Christmas cakes? – they put them in wine for many, many, many days.

Soaked, marinated.

Oh my God, when they make that cake they pour dry vermouth, they soak it every night for like a week or two before they decorate it. So it's a very rich cake. It's used for weddings, first communions, baptisms, you know, very special occasions. So, she made me that cake and then she made a birdhouse out of sugar, and we saved it until we had to leave Colombia. It looked like lace, the little birdhouse. And it had little doves going in and out.

Like a real birdhouse, but in sugar?

Oh yeah. A complete birdhouse, because you're receiving a form of the Holy Spirit when you do your First Communion. Everything with religion for me is like the white bird, you know: peaceful, pure, white.

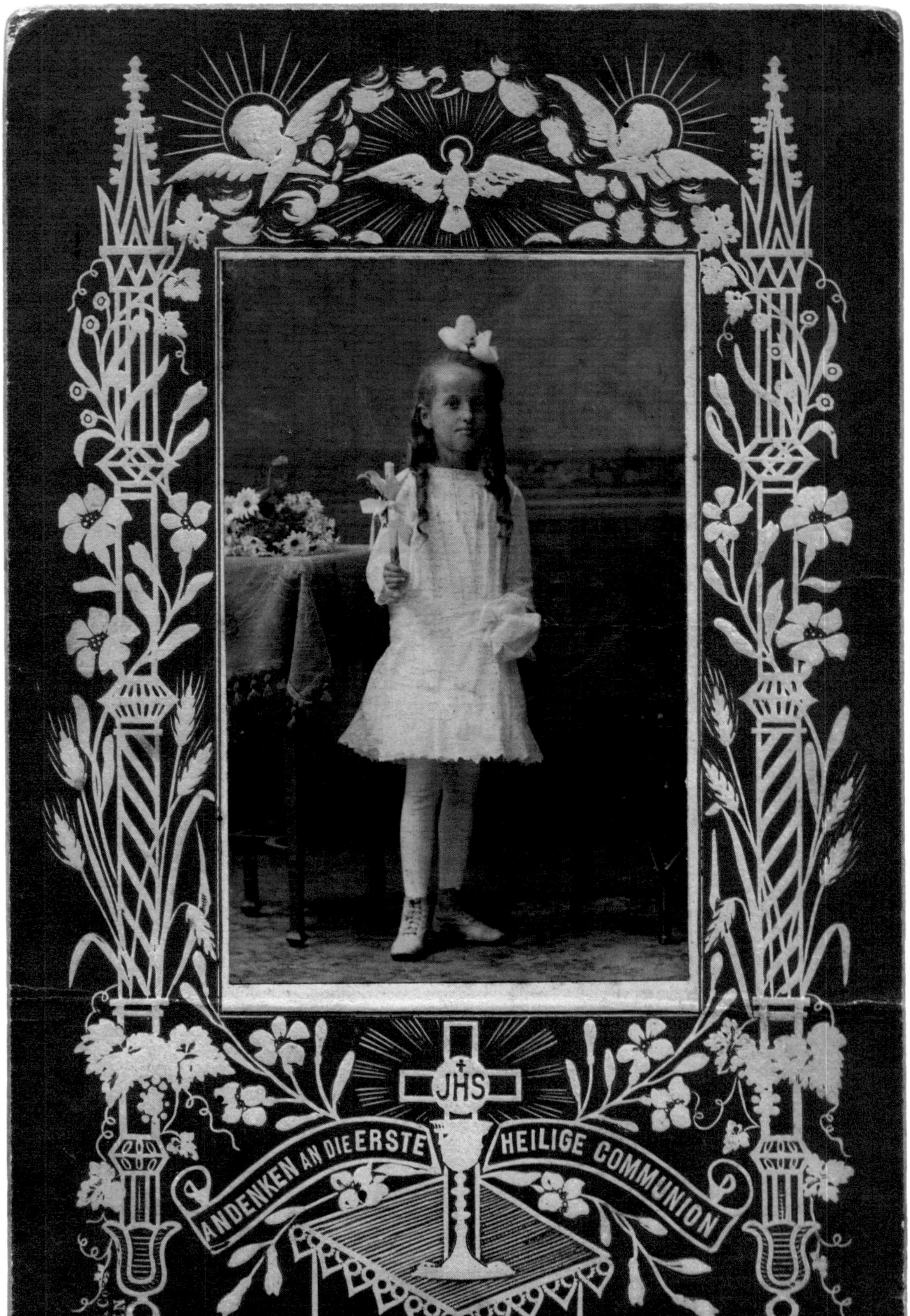
JHS
ANDENKEN AN DIE ERSTE HEILIGE COMMUNION

AFTERWORD

The red is more interesting – there's no red for the girls. You see, the red is the Sacred Heart; that's the symbolism.

Why don't the girls have red?

Not their role, is it? As far as the Church would see it. I mean there is this idea – which I don't support, clearly – that the woman's role is a mothering role, it's a servile role, it's a bride's role. Not to diminish the responsibility, but to define it. There is an idea that Our Lady is incredibly important: a channel for prayers and messages through to the number one man, in the way that, very often, kids will go to Mum to get to Dad. That was how it was presented to us: as somebody who was more approachable, somebody who was a human, who was a mother, who would listen and present your ideas in a way in which they would, perhaps, be heard.

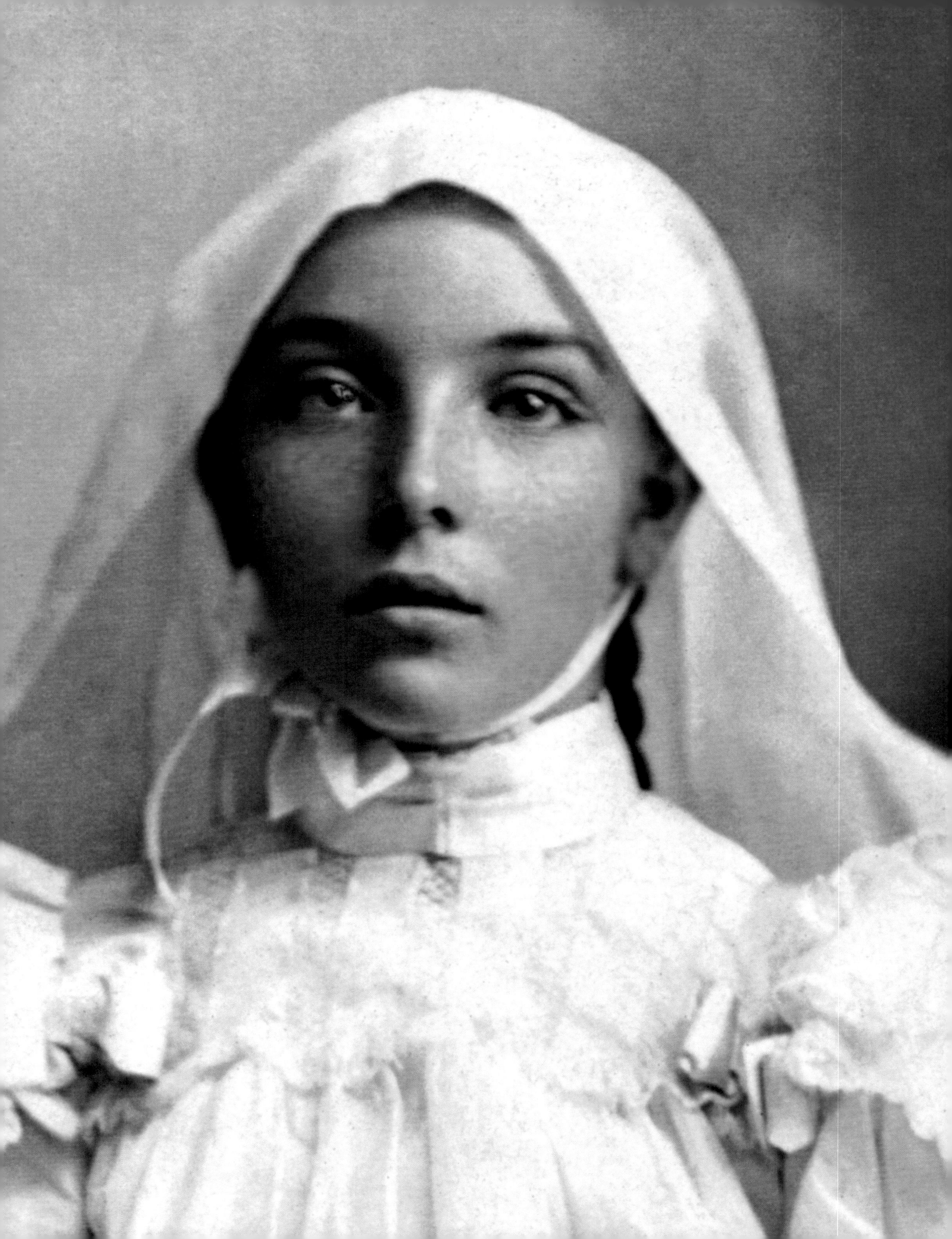

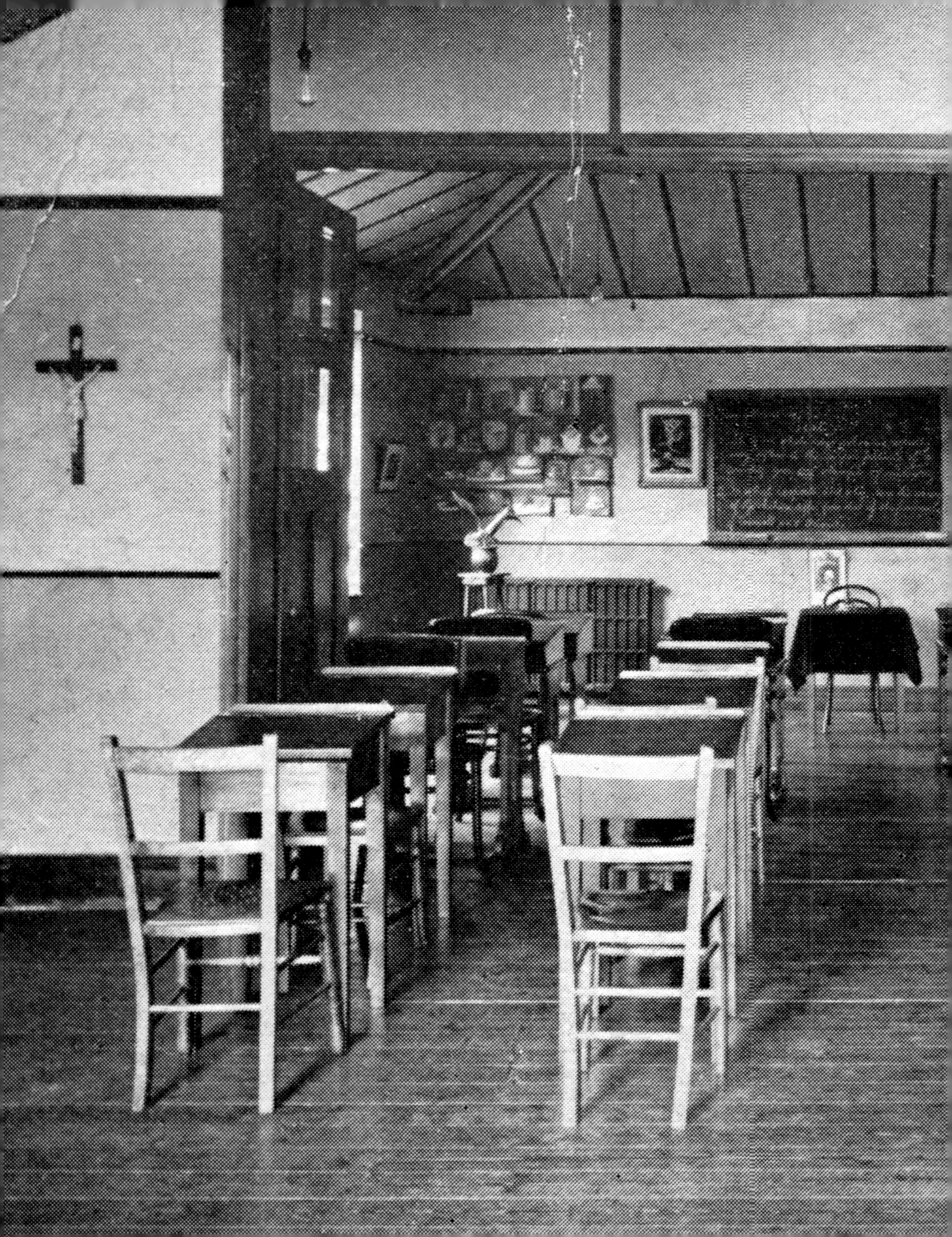

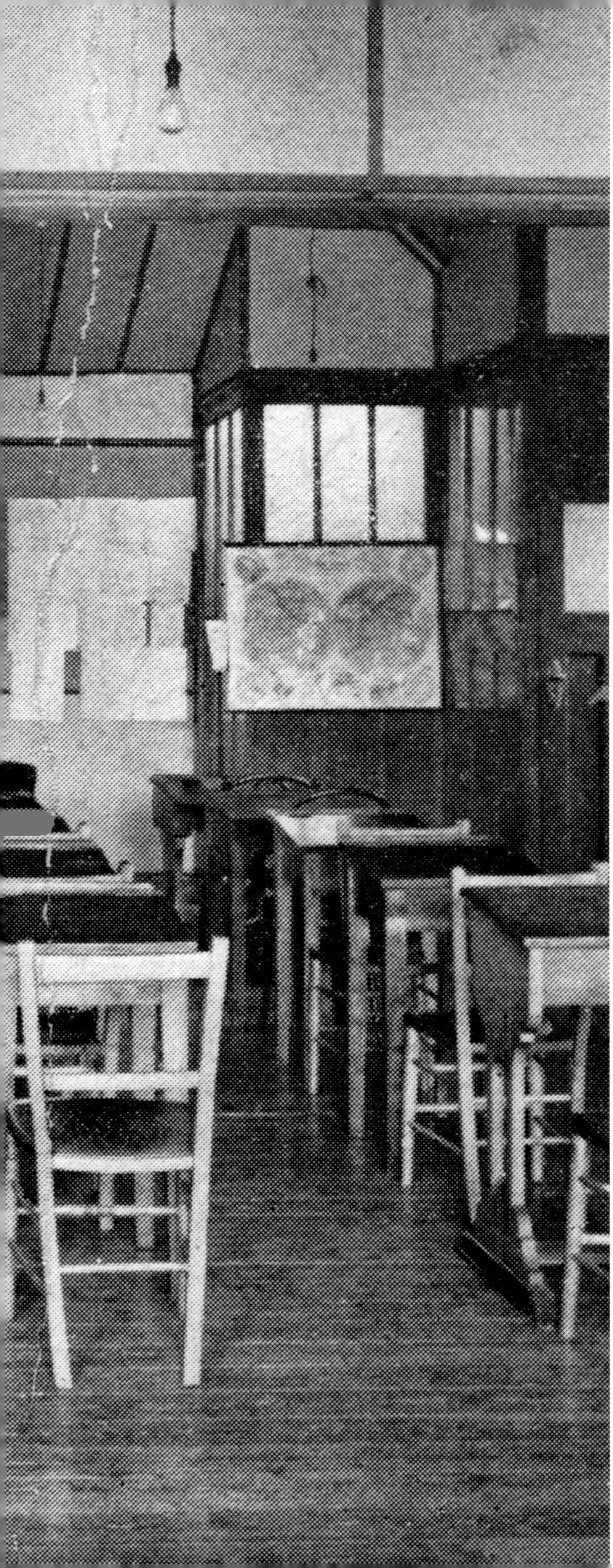

CONFESSORS

Roxanne Aldrich
Anna Bantick
Irma-Jane Caggiano
Olivia Marie Campos
Meinrad Craighead
Caroline Crawford
Adrianna Cruz
Dame Philippa Edwards OSB
Kathleen Godfrey
Emily Hick
Sue Hudson
Safeena Hutchison
Kim Nieve M. Larrichio
Jane Lee
Lucy McHugh
Maria Consuelo Moya-Keller
Irma Murillo
Jacqueline O'Driscoll
Renee Palyo
Kasia Politowicz
Jennifer Reddy
Cindy Rivas
Joan Robinson
Margaret Salter
Jageer Sandhu
Diane Luithly Sawatzke
Ruth Sheehy
Sister Catherine of Siena
Mary Snee
Mary Stockton-Smith
Maria Tannant
Elizabeth Verde
Suzanne Watson

ARCHIVAL MEMORIES – BETWEEN HISTORY AND EXPERIENCE

Margherita Sprio

In the film *Raining Stones* (1993), Ken Loach explores the complex anxieties experienced by the various family members when the daughter of the family is being prepared for her First Holy Communion. The devout father of the family, Bob (played by the actor Bruce Jones) goes to great lengths in order to gather the funds needed for the costly new Communion dress and the added accompaniments that make up the Holy Communion day. The daughter is the innocent onlooker, she bears witness to the parental struggles that can mark such occasions. This particular day remains special to the memory bank that stays with the Catholic daughter for life. The holy day acts as a backdrop to the poverty experienced by this particular Catholic community in the late 1980s in Britain. The out-of-work father is determined to buy his daughter a new Holy Communion dress rather than dress her in one previously worn (as suggested by his priest). We do not learn whether they are able to photograph the event – the narrative resolution is levelled at the emotional poverty of the environment and the roles that the various community members perform within it.

In a comparable way to the temporal image, photography requires performance, and the documenting of any family occasion is fraught with complexities. The occasion is experienced (and hence, remembered) in contradictory ways, by those who are being photographed. What are the photographs for? Who are they for? Colleen, the daughter in *Raining Stones*, is as excited about the prospect of dressing up as some of the daughters appear to be in the disregarded photographs collated here by Johnson. Equally, some of the narratives that accompany other photographs reveal contradictory voices to the smiling images that are being portrayed. Layered voices, our own, those performing within the photographs, those who took the photographs, those who disregarded the photographs (gave them to junk shops, threw them away, sold them) and then finally Johnson, who retrieved the photographs, are all present here.

The aura of shyness is visible as a constant within these images. In Walter Benjamin's essay, *A Short History of Photography*, written in 1931, the strange weaving of space and time, the unique appearance of a semblance of distance (no matter how close the object may be) is how to begin to understand the photographic aura.[1] The shy, childish faces in this work help to ask questions about the original photographer and the new viewing experience through Johnson's reconstruction. The aura of the spaces previously occupied by these photographs, both literal and metaphorical, is what gives this work (as a whole) its edge of melancholia. The sadness of time having passed, and of important moments rendered meaningless through the disregarding of the original photographs by their owners, adds sadness to an already performed world. Why were their owners prepared to give up on these photographs? What circumstances rendered it unnecessary to have these images around them? Unrecognised family members have been tossed aside; others have been digitised and made 'real' once more. That these same images can occupy such different marked spaces in their own right is what also gives Johnson's achievement here its prominence.

Although Johnson works with photographs that document the Holy Communion event for both sons and daughters, it is important to note that all of the written narratives that accompany the work are by daughters. The focus on the apparent bridal day operates at different levels for sons and daughters. The miniature wedding dress alludes to and colludes with specific sets of categorisation that remain with the child (of either gender) forever more. Additionally, all of the thirty-three confessors are daughters, and women feature in every one of the photographs (occasionally there is a lone male priest among the young girls, see for example p. 26; in other photographs, a brother accompanies the girl when it is also his own Holy Communion).

Professional photographers construct some of the photographs resurrected by Johnson, and it is starkly possible to see the tools of their trade (the studio set-up, the contrived backdrops, the posed expressions, the banal physical posturing). Others are staged differently and probably taken by familial, intimate hands (posed for in the street, outside family houses, inside poorly lit rooms). Era and consequences may change slightly in this archive of Holy Communion photographs but some distinctions remain. Aesthetic principals are consistent, whether the photographs have been created by an experienced hand or by one that is assumed to be more subjective. The focus can vary from first-person close-up (final image of the series), to the daughter being at mid-range and alone at the centre of the frame (for example on p. 161), to a distant group shot (such as p. 15). One thing that all the photographs make apparent is the detailing of the paraphernalia that accompanied the Holy Communion dress – the white veil, the white gloves, the white shoes, the white socks or tights, the white bag. Curiously, it is often only possible to tell the period of the photograph because of the technological advances evidenced within the photographs or by the clothing of the non-participants of the Holy Communion – most of the white dresses are remarkably similar.

As Annette Kuhn has argued about her own family photographs, photographs are evidence and in order to show you what they are evidence of, a photograph must always point you away from itself.[2] She continues, 'but the fact that we experience our memories as peculiarly our own sets up a tension between the "personal" moment of memory and the social moment of making memory, or memorising; and indicates that the process of making meaning and making memories are characterised by a certain fluidity'.[3] The photographs in this work operate between history and experience, and they provide a fluid and anonymous autobiography. Where once these images would have been displayed within the private location of home and other familial surroundings, their viewing is now held within an anonymous world. Despite this, what makes them so compelling? The sharp light that is shone upon those in white acts as a metaphor for the surveying, the witnessing that marks the Holy Communion day.

The confessors are divided into seven groups, each of which are enveloped within a particular thematic and continue for eighteen or more pages at a time. The first of these, 'Wash Me Clean from Every Stain of Sin', begins with an epic narrative image of a group of children caught off-guard while queuing to receive the holy bread; the stark shoulders complete with angel wings frames the right of the photograph. Partly evoking a possible still from a Pasolini film, such as the black-and-white *Mamma Roma* (1960), and also reminiscent of a moment possibly shared with those in the image, the photograph is more than a recorder of a Catholic ceremony. 'This Is My Body', the second part of the overall piece, is as with each of the seven sequences more easily narrativised via the accompanying 'confessions' than by the specifics of the photographs choreographed. 'I felt all day like a doll, which has just been taken out of its box with its beautiful white clothes; a bridal doll I suppose' (p. 54). The third of the sequences, 'Blot Out My Iniquity', begins with one of the most moving images from the whole work. A close-up portrait of a child looking passively away from the camera as she holds up for display her rosary beads at the centre of the frame. The performative nature of the photograph, her white-gloved hands clasped together in mock prayer, the cross of her rosary positioned so that the circularity of the fingertips is redrawn through the circular decorativeness of the actual beads, all highlight the innocence that is both lost and gained through the Holy Communion experience.

If photography confirms death then this is most evidenced in the work in the fourth sequencing of these photographs, 'Have a Foretaste of Heaven'. In this section there is an echo of Siegfried Kracauer's assertion that photographic production devastates the memory image.[4] Nameless daughters present themselves to be photographed, to perform a ritual that they themselves have little control over. As Colleen, the daughter in *Raining Stones*, is at the centre of a narrative that is more about the emotional poverty experienced by the world that surrounds her, so the images in this sequence frequent a world that is both lost and present to the contemporary sphere. The memory image that marks each of these works at both an individual and collective level leaves the viewer in a place of strangeness. Recognising the performative nature of an image such as that on p. 83, helps to foster an unease that is not easily digestible. The crinkled edges that help to date this image add to the deathly silence provoked by photographs of every form. The child stands in front of a statue of Christ whose hands are displayed outwards, while her white gloved hands cradle a candle. She stands to the right of the image so that the statue is given the central place in the frame. Her candle is tilted away from her face so that both faces (that of the statue and her own) are in full view. Her innocent smile is made complicated by the tilting of her left foot – how alone she stands, how recognisable is her strange white dress among the memory images that all recall the religious paraphernalia that surrounds her. Her facial expression is so very evocative of a thousand other photographs of children who have no control over the performed images that they are forced to take part in. Some of the other images that surround this one help to further emphasise this feeling of repetition and loss.

How do they do this? The silence in the image on p. 97 of the same sequence is disrupted by the testimonial of one of the confessors who compares the experience of the Holy Communion to that of other forms of meditation – 'where you have to empty your room, empty your mind, then hope for something else'. This work and its specific order of sequencing, enables another space to be constructed. The muteness of the photographs is disrupted by the accompanying texts; the oral narratives that are part of the over-arching photographic project that is *FEAST*. The embittered silence that is communicated via Colleen in *Raining Stones* is often present in these images – enragement often helps the daughters in the images come to life. In the same way that, despite its first impression for Benjamin Buchloh, in 'Gerhard Richter's Atlas': 'neither the private album of the amateur, nor the cumulative projects of documentary photography could identify the discursive order of this photographic collection'.[5]

The line of daughters dressed in white that opens this fifth section is enveloped by the harshness of the surrounding blackness. Within this section, 'From the Abyss of My Nothingness I Adore Thee', a more direct relationship between Johnson and Richter is made apparent. Both works establish 'a cultural model of probing the possibilities of historical memory'[6] and what it is that remains at stake once these images, once cherished, become disregarded. The artist's collecting (which continues[7]) of these disregarded photographs makes possible what once seemed impossible. A re-viewing of these photographs makes the viewer rethink the limits of photographic practice and its collation and archiving. What was once an intimate and hence important image of a Catholic rite of passage for any of the daughters in the images has now become an image for public consumption. The private moment of enragement for those being forced to perform in front of the camera has now become something once again cherished by the artist through this work.

The opening photograph that accompanies the sixth section, 'Print Deep in My Soul the Memory of Thy Bitter Pains', is one that shows a mother and daughter together. The bleached effect of the white dress is heightened by the serious and sensible nature of the dark coat worn by the adult. The bodies could easily have been superimposed next to one another, such is the harshness of the light source – one is forced to construct a narrative even when the actual relationship between the two women can never be known. This photograph makes visible Gillian Rose's assertion that the everlasting melancholia (that provides the framework for the postmodern era that was the twentieth century) accurately monitors the refusal to let go.[8] What she calls 'activity beyond activity'[9] is a useful way of engaging with Johnson's project as a whole and with this section in particular. The constant risk faced by positing and failing and positing again is present here – the work is audible and yet mute, it is mute and yet made audible.

In the seventh and final section, 'The Fruit of Each Mystery', a mute daughter poses alone in a garden; 'June 28 – 1939' is handwritten on the edge of her image. The sun is in her eyes, and like so many of the other daughters, she appears uncomfortable. Like the first photograph that opens this work, the final image in the Afterword leaves a haunted stain no matter how many times it is viewed and re-viewed. The pure white bow envelopes the pre-pubescent daughter's face and her sparkling eyes look beyond the viewer and into another world. A heavy, non-transparent head veil, additionally burdens the angelic tilting of the daughter's head, while also being reminiscent of Colleen's repetitive facial expressions in *Raining Stones*. How weighed down the daughter looks, how enraged by the demands of others – silence is the experience of space. Her lips are slightly parted as though she were wishing to speak – who could know what she would have wanted to say?

What Johnson has created here is supported by the Ricoeurian idea that the most valuable traces are those that were not intended for our information.[10] The known levels of critique applied to the found image, and those images that have previously been understood to be documenting an event remain at the level of involuntary testimony. But Johnson makes problematic the very notion of the testimony. The various types of testimonials or confessions made public in this work operate through and between the different voices that are being displayed both within and around the work. The work as gallery exhibit and the work as a book operate as diverse interchanges between then and now – time past/passed and present. The many Colleens, previously unnamed and newly christened, that appear in this archive, have been given a new and important airing in the world. Moments from other film stills collide with one's family-album pictures (not necessarily of Holy Communion ceremonies) and intermingle with reportage images, perhaps recognised from a multitude of other sources.

In Benjamin's seminal photographic essay (mentioned at the start of this piece[11]), he argues that every age has the passionate inclination of wanting to bring things closer to ourselves or to the masses – this is a useful idea in relation to the over-arching project that is *FEAST*. The more one scrutinises the individual images, the more one is left with the taste of a melancholic experience. The work as a whole acts a memorial to those past frozen moments, shown and re-shown to family, friends and other interested parties, that some time later pass into insignificance. The artist's decision to allow the viewer to get a closer look at the work, her re-creation of it in exhibition and book format, all make for an insightful journey. The question of the role of the historical document – how some images become more significant than others – acts as an entry point into the sadness of this journey.

The experience of each child and their frozen moment having been disregarded and once again re-regarded adds poignancy to this artwork that is very timely. What is the role of this kind of photographic experience in the digital age? The photographs in Johnson's work were printed and displayed – what of our digitised world? How might digitised images be consumed differently – how many of them are ever printed at all? What is perhaps most compelling about *FEAST* is that it marks a possible conclusion to an era when the image was invested with an aura that is not visible in the same way through the endless enhancements that are possible through digitisation. The faded appearance of some of the older images adds historical data to the anonymity of the original photograph (do others like it also exist and if so, why was this copy disregarded?). For Hal Foster the mega archive that is the internet is not necessarily the most appropriate place for archival art.[12] If this work could be labelled as 'archival art', what does its framing through this type of constructed reception (in book format) enable that would not otherwise be rendered possible?

The intimate reading of the body of photographs that is *FEAST* adopts the same coding of the First Communion book held in the hands of so many of the daughters in the photographs. The holy book and the rosary beads are symbols of Catholic consumption that are passed on to the child on the Holy Communion day. Together with the taking of the bread, these cultural markers make the ritual of communion taking (and the assumed maturity that accompanies the Holy Communion day) entangled with the memory of the first occasion. The first taking of the bread, after the first taking part of the confession establishes that the child is now part of a different world order. They are now different to their non-Catholic friends and different again to the child they once were. The shyness (about the rituals that accompany the Holy Communion day) is made apparent through the hands clasping the prayer book which we are being drawn to. As is apparent in the text that accompanies p. 154, the present-giving that is part of the occasion is mystifying to the child (it is neither their birthday or Christmas, but there is a party, a cake and usually plenty of food).

The child's reaction to being at the centre of attention for that day is pivotal to their subsequent memory of the occasion. Our own engagement with the work is specific to the faces we are never able to fully know. Questions of memory are historicised in a variety of forms – this work gives visual focus to identities that would otherwise have been lost or even destroyed forever. The constructions of identities that are deemed worthy of scrutiny are often privileged through the remaining remnant of lives once lived. Photographs, of course play a huge role in the constructions of these histories. The anonymous faces that formulate the many images within *FEAST* present us, the viewers, with questions that we cannot answer. We shall never know who these faces belonged to, what their names were and how their frozen moment became something to disregard. The quality of the re-displaying of this work asks further questions of photography (in the digital age) but little can be added about those who are performing in the images that we address.

For Nicholas Bourriaud this type of art is 'post-production'; the secondary manipulation that creates its very being is innately present in the work.[13] The visibility given to these faces has only been made possible through Johnson's intervention – her voice is of course, also present with those of the confessors. The unnamed faces remain locked in their anonymity until now, when we can at least restore them a place in our minds. The experience of the continual address now made possible through this 'post-produced' work gives it the authority that a disregarded set of photographs would not have had. Curiosity could have given way to disinterest in images already disregarded and here we are once more able to (continually) look. The (sacred) book format, the texts and the images – all lend an air of importance that is imperative to the original experience of the Holy Communion day. The authorial nature of the rituals rehearsed through the holy day are bound up in the consumption of its recording through the photograph – however, this authority escapes into anonymity through the passing of time. Once cherished, now these images are in need of artistic intervention to afford them restoration to their rightful place. Johnson has understood this and has incorporated questions of authority within the construction of both the images and the accompanying texts.

The re-working of the ready-made has a particular and special place in the world of artistic production and some of these histories are better known to us than others. This (personal) history, enveloped in anonymity – the familial resemblance that is coded in the knowledge held by our most immediate family members – is given visibility here. Equally, the many histories of news reportage come with an authority of purpose – one whose premise is too often not questioned. Family photographs came with no such authority – until now. Johnson's welding of identities from a range of eras, while enabling other kinds of voices to co-exist (via the oral narratives that accompany the images) re-figures the work in such a way that it is both part of us and outside of us. *FEAST* has the ability to wound us, to stay with us and to mark us forever. Barthes's idea that a photograph can wound us is made experiential in this work – his writings on photography and mourning are critical to an engagement with private photography (images from the family album) being made public.[14] His own writings about the experience of photography are, in part, through the creation of a memoir of the death of his mother.[15]

When this book is eventually closed, some of the questions *FEAST* evokes remain open. The photographs continue to haunt the onlooker in a similar way to the pained face of Colleen in *Raining Stones*, when she realises the pressures her parents are under in their attempts to ensure that she has a new Communion dress for her First Holy Communion day. The haunting associated with loss is present in all photography and its presence in those images intended for private consumption can make the viewer feel uncomfortable. The more one feels engaged with the level of intimacy demanded by this work, the more one's relationship with it feels disturbed. This disturbance operates at the level of the psychic as well as that of the physical. The ghosting of the present forces one to negotiate with the past, and *FEAST* is a living embodiment of how to experience mourning through the visual. To be visible is to be forever present – the confessors here live on in ways that would have been unimaginable to them. The indelible traces that leave the viewer once the work is away from the gaze live on in the space between history and experience. The non-authority originally experienced by the individual photographs is confronted by the collective endeavour that is made possible through this artistic practice. The newly constructed authority is made present in the rapport that one develops with the unnamed faces and the oral narratives that give structure to the images. The stories that literally surround the images help to evoke signification that might not otherwise be there – equally, the seven sequences give order to lives that might have, otherwise remained without it.

Margherita Sprio *completed her PhD at Goldsmiths College in 2004 and prior to this studied Fine Art at Goldsmiths and the Slade School of Art (both University of London). As well as her continued interest in art practice and theory, her research interests include diverse aspects of transnationalism and visual cultures with a particular focus on both experimental cinema and contemporary art. She is Scheme Director MA Art and Film in the Department of Art History and Theory at the University of Essex, UK.*

Notes

1 Walter Benjamin, reprinted in *Classic Essays on Photography*, ed. Alan Trachtenberg (New Haven, CT: Leete's Island Books, 1980).

2 Annette Kuhn, *Family Secrets, Acts of Memory and Imagination* (London: Verso, 1995, 2002), p. 13.

3 Ibid., p. 14.

4 See Siegfried Kracauer, 'Photography' (1927), in *The Mass Ornament: Weimar Essays*, ed. and trans, Thomas Y. Levin (Cambridge, MA: Harvard University Press, 2005).

5 Benjamin H. D. Buchloh, 'Gerhard Richter's Atlas: The Anomic Archive' (1993), in *Deep Storage*, ed. Ingrid Schaffner and Matthias Winzen (Munich and New York: Prestel, 1998).

6 A shorter version of the original essay is reprinted in *The Archive, Documents of Contemporary Art*, ed. Charles Merewether (London: Whitechapel Gallery; Cambridge, MA: MIT Press, 2006), p. 85.

7 Personal interview conducted with the artist Christy Johnson in London, 15 December 2006.

8 Gillian Rose, *Mourning Becomes the Law: Philosophy and Representation* (Cambridge: Cambridge University Press, 1996), p. 11.

9 Ibid., p. 13.

10 *Time and Narrative*, vol. 3, trans. Kathleen Blamey and David Pellauer (Chicago: University of Chicago Press, 1988), p. 117. English trans. of Paul Ricoeur, *Temps et recit*, vol. 3 (Paris: Editions du Seuil, 1978).

11 See n. 1 above.

12 Hal Foster, 'An Archival Impulse', *October*, 110 (Fall 2004), p. 21.

13 See Nicholas Bourriaud, *Postproduction: Culture as Screenplay: How Art Reprograms the World*, trans. Jeanine Herman (New York: Lukas and Sternberg, 2002).

14 See Roland Barthes, *Camera Lucida* (New York, Hill and Wang, 1981).

15 Ibid.

RETRIEVAL AND TRANSMITTAL IN A FICTIVE PHOTOGRAPHIC EXPERIENCE

Catherine Clinger

On the twenty-eighth day of May in 1894, an Italian photographer Secondo Pia saw a face at the bottom of his developing tray. Right before his eyes, the negative of a photograph of the Shroud of Turin was 'becoming' the indicator of a catastrophic holy event. In its state as the photographically conjured mirror image on ancient cloth, the death mask of Christ appeared through solarisation; converted into a picture of the negation of life as well as light. 'It tells nothing in itself about its origin', states Georges Didi-Huberman in his seminal article on the relic.[1] The critic claimed the shroud documented a trace; a subtle, but an undeniable physicality lending it a material legitimacy and, at the same time, destabilising the claim for miracle. Does Christy Johnson empower images through her digitisation of private memorials to perform similarly? Do the retrieved communion photographs of young Catholic females both document and dispute a holy occasion? One witness to Johnson's process of requisition of the recovered images might not think so, and I believe he was wrong.

'I need to get out of here', said the man fleeing the studio space whose walls displayed testimonials to a fictitious act of divine cannibalism (Fig. 1). It is difficult to imagine a man being so frightened of virgin brides of Christ that he would literally run up a flight of stairs in order to escape the presence of their inky stare. Even more perplexing is that the fearsome virgins, several long since departed, were digital prints from scanned images of found photographs. These powerful harpies are in long-term storage, their survival contingent upon the durability of the paper and dyes that accommodate them. The girls – dressed in white and wearing expressions of beatitude, fear or loathing – surely were unable to harm the man physically, although one supposes their recent feast upon the flesh of a man-god could explain the fleeing man's unfocused dread. Those

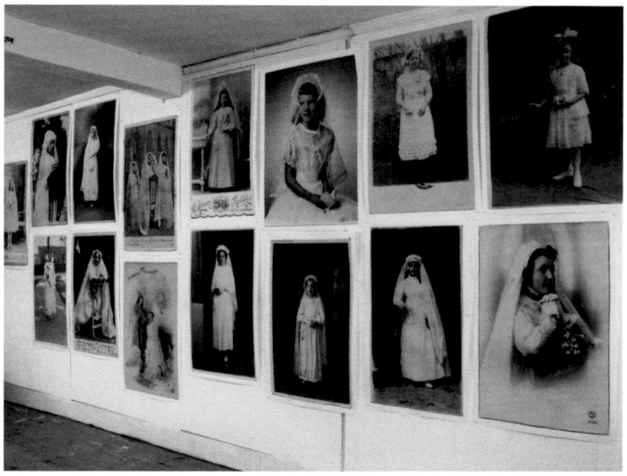

Fig. 1

subtle lips and the chaste intestines hidden under young skin (and doubly veiled by the ritual garment of First Communion) had recently received and digested flesh and blood. When the agitated man arrived in the living quarters at the top of the stairs, he registered his extreme reaction as the result of his rejection of their legitimacy as art objects. He did not admit to any anxiety other than that of aesthetic repulsion.

The setting for this gothic tale of monster virgins and cursory judgement was an artist's studio in Bethnal Green, London. Too bad the event wasn't captured on film, like the monsters, so that the recording could provide evidence for the theory that visceral social analysis tends to 'displace attention from the photograph itself'.[2] The original for each of the large digital prints was itself displaced. The images are only a few of the more than three hundred First Communion commemorative pictures collected by artist Christy Johnson. Presumably, most resided at one time in a family album or on a mantelpiece, then were passed down to heirs, discarded upon death, thrown away or sold, eventually finding their way to bins and boxes in markets, junk shops, antique and book stores in New

York, London, Paris, Rome, Prague, Berlin, Vienna, Los Angeles … and Santa Fe, New Mexico.

After meticulous archiving by the artist, the photographs were then matched with text generated from a series of interviews with thirty-three women ranging from the age of eight to eighty who had partaken of First Communion – the ultimate takeaway – an ecclesiolatric, mnemonic devotion consisting of the consumption of a son whose father had ritually sacrificed him. Through the miracle of Transubstantiation, his flesh and blood remain hidden in the form of a stale biscuit known as the Host. The Catholic dogma of the Real Presence advocates that Christ meta-spatially occupies the material substance of the bread. The Host consists of wheat flour and water that has been baked at 120°C by nuns on a flat iron pan, then steamed and cut into specified sizes using a stamping process. Despite the possibility of killing a member of the flock with a severe wheat allergy, the Vatican's Congregation for the Doctrine of the Faith in August 2004 made firm the requirement for the grain's inclusion in the communion host. On the Vatican's behalf, Father Williams stated, 'the church would not deliberately attempt to poison its communicant members' – although Father Tony Doherty of St Mary's Cathedral in Sydney, Australia suggested that 'the Vatican's instruction reflected a Latin-American mindset that considered gluten-free hosts an expression of *American excess*', thus signalling another dietetic rift in the international community.[3] Apparently the host production process is delicate – any sudden change in temperature will spoil the batch, so an infernal presence would likely not be welcome – hence, it is doubtful Father Doherty would be allowed into the wafer kitchen of a Carmelite convent in Guatemala.

The sacrilege of desecrating the unlikely Host of such a celebrated Guest is a major topic in the catechism preparing the youth for Communion. The ubiquitous anecdote of the over-heated or overly-excited child involuntarily heaving up the Host and the ensuing thrashing by a nun or priest as punishment for such a heinous act figures prominently in Catholic oral folklore. Contributing a more provocative yarn, one of the women interviewed by Johnson recollects a story invented during World War II that told of Nazi soldiers who entered a Catholic church and stomped on the Host resulting in a torrent of blood gushing out from under their boots – a malodorous reversal of the event in Genesis 3.14–15, a popular typological tale in fifteenth-century picture-books of the *Biblia Pauperum*, where the serpent who successfully tempted the Original Sinners was warned that it would be his head that found itself crushed under the heel of a woman. The implausibility of such phenomena must be hard for the priest to explain to a young child, 'when I say Body of Christ, don't think you're actually going to eat Jesus Christ's little finger'. The woman who recalled this pearl of priestly wisdom said she could not get that image out of her head. 'I was completely OK with the symbolism before he tried to dismantle it.'[4]

The re-enactment of the Last Supper before the mystical slaying is not the matter the children are supposed to focus on – instead they are to concentrate on the separation of the blood (wine) from the flesh (bread) that symbolises the sacrifice of the man-god. His death is equated with the liquidity of a spirit leaving a vessel. This action of haemorrhage is remedied by the provision of a new vessel, the communicant. By concentrating on the two materials rendered apart from one another, the supplicant performs a gastronomic remembrance of the physical form of the sacrifice. It wasn't the killing of the divine progeny by the Roman soldiers or asphyxiation on the cross; it was bucking up and swallowing his fate, his *surrender* to bloodletting, that is to be remembered by the child trying not to think of the wafer as Jesus' little finger. 'By the power of the Holy Spirit, the bread would turn into, symbolically and energetically, the Body of Christ … I do remember the three persons and all of that and just trying to, trying to grasp the concept of the Trinity. It blew the sockets in my brain. It was too big for me to understand, so you just sort of had to accept it.'[5]

In a rite of secular remembrance, the artist transcribed over one hundred and seventy-five pages of taped dialogue with the help of editor Victoria Millar of

Bloomsbury Publishing. When the two women sat down to edit the transcription, they re-enacted the interview, performing the dialogue together so as to reclaim the conversational quality of the discourse while they minimised the intervention of the interrogator and left the answers intact. They did not rewrite or remove anything from the responses except for the occasional 'h-mm' or pause for breath. No one put words into anyone's mouth ... except the interviewees themselves, who entered the photographs by way of a subversive dialectic structure, thus sanctioning the real experience of the repressed object in the image rather than subjecting herself and her chemically encapsulated counterpart once again to the fiction pictured by the surveillant authority. The mechanism for authority was the trade photographer who transubstantiated not the body of Christ but the virgin's spiritual passage to adulthood without tangible penetration by anything other than wheat, water and wine. He adopted the role of the priest in his quest to materialise the spiritual in a fabricated after-glow following her opening act of ritualised anthropophagy. Strangers to one another, interviewee and pictured communicant unwittingly conspired to create an authentic fictional state through the fusion of a factual document with a true story. Johnson assembled these two distinct archives into the artist's book *FEAST* and, together they tell a multifarious tale of seduction, revulsion and redemption.

Returning to the Shroud of Turin ... the image of the Christ countenance was created, as the story goes, through direct physical contact. It is, in a sense, the negation of the iconic through touch. Secondo Pia's photograph of the Shroud is only a document; the image provides proof of touch. In anthropological science, evidence is sought to support or document cultural practice – and in Western tradition, it is the archive that substitutes for the real subject. Rejecting the 1980s model of the objective archivist/anthropologist artist (over-used to the point of pointlessness in the 1990s), Johnson commandeered these commemorative documents and refused to dismiss them as afterthoughts. In *Camera Lucida*, Roland Barthes declares that the 'death of the subject' is evidenced in objective studio portrait photography, where the photographer is absent as narrator and the subject is recorded without symbolic value.[6] In the *FEAST* project, the narrator, 'nobody', is resurrected as 'somebody' in the text of memories. Johnson's reinstatement of irony in the act of appropriation, in a sense, restores subjectivity to its rightful place in structured arrangements that are 'firmly embedded in the particular and the real rather than the universal and symbolic'.[7] Her gesture of exposure, however, is a Romantic trope not an anthropological one, thus the particular becomes peculiar and the real, imaginary. In Johnson's method of fieldwork, the subject of the photograph is not interviewed and, the interviewee is not photographed. This would not please Margaret Mead who said the best method for telling others' stories was to accompany the text with a picture or film of the actual narrator.[8] Michael Taussig suggests that most ethnography tells other peoples' stories rather badly and *FEAST* steers clear of this methodological blunder.[9]

As evidenced by the reaction of the man in the studio space, however, clearly this was not a Boltanskian site for shared collective memory. Unlike an exhibition of private materials by Christian Boltanski, a self-styled recycler artist, the *FEAST* project does not try to 'create democratic kinds of cultural identification' (pp. 150–1).[10] Johnson did not show the interviewees the First Communion pictures. They were not reacting to, or identifying with anything other than their own experiences. The women interviewed – American, Colombian, East Indian, English, Irish, Italian, Mexican, Polish and South African – were humorous as well as reflective. The photographs can be amusing too. On pp. 58–9 of *FEAST*, I am certain that we are looking at Björk at the opening ceremony of the 2004 Summer Olympics in Athens, who tells us, 'It's a funny affair this Communion thing because first of all you stand outside of yourself and examine your conscience, as Marcus Aurelius did, like a Roman general, and then the next day you turn up like a Baroque marshmallow.'[11] Sometimes the comedy is disconcerting, 'Getting seven-year-olds to examine their conscience must be kind of funny. You had a list of sins and you asked yourself

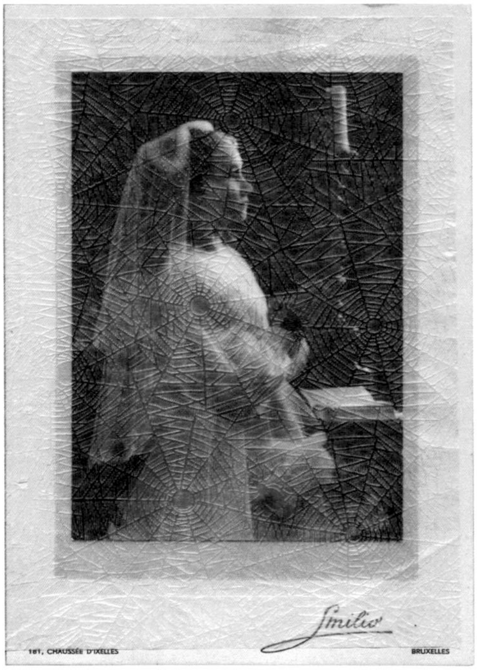

Fig. 2

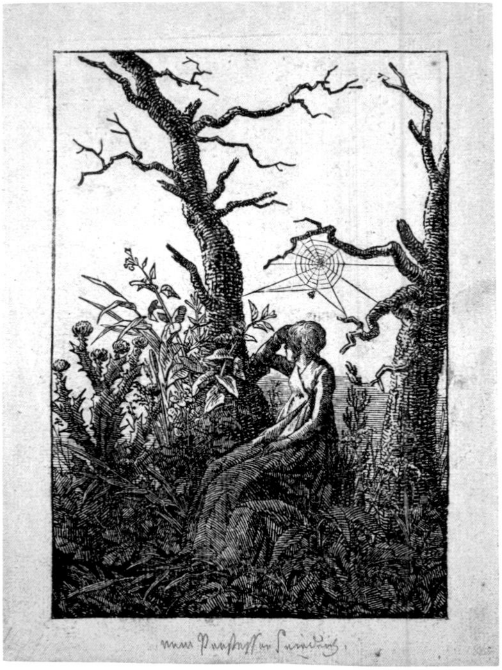

Fig. 3 bpk/Hamburger Kunsthalle Photo: Elke Walford

whether you'd committed any of these. Of course you were horrified to find that, because the list had been specially prepared for seven-year-olds, you'd committed all of them.'[12] It was not until 1910, when the age was lowered to seven years old, that the Church allowed children younger than twelve to attend First Communion. In France, employers required proof of this rite of passage to adulthood and one must worry why the age limit was lowered.[13]

Johnson's treatment of the transition from childhood to adulthood through the socially identified circumstance of a shared meal in a religious context is without guile. Her engagement with the text and image is skilful, yet she does not attempt to construct a narrative out of some covert, postmodern position. However, there is a theoretical attitude embedded in the work. Johnson insists on the priority of seeing the subjects as autonomous beings, in the spirit of Adorno's *Sache* and in the process of cultural reformation through a dialectic structure.[14] The theorist Baudrillard committed the blunder – which a theorist sometimes does in order to make his or her theory more plausible – of distorting the character of an image through dislocation. In *FEAST,* there is dislocation, however, distortion is absent. The historian of photography, Geoffrey Batchen, states notably that 'we need to invent a way of dealing with the photographs that emulates its own way of being, that acknowledges rather than represses photography's particular qualities and characteristics'.[15] The photograph of the Shroud allows us to discern, sift and decide what it is that happened. Its particular quality of detail is a commemoration that acts as an anthropologist would – archiving the event through documentation. By combining the archive of commemorative images with one of text shaped by interviews with invisible communicants, Christy Johnson invents a fictive location of experience and memory – a buffered space that shields the girls and the women from the social, religious and familial forces.

Children did not always go to First Communion with the full blessings of the parents. Communist party members in Italy who rejected Catholic principles still allowed their children to participate in communal rites of passage; they tried to supply new ones in the 1950s but failed.[16] The French Socialists came closer to relinquishing the symbolic rituals so beloved by them. Early in the century, they invented a new holiday to replace Whitsunday, a favourite time for the Communion ceremony, with the 'Feast of Reason' substituting a diet of knowledge for the consumption of a deity. In Paris, the hostility towards the Church had grown to the extent that the tone was 'the worst it had been in twenty-five years' and this is supported by the author of an 1904 article in *The American Journal of Theology* (he asked then that his name be withheld), who stated that 'clergymen are treated as rebels and their monks and nuns as outlaws'.[17] The abuses of the Church in 1904 were seen as universal not personal. Citizens of France in the first quarter of the century objected to the moral education of children in the guise of secular pedagogy. In the late twentieth century, the laity's hostility developed out of reports that aberrant priests were providing a less sacred lesson for their young flock.

Often, the *FEAST* images are starkly beautiful, and one cannot help but to fall in love with some of the young women who appear haunted, noble, pure or immensely happy. A number of the ephemera are beautiful as objects and they evoke memories of other works on paper, such as the image with a faux spider-web treatment on the gossamer overleaf protecting the photograph's surface (Fig. 2). The network of lines reminds one at once of Odilon Redon's *Reader of the Ramayana* (1869) or the melancholic woodcut of Caspar David Friedrich's *Woman beneath the Web* (Fig.3). Some Church Fathers have used the spider's web as a metaphor for their descriptions of the doctrine of Emanation; the word from the Latin *emanare*, 'to flow from'. The image of water from a spring and light from the sun have been used to describe the doctrine; however, use of the spider's web as an example is unique in that the emanation produces a dwelling at best and, at worst, a deadly snare. The Fourth Lateran Council in 1215 roundly condemned the doctrine of Emanation. At the same time, they took care of other business such as confirming the requirement of Jews and Muslims to wear special dress

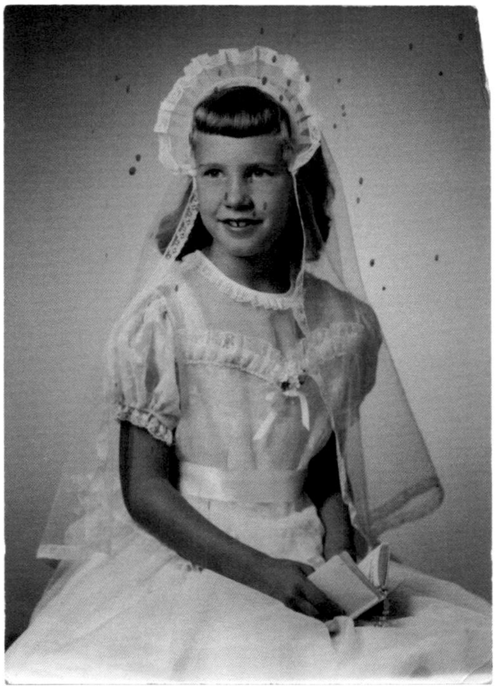

Fig.4

in order to distinguish them from Christians (Canons 78 and 79) and, creating the rules of engagement for the anticipated crusades to follow.[18] Emanation was seen as an excessively mystical metaphor that could interfere with both exclusionary and expansionist agendas.

Needless to say, the doctrine of Emanation (giving off) is not taught in the catechism, only the idea of consumption (taking in) of a man-god's flesh and blood through remembrance (giving in). In *Moses and Monotheism* (1939), Sigmund Freud believed the consumption of the son gave rise to the consciousness of guilt prevalent in Christianised Europe; though it didn't seem to prevent events that should have warranted remorse. 'I remember something about them telling us that our soul – was it our soul? Yeah, it was – was like this white mass … with lots of little black dots on, which were the sins. And there was always loads of black and you had to try and get rid of all the black' (Fig.4).[19]

Avicenna, the Persian philosopher/physician, celebrated the release of the Soul in his *Treatise of the Bird (Risâlat at-Tair)*.[20] His story tells of doves who, when ensnared by hunters, grow complaisant in captivity until a few succeed in escaping the net and the others long to follow. The story is an allegory for the soul's (the spiritual world) containment in the body (the material world). It is the remembrance of the protected park (heaven) that invests the bird with the longing to ascend and eschew captivity. Avicenna states that the gain of metaphysical knowledge reminds the soul of its origin and longing signals its desire to return to the Godhead. This early Islamic idea differs radically from the Christian Doctrine of Original Sin that was generated from the famed consumption of fruit from the Tree of Knowledge. Guilt is not associated with the ingestion of knowledge according to Avicenna. It is in the abuse of intelligence that Avicenna finds fault. 'It's used for weddings, first communions, baptisms, you know, very special occasions. So, she made me that cake and then she made a birdhouse out of sugar … It looked like lace, the little birdhouse. And it had little doves going in and out … A complete birdhouse, because you're receiving a form of the Holy Spirit when you do your First Communion. Everything with religion for me is like the white bird, you know: peaceful, pure, white.'[21] Christy Johnson's *FEAST* is a birdhouse that doesn't ensnare the doves – rather it releases them. Too bad the man running up the stairs was afraid of birds.

Catherine Clinger *is an artist/scholar living in London. Her work has been exhibited in North America and Europe. She recently completed her PhD at University College London, History of Art. Her research interests are German Romanticism, the History of the Print in Northern Europe, and representations of subterranea.*

Notes

1 Georges Didi-Huberman, 'The Index of the Absent Wound (Monograph on a Stain)', *October*, 29 (Summer 1984), pp. 63–81.

2 Geoffrey Batchen, *Burning with Desire* (Cambridge: MIT Press, 1997), p. 10.

3 Barney Zwartz, 'Wafers must have wheat, says Vatican', *The Age*, 20 August 2004.

4 Christy Johnson, see p. 88 of this volume.

5 Ibid., p. 86.

6 Barthes suggests photography suppresses narration. However, Baudrillard claims that historical photographs like historical objects function only to suppress time. He also argues that collecting such objects is too concrete and discontinuous for the collection to create texts, that they can only be possessed. See Jean Baudrillard, *System of Objects*, trans. James Benedict (London: Verso, 1996), p. 106.

7 Sheryl Conkelton, 'The Deceptive Play of the Individual, or In the Archive', in *Deep Storage*, ed. Ingrid Schaffner and Mätthias Winzen (Munich and New York: Prestel, 1998).

8 Margaret Mead, 'Visual Anthropology in a Discipline of Words', in *Principles of Visual Anthropology*, ed. Paul Hockings (The Hague: Mouton, 1975).

9 Michael Taussig, from author's notes at *Fieldworks*, a symposium at the Tate Modern, London, 27 September 2003.

10 Rebecca J. DeRoo, 'Christian Boltanski's Memory Images: Remaking French Museums in the Aftermath of '68', *Oxford Art Journal*, 27, 2 (2004), pp. 219–38. See also Didier Semin, Donald Kuspit and Tamar Garb, *Christian Boltanski* (London: Phaidon, 1997).

11 Christy Johnson, see p. 59 of this volume.

12 Ibid., p. 64.

13 Ralph Gibson, *A Social History of French Catholicism 1789–1914* (New York: Routledge, 1979), p. 165.

14 Theodor Adorno, *Negative Dialectics*, trans. E. B. Ashton (New York: Routledge, 1973), p. 144. Baudrillard uses visual representations accompanied by discursive verbal texts to give an account of postmodern uses of the photograph.

15 Geoffrey Batchen quoted in Brian Dillon, 'Forget Me Not: An Interview with Geoffrey Batchen', *Cabinet*, 14 (Summer 2004), pp. 40–2.

16 David I. Kertzer, 'The Liberation of Evelina Zaghi: The Life of an Italian Communist', *Signs*, 8, 1 (Autumn 1982), pp. 45–67.

17 A. G. B., 'The Religious Situation in Paris (July–August 1903)', *The American Journal of Theology*, 8, 1 (January 1904), p. 1.

18 *Sources of Catholic Dogma*, trans. Heinrich Denzinger (St Louis, MO: Herder, 1957). English trans. of Roy Deferrari, *Enchiridion Symbolorum et Definitionum* (Würzburg: Sumptibus Stahelianis, 1854).

19 Christy Johnson, see p. 31 of this volume.

20 Abu Ali al-Husain ibn Abdallah ibn Sina (973–1037), one of the leading philosophers of the golden age of Islamic tradition was born in present-day Uzbekistan and died in his adopted Persia (Iran). His influence on intellectual thought was immense, from Thomas Aquinas to Spinoza. He was a master of mathematics, physics and medical science. His treatises on the Soul and Love are among the most beautiful of philosophical texts.

21 Christy Johnson, see pp. 174–5 of this volume.

ALL IN WHITE FOR THE FEAST: WHITENESS IN THE CHRISTIAN IMAGINARY

Jenny Daggers

> The Mass is a dramatic performance that is at one and the same time an incarnation, a crucifixion, a resurrection, a birth, a wedding and a feast.[1]

Christy Johnson's *FEAST* is rich fare indeed. Clinger's intriguing musings reflect on photographs of First Communicants, which she perceives as being divested of their symbolic value through their relocation by Johnson in the discursive site of *FEAST*. In contrast, this essay reappropriates both images and text for the Christian imaginary, and enquires of their symbolism in that context.

Johnson's *FEAST* is an abundant panorama of symbolism and imagery associated with the liturgical event of Catholic First Communion. An over-riding impression, on viewing images and reading text, is of whiteness. Adolescent girls, in the older images, are succeeded by little girls of six to eight years, all caught by the camera in their dresses of white. Some wear veils, some carry lighted candles, others are set against an arrangement of flowers, often white lilies. One figure attracts my gaze – a white girl dressed in white with both lighted candle and lilies (p. 163). A text catches my attention – the recounted experience of a girl, her photograph an epiphany of herself as a single brown face immersed in white veils, dresses and faces: this sole black witness tells of how odd she felt to be 'the only little brown face stuck in a sea of white faces'. After fasting to cleanse body and soul her thought was 'Well, I haven't changed colour so I can't be pure'. She, with her brown mum and white dad, had never before seen herself 'as a colour' (p. 27).

Her transgression of normative whiteness is reflected in only two images and one other confession within the entire collection: here the colour symbolism is ambiguous – a black girl in a white dress ... boys of colour, some in frilly white shirts (p. 70); there the confessor remembers being called 'La Negrita Consentita' by her grandmother; 'I was the favourite grandchild ... And I think it had to do with being the darkest one'; the confession perfectly matched by the image (p. 28). But these instances disturb an otherwise consistent gender symbolism: (white) girl in white dress; (white) boy in black.

One confessor remembers being told the soul was like a white mass, covered in black dots – your sins – which you must eradicate (p. 31); just as the perfect dress must remain unmarked, and unspoilt. Another tells how the whiteness of the lily or dress 'always signifies purity' (p. 15). Yet another speaks of feeling cleansed that day (p. 25). On the one hand, the flowers were themselves symbolic of the child in white: 'you were an angel, a flower' (p. 108). On the other, the imagery blends the poetry of the late Franciscan saints, where flowers fall from heaven, lilies and roses, with the pagan spring rituals of the May Queen, taken up into mariological May celebrations – 'Oh Mary we crown thee with blossoms today' – the wearing of white at Whit festivals, all associated with the young girl in her dress. This voice confirms the link between the First Communicant's dress, and the white dress already worn in the Whit procession (pp. 110–11).

Another confession discloses the subject's naive attempt at living her married life in the image of the Virgin: 'When I first got married, I thought I had to be pure, just like Mary. I didn't think sex was part of marriage ... I wanted to be just like her' (p. 52). Yet another voice established the link between the First Communion dress and the white wedding dress: 'it's something about the significance of white that happens again when you get married ... whether it's the lily or the dress or whatever, it always signifies purity (p. 15)'. The wedding symbolism is powerfully present in one (com)posed studio photograph: First Communicant girl and boy stand alongside, facing the camera, each holding candle and book; she in white, he in black. But, between them and behind, is an altar with the figures of Mary and Jesus, placed either side of a crucifix. The wedding trope is thus interrupted, by the Mother–Son relationship binding Second Eve with Second Adam (p. 102).

As with the slide from Franciscan to pagan imagery, the bridal references slip into other meanings, crossing and recrossing the boundaries of a distinctive Christian imaginary. For the little girl drawn into romantic dressing up, 'there's a slightly bridal thing, but also a sort of princess thing, you know ... being really special' (p. 48). And again, 'the bridal thing' but also 'a sacrificial lamb thing as well, because lambs are white and fluffy and you're going up to eat the Lamb of God' (p. 117).

Then a different genre of bridal imagery appears, steeped in the mystical tradition, where the bridal experience is infused with St Teresa of Avila's breast pierced by the shaft of burning love, a kind of eroticism where celibate nuns keep themselves for Jesus, spousa and spouse. 'There's something erotic in terms of the look – the gaze' (p. 118). Here the little girl is the 'archetypal spousa', 'the image of the purity of the soul' (p. 121).

An altogether different kind of slippage is evident in the reflection: 'this row of very pretty little brides ... looked so good in that dark, ecclesiastical kind of way ... there is that kind of slightly sado-erotic-y sexual thing of a woman in white in a dark, dark space. Strange' (p. 117). One commented that the religious experience, the church, the confessional, is dark (p. 65), whereas for another religion is 'peaceful, pure, white' (p. 174).

Entwined in image and text, and deeply embedded in the Christian imaginary, lie over-determined Eurocentric notions of whiteness in relation to purity, sexuality and the continuing discourse of 'race', these three being themselves entangled. The Platonic binary, light and dark, with light as the superior, elevated term, informs the binary white and black of the self-confident racial discourse arising from the nineteenth-century colonial heyday. Notions of purity are already implicated here, as epitomised in the imagery of whiteness and purity associated with the marketing of cleansing products, where the inferior black body was portrayed as scrubbed 'white' and therefore clean.[2] Sexuality also already animates this racialised binary.

According to Alistair Bonnett, as early as the period 1890 to 1930, white self-confidence was giving way to white crisis, evident in a growing literature attempting to defend and affirm white identity.[3] In contrast, a renewed discourse of 'whiteness' in the final decade of the twentieth-century again attempts to problematise whiteness as the unmarked norm, or, as Mason Boyd Stokes puts it, to place critical emphasis on whiteness 'as a form of textual, political and sexual anxiety'.[4] Despite the focus of both early and late twentieth century discourses on (differently perceived) problematics of 'race', entwining of purity issues and questions of sexuality with anxieties around whiteness is palpable. Thus, for Stokes, whiteness is situated 'within a larger system of oppressive and normalizing structures',[5] with heterosexuality being the main ally in its normalising mission. Richard Dyer makes a stronger case for heterosexuality as 'the cradle of whiteness',[6] with concepts of race being 'always concepts of the body and of heterosexuality'.[7] Stokes points out the 'amalgamationist terror' evident in nineteenth-century racial theory, and explores the way in which white women become silent markers in the homosocial systems of exchange that produce both whiteness and heterosexuality as cultural givens.[8] Women's subjectivity is severely curtailed by their location in this masculine white supremacist and heterosexual symbolic order.

Stokes focuses attention on the significance of the shift from 'reproduction-based' to 'pleasure-based' heterosexuality, wherein heterosexuality is simultaneously the means of ensuring, and the site of endangering, the reproduction of 'racial' difference.[9] A slogan adopted in 1885 by the Women's Christian

Temperance Union, in the US, exemplifies not only this relation between whiteness and heterosexuality, but also whiteness as a symbol of Purity. As D'Emilio and Freedman point out, the slogan, 'The White Life for Two' signals the centrality of heterosexuality to maintaining both the white race, and a white – in the sense of pure – morality.[10] Yet racist fears of 'amalgamation' highlight the fact that 'to reproduce whiteness sexually is to risk contamination', and thus, paradoxically, homoeroticism becomes the only structure of desire that can be sure to keep whiteness white.[11]

There have been historical moments when the Christian imaginary has been seduced by racial theory, and annexed to the racist cause. Toni Morrison perceives an unacknowledged, but never silent, Africanist presence, or blackness, as underpinning the [American] white literary imagination of freedom, autonomy and individualism.[12] Stokes examines nineteenth-century racist renderings of the Eden Genesis myth, and concludes, in the light of Morrison's insight, that retellings of the Eden mythos, which portray a black tempter in the garden, are central to the American imagination.[13] The history of apartheid in South Africa is a second example of racist appropriation of Christian imagery, also now discredited.

A welcome counterbalance is supplied by Brigalia Bam's figuration of the 'Mitochondrial Eve' as the black woman of Africa, common mother of the human race.[14] Here humanity's debt to blackness is made explicit in figuring the mother of the race as black, in contrast with the amalgamationist horror of the pure, white Eve, in danger of contamination by the black tempter. Here, too, the white–black binary relation is subverted.

As David Roediger puts it, whiteness is the 'terrifying attempt to build an identity based on what one isn't and on whom one can hold back'.[15] White symbolises the light, and black the dark: light, white and sacred stand over against dark, black and the profane. It is clear that Christianity has been implicated in the binary of light and dark, as it has informed normative whiteness, heterosexuality and purity. Under the conditions of late modernity, the binary relation between light and dark, man and woman, pure and impure dissolves, allowing us to glimpse new possibilities in relationality and therefore in subjectivity. Is Christ, the light of the world, locked within this crumbling binary?

Peter McGrail, in his study of First Communion, investigates the way in which 'the community's self-understanding, and its concerns, filter through the highly permeable boundaries of the ritual and become embedded in the event'.[16] McGrail examines the competing discourses dispersed within the discursive space of the First Communion ritual.[17] Traditional ecclesiastical discourse demonstrates anxiety over the potentiality for a sacrilegious First Communion. An example of this anxiety is the cautionary tale rendered by Mary Loyola, in 1896. A girl eats a chocolate on her way to First Communion; ignoring warnings from her guardian angel, she approaches the communion rail 'in her white dress, her white veil and her wreath … her soul dead in that whited sepulchre'.[18]

However, McGrail argues that 'the broad range of mortal sins found in the early texts is … reduced to a single focus upon sexual fallibility',[19] providing the impetus for the *Quam Singulari* reform of 1910 'to permit the reduction in age that guaranteed innocence'.[20] As McGrail demonstrates, even as Catholic primary school children in the 1990s are taught that light and a new garment are symbols of initiation into the faith,[21] the reality for many who take part in the First Communion is that this is an elaborate social, as opposed to religious ritual. Thus a mother, herself never married, inducts her young daughter into womanhood through the wearing of a substitute wedding dress that she, the mother, has never worn.[22]

McGrail's study can be read as a document of the decline in the power of the Catholic imaginary, as given expression in the Mass, to capture the imagination of contemporary Catholics undergoing the formal process of induction into the faith. But, elsewhere, the conditions of late modernity are bringing about imaginative refigurations of Catholic sacramentality.

Morrison's identification of the black surrogacy that underpins the white literary imagination, is reminiscent of the insights of both Luce Irigaray and Julia Kristeva in recognising the unacknowledged cultural debt to the mother in a social order founded on matricide (Irigaray), and the secret, or phallic, mother (Kristeva). Kristeva's work elucidates my use of the terms 'imagination' and 'imaginary'. In suggesting that the psychoanalytic subject be understood as a 'work in progress', Kristeva, recommends imaginary, imaginative speaking and writing to support this fluidity of identity.[23] Though pessimistic about the possibility of feminine subjectivity, Kristeva is clear that 'in the imaginary, maternal continuity is what guarantees identity'. The imagination of the work of art is an inhuman substitution for the continuing, yet unacknowledged, dependence of the (now adult) child upon the mother: this sublimation is constructed upon the secret mother.[24] The subject participating in Christian liturgy may be seen as such a 'work in progress', if symbol and liturgical performance are situated in place of Kristeva's 'art'.

Kristeva's pessimism over the prospects of women's subjectivity contrasts with Melissa Raphael's thealogical perspective.[25] Raphael's project is the redrawing of boundaries between the sacred and profane, by means of the feminist spirituality associated with the Goddess. As Cynthia Eller puts it, this feminist religion sets out to 'glory in femaleness, to proclaim the spiritual potential inherent in womanhood, to take the "weak vessel" of Christianity and make her the holy chalice of the great goddess'.[26] Where disenchanted nature and *de*sacralised woman are profaned by patriarchal order, feminist goddess spirituality, centred on the Goddess who is holy, *re*sacralises woman and the earth. (Sacred-profane boundaries are redrawn, rather than abolished, so that, for example, holy war is perceived as profane).[27] Significantly, Raphael refers to the 'maternal' dissolution of boundaries separating powerful patriarchal subject, and powerless natural or female object, within the patriarchal sacred/profane dualism.[28] Thealogical resacralisation, in a recreative act, restores life where patriarchy has desecrated and profaned.[29]

Connecting these insights to the practice of Christian liturgy, patriarchal Christianity can be seen to rest on the unacknowledged debt to the murdered (secret) mother, just as Morrison perceives the white literary imagination to rest on unacknowledged Africanist presence. As the Church building rests on foundations dug deep into mother earth, so the sublimation in the patriarchal Christian imaginary, expressed in liturgy and symbol, is constructed upon the secret mother.

Kristeva's dolorous 'Stabat Mater' sites the Virgin Mary as the phallic mother, whose own subjectivity is sacrificed to the boundary role she performs in underwriting the entry of the (male) child into the symbolic order. *FEAST*'s images are redolent of Mary. Our Lady as channel for prayers and messages to God, 'the number one man' (p. 178) to whom Hail Marys were addressed as penance – an extra five to an eight-year-old for her lies in confessing to adultery (p. 69). 'Oh Mary we crown thee with blossoms today' (p. 111), white lilies and roses, for Mary, the mystic rose. As Tina Beattie reminds us, 'The rose, symbol of love and fertility, of mysticism and the Virgin Mary, is also a symbol of the female genitals.'[30] Can those be *red* roses among the white, below the white lilies and the lighted candle held before them by the little girl (p. 163)? Has the colour of the Sacred Heart – 'there's no red for girls' (p. 178) – seeped into the sepia, to confuse the gendered imagery?

Beattie offers a feminist reading of Hans Urs von Balthasar's voluptuous neo-orthodox masculine imaginary, wherein the Church is both 'cosmic Mother and the holy heart'.[31] Her project is one of 'sacramental transfiguration'[32] wherein the female body, and thus female sexuality, are returned to the scene of salvation,[33] through their symbolisation in 'a maternal, Marian sacramental priesthood'.[34] If, in the words of Pope John Paul II 'At the root of the Eucharist ... there is the virginal and maternal life of Mary',[35] then von Balthasar's notion, that 'Mary surrenders her identity to Christ on Calvary, in a nuptial union in which she becomes "one flesh" with him in the motherhood of the Church',[36] Beattie argues, can be deployed in this sacramentalisation of woman's body, so resisting the reassertion of its sacramental exclusion, by Catholic neo-orthodox sexual theology.

Thus it is not imperative to turn away from Christian patriarchal religion, with its symbolism of sacrifice, to matriarchal thealogy, in search of the fecundity associated with the female body: rather maternal feminine symbols are retained at the heart of the Catholic Christian tradition; there is a pressing need to '[restore] the sacrificed mother to language and meaning',[37] with the figure of the maternal priest as vehicle for this sacramentalisation. Where Raphael speaks of resacralisation of woman, Beattie speaks of God 'incarnate at last in the divinisation of the female body'.[38] The 'weak vessel' of patriarchal Christianity may indeed be transformed.

The dual impossibilities of the patriarchal Virgin Mary as model for adult womanhood – 'I didn't think sex was part of marriage … I wanted to be just like her' (p. 52) – and of purity as a state of female subjectivity, haunt the young girls and women of *FEAST*. Meanwhile, modernity, with its confident Protestant and feminist partners, marches on towards its point of exhaustion, where its repressed Other – Catholicism[39] – joins forces with postmodern 'feminisms' of Irigaray and Kristeva to facilitate the construction of a revitalised imaginary, where the male privilege of the ancient gender binary is cast down, and relational and corporeal figurations of subjectivity are invited in its place. In the light of this imaginary, for the girl and boy posed before Mary, Jesus and the crucifix (p. 103), or for we who gaze on their image, the nuptial union of Mary with Christ on Calvary, and the maternal Church coming to birth in this event, offers the possibility of open-ended refigurations of identity: a space for negotiation of subjectivity as both 'relational and corporeal'.[40]

As Kathy Rudy suggests, whiteness studies challenge not only the privilege of white culture, but also its emptiness.[41] Whiteness, with its entwined threads of racist discourse, compulsory heterosexuality and feminine purity – the latter that impossible pedestal on which the privileged white woman is installed while the female is profaned – can be perceived as inscribing an emptiness, an absence. A theme runs through my swift survey, a theme of fluidity across the binary boundary, of a silent blackness and secret mother informing the white and patriarchal imaginaries constructed upon them, of Raphael's 'maternal' dissolution of the patriarchally defined sacred/profane boundary, and of Beattie's parallel task within the Catholic sacramental imaginary.

As Raphael reminds us, 'One has moral obligations to the holy'.[42] And the holy within the Christian imaginary may, in the end, assist us in the necessary challenge to the emptiness and privilege of whiteness, by resourcing identities beyond the knotted white, heterosexual matrix. Here Christian reflections which exceed those homed in Catholicism join with Catholic reflections. As William Cavanagh suggests, 'to participate in the Eucharist is to live inside God's imagination'.[43] Thus Jeremy Ayers sees primary Christian identity, centred on Eucharistic participation, drawing black bodies into the 'Triune life of God in the broken body of Christ'[44] as helping black Christians to negotiate the constructs of race and sexuality.[45]

A 'White Mass', celebrated in 1995 in St Peter's Church, Cologne, found a different way of living inside God's imagination. Collaboration with the artist James Lee Byars transformed the church into an empty space where whiteness, in vestments, sculpture and the bleached host, symbolised a spirituality where identity is thrown into question.[46] The Mass or Holy Communion as opening is here restated. Denys Turner finds in his theology of Eucharistic presence, primordially located and sourced, the dialectic of the darkness of God and the light of Christ.[47] In this dialectic, light and dark as binary opposition is dissolved in the tension between affirmation and negation which is the hallmark of 'mystical' theological speech.[48] The emptiness and privilege of whiteness have no stability amid this tension.

In this emptiness, where the patriarchal mindset has made women the simultaneous bearers of an impossible purity, and of responsibility for sin, particularly the central mortal sin of sexual fallibility, Johnson has, as Clinger asserts, insisted on the autonomous subjectivity of the young girls in the images and text of *FEAST.* In Irigaray's nascent female imaginary, angels cross and recross the space between human and divine, body and language: 'As if the angel were a representation of a sexuality that has never been incarnated'.[49] Might the angelic girls in white dresses, who confront us with their gaze, be capable of traversing the space between the community's secular self-understanding and concerns, as they filter through the permeable ritual boundaries, and a re-enchanted liturgical sacramentality, in which patriarchal gender relations are reordered? May they indeed 'become the bearers of good news, messengers of annunciations that open the way to a new birthing of God among us, incarnate at last in the divinisation of the female body?'[50]

Jenny Daggers *is Senior Lecturer in Theology and Religious Studies at Liverpool Hope University, UK. Jenny holds a PhD in Theology awarded by the University of Manchester. She is author of* The British Christian Women's Movement: A Rehabilitation of Eve *(Aldershot: Ashgate, 2002) and co-editor, with Diana Neal, of* Sex, Gender and Religion: Josephine Butler Revisited *(New York: Peter Lang, 2006), as well as author of a number of articles on feminist theology, and women and religion.*

Notes

1 Tina Beattie, *New Catholic Feminism: Theology and Theory* (London: Routledge, 2006), p. 300.

2 S. Moore and J. Williamson, 'Coming Clean: The Rise of the White King', in *New Statesman*, 130, 4550 (13 August 2001), pp. 27–9.

3 Alistair Bonnett, 'From White to Western: "Racial Decline" and the Idea of the West in Britain, 1890–1930', in *Journal of Historical Sociology*, 16, 3 (September 2003), pp. 320–48.

4 Mason Boyd Stokes, *The Color of Sex: Whiteness, Heterosexuality and the Fictions of White Supremacy* (Durham, NC: Duke University Press, 2000), p. 11.

5 Ibid., p. 13.

6 Richard Dyer, *White* (London: Routledge, 1997), p. 20.

7 Ibid., p. 140.

8 Stokes, *Color of Sex*, p. 18. Stokes draws on Sedgwick's concept of homosociality.

9 Ibid., p. 16.

10 Ibid., p. 16.

11 Ibid., p. 18.

12 Ibid., p. 107.

13 Ibid., p. 107.

14 Brigalia Bam, 'All About Eve: Woman of Africa', in *Anglicanism: A Global Communion*, ed. Andrew Wingate, Kevin Ward, Carrie Pemberton and Wilson Sitshebo (London: Mowbray-Cassall, 1998), pp. 347–53.

15 Cited in Kathy Rudy, 'Subjectivity and Belief', in *Literature and Theology*, 15, 3 (September 2001), pp. 224–40, esp. p. 238.

16 Simon Peter McGrail, 'The Celebration of First Communion in Liverpool: A Lens to View the Structural Decline of the Roman Catholic Parish', unpublished PhD thesis, University of Birmingham, 2003, p. 33. McGrail's study investigates First Communion in the 1990s, over twenty years after the most recent images in Johnson's collection.

17 Ibid., p. 35.

18 Ibid., p. 58.

19 Ibid., p. 61.

20 Ibid., p. 67.

21 Ibid., p. 154.

22 Ibid., p. 167.

23 Toril Moi, 'Introduction', in *The Kristeva Reader*, ed. Toril Moi (Oxford: Blackwell, 1986), pp. 1–22, esp. p. 14.

24 Interview with Kristeva by Francoise Collin, in *Les Cahiers du GRIF*, 32, pp. 7–23, cited in *The Kristeva Reader*, p. 14.

25 Melissa Raphael, *Thealogy and Embodiment: The Post-Patriarchal Reconstruction of Female Sacrality* (Sheffield: SAP, 1996). The term 'thealogy' denotes matriarchal divinity, associated with Goddess spirituality.

26 Ibid., p. 41.

27 Ibid., pp. 34–43.

28 Ibid., p. 43.

29 Ibid., p. 43.

30 Beattie, *New Catholic Feminism*, p. 293.

31 These are Beattie's words, encapsulating an elaborate paragraph from von Balthasar's theodramatic *Heart of the World*; ibid., p. 286.

32 Ibid., p. 48.

33 Beattie argues von Balthasar eliminates the female body from this site; ibid., p. 111.

34 Ibid., p. 309.

35 Ibid., p. 275.

36 Ibid., p. 275.

37 Ibid., p. 275.

38 Ibid., p. 294.

39 Ibid., p. 257 for this perspective on Catholicism as repressed 'other'.

40 Ibid., p. 257.

41 Rudy, 'Subjectivity', p. 238.

42 Raphael, *Thealogy*, p. 42.

43 Cited in Jeremy Ayers, 'Towards a Eucharistic Politics of the Black Body: Black Sexuality in the Horizons of Christian Theology', *Theology and Sexuality*, 10, 2 (March 2004), pp. 99–113, p. 108.

44 Ibid., p. 113.

45 Ibid., p. 110, fn. 46.

46 Friedhelm Mennekes, 'Liturgy as Question: James Lee Byars' *The White Mass*', in *The Month* (July 1999), pp. 266–71.

47 Denys Turner, 'The Darkness of God and the Light of Christ: Negative Theology and Eucharistic Presence', in *Modern Theology*, 15, 2 (April 1999), pp. 143–58, esp. p. 158.

48 Ibid., p. 147.

49 Luce Irigaray, *An Ethics of Sexual Difference*, trans. Carolyn Burke and Gillian C. Gill (London: Athlone Press, 1993), p. 16.

50 Beattie, *New Catholic Feminism*, p. 294.

ACKNOWLEDGEMENTS

THANKS TO

Arts & Humanities Research Council, British Council, UCR California Museum of Photography, U-Frame-It (Adrianna Cruz), and the Research Office, University College for the Creative Arts: for whose funding and support made the *FEAST* project possible.

33 Confessors (p. 181): for sharing their intimate and poignant memories with me – graciously offering 'material'.

Julien Lesage: for bringing energy and creative vision to the procession – generously giving time and commitment to the project.

David Gray Gardner: for his enthusiasm, making this book possible – a consummate printer.

Victoria Millar: for her editing finesse – an enjoyable collaborative performance and journey.

Liz Barton: for hours of patience and skill – putting voice to paper.

Catherine Clinger, Jenny Daggers, Margherita Sprio: for contributing innovative, challenging and thought-provoking discourse.

Joanna Lowry: for useful guidance and research support.

Ciara Ennis: for believing in the work and launching the *FEAST* project internationally at UCR/CMP.

Suzanne Watson: for introducing me to David Gardner and generously helping me understand the complexities of book production – my dearest friend.

Jeremy Williams: for the preliminary design work – giving the text/image archive form and shape for public view, thus crucially helping elicit interest in the project as a whole.

Sarah Hall: for expedient and expert proofing.

Confessor Scouts: for making those most helpful connections and introductions.
Peter DeBarra, Vicki Johnson,
Susanna Kearney, Searle Kochberg,
Pam Posner, Edna Sprague, Jane Sprague

Photographic Scavengers: for enthusiastically sharing their 'finds'.
Nick Abdalla, Shaun Barnett, Roz Mortimer,
Andrea Silvestri, Adolfo 'Rudy' Silvestri,
Angela Villalba

To all those others who have supported the *FEAST* project in various guises:
Rowan Taliesin Appleton-Wickens,
René Bach, Martin Berry, Imogen Bloor,
Tim Borton, Darren Cayley, John Everest,
Beverley Ferrell, Pearl Fish, Andy Garcia,
Mark Hamilton, Gareth Jasper, Conor Kelly,
Andrew Kötting, Rachel Matthews,
Fergus Moloney, Sophia Phoca, Frank Sieber,
Martin Verrier, Ken Wood

And finally … heartfelt thanks to my family for their love, encouragement and support.

CONCEPT Christy Johnson

DESIGN Julien Lesage www.brett-lesage.com

PRINT Dual Graphics, USA www.dualgraphics.com

EDITOR Victoria Millar

TRANSCRIPTION Liz Barton

PREFACE Bernard of Clairvaux. *On the Song of Songs II*,
vol. 3, trans. Kilian Walsh, OCSO (Kalamazoo, MI:
Cistercian Publications Inc., 1983), p. 199.

WITH SUPPORT FROM
Arts & Humanities Research Council, UK
British Council, UK
UCR, California Museum of Photography, USA
U-Frame-It, USA
University College for the Creative Arts, UK

FEAST: Christy Johnson and 33 Confessors

Published in 2007 by
University College for the Creative Arts
at Canterbury, Epsom, Farnham, Maidstone and Rochester, UK

ISBN 978-1-870522-49-6

Edition of 1,000
Distribution: Art Data, London, UK www.artdata.co.uk

Typeset in Gill Sans and printed on Sterling Ultra Matte 80 lb